Antisemitism in the
Contemporary World

About the Book and Editor

This collection of original essays by renowned scholars deals in a thematic fashion with the ways in which antisemitism is currently expressed. The book addresses the questions of whether there are new forms of antisemitism, whether there has been a resurgence of antisemitism in the current age, and whether critical attitudes toward Zionism or opposition to the State of Israel and its policies have given new impetus to antisemitism. The contributors also examine the complex relationship between the State of Israel and the Jewish community worldwide.

Michael Curtis is a professor of political science at Rutgers University and was the 1984 Lady Davis Visiting Professor at The Hebrew University in Jerusalem. He organized the conference "Antisemitism in the Contemporary World," held at Rutgers, November 1983, from which this book grew.

To the memory of

Terence Prittie

Antisemitism in the Contemporary World

edited by Michael Curtis

Westview Press / Boulder and London

Copyright © 1986 by Westview Press, Inc.

Published in 1986 in the United States of America by Westview Press, Inc.; Frederick A. Praeger, Publisher; 5500 Central Avenue, Boulder, Colorado 80301

Library of Congress Cataloging in Publication Data
Main entry under title:
Antisemitism in the contemporary world.
    Papers originally presented at a conference sponsored by the International Center at Rutgers University in association with the American Jewish Congress, held at Rutgers University, Nov. 1983.
    Bibliography: p.
    Includes index.
    1. Antisemitism—Congresses. I. Curtis, Michael, 1923–   . II. Rutgers University. International Center. III. American Jewish Congress.
DS145.A64 1986   305.8′924   85-13919
ISBN 0-8133-0157-2

Printed and bound in the United States of America

10   9   8   7   6   5   4   3   2   1

Contents

Part Five
Contemporary Perceptions

Preface

This volume stems from papers originally presented at a conference sponsored by the International Center at Rutgers University in association with the American Jewish Congress, held at the university in New Brunswick in November 1983.

As organizer of the conference, I am indebted to a number of organizations and individuals for financial assistance and logistical support. In addition to the sponsoring bodies, these include the New Jersey Committee for the Humanities; the Anti-Defamation League of B'nai B'rith; the Bronfman Foundation; Alvin Rockoff; Joseph Littenberg; Bernard A. Mollen; Edward Weiss; Kenneth Wolfson, dean of the Graduate School; Tilden Edelstein, dean of the Faculty of Arts and Sciences; and Kenneth Wheeler, provost at New Brunswick, Rutgers University.

I am also indebted to a large number of individuals for advice and help in facilitating arrangements for the conference. In particular I want to thank Henry Siegman, Philip Baum, and Raphael Danziger of the American Jewish Congress; Jeffrey Maas of the ADL; and Bernard Lewis, Alvin Rockoff, Carole Levin, and Miriam Murphy for their support and enthusiasm. I very much appreciate the interest of the members of the International Center and the participation of the colleagues in the Rutgers faculty who chaired the six panels of the conference. Above all, I am grateful for the dedication and effort beyond any reasonable expectation of Henriette Cohen of the International Center, who contributed so greatly to the success of the conference.

These papers are presented here in the belief that it is important to inquire into the question of whether there has been a resurgence of antisemitism or whether new forms have appeared in the current age. The papers are not concerned primarily with the history of the subject nor with localized manifestations, but deal instead in a thematic fashion with the ways in which antisemitism has been expressed or implemented. The different views expressed about the nature and significance of antisemitism today, and in particular about the relationship between antisemitism and anti-Zionism, provide the basis for a new analysis of a historic phenomenon.

Michael Curtis
New Brunswick, N.J.

1
Introduction:
Antisemitism—The Baffling Obsession

Michael Curtis

The History of Antisemitism

Discrimination, bias, hatred of outsiders, patterns of prejudice, bigotry, racism, denial of equal rights, and xenophobia have existed in all historical eras and in all countries. Racial, religious, national, social, and cultural minorities have suffered from past and present injustices. Slavery, caste systems, denial of civil and political rights, lack of economic opportunity, and deliberate massacre have been familiar parts of social experience. All countries have been subject to the lunacy of believing that whole races or nations were mysteriously good or evil.[1]

Hegel saw history as a slaughterbench. Yet, notwithstanding the horrors and bitterness of past experience and recent example, there is something distinctive and compelling in the extraordinary persistence of antisemitism, or hatred of Jews, historically and spatially. Indeed, much of the case made by early Zionist proponents such as Theodor Herzl and Leo Pinsker for an independent Jewish state rested on the normality of antisemitism. Only with the creation of such a state, which would end the role of Jews as an external minority, would the anti-Jewish attitude change.

A wholly disproportionate amount of the attention given to the existence of Jews has been critical in character, irrespective of any specific behavior. Or it has focused for varied and often contradictory reasons on the alleged negative qualities of Jews. No other group of people has suffered from a regime like that of Nazi Germany, whose leaders had the total extermination of a whole people as their main ideological motivation.

Expectation that the unprecedented horrors of the Nazi regime and the scale of the Holocaust would lead to a climate of opinion that would not countenance antisemitism has been sadly disappointed. It is true that all surveys, using such customary indexes as non-Jewish attitudes toward work relationships, housing, college admission, employment, and intermarriage with Jews, show a decline in the post–World War II period in discriminatory attitudes and in the numbers of those who are strongly prejudiced against Jews. Moreover, antisemitic prejudice appears to be less prevalent among young white non-Jews than among middle-aged and older persons.

Antisemitism is now not politically or intellectually respectable in an era when Jews form part of the political elite. In the U.S. Congress of 1982–1984 eight Jews were members of the Senate and thirty of the House of Representatives. The British Conservative government in 1984 included four Jews in senior positions. The prime minister appointed in France in 1984 was of Jewish origin. No important political organization in the United States or in other democratic countries openly advocates antisemitic views; nor are Jews denied civil or political rights in those countries; nor is much overt public expression of antisemitism heard.

The medieval conception of Jews as the demonic, accursed people who killed Christ, or as cannibals and blasphemers, is rarely present in the pluralistic societies of the Western world. Historical solutions proposed for the "Jewish problem"—forced conversion, expulsion, strict segregation, or extermination—are seldom advocated. Extreme passions of antisemitism, familiar until the end of World War II, are limited to the lunatic fringe in politics or the literary world.

Yet an atmosphere of disquiet persists. The phenomenon of antisemitism has still not disappeared, even if a Richter scale would show it to be less violent than in the past.[2] A survey in 1981 revealed that in the United States, some 53 percent of the population felt "Jews stick together too much," 22 percent believed that "Jews are not as honest as other businessmen," and 40 percent believed that "Jews should stop complaining about what happened to them in Nazi Germany." Recent incidents and political activity suggest that temporary immunization against the virus may be wearing off and that any guilt felt by non-Jews about the Holocaust may be lessening.

Small political parties of a neo-Nazi tendency have erupted in Western Europe and the United States. Atrocities, including bombing of synagogues, desecration of cemeteries, attacks on or assassinations of Jews, and destruction of Jewish property, have occurred in a number of countries. Verbal violence has taken the form of fundamentalist preaching that God does not hear the prayers of Jews and of racial slurs by a candidate for the U.S. presidency. Political writings of the French New Right, couched in the language of sociobiology, have denigrated the Judeo-Christian heritage, blamed Jews for the creation of Christianity, and argued for a return to the Aryan roots of European civilization. Books in the United States, Britain, and France (for one of which, Robert Faurisson's *Mémoire en Défense contre ceux qui m'accusent de falsifier l'histoire*, Noam Chomsky wrote an introduction), as well as in the Communist countries, have denied or minimized the reality of the Holocaust; other works have suggested that the *Diary of Anne Frank* was a forgery. By contrast, the real forgery, the *Protocols of the Elders of Zion*, has been republished in a variety of countries since the war. Recent literary works and films have, perhaps inadvertently, expressed a change in sensibility about Jews, who are now sometimes portrayed as aggressors who take pleasure in killing. Prejudice has come not only from the Soviet Union and the Arab and Islamic countries, as might be expected, but also from the black community of the United States, Third World countries, the United Nations, and, above all, the political left and some of the opponents of Israel.

What can account for the extraordinary persistence of antisemitism in world history? How can one explain its protean character? How can one understand the avidity of so many to believe in the killing by Jews of non-Jewish children, in ritual murders, or in Jewish responsibility for events such as the Black Death in 1347 and false accusations such as treason in France in 1894 (the Dreyfus affair) or the murder in Georgia in 1913 (the Leo Frank case)? What explains the massacres, burning of Jews, expropriation of property, expulsions, wearing of special badges, imposition of quotas, legal and social discrimination, and denial of and limits on emancipation?

Antisemitism has emanated from all political persuasions, from holders of all religious beliefs, from those critical of Christianity or Judaism, and from all social groups. Even a document like the Magna Carta, which has been of such symbolic significance in the struggle for human freedom, has its antisemitic clauses. Hatred of Jews has been manifested when they lived in segregated ghettoes and when they shared emancipated environments with non-Jews. It has persisted in an age of universal suffrage and change in the nature of economic systems and social relationships in postindustrial societies. Although higher education has had some impact in reducing the intensity of antisemitism, the belief that antisemitism would disappear with the spread of education, which would bring with it more humane and tolerant values, has not been fulfilled.

What distinguishes antisemitism from the ever-present prejudice or hostility directed against other (non-Jewish) people and groups is not so much the strength and passion of this hatred as its many-faceted character and the range of arguments and doctrines that see Jews at best as peripheral (or as pariahs, to use Max Weber's term) in society and at worst as destructive monsters and forces of evil. In its lowest form, as in the hands of a Julius Streicher, antisemitism takes the form of pornography depicting a struggle between Aryans and Jews for women.[3] Elsewhere, arguments—whether of a political, economic, social, religious, or psychological nature—make a greater claim to rationality. Always the claim is that the Jews, because of their religious customs or insistence on monotheism or dietary habits or tribal exclusiveness, were alien to the traditions and ways of life of the societies in which they lived or tried to subvert those societies or were able to control both these societies and other diabolical forces in the world.

But the charges against Jews cannot be true, partly because they are mutually contradictory and partly because no one people can have a monopoly on evil. The uniqueness of antisemitism is that no other group of people in the world has been charged simultaneously with alienation from society and with cosmopolitanism, with being capitalist exploiters and agents of international finance and also revolutionary agitators, with having a materialist mentality and with being people of the Book, with acting as militant aggressors and with being cowardly pacifists uttering (in Michelet's phrase) "the groan of the slave," with adherence to a superstitious religion and with being agents of modernism, with upholding a rigid law and also being morally decadent, with being a chosen people and also having an inferior human nature, with both arrogance and timidity, with both individualism and communal adherence, with being guilty of the crucifixion of Christ and at the same time held to account for the invention of Christianity—as Nietzsche put it, "the ultimate Jewish consequence"?

The Obsession with Jews

Ever present is what Jacob Talmon called the "baffling obsession with the Satanic ubiquitousness and malignant effectiveness of the Jews."[4] Sometimes the obsession is directed to Jews as a category; at other times it pertains to particular groups of Jews, impoverished masses of alien immigrants with a culture of their own, or a financial elite, or shopkeepers denounced as nonproducing parasites. Sometimes the concern is with the defects of Jews—their physique, odor, or health or their moral and social inadequacies. At other times it is their economic, intellectual, or cultural prominence that disturbs, as in the case of Charles de Gaulle, who spoke of "un peuple élite, dominateur et sûr de lui-même."

Underlying the obsession with Jews are a number of difficult issues: the tension between the principle of universality and the particularity of Jews, the unique status of Jews as members of a nation as well as of a religion, the role or burden of being a chosen people, the relegation to inferiority in a racial hierarchy, and the role accorded to Jews in a world conspiracy.

The Charge of Particularity

Universality, with its practical connotation of a homogeneous political culture and of devotion to a national unity or to a concern for all humanity, is in dialectical tension with the particularity of Jews, "a people that dwells apart," having marked differences from the beliefs and practices of the majority. The tension exists for those Jews whose commitment to a left-wing political ideology often provides them with a new universal religion to replace any attachment to the religion of their origin.[5] In his celebrated essay "The Non-Jewish Jew," Isaac

Deutscher typifies those who identify with the brotherhood of all "humanity" rather than with Jewry.[6] The cosmopolitan Arthur Koestler left his early Zionism to search "for the knowing Shaman, then . . . the pursuit of utopia . . . to embrace the perfect cause."[7]

But the issue has been more important for non-Jews and their consequent intolerance toward Jews. Even in ancient Greece and Rome, the refusal of Jews to recognize pagan gods and their different rituals, their practice of circumcision, their observance of Sabbath, their dietary laws, and intermarriage among Jews set them apart from those who conformed to the universal beliefs and patterns of behavior in their societies.[8] Christian hostility, expressed at its strongest by Chrysostom (ca. 347–407), was based on the responsibility of Jews ("deformed monsters" who rejected Christianity and the Messiah) for the crucifixion of Jesus, which justified their "perpetual servitude." For Augustine, Jews were carnal beings who had rejected the spiritual truth of Christianity. The Spanish insistence on purity of the blood, *limpieza de sangre*, largely stemmed from fear that the blood of an inferior people transmitted by the Marranos might taint the Spanish populace. From early modern European history on, Jews were castigated for their ethnic separation, culture, and autonomous community. This separation, accompanied by a purported Jewish personality or character type, occasioned the denial of equal rights to Jews.

Logically, it might have been expected that the criticism of Jewish particularity would cease in the more enlightened era that brought with it the first "civic betterment of the Jews,"[9] emancipation, and the gradual removal of many traditional restrictions and forms of discrimination. Emancipation would, it was believed, bring with it assimilation, if not religious conversion, and the elimination of supposedly Jewish behavioral characteristics.[10] The assimilation process, or, in Walter Rathenau's phrase, "the conscious self-education of a race for its adaption to outside demands,"[11] would transform the nature of the Jewish community such that it became indistinguishable from the rest.

The religious element of antisemitism, resting on Jewish rejection of the true faith, may indeed have been reduced, if not eliminated, since the Enlightenment either through growth of tolerance, increasing skepticism about religion, or expectation of conversion. But in its place greater prominence was placed on Jewish characteristics, which were partly genetic in nature and partly the result of alien cultural and ethnic traditions. Purported characteristics such as moral insensitivity, superstitious habits, lack of social graces, and cultural inferiority now rendered Jews incapable of true citizenship.

Unexpectedly, the Enlightenment helped produce a new rationale for antisemitism. Some of its major figures—including Diderot, Holbach, and especially Voltaire, who believed Jews to be an ignorant and crude people without art or science and Judaism to be an obscurantist and intolerant religion—were instrumental in providing a secular anti-Jewish rhetoric in the name of European culture rather than religion. Although the medieval assignment of perpetual servitude had largely ended—indeed, Judaism was now condemned as the foundation of Christianity—and their legal status had improved, Jews were still incapable of true citizenship because of the innate nature attributed to them and their inability to belong to communities characterized by blood ties, common race, and historic memories.

Not surprisingly, the very prominence of the Jewish community, especially in Central Europe, accentuated the argument that Jews were aliens who were disproportionately prominent in elite positions. Envy of economic success by Jews, resentment of their position in certain businesses and professions, criticism of their prominent role in the sphere of distribution and of their crucial situation as intermediaries, and jealousy of their prominent role in cultural and intellectual life led to the charge that Jews were subverting the economic basis of society and were responsible for its problems, economic crises, dislocation of individuals, and any reduction in the standard of living. To this charge was added that of cultural alien. Xenophobic attitudes might have excluded the prosperous "cravat Jews" of Central Europe, but the larger number of Eastern European Jews, the "caftan Jews," immediately discernible by appearance, were severely castigated.[12] It was the black caftan that Hitler said first drew his attention to the "alien" face, which from then on he could distinguish from other faces.

The Charge of Racial Inferiority

Reinforcing this charge of the particularity, or alien nature, of Jews has been a second one, more recent in history, of racial inferiority. Greater insistence after the Enlightenment on supposed Jewish genetic characteristics coincided with the formulation of racial theories by Renan, Gobineau, Houston Stewart Chamberlain, Nietzsche, Wagner, and the Social Darwinists and with the rise of anthropological thought.

The concept of race may never have been completely neutral in its allocation of character, physical, and even moral qualities to peoples. A theoretical basis was now available for different peoples not only to be regarded as distinct but also to be ranked in order of superiority. And those using racial theory usually applied it only to the Jewish people. Jewish racial qualities were thought to be a negative and inferior nature that merited exclusion, discrimination, and, at the most extreme, extermination. Religious conversion was insufficient if behavior resulted from the inherited characteristics of racial groups. The very coining of the term *antisemitism* by Wilhelm Marr in 1879 suggested that it was racial characteristics rather than religious beliefs to which opposition was being registered. In reality, of course, there is no such thing as a "semitism" that is characteristic of Jews. The original opposition between Semite and Aryan made by Renan and others was concerned with differences in languages, but in debased form it coincided with the distinction between Jews and non-Jews, secular as well as Christian. Secular racial antisemitism has never really been anything else than antagonism to Jews. The myth of Jewish biological inferiority justified the systematization of antisemitism and the continuing attacks in a more secular age since evils in society supposedly resulted from the presence of the Jewish race. The argument of biological differences propounded by anti-Christians marks the emergence of the genocidal strain in modern antisemitism. The world, it was concluded, must be saved from Judaization.

In other words, Jews were considered a threat to culture itself, as the materialist spirit of their race presumably eroded true values. Much of the original support for Nazism rested on its claim that it was defending the true European values against the threat to Aryan virility—a claim that stemmed from the inculcation of the nineteenth- and twentieth-century German ideology of the *Volk* in both racial and nonracial forms. The *Volk*, which embodies feeling and inward spiritual growth, the true and the beautiful, must overcome and reject the materialism and capitalism symbolized by the urban and rationalistic Jew, whose religion had no ethical foundation.[13] In this view, Jews at best might exemplify materialism and unspirituality—both inferior to culture, a living organism. If in the Enlightenment a distinction could still be made between Judaism as a fossil and the possibility of assimilation for individual Jews, the stress on inherent differences between races meant the erosion of the distinction.

Ironically, the whole argument rests on a misnomer, inasmuch as Jews do not constitute a race as that term is used today but include people from many races. Composed of individuals of different colors, backgrounds, religious views, and countries of origin, Jews are a heterogeneous people made up not only of those born to Jewish mothers but also of converts. They cease to be Jews by conversion to other religions. They are also unique in being members of both a religion and a nation with common experiences—historical, recent, and current—that have been welded together by shared tragedy and aspiration.

Paradoxically, the charge that Jews were a separate ethnic group, thus justifying denial of their individual rights, did not lead to a recognition that they were also members of a collective entity with its own self-consciousness and interest in collective self-determination as a nation-state. It was inequitable already that the criticism of individual particularity was confined, with rare exceptions, only to Jews, who were therefore seen as aliens. But it was even more inequitable that recognition was not accorded to the national particularity of Jews nor to the legitimacy of a Jewish political entity in its own nation-state. If the historical experience of Jews has been a varying combination of adherence to God, Torah, or Law, and to Israel or Jewish nationhood,[14] recognition of that nationhood is just as important in demonstrating toleration of Jews as a function of understanding Jewish ethical monotheism or the significance of Jewish law for the behavior of Jews.

But recognition of Jewish nationhood was denied as early as 1789 when Count Stanislas de Clermont-Tonnerre in the French National Assembly argued that "the Jews should be denied everything as a nation, but granted everything as individuals. . . . There cannot be one nation within another nation." Emancipation would thus mean the end of Jewish national identity. The price of civil and political equality in this view was renunciation of any collective identification by Jews. For two centuries this argument has been made, but in the present it has another dimension. The question of Jewish nationhood or collective identity is now, of course, linked with the state of Israel. Most Jews are committed to the existence of the state; to be anti-Israeli in principle is to be anti-Jewish as Jews now understand Jewishness.

Anti-Zionism

In world politics, the principle of Jewish self-determination as a people with the right to form its own state has often been regarded less sympathetically than in the case of other peoples. Not only has the creation of Israel been opposed by Arab and Muslim countries, which usually only refer to it as "the Zionist entity," but its claim to legitimacy as a sovereign state also troubles left-wing Western intellectuals who have no similar difficulty with the claims of other groups. The equation of Zionism with illegitimacy has now turned to farce, with the Soviet Union in Outer Mongolia denouncing the Chinese as Zionists and Haitian exiles attacking the Zionism of the ruler Papa Doc Duvalier.

More recently, anti-Zionism has taken another form in addition to its rejection of the collective right of Jews to form their own state. Now it also embraces an attack on a state of a particular kind—a conspiratorial and imperialistic state as well as a tool of colonialism, with demonic qualities.[15] The historic complaint from Tacitus on the "intransigence" of Jews has now been transferred to the state of Israel.

The establishment of the state led in part to the transformation of the traditionally perceived image of Jews. That image—of the sinister economic force, usurer, moneylender, landlord, parasite—still survives, if in much reduced fashion, but it has now been superseded by that of the Israelis, or Zionists, who are criticized as arrogant, colonialist, imperialist, and racist. Political anti-Zionism is not synonymous with traditional antisemitism. Surveys in the United States show that the attitudes of a group toward antisemitism and toward Israel may not coincide. Moreover, criticism of the acts of Israel cannot and must not be taken per se as examples of antisemitism. Individuals may oppose Israel because they are honestly convinced of its errors, or for commercial reasons, or by following currently intellectually fashionable position. Nevertheless, many current examples show that one reason is not readily distinguishable from the other.

Soviet persecution of its own Jews is accompanied by leadership of an anti-Israeli bloc at the United Nations. Polish antisemitism remains in a country where only 6,000 Jews are left of the former 3 million.[16] In some Third World countries antisemitism exists without any experience, past or present, of Jews. The myth of worldwide Jewish conspiracy survives with the continuing publication of the forgery entitled *Protocols of the Elders of Zion* in a number of countries, including not only the Soviet Union but also Saudi Arabia, whose late king viewed international politics as dominated by the Zionist-Communist conspiracy.

In the Arab and Islamic countries, antisemitism, once less violent than in Christian countries, has dramatically increased since 1948. This increase is evidenced not only by the rhetoric used internally in those countries but also by actions on the international level. The Arab economic boycott of Israel extends (erratically, it must be admitted) to non-Israeli businesses under Jewish control and to individuals of Jewish origin. And the continual Arab attacks on Israel at the United Nations have degenerated into antisemitic utterances. Particularly flagrant examples of these attacks can be witnessed in the speeches by the Libyan ambassador, Ali Treiki, on December 6, 1983, and by the Jordanian representative Hazzem Nusseibah on December 8, 1980. The former stated that "the Jewish Zionists here in the United States attempt to destroy Americans. Who are the owners of pornographic film operations and houses? Is it not the Jews who are exploiting the American people and trying to debase them?" The latter attacked "the representative of the Zionist entity" and "his own people's cabal which controls and manipulates the rest of humanity by controlling the money and wealth of the world."

A conference in Germany in 1981 attempted to define the "New Anti-Semitism." Included in the definition were the following points: that antisemitism exists when Israeli politics is judged without regard to the special problem of the state of Israel threatened by hostile states, and that it exists when actions by the Israeli government are automatically judged one-sidedly. Examples of this new antisemitism now abound; probably the most explicit of these were the political attacks on Israel for its actions in Lebanon in 1982, attacks in which a similarity between Israel and Nazi Germany was often asserted. In this "semantic hysteria," as Bernard-Henri Lévy called it, Israel was accused of racial genocide and "final solutions" against the Palestinians; the Israeli government was also said to be "pounding the Star of David into a Swastika."[17] The litmus test proposed by Conor Cruise O'Brien is a useful one.[18] An individual is anti-Jewish if that person cannot keep the name of Hitler out of conversation, or compares Jews, whether Israelis or not, to Nazis, or characterizes Israel as a racist, Nazi, fascist, or imperialist state.

The Chosen People

In addition to the criticism of Jewish particularity, a constant and continuing source of antagonism has proceeded from the concept of Jews as the "chosen people." The concept was meaningful for the early leaders of the Church and by Islam, following from their recognition of its significance for spiritual leadership and, in a sense, from their attempt to supplant Jews in this role. But the concept is usually misunderstood by antisemites. For them the chosen people embody fanaticism, evil, or an attitude of superiority to other peoples. They perceive the Old Testament as the source of Jewish fanaticism, tribal nationalism, and communal exclusivism, and as the basis for the aggressive attitude of the state of Israel, whereas the New Testament represents for many such antisemites a universal belief and community.

The "chosen people" must shoulder yet another burden—the imposition of adherence to stricter rules and to the highest standards of conduct from which other peoples and groups may be exempted. Departure from or failure to reach those standards has been subjected to castigation in ample fashion, as evidenced not only by the Western use of double standards of behavior but also more recently by the media commentary on Israeli actions in Lebanon in 1982.

The concept of chosen people may reflect "the envy and admiration of the world," but it is not a claim of superiority of a people or a racist belief, nor does it confer any privilege. It is only an assertion that Jews have been chosen by God to uphold ethical monotheism, to show "a light unto the nations" (Isaiah 49:6) on moral questions, and to spread "God's salvation unto the end of the earth."[19] It is a charge to perform special duties and to bear responsibility—even suffering.

Yet the antisemitic argument has always been that Jews perceive themselves as superior to other peoples. It did not come as a surprise when Yakov Malik, the Soviet ambassador to the United Nations, said in 1973 that "the Zionists have come forward with the theory of the Chosen People, an absurd ideology." It is more surprising that 59 percent of those questioned in a 1969 survey in the United States agreed that "Jews still think of themselves as God's chosen people."[20] Given the abundant evidence of the misunderstanding of the concept, Sholem Aleichem's character Tevye is, indeed, not the only Jew to urge God, "Please, next time choose someone else."

To explain the pathological obsession with Jews some have resorted to psychological factors, as did Sartre in his famous definition of the antisemite as a person who is afraid.[21] Troubled people project their own anxieties, drives, impulses of which they are ashamed, and negative self-images onto Jews, who are then seen as aggressive, competitive, and secretive; are resented as a "chosen people"; and are made a scapegoat for the failures of society and themselves.[22] Indeed, sadism is a powerful force behind antisemitism. But not all those interested in the psychological explanation can accept the Freudian view that the Christian charge against Jews of deicide has been transformed into a secular one of parricide. More, however, will agree that collective psychopathology is at work when Jews are seen as the embodiment of evil aiming at the domination of mankind.

This paranoiac fear of a worldwide Jewish plot or conspiracy, which Norman Cohn has called the heart of antisemitism,[23] has been manifested in a variety of ways, whether Christian, Enlightenment, Socialist, Marxist, Third World, or Nazi in form. Yet even here there are crucial differences. Arguments by the Russian Orthodox Church that the Christian religion or order was being subverted, or by Holbach that Jews were the enemies of the human race, or by Marx that money had become "a world power," or by Soviet polemists that joint American-Zionist imperialist forces were at large in the world, or by Stalin in 1953 that Jewish doctors were planning to poison the Communist party leadership are all qualitatively different from Hitler's outlook in his final document that international Jewry is "the universal poisoner of all people."

The Nazi version was not only that Jews were destroyers of culture and constituted a race whose communal solidarity and exclusivity formed the basis of a worldwide conspiracy. More tragic was the conclusion that the Jewish race was a microbe or bacillus that had to be eliminated so that purification could be obtained. The constant insistence on Jewish identification with evil and poison is the main factor differentiating Nazi actions toward Jews from those toward other peoples and groups. It also distinguishes the Nazi ideology and policy of total extermination or Holocaust of an entire people from the massacres and horror other peoples have experienced throughout history.[24]

In the contemporary world the virus of antisemitism continues to infect the rhetoric and actions of heterogeneous groups: religious fundamentalists, elements of the right, blacks, Arab and Islamic countries, the Third World, the Soviet Union, the political left, and those, particularly intellectuals, who are critical of liberal democratic systems.

Religious, Political, and Social Prejudices

Christian hostility toward Jews has declined considerably. A study of American attitudes in 1979 shows that liberal white Protestants are the least antisemitic—less so than white Catholics, who in turn register less than conservative white Protestants.[25] Particularly heartening was the acknowledgment by Catholic bishops in Germany in 1980 of the harm done for 2,000 years to the Jewish people by the Church. But the 2,000-year-old Christian prejudice, with its negative moral and spiritual conception of Jews, has still not ended. Moreover, the image of the Jews inherited from Christianity has shaped the secular perception of Jews, as well as that of the state of Israel, as outsiders.[26] In Western societies, now that Jews, the former pariahs, have moved into the center of society and compete on equal terms for its key positions, the perception has become alloyed with resentment. And in Israel, now that Jews are the object of history and not victims or scapegoats, it is not surprising that antisemites treat it as a "pariah state."

Antisemitism has customarily been associated with the political right and with the upholders of traditional values who were suspicious of new elements and alien intrusions. As a corollary, it was assumed that the left, associated with emancipation and nondiscrimination, would be unsympathetic to antisemitism in theory and practice. In their *Anti-Semitism in America*, Harold E. Quinley and Charles Y. Glock summarize the antisemitism of right-wing extremists and ignore left-wing groups.[27]

Certainly the antisemitism of the right has been significant in the nineteenth and twentieth centuries. Even today it is manifested in a group like the French National Front party under Jean-Marie Le Pen, which received over 10 percent of the vote in France in 1984. The views of the antisemitic right are spread by writers who argue that no genocide of Jews by the Nazis occurred, that the "final solution" was only the expulsion of Jews to Eastern Europe, that the numbers of Nazi victims have been greatly exaggerated, and that Jews bear part of the responsibility for World War II.[28]

Yet the criticism of or hostility toward Jews has often come from the political left. Even during the French Revolution the leftist groups took the most anti-Jewish view.[29] With the Socialist movement in the nineteenth century came sharp criticism of the role of Jews in capitalist systems. In this criticism Marx (among others) was an influential figure in his argument that Judaism constituted the essence of capitalism: "The God of the Jews has become secularized and has become a World God." As he cryptically put it, "The emancipation of the Jews is in its final significance the emancipation of mankind from Judaism."

Socialist writers, from Leroux and Fourier to the present, rarely refer to Jews except in a negative or hostile fashion. The most charitable conclusion one could draw about this surprising attitude is that if socialism is not responsible for antisemitism, neither is it a consistent defender of Jews.[30] Perhaps the political left once genuinely believed that the Jewish problem could be solved only by the assimilation of Jews into a Socialist society. But the contemporary automatic hostility to Israel by the left, which has associated it with imperialism, pronounced it a racist state, and regarded Zionism as the only national liberation movement that is "reactionary" rather than progressive, suggests deeper emotions.

The left not only objects to Israel's association with any nonleftist foreign systems, especially the United States and its supposed policies of colonization, but it is also critical of the ethnic and religious identity, the "Jewishness," of Israel, which the left considers a theocracy. This criticism undermines the existence of Israel for two reasons. It suggests that the Jews constitute only a religion, not a nation with a collective identity and a right to self-determination; by implication it denies the validity of their claim to the status of an independent state. Moreover, since the argument is made by those who are hostile to religion as such, it is really a case against the existence of Jewry.

Jews, who have been associated for so long with progressive causes, have been sadly disappointed by the hostility of the intellectual left to

Israel. It is interesting to recall that in 1960 the first Congress of the Socialist International to be held outside of Europe took place in Haifa. As Jews have moved more solidly into the middle class and elite positions in the West, they have tended to move slowly to the right politically.[31] This trend has been reinforced by the present views of the Socialist International on Middle Eastern issues and by the more apparent hostility shown by minority groups.

Antisemitism in the Black Community

A distressing increase in antisemitic attitudes, particularly in the United States, has been registered in the black community, with which Jews had allied so strongly in the struggle against racial discrimination and which had gone through similar historical experiences in an effort to emancipate itself from the ghetto.[32] The 1979 study by William Schneider reveals an increase in black antisemitism that largely reflects the attitudes of younger blacks, who are more negatively inclined than younger whites at the same educational level as well as older blacks.[33]

Two factors cause anxiety. The first is that, contrary to the situation with American whites, black antisemitism is inversely related both to age (the strongest antisemitism is expressed by young blacks) and to educational level, as better-educated blacks are more negative than the less educated. The Selznick-Steinberg survey[34] reveals on every social, economic, and political indicator a more negative image of Jews held by blacks than by whites. The second factor is that black leaders (other than members of Congress) and the more politically conscious blacks are more negative than the majority of blacks. This more negative attitude toward Jews overlaps in general with a more unsympathetic attitude than that held by whites to Israel and its policies. This is especially ironic in view of Theodor Herzl's words, in his novel *Old-New Land*, that "once I have witnessed the redemption of the Jews, my people, I wish also to assist in the redemption of the Africans."

Although Jews are less visible as economic merchants or as landlords in black communities, formerly a source of hostility, antisemitism has increased, not diminished. Memories of common fellowship in the struggle for civil rights are fading. What these surveys seem to show is that any special relationship between Jews and blacks is now drawing to an end, partly as a result of differences between the two communities on social issues such as quota systems and forced busing, and partly because of the different attitudes toward Israel.

Much of the black attitude to Israel stems from an understandable sympathy with the countries of the Third World and a less understandable identification with Arab states. Although many of these countries benefited from Israeli help in dealing with developmental problems until 1973, they now largely, if sometimes unenthusiastically, support the Arab view in the Arab-Israeli conflict for reasons of belief, profit, or convenience. In their general anti-Western and anti-American posture,

Israel is seen as the symbol of Western political values. Through the unending series of critical resolutions at the United Nations, the new antisemitism has been internationalized.

The Muslim Attitude

In the Islamic world, Jews no longer conform to the stereotype of a tolerated but subordinated minority. The Muslim attitude toward non-Muslims has historically been one "not of hate or fear but simply of contempt."[35] Throughout the centuries the *dhimma* principle provided tolerance and protection to non-Muslims, who were allowed a subordinate status while recognizing the primacy of Islam and the supremacy of Muslims. Although anti-Jewish discrimination existed in the enforcement of laws and rules in Muslim countries and in special taxes levied against them, Jews also enjoyed social autonomy and religious freedom to some degree.[36] Islamic treatment of Jews has generally been less harsh than that in Western countries or that accorded Christians in Muslim countries, partly because Jews did not challenge the political supremacy of Muslims. But now, instead of their *dhimmi* status, Jews rule over Muslims. To the abhorrence of this reversal of relationships has been added the growing antisemitism, first introduced by diplomatic and Christian missions to Arab countries and by European works such as the *Protocols*. A combination of factors—such as the breakdown of Islamic consensus on minorities, the effect of Nazi propaganda, the resentment directed against the economic power of Americans, including Jews, and the unrelenting hostility toward Israel—has magnified that antisemitism. It is discouraging to read in recent works published in Egypt, at peace with Israel, that Jews "are enjoined by their faith to ravish all women of other religions" and that they still stand accused of the 1840 Damascus blood libel and other similar "crimes."

Antisemitism in the Soviet Union

In the Soviet Union antisemitism flourishes for a variety of reasons: jealousy of citizens who want to replace Jews occupationally, annoyance at Jews who are critical of the system or who struggle for human rights, inherited prejudice from czarist times, rancor at the desire of Jews to emigrate (thus setting a precedent with respect to other groups), fear of the attraction of Israel as a competing way of life, and the appeal of antisemitism as an instrument to gain popularity among the population and to deflect attention from the country's pressing problems.

It is symptomatic that in 1983 a supposedly open letter was written by fifty Soviet citizens of Jewish origin, addressed to American Jews and denying that antisemitism now exists in their country. Yet, although antisemitism is forbidden in the Constitution, it is wielded cynically by the rulers as a policy weapon. Indeed, Jews in the USSR have been subjected to violence, often refused access to higher education, prevented from emigrating, and denied the right to study or teach Hebrew.

An officially sponsored literature in the USSR, in which Lev Korneev, Vladimir Begun, and Trofim Kichko are familiar figures, concentrates on a number of themes: a Jewish conspiracy directed against the Communist countries, an attack on Jewish history and religion, and the allegation that Jews collaborated with Nazis in murdering the Jewish people during the Holocaust.[37] It argues that czarism was under the yoke of Jewish bankers and industrialists, that Jews are now "a fifth column" in any country, that they are stateless "cosmopolitans" and exploiters, that a huge and powerful empire of Zionist financiers and industrialists, "blood-sucking spiders, lie in wait for their prey." Throughout history the Jewish bourgeoisie has attempted to control the world. One book deals with Judaism's poisonous hatred of all peoples. Another argues that the Jewish Torah was unequalled in its bloodthirstiness, hypocrisy, treachery, flattery, and moral baseness. Yet another traces the ideological roots of "Zionist gangsterism" back to the Torah scrolls and doctrines of the Talmud.

The callous Soviet antisemitism has directly infected current thought in the rest of the world through its criticism of Jewish traits and behavior; moreover, Soviet attacks on the actions of Israel have affected the international community, especially the United Nations, which reached its lowest point with the 1975 "Zionism is racism" resolution. The Communist world has also used Israel as a surrogate for attacks on liberal democratic systems.

Conclusion

As the fate of Jews is linked with that of democracy, two troublesome problems now exist. One is the assertion of new principles—for redistribution of wealth internally and internationally, and for society to be based on equality of result. The values of a pluralistic society and the principle of equality of opportunity have allowed Jews, through education and effort, to reach high levels of achievement in open competition. Criticism of the removal or reduction of the competitive process as the basis for success has already produced resentment of the status of Jews in democratic countries. The other problem is a possible decline in tolerance, contingent on the tendency of certain factors—including rapidly changing technologies, economic pressures, a mood of neo-isolationism among intellectuals, the enormous oil wealth of Arab countries, Islamic fundamentalism, the assertion of ethnic or group rights in many countries, and the large number of nondemocratic countries—to lead to social discontent and to actions not consonant with the values of pluralistic societies.

This rejection of democracy is not a new problem. From the late nineteenth century on, a variety of political and social attitudes stemmed from those affected or feeling threatened by changing social conditions, economic depression, and modernization.[38] The social strata who felt insecure—the populist demagogues, critics of capitalism, neopagans, and anti-Christians who sought different moral values; the social radicals, conservative nationalists, aggressive imperialists, and racists—all could join forces against the dominant liberal, democratic ethos that, along with other factors, had allowed the emancipation of the Jews. In its various forms today, antisemitism is linked to criticism or rejection of liberal, tolerant, democratic political systems, to unrelenting attacks on Western values and practice in general and on the United States in particular, to demands for group or national privileges, and to the intransigent hostility of so many countries toward what is the only democracy in the Middle East. With all these factors fostering hatred and prejudice, with democratic systems under great pressure, and with the United States under constant attack by antidemocrats, both internally and externally, there exists a critical need to analyze antisemitism in the contemporary world.

Notes

1. George Orwell, *The Collected Essays, Journalism and Letters*, edited by Sonia Orwell and Ian Angus (New York: Harcourt, Brace, 1968), p. 340.

2. Nathan Perlmutter and Ruth Ann Perlmutter, *The Real Anti-Semitism in America* (New York: Arbor House, 1982), pp. 71–102.

3. Dennis E. Showalter, *Little Man, What Now? Der Stürmer in the Weimar Republic* (Hamdon, Conn.: Archon, 1983).

4. Jacob Talmon, *The Myth of the Nation and the Vision of Revolution* (Berkeley: University of California Press, 1981), p. 551.

5. George Mosse, *Germans and Jews* (New York: Fertig, 1970), p. 206.

6. Isaac Deutscher, *The Non-Jewish Jew and Other Essays* (New York: Oxford University Press, 1968), pp. 11–12.

7. Arthur Koestler, *Arrow in the Blue* (New York: Macmillan, 1952), p. 244.

8. Jacob Katz, *From Prejudice to Destruction: Anti-Semitism, 1700–1933* (Cambridge, Mass.: Harvard University Press, 1980), p. 322.

9. Jacob Katz, "Post-Emancipation Development of Rights: Liberalism and Universalism," in David Sidorsky, ed., *Essays on Human Rights* (Philadelphia: Jewish Publication Society, 1979), p. 287.

10. Arthur Hertzberg, *The French Enlightenment and the Jews* (New York: Columbia University Press, 1968), p. 313.

11. Walter Rathenau, quoted in Theodore S. Hamerow, "Cravat Jews and Caftan Jews," *Commentary* (May 1984), p. 35.

12. Hamerow, op. cit., p. 35.

13. Mosse, op. cit., p. 35.

14. Dennis Prager and Joseph Telushkin, *Why the Jews? The Reason for Antisemitism* (New York: Simon & Schuster, 1983), p. 27.

15. Robert Wistrich, "The Anti-Zionist Masquerade," *Midstream* (August-September 1983), p. 10.

16. Paul Lendvai, *Antisemitism Without Jews: Communist Eastern Europe* (Garden City, N.Y.: Doubleday, 1971).

17. *Spectator*, 19 June 1982.

18. *Observer*, 26 June 1982.

19. Prager and Telushkin, op. cit., p. 43.

20. Gertrude J. Selznick and Stephen Steinberg, *The Tenacity of Prejudice* (New York: Harper & Row, 1969), p. 6.

21. Jean-Paul Sartre, *Anti-Semite and Jew* (New York: Schocken, 1948), p. 53.

22. Rodolphe Loewenstein, *Psychanalzse de l'Antisémitisme* (Paris: Presses Universitaires de France, 1952), p. 137.

23. Norman Cohn, *Warrant for Genocide: The Myth of the Jewish World-Conspiracy and the Protocols of the Elders of Zion* (New York: Harper & Row, 1967), pp. 16, 266.

24. Yehuda Bauer, *The Holocaust in Historical Perspective* (Seattle: University of Washington Press, 1978), p. 35.

25. American Jewish Committee Study by William Schneider, quoted in Perlmutter and Perlmutter, op. cit., p. 168.

26. Katz, *From Prejudice to Destruction*, op. cit., p. 320.

27. Harold E. Quinley and Charles Y. Glock, *Anti-Semitism in America* (New York: Free Press, 1979), pp. 158–183.

28. Pierre Vidal-Nacquet, *Les Juifs, la mémoire et le présent* (Paris: Maspero, 1981), pp. 218–220.

29. Hertzberg, op. cit., p. 353.

30. Jacob Talmon, "Mission and Testimony: The Universal Significance of Modern Anti-Semitism," in Sidorsky, op. cit., p. 341.

31. W. D. Rubinstein, *The Left, the Right and the Jews* (New York: Universe Books, 1982), pp. 11–12.

32. Annie Kriegel, *Les Juifs et le Monde Moderne* (Paris: Editions du Seuil, 1977), p. 47.

33. Perlmutter and Perlmutter, op. cit., p. 90.

34. Selznick and Steinberg, op. cit., p. 119.

35. Bernard Lewis, *The Jews of Islam* (Princeton, N.J.: Princeton University Press, 1984), p. 33.

36. Amnon Cohen, *Jewish Life Under Islam: Jerusalem in the Sixteenth Century* (Cambridge, Mass.: Harvard University Press, 1984).

37. Yehuda Bauer, "Anti-Semitism Today," *Midstream* (October 1984), p. 25.

38. Wistrich, op. cit., p. 9.

Part One

Philosophy and Ideology

2

Philosophical Reflections on Antisemitism

Emil L. Fackenheim

I would like to begin with a personal anecdote dating back some forty years. I was a Reform rabbi in Hamilton, Canada, and by tradition in that city the Reform rabbi is almost automatically chairman of the Public Relations Committee of the Jewish community. One afternoon, in that capacity, I got an urgent phone call from some members of a small Orthodox synagogue. It was a great emergency, they said, and I had to come right over. So I jumped on the bus and went there. There I was told that a terrible catastrophe had occurred, and that I had to write letters to newspapers all over Canada. What had happened? A window had been broken! So I told them not to worry, that some kids had thrown stones, and that they might have done it just as easily at a church. And I went home thinking there were still some Jews who saw an antisemite behind every tree.

I report this anecdote because although in a superficial sense I was right, I now think that in a profound sense these old East European Jews were right and I was wrong. Remember, that was the time when one part of the world was murdering every available Jew while the rest of the world was doing very little about it. It has taken researchers a long time to find out what the government of Canada, our country, was doing—or rather was *not* doing—about saving some Jewish souls. These old Jews, I think, knew the depressing facts in their guts. They had relatives being murdered on the other side, and they were helpless. Compared to that monumental manifestation of antisemitism, the reason for which the kids threw stones and whether they would have been equally likely to throw those stones at a church constituted a very minor point.

So I now repent of my "liberal" folly of forty years ago. I also distance myself from the kind of Jewish intellectuals who place liberal

This chapter is an edited version of a paper delivered at a symposium at York University, Toronto, in honor of the late Professor Harry Crowe.

slogans and ideologies between themselves and the stark particularity of the phenomenon known as antisemitism. There are those quick conclusions that antisemitism is a "prejudice," and of course one removes prejudice with "enlightenment." Then there is the quick resort to the "scapegoat theory," which never bothers to explain why the scapegoats are always, or for the most part, the Jews. There is a certain mentality among many liberal Jewish intellectuals that is unable to face reality and instead places ideologies between itself and that reality. I have learned to reject such escapist ideologies from ordinary Jewish people, and in particular from survivors—the very people who are often pictured by these intellectuals as "traumatized." Yet the survivors are the ones who know best that we cannot afford to see an antisemite behind a tree when one isn't there.

I have also learned a lot from some Gentile scholars who, because they are Gentiles, are free of the Jewish hangups I am alluding to. Perhaps foremost among them is the man in whose honor this chapter was originally written. I have never participated in the annual University of Toronto Zionist Symposium when the committee would have dreamt of choosing anyone except Harry Crowe as chairman and when Harry did not bring profound insights to bear on whatever the topic was. I also want to mention—especially because this chapter will involve a great deal of criticism of Christianity—a great Christian thinker, probably the greatest of our time. In the 1940s Reinhold Niebuhr wrote the following: "When a minority group is hated for its virtues as well as its vices, and when its vices are hated, not so much because they are vices, but because they bear the stamp of uniqueness, we are obviously dealing with a collective psychology that is not easily altered by a little more enlightenment."[1] I have pondered this statement many times and concluded that what is needed is philosophical reflection. (I distinguish this sharply from ideology, which is escapist and, in this case, flees into generalities. Philosophy must be anything but escapist.) When there is something unique to wonder at, it is precisely then that philosophy must not resort to generalities but, rather, must stop at the phenomenon in question.

I

To begin with, let me therefore list some peculiarities of antisemitism that would seem to call for philosophical reflection. The first one Niebuhr has already brought to our attention: the peculiarity that Jews are criticized by antisemites for their virtues as well as for their vices. For example, nineteenth-century antisemites claimed to hate Jews because they were a "nation within a nation" (i.e., still had some collective vitality) and a "bloodless shadow" (i.e., because they did not have it). The familiar shout was "Hep! Hep!" which is the abbreviation of a Latin phrase ("*Hyroselyma Est Perdita*") meaning "Jerusalem is destroyed." They gloated over that, that Jews were not a nation! The Jews, in other words, must not be a nation like other nations and also must not *not* be a nation like other nations. One feels like saying, "Antisemite, please make up your mind. Which is the virtue and which is the vice? Take your pick, criticize Jews for the vice, but not for the virtue!"

In our own century, a generation ago, Jews were criticized for supposedly flocking like sheep to the slaughter, when others in the same situation might have been praised for the martyrdom with which they faced death without resisting their persecutors when this was futile. Yet today Jews are criticized for being militarists, when others in the same situation would surely be praised for the courage with which they defend themselves against those who want to destroy them. Once again, one would like to say to the antisemite, "Make up your mind. Which is the virtue, which is the vice?" Here, then, is one phenomenon for which I see no counterpart in any other form of "prejudice" or in any of the countless other evils that beset our world. Of course, it is very easy to mention antisemitism and then immediately to talk about other evils, like racism, or the war in Vietnam, or Hiroshima. The typical liberal intellectual or clergyman quickly draws parallels between them and antisemitism! The liberal, as Jean-Paul Sartre has said, is a very busy man, fighting as he does many evils. However, when we talk about antisemitism, let us not talk about other evils—which is not to say, of course, that other evils might not be equally bad or even worse.

The next unique, and perhaps related, characteristic of antisemitism is its extraordinary persistence. Civilizations change, yet antisemitism persists. Again and again, a new world comes into being and it is said that antisemitism was only a "medieval" thing, now past. (Maybe it was just "religious prejudice.") And then, after a while, along comes a Voltaire, and in the new world antisemitism reappears as an antireligious prejudice.

Third, and presumably related to the second characteristic, there seems to be an extraordinary mutability to the phenomenon, such that many would say the various forms are not the same at all. ("Religious" antisemitism, say, has no connection with "racist" antisemitism.) Undoubtedly, there are profound differences. But no one reflecting deeply on the issue can say that the two are not the same phenomenon at all.

Next, I have used the word "prejudice" in quotation marks. Unlike a genuine prejudice, antisemitism does not seem to disappear when knowledge comes on the scene. Let me give two examples, one at the lowest, most horrendous level, the other at the highest and most exalted, if indeed not saintly, level. In 1944, Joseph Goebbels declared in a public speech in the Berlin Sportpalast that in this war all the nations of Europe had suffered, but that there was one people who had not suffered but only profited from the war—the Jews. Of course, Goebbels, if anyone, knew that when he was uttering these words most of the Jews of Europe had already been murdered. This did not stop him from saying what he did with every sign of conviction.

That was the horrendous. Let me turn now to the most exalted. Among recent Christian theologians few have been more saintly, more courageous than Karl Barth. In his *Dogmatics,* Barth described a visit to a synagogue in Prague, the famous Altneuschul. He remarked that when he saw the synagogue surrounded by a cemetery, he realized that Jews were the shadow of a people no longer alive. A few friends and I once had a meeting with Barth, one of the few if not the only Jewish-Christian dialogue in which the great thinker ever participated. One of us, perhaps the most forward of the lot, and in this it was proper to be forward—Steven Schwarzschild—said to Barth: "Professor Barth, did you go inside that synagogue? If you had, you would have seen Jews profoundly alive, Jews studying the Talmud." In retrospect, I wonder whether, had Barth gone inside that synagogue, it would have made any difference. Jews would still have been a shadow. Knowledge apparently does not by itself remove antisemitism, which is why one cannot call it a prejudice. ("Prejudice" is judgment before knowledge.) And one could give a long list of saints as well as sinners, of the experts as well as the ignorant, who were and are antisemites.

All the above aspects of uniqueness pale in comparison to yet another. This climactic one no discussion of antisemitism in our time can ignore. It is clearly present in the unsurpassable form of antisemitism—the Nazi Holocaust. And while one hates to mention any other form of antisemitism in the same breath as Nazism, to say that there is no connection would be absurd. Hence the need for philosophical reflection.

Not many philosophers have given it that. Among those few was Jean-Paul Sartre. And his book, *Anti-Semite and Jew,* deserves serious attention.[2] What he concluded from the facts as he knew them is that antisemitism is not a legitimate opinion, not a prejudice, but, rather, a criminal passion and that it is criminal because its ultimate goal is the death of the Jew. Here a searching philosopher has come to the bottom of things: What else can the real goal be when the enemy of Jews hates their virtues as well as their vices? Their vices as well as their virtues?

Sartre saw this very clearly. What he did not see is where this strange and unique phenomenon comes from, and how it could have arisen at all. The reason Sartre did not see this lies in his failure to consider history. To explain and understand the phenomenon without history is impossible.

II

A profound historian of the Holocaust, Raul Hilberg, early in his monumental work *The Destruction of the European Jews,* wrote a sentence that, when I first read it, shocked me profoundly. It continues to shock me but, pondering it again and again, I now find it necessary to quote it because I think it is true: "The missionaries of Christianity had said in effect 'you have no right to live among us as Jews.' The secular rulers who followed had proclaimed: 'You have no right to live among us.' The German Nazis at last decreed: 'You have no right to live.'"[3] I find this statement shocking yet true for two reasons. First, it asserts the persistence of Jew-hatred, during long centuries when many times it seemed to have virtually disappeared. The Middle Ages were by no means, as far as Jews are concerned, a uniformly black period. There were long periods of Christian-Jewish tolerance, if not friendship. The early vitriolic sermons of, say, Saint John Chrysostom seemed to have been forgotten. This, however, does not alter the shocking fact that during the Crusades Jew-hatred suddenly reappeared as if from underground. Again, before 1933 in Germany, if anyone had suggested to me that there was some connection between contemporary life and medieval church legislation against the Jews I would have laughed. Anyone would have laughed. Yet Hilberg has chilling tables of comparison between medieval-Christian and Nazi-German anti-Jewish legislation.

Persistence, then, is the first fact brought out by Hilberg, and it teaches a fundamental lesson—that it won't do to sweep Jew-hatred under the carpet. I am reminded of my student days some forty years ago, when I studied the writings of St. Thomas Aquinas, with a very beloved teacher at the Toronto Institute of Medieval Studies. One day I came to his office to study St. Thomas and there on his desk was a pamphlet in French entitled "St. Thomas and the Jews." I said that I was interested and asked if I could borrow it. He replied that he didn't want me to see it. I insisted, and he gave it to me. It was written by a Catholic writer from Quebec who was deriving from St. Thomas the available anti-Jewish sentiments for modern application, to the effect that Jews do not deserve equal rights in a democratic but somehow Christian state. I think now that although my teacher had the right moral sensibility, he was wrong in thinking that I should not see the document or, more important, the anti-Jewish passages in Aquinas's work itself. Perhaps what we really should have studied was not St. Thomas's doctrine of analogy but rather how Jews and Christians together can cope with the phenomenon of Christian Jew-hatred that has been between them for so many centuries. No, sweeping the past under the carpet, though no doubt well-intentioned, won't do. That is the first lesson.

The second lesson comes when we consider the second fact implied in Hilberg's statement. If the persistence of antisemitism through the centuries is shocking, then what shall we say of the escalation of it? We have been told by the Catholic theologian Rosemary Ruether that even St. Chrysostom never preached violence against Jews. (After all, the man was a saint.) Yet without those sermons of his, or others like them, the expulsions of Jews in the Middle Ages—surely acts of violence— could not have occurred. One can picture St. Chrysostom actually protesting against these violent acts while having to admit to himself that without his preachings they could not have taken place.

Yet, concerning escalation, the medieval version was dwarfed by the unsurpassable modern one, which did not occur until our own time. Torquemada burnt Jewish bodies in order to save Jewish souls. The Eichmanns of this world did their best to destroy Jewish souls before consigning Jewish bodies to the gas chambers. From this terrible process of escalation we must derive our second lesson. If the first lesson is not to sweep the past evil under the carpet, the second is that nothing less will do than to deescalate the escalation, unless the new escalation is to win the victory. We may think that we live in a modern, postmedieval world, yet it is still a world in which it is widely taken for granted that Jews are supposed to be homeless. That was not so before the medieval expulsions. Shall the post-Holocaust world be one in which the very right of Jews to exist is debatable?

III

I have used Hilberg's thesis, yet there is a most obvious objection to it: What of ancient pagan antisemitism, prior to the Christian variety? There were accusations of antisemitism such as those of Manetho, the Egyptian priest, and of Apion, against whom Josephus wrote. Writers such as these balked at "Jewish exclusiveness." In wider circles, a great deal of anti-Jewishness undoubtedly resulted from the wars that the Jewish people waged in order not to be engulfed by the flood of Hellenism—namely, the Maccabean War, the anti-Roman War ending in the second destruction of Jerusalem, and finally the Bar Kochba War. Reflecting on those early phenomena, I have found myself in the rare position of answering in the affirmative a most crucial question, "Do Jews themselves cause antisemitism?" Yes, maybe in one respect they do! Significantly, this issue was articulated for me by a philosopher, the late Leo Strauss. If there is a people who reject what other nations consider holiest, namely their gods, and scorn them as idols or nothings, then there is bound to be a deep resentment. We hear of ancient Jews not wanting Roman emperor statues in their temples. That attitude must have caused much resentment.

There is, then, a considerable case to be made for the significance of ancient antisemitism. Yet in weighing this case, I conclude that had the Christian transfiguration of antisemitism not occurred in the ancient world, it would have died with the ancient world. It was, in fact, well on the way to happening. To give an example on the side of the Jews, the bitter opposition to idolatry was becoming milder. Corresponding to this milder attitude on the part of the rabbis, of course, is a demythologization on the part of the Greco-Roman world itself. I will give a few examples of relative Roman tolerance. Hadrian, the most anti-Jewish Roman emperor, went so far as to make Jerusalem into a pagan city and to forbid Jews to live in it; yet four years later, his successor, Emperor Antoninus, revoked the decree. Later in the Roman

Empire, Jews were permitted to remain Jews and yet to become Roman citizens. Perhaps one could say that the ancient pagans criticized Jews for their presumed vices but not for their presumed virtues. Theophrastus, the disciple of Aristotle, attacked what he considered the barbaric Jewish institution of animal sacrifices, but he praised Jews for their monotheism—for being, as he put it, "philosophers by race."

Now compare all this to early Christianity. When I say "early Christianity," I confine myself to the Church Fathers. One could make a very large case about the New Testament. But let us assume, for the purposes of this argument, that many of the anti-Jewish elements in the New Testament would not have become effective unless there had been a need to reiterate them in later generations—and this is what happened in the case of the Church Fathers. The Roman Empire, as I have said, admitted Jews to citizenship; it had hardly become "holy" in the fourth century when their citizenship was revoked. More significant still, the expulsion of Jews from Jerusalem under Hadrian lasted only four years; but for more than one Church Father, "circumcision was given by God to the Jews not as a sign of Divine favour, but as a mark of their future reprobation, so that they might be recognized by those presently occupying the city and preventing them from entering it."[4] God Himself, then, presumably wanted the Jews to be expelled from Jerusalem, and the Roman Empire revoked what, in the mind of the Church, was not being revoked by God! One can see here a connection with the nineteenth-century anti-Jewish insult in Germany, "Hep! Hep! ("Jerusalem is destroyed").

Let me give you a few examples from the Patristic anti-Judaic literature. Rosemary Ruether deserves great credit for having brought this literature out from under the carpet, and in what follows I rely on her entirely. St. Augustine, a thinker I have always cherished, appropriated the Old Testament for Christianity. What does this mean? In the Old Testament itself there are both curses and blessings for Jews. In the Christian appropriation, all the curses go to the Jews, and the blessings to the Christians—a transformation that at once produces two evils: self-righteousness among the Christians and condemnation of the Jews. For St. Chrysostom it was not enough even to appropriate the Old Testament in this manner. For him even the Maccabees become martyrs for Christ's sake. When confronted with such a stance, a Jew might understandably exclaim, "If you must rob us of our Bible, won't you at least leave our post-Biblical heritage alone?" "No," the Church replied; "if you have saints, they belong to us." Here, in essence, is the much-quoted modern antisemitic statement, the significance of which is much deeper than is commonly realized: "Some of my best friends are Jews." This, supposedly a refutation of the charge of antisemitism, is in fact an expression of it. It means that anyone who is a good friend isn't really a Jew. Jews may be saints; the very fact that they are saints makes them an exception, and what that means is that they are not Jews at all. Antisemites who say that some of their best friends are Jews could maintain, theoretically, that 99 percent of all Jews are their friends. But that would still leave the *real* Jews, who are not.

In the following example what I said previously about Jewish vices and virtues really comes clear. The present virtues of the Jews, St. Chrysostom wrote, are worse than their past vices. In the past, as we read in the Old Testament, the Jews perpetually broke the Law, which is why they were reprimanded by God. What are they doing now? Why, they are *keeping* the Law! And that they should keep the Law now is worse than to have broken it in the past. In fact, who are the Jews? They are the ones who forever do what God does not want them to do. For Chrysostom, that is almost the definition of Jews. And from here there is only one step to the statement that the father of the Jews is not Abraham but Cain. This is said by none other than that beloved friend from my student days, St. Augustine. Justin Martyr took up the issue from here in asserting that if their father is Cain, the Jews must be landless. Their city and their land are not only desolate, but now they must remain so forever. Not surprisingly, it is St. Chrysostom with whom the logic of this kind of thought reached the ultimate conclusion: that the Jews are "fit for slaughter." Here we have the roots of the phenomenon described by Sartre, who did not however, get to the roots because he ignored history.

Now, what should we conclude from all this? Obviously the Church Fathers went much further than the New Testament. For example, when it comes to the argument of whether St. Paul was an antisemite, it is always possible to stress that he did not reject his own people forever. There is a qualitative difference involved when the father of the Jews is regarded as Cain rather than Abraham, and when their land is not only desolate now but must stay so forever. How is this to be explained? As Ruether writes, "For the Christianity of the Fathers, Anti-Judaism is not merely a defence against attacks but an intrinsic need of Christian self-affirmation."[5]

IV

So much for the first part of Hilberg's statement. Let me now come to the second, that pertaining to the "secular rulers"—those who, in effect, said to the Jews: "You have no right to live among us." I previously mentioned that even St. Chrysostom never incited to violence. Of course, violence is, potentially at least, in his very words. Moreover, it would be a mistake to generalize that the saints, just because they were saints, never advocated violence. Thus, in the first century when a synagogue in Callinuum was destroyed and the Roman emperor demanded that compensation should be paid to have it rebuilt, St. Ambrose protested strongly and thereby, at least implicitly, endorsed the violence.

Still, there is a quantum leap from words to deeds when the latter are no longer sporadic—from the position "you have the right to live among us as Jews," to the position "you have no right to live among us." This leap occurred when beliefs and words became enacted into law. Law creates a world, and in the new world Jews have no right to live. Moreover, the escalation creating a new world creates precedents for later times. In this connection one hesitates to mention, but cannot help mentioning, that in 1919 Adolf Hitler wrote a notorious letter in which he said that pogroms were not enough. They were emotional, unsystematic, and therefore ineffective. Needed was "the removal of the Jews as a whole," and this required the action of law. Hitler did not specify at that time what kind of "removal" he had in mind—whether it was medieval or modern. Still, the medieval precedent was there.

What sort of world is created by the law? In this case, it was a world in which antisemitism was a self-fulfilling prophecy. Jews were supposed to be landless, so the law had to make them landless, by prohibiting them from owning it. Jews were supposed to be cursed, so the law had to make them cursed. Jews were supposed to suffer, so the law had to make them suffer. This sort of logic led to the medieval expulsions, and thus the Jews were no longer at home in the lands of their domicile; yet they also could not return to their own land for it had been devastated, and Jerusalem, too, had been destroyed, so they became "eternal wanderers." (Ahasuerus, the Jew as restless wanderer, is a legend not of Jewish making but, rather, one of Christian making.)

This, then, is the world produced by medieval Christian law, and once it has been produced it tends to seem right and natural. It has been taken for natural even though, of course, it is historical. And, unless the whole escalation is deescalated, the precedent will persist and continue to exert its power. To quote from my recent *To Mend the World*:

> [In 1933] Martin Buber was forced to write to the Nazi Christian theologian Gerhard Kittel as follows: "Authentic Jewry, you say, remains faithful to the symbol of the restless and homeless alien who wanders the earth. Judaism does not know such a symbol. The wandering Jew is a figure in Christian legend, not a Jewish figure." Kittel had invoked the image of the wandering Jew, not only to justify the Nazi reversal of the emancipation of German Jews, but also to argue that "authentic" Jews (and needless to say, Christians) were religiously required to accept it. Close to forty years later Father Daniel Berrigan asserted that in Israel "the wandering Jew became the settler Jew . . . [and] the slave became master and created slaves." Just as Kittel had no need to investigate whether German Jews had behaved like a "foreign people," so Berrigan had no need to find out whether kibbutzniks were "settlers" and Israel in general "masters" who "created slaves." In both cases the "eternal wanderer" stereotype was quite enough.[6]

The stereotype has power over the nice people as well as the nasty ones. Ours is a grim age in which there are many groups and vast numbers of refugees. All of them together do not attract the attention of the Palestinian Arabs alone. Why is this so? Correspondingly, why doesn't anybody ever stop to consider that more than half of the Jewish population of Israel consists of Jewish refugees from Arab countries? Why is this so? Are all those guilty of one or both of these errors to be called antisemites? No, but they are heirs to the medieval world. That there are Jewish refugees is a fact of life accepted as natural even by those who do not like it. That the Jewish self-liberation in the former Palestine should, unhappily, have created refugees who are not Jewish is unnatural even in the eyes of many who endorse the collective Jewish self-liberation. As the saying goes, it doesn't make news when a dog bites a man, but it does make news when a man bites a dog. The difference, of course, is that the proverbial man-dog case is based on nature but there is nothing natural about the other case. It is a case of history having regrettably become second nature.

V

I now come to Hilberg's third point—a concept that boggles the mind. As the Nazi policy represents the unprecedented with which we still are struggling, and as we are not very close to understanding it, I can only try my best to explain.

In the beginning was the word—the code word *antisemitism*. Somebody concocted that code word way back in the nineteenth century, but it does not matter who it was.[7] What really matters is that it caught on. (It is still being used, in fact.) As the nineteenth century was a scientific age in which many people no longer believed in Christ, it became difficult to call Jews "Christ-killers." Hence it became necessary to find a new—and, if possible, scientific-sounding—word to rationalize the old hatred. The word found was *antisemitism*.

James Parkes has argued for many years that we shouldn't spell *antisemitism* with a hyphen because that suggests there is something called *semitism* that the *anti* is against. But of course there is no such thing as semitism, nor has antisemitism ever been directed against the Arabs.[8]

In nineteenth-century Germany, there were three kinds of antisemite: the right-wing antisemites, for whom the Jews were all revolutionaries; the left-wing antisemites, for whom the Jews were all money-bags and capitalists; and the liberal antisemites, who didn't actually hate Jews but did disapprove of them. Given that two kinds of liberals existed in Germany at the time, there were two reasons for disapproval. The internationalist liberals disapproved of Jews because they were too clannish and did not take part in the concerns of mankind. The nationalist liberals, who were more typically German, complained that the Jews were not clannish enough, that they mixed with German culture.

Now that was an extraordinary situation. Jews couldn't be both all Marxists and capitalists, too clannish and not clannish enough. And one should have thought that these contradictory accusations would cancel each other out. That is what the Jewish defense organizations of those days believed, which is why they proposed to refute these accusations—an activity that proved totally useless. These organizations believed in what one might call the logic of God—a logic in the service of the truth. What they did not realize is that there is also a logic of the devil. The latter serves the lie, and tries to preserve the hatred that lies underneath by creating from the lie a consistent system. That, in this case, was quite a job—but the *Protocols of the Elders of Zion*, that notorious forgery, caught on like wildfire nevertheless. Even the *London Times* thought for a while there was something to the *Protocols*.[9] And Henry Ford peddled the book in the United States.[10] Why, according to the *Protocols*, the Jews only pretend to be revolutionaries concerned with the poor or, alternatively, to be interested only in money. They only pretend to love German culture. It's all part of a secret Jewish plot to dominate the world.

Here you see what has been happening all along. When an escalation takes place, the hatred is not only preserved; it is escalated and transfigured. Great as their Jew-hatred was, the Church Fathers would have said that there was one way in which a Jew could save himself, and that was by accepting redemption in Christ. But what would be said within the modern plot theory when a Jew became a Christian and joined a church? Why, now they are infiltrating the Church! So the hatred itself becomes transformed and escalated.

Now, from the standpoint of the "devil," there is still one stage left if the hatred is to become ultimate and unsurpassable. This I recognized one day in a flash, when the Canadian Broadcasting Corporation (which at one time loved to include Nazis in its shows as they were good for the ratings) featured Norman Lincoln Rockwell. One American Nazi maintained that "Hitler never murdered all the Jews, only Jewish traitors!" And the fellow who interviewed him did not have the wit or gumption to ask: "What about the children?" Children, even Jewish ones, are not plotters or traitors. So from the standpoint of the "devil," if the hatred was to reach the ultimate, one had to produce an equation without precedent and equal anywhere in human history: *For Jews and for Jews only, existence itself is a crime, punishable by torture and death.* That is what happened in the Nazi regime; on the one hand, Jews were "vermin" to be "exterminated" and, on the other hand, devils to be tortured. Nazi antisemitism is improperly called racism—a great evil, of course, but an evil different from antisemitism. Racism holds that there are lower races who, nevertheless, are still human. For Nazis, Jews are not of the human race at all, as neither vermin nor devils are human.

The Nazis often did not understand this equation themselves. There was one fearful moment in an interview with Franz Stangl, the commandant of Treblinka. The interviewer asked this question: "If they were going to murder them anyway, what was the purpose of those terrible tortures that preceded the murders?" Stangl replied to the effect that the Nazis had tried to condition the murderers to the terrible deeds they had to do. But this does not make any sense at all. Which would have been easier on the stomachs of all those Nazi murderers—to kill people with clean rifle or machine gun shots? Or to go through endless processes of torture? Generals Patton and Eisenhower witnessed some of the evidence when they entered the concentration camp at Ohrdruf. Patton became sick, and Eisenhower said, "I want every American unit not actually in the front lines to see this place. We are told that the American soldier does not know what he is fighting for. At least he will know what he is fighting against." He added that the American mind cannot understand this. He should have said "the human mind." And yet it happened.[11]

I must discuss this terrible escalation once more, this time not from the standpoint of the Jewish victims but from that of the German people themselves. Those nineteenth-century right-wing antisemites, however absurd their belief that the German Jews who loved German culture actually wanted to destroy it, at least loved German culture themselves. In turn, the left-wing antisemites, however absurd their belief that the Jews were all in league with Rothschild, were at least concerned with the poor.

But what, one must ask, was the positive counterpart to the Nazi murder of the Jews? Superficially it seems that there was such a counterpart: "Today we have Germany, tomorrow the world." This slogan was shouted from the house tops. But when one asks what the Nazis were going to do with the world once they had it, no answer is available. Hermann Rauschning called the Nazi revolution a "revolution of nihilism." And except for one matter he was right. At the height of the Nazi regime, however, it looked as if there were two points: murder of Jews and domination of the world. These two points were no longer true, however, at the time of the apocalypse. In the Berlin bunker, Hitler and Goebbels, the only true Nazis left in the last days of the war, expressed ghoulish satisfaction at what they thought was the imminent demise not of their enemies, to say nothing of the Jews, but of the German people themselves. And there were two significant last acts that Hitler performed. One was a last will and testament spouting once more a murderous hatred of Jews. The other was an order, no longer obeyed, to flood the Berlin subways in a last attempt to stop the Russian armies. Visualize the apocalyptic scene: Berlin was surrounded by the Russian armies. Bombs were falling from the skies. And German civilians were hiding in the subways. The officer given the order said to Hitler, "But *mein Führer*, if we flood those subways, we shall drown German men, women and children!" And Hitler, that great lover of German children, replied, "Let them drown!" Of all the world's empires, the German Nazi Empire was the only one that left not a single positive accomplishment in its wake—for which reason we cannot entirely blame the German people when they act as if those twelve years that were equal to a thousand never happened at all. There is just one lasting monument, and that one is a negative. It is the presence of an absence—6 million murdered Jews.

VI

After all this there was a moment of great repose when the death camps were revealed and many, myself included, were prepared to declare that this was the end of antisemitism everywhere—that it was the ultimate revelation of an evil that had haunted Europe and much of the rest of the world for far too long a time. And in that moment of repose occurred some glorious achievements. In that moment the State of Israel was declared by the United Nations. (Now that organization is rightly called by the Christian theologian Roy Eckardt "the effective world centre of antisemitism.") Then there was also a deep soul-searching in the churches in an attempt to remove, to root out, the "teaching of contempt" (as it was called) for the Jewish people—an effort culminating, perhaps, in Vatican II, (the council, convened by Pope John XXIII (1962–1965), that repudiated the idea of collective Jewish guilt for the crucifixion and stressed the spiritual bond between Catholics and Jews). Then there was an acceptance of the Jewish collective right to a state of their own, not only by the West but by the East as well. If one reads Gromyko's UN speech of May 14, 1947, supporting partition of the area of Palestine and the creation of a Jewish state (which took place at the time of the vote in behalf of a Jewish state), one can hardly believe it.

The repose was soon destroyed. It was destroyed, or beginning to be destroyed, in the three weeks preceding the Six-Day War, when the same sort of words emanated from Cairo, Amman, and Damascus that had once emanated from Berlin and Vienna. The man who said at that time, "Kill the Jews wherever you find them, kill them with your nails and with your teeth"—that was King Hussein of Jordan. Another moderate, Faisal of Saudi Arabia, said in 1971 that Jews had strayed from the Law of Moses, killed Jesus, and were cursed by God through the Prophets forever. Yet another, Anwar Sadat, maintained as early as 1955 that "our war against the Jews is an old battle which Mohammed began. It is our duty to fight the Jews, in the name of Allah and in the name of our religion. It is our duty to finish the war which we have begun." (One wonders what "finishing it" would mean.) That same statesman declared in 1972 that Israel must be returned to the humiliation and wretchedness that was established in the Koran, and that Jews are a nation of liars, and traitors, a people born for deeds of treachery.[12] Jews reading such words can only conclude that just as one "daughter religion" of Judaism—Christianity—has found it difficult to tolerate her "mother," so, to put it mildly, did the other (namely, Islam).

This hostile rhetoric is one kind of thing that destroyed repose for Jews in those three weeks preceding the Six-Day War. Another was the silence in the churches. Some Jewish people had been in dialogue with Christians for a long time; for me personally, the dialogue began in the concentration camp of Sachsenhausen in 1938 with a few Christians who were there for much nobler reasons than such as I. Yet now, when there seemed to be the threat of a second Holocaust, there was a silence in the churches. All these years we had talked theology—and there was silence now because the subject that concerned us was "politics."

This experience of silence prompted me to think up a parable. Two friends walk in a forest, engaged in friendly conversation. Suddenly, one falls into a swamp and shouts "Help!" But the other cannot hear him. Well, since all great parables must have at least two versions, here is the second: The one falls into the swamp, and the other hears him but asks, "What is the matter? We had such a nice conversation, so why are you changing the subject?" That was my parable in 1967. Since then, with the resurgence of the old antisemitism and the appearance of a new, I changed the parable. The one falling into the swamp shouts: "Help—and watch out, my friend! You too may fall into a swamp—and the swamp will be the same." After the Holocaust, any new antisemitism tolerated within Christianity may destroy what is left of the reality of the religion of love.

This year I wonder whether the parable might have to be changed again—whether, perhaps, the other hears his friend but falls into the swamp all the same and, in his attempt to get out, accidentally—or perhaps not so accidentally—steps on his friend and shoves him down deeper. That possibility occurred to me when I read with shock of the pope's granting of an interview with Yasser Arafat. This is a subject to which I shall have to return in a few moments.

Meanwhile, I must first face the logically and morally impossible fact of a post-Holocaust antisemitism. Surely such a thing is impossible following the ultimate revelation of antisemitism given to the whole world! Of course, here and there may be those who have never heard of the Holocaust or else have truly forgotten it. Can post-Holocaust antisemitism exist when antisemites themselves invoke the Holocaust and turn it against the Jewish people? How is such a thing possible? The conclusion to which I am driven is this: that there has been a resurrection of the devil's logic. In effect, the present right-wing version of the devil's logic states that Hitler never murdered any Jews—and that he should have finished the job.

So much for the devil's new logic on the extreme right. We now turn to the extreme left. If for the right, Hitler never murdered any Jews, for the left he murdered, yes, not Jews but his victims were human beings-in-general. Hence Jews today are thought by some to be guilty of parochialism if they so much as mention the Jewish identity of the Jewish victims, if indeed not guilty of a racism that sets the Jewish above all the other "victims of fascism."

Five years ago, my wife and I went to visit refuseniks in the Soviet Union. When we arrived in Riga, a refusenik urged us to visit Salaspils, a nearby concentration camp site, but after that to go as well to Rumbula, a camp where, as was not the case at Salaspils, only Jews were murdered. So we went to Salaspils, a tremendous memorial site where no expenditure has been spared to keep memory alive. (Not the slightest evidence remained, however, that any Jews were murdered there.) We stayed on at Salaspils for such a long time that the head of the place noticed us and asked us to sign the visitor's book. So we opened the book, and the first statement was a very moving one in Hungarian, saying that the world must see to it that such terrible things can never happen again. We then opened the next page and saw a long statement in Arabic, with a translation in English attached, to the effect that "We too have suffered, at the hands of the Israeli Nazis, and mourn for those who suffered at the hands of the German Nazis." I wrote in response, "Let no one pervert, for whatever cause, what happened here."

We then asked our tourist guide to stop at Rumbula, a totally neglected place. We got out of the car, looked at the miserable stone, and asked our guide to translate for us. And this is what it said: "To the memory of concentration camp inmates, political prisoners, etc." Jews are the "etc."

Soon after that, in Minsk, we stood before the only memorial (so far as I know) in the whole Soviet Union in which Jews are mentioned, which says in Yiddish: "In memory of the 3,000 Jews murdered here, by the greatest enemies of all mankind." Rather universalistic, yes? But not universalistic enough for Stalin, for it is in Yiddish and it mentions Jews. So the man who put it up was sent to Siberia. Throughout the Soviet Union the memory of Hitler's Jewish victims is systematically suppressed! Thus they are murdered a second time. But then, all this is no different from what happened on the University of Toronto campus in the autumn of 1982 with the emergence of the Trotskyite slogan "Lebanon is the Holocaust, and Beirut the Warsaw Ghetto." This is stealing the Holocaust, for whatever the sufferings and evils in Lebanon, they bear no resemblance to the Holocaust. And the theft can only have one purpose: to do on the left what the neo-Nazis are doing on the right. For the right, the Holocaust never happened, yet the job should be finished. For the left, it happened, yes, but it did not happen to the Jews; rather, it happened to humans-in-general or, perhaps more precisely, to all humankind except Jews.

But what about the people who really matter to the Jewish people and the fight against antisemitism—their friends the liberals? Perhaps we should have guessed all along that this liberal friendship wouldn't always be easy, either, given that in the 1950s Arnold Toynbee compared what the Israelis supposedly were doing to the Palestinian Arabs with what the Nazis had done to the Jews. The same thing happened in Montreal, and the public debate that ensued between Toynbee and the then Israeli Ambassador Yaacov Herzog is available in print as well as on two long-playing records.[13] There, one may hear Toynbee saying twice: "What the Nazis did to Jews was nothing peculiar." Here we have a supposedly great historian who is blotting out the uniqueness of the Holocaust—the murder trains, the gas chambers, the poisonous propaganda leading up to it, to say nothing of its background in Christian Jew-hatred. In 1974, too, Yasser Arafat appeared before the United Nations and committed a systematic theft of the Holocaust; but it was hardly noticed: "If you want to understand it in your terms" [of course, he was addressing the liberal Western democracies, not the Arabs], "the number of Palestinian victims at the hands of the Israeli fascists . . . would be 6,000,000." Nobody can understand the mathematics or should attempt to do so, for the purpose is clear enough. This statement was a bare-faced theft of the Holocaust and a rape of the Western conscience, for of course everyone is familiar with the figure 6,000,000.

So we come to the recent news out of Lebanon that there were supposedly 600,000 homeless Lebanese in the recent war. How many casualties were there? Sixty thousand (*Barrie Examiner*). How many PLO prisoners were there in places in Israel that "could only be called concentration camps"? Six thousand (*Edmonton Sun*). The *Sun* apparently knows what a concentration camp is. It is impossible to consider the number 6 in these cases as incidental. And this is confirmed when one reads that maybe the number in the Nazi Holocaust was only 60,000, that maybe somebody added "00" at the end. And the obscenity of it all reached a climax when, in supposedly respectable magazines, the PLO in Beirut was compared to the Warsaw Ghetto uprising. Of course, unlike the PLO, the Jews in Warsaw had not murdered children; and unlike the Jews in Warsaw, the PLO could get out of Beirut and did get out, with great applause by the world. But this difference in behavior failed to stop the journalists not only from making the comparison but also, in one case, from adding that the Israelis were obtuse to the "irony" of it all.

What is the upshot of these somber recent developments? Despite all protestations to the contrary, the post-Holocaust transfiguration of antisemitism is "anti-Zionism." A qualitative change has once again occurred, of course, but it is the same reality. For pre-Holocaust antisemites, Jews, and Jews only, have no right to exist—or, at any rate, their right to exist is debatable. For post-Holocaust antisemites the Jewish state, and that state alone, has no right to exist—or, at any rate, in its case alone the right to exist is debatable. In a way, the most shocking phenomenon of all concerns those people who forever keep repeating that Israel has a right to exist, and who in saying this legitimate those who say the opposite or act on it. What would anyone think of a person who got up and said "Canada has a right to exist!" Or Ghana?

This is why, in the minds of Jewish people, the pope's recent meeting with Yasser Arafat was a shocking episode and one, indeed, that may have caused a severe setback in Catholic-Jewish relations. For if in this meeting the pope asked Arafat to abrogate the PLO's Palestinian National

Covenant (which clearly calls for Israel's destruction through "armed struggle"), the media did not report it. Would the pope meet with the IRA? Yet the IRA does not seek to destroy Britain.

In my view, one element of that meeting was worse even than the meeting itself. The pope used the occasion to express, once again, the Vatican's wish for the internationalization of Jerusalem. That, of course, may seem a humane, universalistic gesture. However, after 2,000 years of Christian antisemitism, much of it institutionalized, one must ask a few tough questions. The late King Saud of Saudi Arabia lamented that he could not worship in the al-Aksa Mosque because Jerusalem was in Jewish hands; yet he never bothered to go there even once in the nineteen years that it remained in Muslim hands. This is only one striking piece of evidence indicating that Muslim anti-Jewishness is not dead, that it is Jewish Jerusalem that must be negated. So I must ask this question: Why, in the nineteen years that Jerusalem was in Jordanian hands, did the Vatican never once call for the internationalization of Jerusalem?

The Christian theologian Krister Stendahl of Harvard University has noted that in the view of Muslims and Christians Jerusalem has holy sites, but that for Jews Jerusalem itself is holy. That is why the present rebuilding of Jewish Jerusalem is of religious as well as secular significance—almost 2,000 years after the Jewish Jerusalem was destroyed. Yet this is the time that the Vatican chooses to call for the internationalization of Jerusalem—surely a fact requiring the deepest soul-searching on the part of many Christians.

The matter goes beyond ecclesiastical establishments, however. Reporters are keenly interested in all sorts of Arab opinions. Regarding Israelis they seem most interested in critics of the Begin government. But they must begin to ask what Israelis themselves think about Jerusalem. In a recent poll, half the Israeli population was in favor of territorial accommodation in return for peace. On the subject of Jerusalem, the opinions were almost unanimous that the city must remain both united and Jewish.

VII

This brings me to my conclusion, which necessarily concerns not the phenomenon of antisemitism but rather the response to it by Jews themselves. Again and again the sickness of antisemitism, though often thought dead, acquires a new lease on life. How should Jews respond to this depressing fact? Perhaps the medieval philosopher-poet Yehuda Halevi put it best. Living at a time, he says, in which Christians and Muslims are fighting each other, dragging Jews down to doom, he was nevertheless able to write a glowing account of Judaism. In this account, a pagan king who has studied philosophy, Christianity, Islam, and Judaism and finally converts to Judaism asks this deep question of a rabbi: Has he correctly observed that Christians and Muslims are superior in saintliness to Jews? The former have monks and saints, but Jews do not even have monasteries. The rabbi agrees but stresses that the great Jewish virtue is different. It is fidelity. How easy would it be for Jews to escape persecution by converting to Islam or Christianity! Yet only because of fidelity do they still exist at all. Fidelity, therefore, is the virtue of the Jewish people *as a whole*, not just that of the saints or prophets among them. Without fidelity they would have ceased to be.

The focus of this fidelity today is Jerusalem. As Yehuda Haleir once wrote, "Jerusalem will not be redeemed, until Jews yearn for her very dust and stones."

Jews who walk the streets of Jerusalem today are filled with the pain of 2,000 years, but also with a sense of wonder and a great rejoicing. They must surely recall the words of *Lamentations*, which describe from the Jewish side what from the anti-Jewish side is meant by the cry, "Hep! Hep!"—namely, "How solitary doeth the city sit that was full of people." If they look around, they would see Jews from Western countries as well as Muslim and Arab countries—Jews from as far away as India and China. They would be filled with a profound astonishment, as if to say: "The city that sat solitary yesterday, that was ruins even if holy ruins—how full of people it is now!" "Hep! Hep!"—the deepest Jewish response to this in our time is Jewish Jerusalem rebuilt. It is today the most profound expression of the Jewish faith that the long but not incurable disease of Jew-hatred will one day come to an end.

Notes

1. D. B. Robertson, ed., *Love and Justice: Selection from the Shorter Writings of Reinhold Niebuhr* (Cleveland: World Publishing Co., 1967), p. 133.

2. Jean-Paul Sartre, *Anti-Semite and Jew* (New York: Schocken, 1948).

3. Raul Hilberg, *The Destruction of the European Jews* (Chicago: Quadrangle, 1978), pp. 3ff.

4. Rosemary Ruether, *Faith and Fratricide* (New York: Seabury, 1979), p. 147.

5. Ibid., p. 181.

6. Emil L. Fackenheim, *To Mend the World* (New York: Schocken, 1982), p. 93.

7. A rabble-rouser by the name of Wilhelm Marr made the word prominent, but he may not have been the first to use it.

8. See the related discussion in Fackenheim, *To Mend the World*, p. 214.

9. Ralph Lord Roy, *Apostles of Discord* (Boston: Beacon Press, 1953).

10. Albert Lee, *Henry Ford and the Jews* (New York: Stein & Day, 1980).

11. Quoted and discussed in Fackenheim, *To Mend the World*, pp. 202ff.

12. See M. Maoz, "Anti-Jewishness in Official Arab Literature and Communications," in M. Davis, ed., *World Jewry and the State of Israel* (New York: Arno Press, 1977), pp. 33ff.

13. CBS Records, CP 13–14. See also Yaacov Herzog, *A People That Dwells Alone* (London: Weidenfeld Nicolson, 1975), pp. 21–47.

3
Marxism Versus the Jews

Paul Johnson

Why is antisemitism, at least in its new "respectable" form of anti-Zionism, now found predominantly on the left of the political spectrum? Why in particular is this new form increasingly common among intellectuals? If we begin by tackling the second question first, we find a curious paradox. Antisemitism is one of the oldest and most persistent forms of human irrationality; yet its theoretical basis has always been the work of intellectuals. The paradox can be explained. It is true that intellectuals seek to understand phenomena by reason. But in their search for radical explanations, which excite the mind by their audacity and comprehensiveness, they tend to stumble into gigantic fallacies. Inside many intellectuals there is a conspiracy theory of the universe struggling to get out, and sometimes succeeding. And antisemitism is the father of all conspiracy theory.

The first layer of antisemitism, itself a form of anti-Zionism, was laid down by Manetho, a priest from the intellectual community of Heliopolis in Ptolemaic Egypt, about 280 B.C. He presented the Jews as wanderers by nature, descendants of an outcast tribe of lepers, who had no natural land of their own. His theory underlay the response of Hellenistic intellectuals to the disquieting phenomenon of Judaism: They argued that the Jewish rejection of Greek syncretism and universalism was a form of misanthropy, that the Jews were a dislocated people without true territorial title deeds, and that their Diaspora was a conspiracy against humankind. This was the intellectual justification for the first systematic persecution of Jews by Antiochus Epiphanes in the second century B.C. In Roman times a second layer of theory was added by both Greek and Latin writers: Lysimachus of Alexandria; Apion; Nero's tutor Chaeremon, who inspired the second great wave of persecutions; and Horace, Martial, Tacitus, and Juvenal.

A third layer was contributed by Christian writers, including some of the greatest doctors of the Church, such as Gregory of Nyssa, John Chrysostom, Ambrose, Augustine, and Gregory the Great. Some Christians taught that the deicidal Jews were in both local and universal conspiracies with Satan, a notion later explored in innumerable plots and subplots by the investigators of the Inquisition. The writings of Luther added yet another layer of antisemitic theory, which became the pattern for prejudice in Protestant Europe. When the intellectuals of the Enlightenment came to undermine Christianity in the eighteenth century, they produced the first secular layer of antisemitism: Diderot and, to a greater extent, Voltaire engaged in the most virulent attacks on Judaism, partly as an indirect but safer way of attacking the more dangerous target of Christianity.

The implication was that the intellectual foundations of the modern world were warped by antisemitism, for virtually all modern writers were influenced, directly or indirectly, by Voltaire. So at a time when the old Christian myth of the Jews in conspiracy with the Devil was losing force, at least in Western and Central Europe, antisemitism acquired a nonreligious dynamism. It was at this point that a connection between the left and antisemitic theory was first established. The early French Socialists linked the Jews to the new Industrial Revolution and the vast increase in world commerce that marked the beginning of the nineteenth century. In a book published in 1808, François Fourier identified commerce as "the source of all evil" and the Jews as "the incarnation of commerce." The same line was taken by Pierre Joseph Proudhon: In a world poisoned by greed and materialism, the Jews were "the source of evil," who had "rendered the bourgeoisie, high and low, similar to them all over Europe. . . . We should send this race back to Asia or exterminate it." Fourier's pupil, Alphonse Toussenel, worked out in detail the notion of a worldwide financial conspiracy against humanity, run by Jews.

These ideas of the early French Socialists became part of the mainstream of French antisemitism, later reflected in the propaganda of Edouard Drumont and Charles Maurras's Action Française. They were also an early prototype of the National Socialism of Hitler's Germany. Equally important, however, they formed part of the background to Karl Marx's notions of how the world economy worked. The main element in Marx's intellectual formation was, of course, German idealism. Thanks partly to Voltaire, this had always possessed a certain anti-Jewish coloring. As Robert Wistrich has pointed out, the antagonism toward the Jewish religion of the German idealists underwent "a progressive vulgarization" through Kant, Fichte, Hegel, and then Ludwig Feuerbach and the Young Hegelian Bruno Bauer, the last of whom was Marx's particular mentor. It was Marx's sinister achievement to marry the economic antisemitism of the French Socialists to the philosophical antisemitism of the German idealists and thereby to construct a new kind of antisemitic conspiracy theory, which was to be an intellectual rehearsal for his general theory of capital.

Here it is not amiss to reflect on the rational frailty of intellectuals. The moment they emerge from one form of obscurantism, they plunge eagerly into another. In the second quarter of the nineteenth century they were stripping away, as they saw it, the accumulated layers of millennia of religious superstition. But almost in the same moment they substituted new, secular ones. Satan was dead but lo! legions of new devils were everywhere conspiring against humankind. In Italy it was the Freemasons, in France it was the Protestants, in Germany it was the Jesuits; and always, everywhere, it was the Jews, too. If one conflated these various conspiracy theories, the Jews were revealed as simultaneously in league with the Freemasons, Protestants, and Jesuits. Satan might be dead, but Rothschild had taken his place. Jewish intellectuals abandoning their Judaism were almost as prone to these fantasies as Christian intellectuals abandoning their Christianity. It was Heinrich Heine who coined the characteristic epigram of the epoch: "Money is the God of our time and Rothschild is his prophet."

Marx, the self-elected scourge of all superstition, religious or secular, the paladin of rationality, who set out to sweep away all the cobwebs of the past from the face of the world and to reveal it as it really was, might not Marx of all people—himself descended from long lines of rabbis on both sides—have disposed of this particular superstition once and for all and finally rid the world of its two-thousand-year-old burden of antisemitic fantasy? In fact he did the opposite. He reinforced it. He gave it a whole new lease on life and new, respectable garments of pseudorationality, calculated to appeal to the young of successive generations.

There can be no doubt that as a young man Marx was antisemitic. He got his theoretical antisemitism from Bruno Bauer, a lifelong antisemite. In the early and mid-1840s, when Marx was in his twenties, his antisemitism was acute. It is true that, later, antisemitism ceased to be, for Marx, one of the keys to the universe. But there is ample evidence that his prejudice remained. In 1861, to quote only one significant example of many, we find him in a letter to Engels repeating as "proved" Manetho's original claim that the Jews were a race of lepers, a rootless people without a country—what might be called the primeval matrix of antisemitism.

Like most cases of antisemitism, Marx's was based on ignorance, reinforced by a personal experience from which he generalized. His father was baptized a Lutheran the year before Marx was born. His education was classical, not Jewish, and took place mainly at a former Jesuit academy whose other pupils were predominantly Catholic. Marx knew very little about Jewish religion, history, and culture, and never showed any desire to acquire any such knowledge. He knew very few Jews. His mother remained more attached to Judaism than his father, and when Marx married a Christian girl in 1843 he quarreled with his mother about this matter as well as about money. When Marx wrote about the Jews in 1843–1844, this quarrel gave a personal edge to his anti-Jewish prejudice, which otherwise was based on the common antisemitism of the cafe and the university, and on certain specific writings, such as those of Bauer. Shorn of its Hegelian idealism, Marx's tract, "On the Jewish Question," had the same factual basis as Toussenel's philippic, published the following year, entitled *Les Juifs, rois de l'époque: histoire de la féodalité financière* (The Jews, Kings of the Era: A History of Financial Feudalism)—a work that later inspired Drumont to write perhaps the most influential of all antisemitic books, *La France juive.*

I find it hard to believe that those who deny Marx's antisemitism can have read this essay, or at any rate progressed beyond the first part. As Wistrich has pointed out, the attempts by later Jewish Socialists, such as Rosa Luxemburg, to present it as a scientific demystification of the Jewish problem can be sustained only by deliberate misquotation or willful misunderstanding of what Marx wrote. In any case, the word *scientific* is absurdly misplaced given that Marx wrote without any attempt at an objective inquiry.

The second part of Marx's essay is an almost classic antisemitic tract, based on a fantasied Jewish archetype and a conspiracy to corrupt the world. Marx wrote that he was concerned with "the real Jew: not the *sabbath Jew . . .* but the *everyday* Jew" (Marx's emphasis throughout). He asks: "What is the profane basis of Judaism? *Practical* need, *self-interest.* What is the worldly cult of the Jew? *Huckstering.* What is his worldly God? *Money.*" This point is repeated again and again. What was "the basis of the Jewish religion? Practical need, egoism," and "the god of *practical need and self-interest* is *money.* Money is the jealous god of Israel, beside which no other god may exist. Money abases all the gods of mankind and changes them into commodities. . . . Money is the alienated essence of Man's work and existence; this essence dominates him and he worships it. The god of the Jews has been secularized and has become the god of this world. The bill of exchange is the real god of the Jews."

The Jews, Marx maintained, had corrupted the Christians—indeed, the whole world. Jews did not need emancipating since the Jew "has already emancipated himself in a Jewish fashion" by using the power of money. Marx quoted with approval Bauer's assertion that the Jew already "determines the fate of the whole [Austrian] empire by his financial power . . . [and] decides the destiny of Europe." Indeed, he adds, the Jew "by acquiring the power of money" has turned money itself into "a world power."

There are, needless to say, fundamental confusions in Marx's reckless analysis of the world's ills. He says that the characteristics of the Jew are to be explained "not by his religion, but rather by the human basis of his religion—practical need and egoism." Hence the problem is a cultural one. On the other hand, he seems to be arguing that, inasmuch as the essence of Jews is not their religion but their attitude toward money, by abolishing property, society would automatically destroy the Jewish religion and in so doing free not only the Jews but all of humankind: "In emancipating itself from *hucksterism* and *money,* and thus from real and practical Judaism, our age would emancipate itself."

Marx's essay on the Jews thus contains, in embryonic form, the essence of his theory of human regeneration: By abolishing private property, society would transform human relationships and thus the human personality. Marx's form of antisemitism was a dress rehearsal for Marxism itself. Later in the century, August Bebel would coin the phrase, much used by Lenin: "Anti-Semitism is the socialism of fools." Behind this revealing epigram lay the following crude argument, which might be paraphrased thus: We all know that Jewish middlemen, who never soil their hands with toil, exploit the poor workers and peasants. But only a fool blames the Jews alone. The mature man, the Socialist, has grasped the point that the Jews are only the symptoms of the disease, not the disease itself. The disease is the religion of money, and its modern form is capitalism. Workers and peasants are exploited not just by the Jews but by the bourgeois-capitalist class as a whole—and it is that entire class, not only its Jewish element, that must be destroyed.

Thus understood, the militant socialism that Marx adopted in the later 1840s can be seen as an expanded and transmuted form of his earlier antisemitism. The Jewish world-conspiracy theory was not so much abandoned as extended to include the entire bourgeois class. Marx retained the fundamental fallacy that the making of money through trade and finance is essentially a parasitical activity, but he now placed it on the basis not of race or religion, but of class.

Such refinement or enlargement does not improve the validity of the theory. It merely makes the theory more dangerous, if put into practice, because it expands its scope and multiplies the number of those to be treated as conspirators, and thus as victims. Marx was no longer concerned with specifically Jewish witches to be hunted; he generalized the category to encompass human witches. The theory is still fundamentally irrational, but it has a more sophisticated appearance. To reverse Bebel's epigram, if antisemitism is the socialism of fools, socialism is the antisemitism of intellectuals. An intellectual like Lenin, who clearly perceived the irrationality of antisemitism and would have been ashamed to be heard defending a pogrom, let alone conducting one, nevertheless fully accepted its spirit once the target was generalized into the capitalist class as a whole—and he went on to conduct pogroms against the bourgeoisie on an infinitely greater scale, murdering hundreds of thousands on the basis not of individual guilt but merely of membership in a condemned group.

It is misleading to contrast the activist violence of Lenin with the theoretical abstractions of Marx, who seems to have imagined that the capitalist class would be eliminated by the painless process of historical determinism. Marxist theory cannot be divorced from the verbal violence with which Marx expressed it. Nor is it possible to make absolute distinctions between violence against a race and violence against a class—between genocide and class warfare. The two concepts were in fact confused in Marx's own mind. As he saw it, races, peoples, and nations were subjected to the same Hegelian processes as classes. He often discussed with Engels the notion of inferior or superior nations or races, and of races in the process of decay and disappearance—what Engels called "dying nationalities." Engels liked to quote a saying of Hegel's that "residual fragments of peoples" always become "fanatical standard-bearers of counterrevolution." Thus a reactionary people as well as a reactionary class could exist—a thought that appealed strongly to Stalin as well as Hitler, and indeed to Mao Tse-tung as well, when he dealt in 1950 with that reactionary little people, the Tibetans. Engels wrote in Marx's newspaper, the *Neue Rheinische Zeitung*, that "the next world war will result in the disappearance from the face of the earth not only of reactionary classes and dynasties, but also of entire reactionary peoples. And that, too, is a step forward." Thus Engels, who specifically repudiated political antisemitism in 1879, saw Marxism as a sufficient warrant for genocide as well as class warfare.

Equally important, I think, is the fact that the emotional tone remained similar both in Marx's antisemitic essay and in his subsequent writings about the capitalist class as a whole. The archetypal Jew was replaced by the archetypal capitalist, but the features of the caricature were essentially the same and the venom with which Marx portrayed them was, if anything, greater. Take, for instance, the presentation of Marx's capitalist monster in *Das Kapital* (Volume II, Part VII, Chapter 22, Section 3):

> Only insofar as the capitalist is personified capital has he a historical value; only as such has he that historical right to exist. . . . Fanatically bent upon the exploitation of value, he relentlessly drives human beings to production for production's sake. . . . Only as the personification of capital is the capitalist respectable. As such he shares with the miser the passion for wealth as wealth. But that which in the miser assumes the aspect of mania, is in the capitalist the effect of the social mechanism in which he is only a driving wheel. . . . His actions are a mere function of the capital which, through his instrumentality, is endowed with will and consciousness, so that his own private consumption must be regarded by him as a robbery perpetrated on accumulation.

Could such a weird personification of inhumanity ever have existed? Did Marx actually believe in such a creature? But then, when had an antisemitic propagandist believed in the archetypal hate figure he presented as a living person? That Marx still saw, in his mind, the capitalist archetype as essentially the Jewish archetype is suggested to me by the footnote he added to the passage just quoted. It deals with the usurer, whom Marx terms "the old-fashioned but perennially renewed form of the capitalist." Marx knew that, in the minds of most of his readers, the usurer was the Jew; as Toussenel put it, the terms *usurer* and *Jew* are interchangeable. Most of the footnote consists of a violent quotation from Luther, who, as Marx was well aware, numbered among the most furious antisemitic writers. A usurer, Marx quotes Luther as saying, is a double-died thief and murderer. . . . Whoever eats up, rots, and steals the nourishment of another, that man commits as great a murder (so far as in him lies) as he who starves a man or utterly undoes him. Such does a usurer, and sits there while safe on his stool when he ought rather to be hanging on the gallows, and be eaten by as many ravens as he has stolen guilders, if only there were so much flesh on him, that so many ravens could stick their beaks in and share it. . . . Therefore is there, on this earth, no greater enemy of man (after the Devil) than a gripe-money and usurer, for he wants to be God over all men. . . . Such a one would have the whole world perish of hunger and thirst, misery and want. . . . Usury is a great huge monster, like a werewolf. . . . And since we break on the wheel and behead highwaymen, murderers, and housebreakers, how much more ought we to break on the wheel and kill . . . hunt down, curse, and behead all usurers!

I find it suggestive that Marx should quote in a work purporting to be scientific this brutal exhortation to kill from an antisemitic writer; both Marx's own violence and that of the emotional irrationality that expressed itself first as antisemitism and then as generalized anticapitalism are called to mind.

The origins of Marxism in antisemitic conspiracy theory can never be wholly erased. Whatever guise Marxism may take, it retains this stigma, like a mark of Cain; sometimes palimpsest, sometimes brazen. Marxism always was, and it remains, a theory and practice that will not accommodate the Jews as they are.

Lenin not only repudiated antisemitism but took steps to stamp it out. How then could such a tradition carry with it, uncured, indeed undiagnosed and untreated, the antisemitic virus? The answer is that the secularized, or non-Jewish, Jews who were among the principal architects of the Leninist state shared with Lenin a fallacy almost as egregious as the fallacies of traditional antisemitism, or those of the variety peddled by Marx in 1844. They did not see the Jews as a world conspiracy but went almost to the opposite extreme: They denied that Jews had any cultural particularity at all. The notion of Jewishness would simply disappear after the revolution. The Jews, and their doppelgänger the antisemites, were transient phenomena to be erased by the ineluctable logic of history. Hence Jewish Socialists were not entitled to their own Bund, or party. Still less were Jews, as a nation or race, entitled to their own nationality status in the Socialist community, and least of all to their own Zionist state.

Most of these non-Jewish Jews, though Socialists, knew nothing about the proletariat as it actually existed. Like Lenin, they had no direct experience of working-class society. They came from Poland and Russia, but they had left the ghetto; they led the lives of students, cafe agitators, political activists in a middle-class or bohemian environment far from the Jewish masses. By denying the undoubted fact of the Jewish proletariat, of Jewish society, of Jewish culture, they made trouble inevitable. For facts that are denied by authority yet obstinately make their reappearance are liable to be treated as hostile or malevolent phenomena. Hence, when, in the Soviet Union, Jewish religion and culture, and even Zionism itself, far from disappearing, persisted and sought to express themselves, they were interpreted by the ruling elite—above all, by Stalin but to some degree by all his successors—as a conspiracy. Thus antisemitic conspiracy theory was revived, within the wider conspiracy theory of Marxism itself.

Stalin termed the new Jewish conspiracy "cosmopolitanism." He thus reunited two streams of antisemitism, which had diverged in Napoleonic times but now flowed together again. As previously noted, the crime of "rootlessness" was the oldest of all accusations, from Manetho to Marx, hurled against the Jews. The Socialist progeny of Voltaire saw the Jewish threat as a conspiracy of rich exploiters. But the French Revolution and empire, in provoking reactions among the traditionalist forces in Europe, brought into existence yet another variety of antisemitism.

Like all children of the Enlightenment, Napoleon sought a rational "solution" to the "Jewish problem." He liberated Jews just as he liberated nations. He also conceived the idea of convoking a "Grand Sanhedrin" in Paris in 1807 to help him solve the "problem." The idea was unfortunate because it did nothing for the Jews; but it did set up terrifying vibrations among their conservative enemies. Traditional antisemitic conspiracy theory had been kept alive by the ecclesiastical inquisitions of Spain and Rome. When they fell in the revolutionary convulsions, the torch was handed to the new and growing secret-police forces of the European empires, especially Austria and Russia. They saw all Jews as potential or actual partisans of Napoleon and took a close interest in covert Jewish activities. The idea of the Grand Sanhedrin fed their paranoia.

So, in addition to the radical antisemitic conspiracy theory of the type favored by Marx, there grew up a "reactionary" theory of Jewish elders meeting in secret to overthrow established society. The actual *Protocols of the Elders of Zion* were forged by the czarist secret police, who also arranged for their publication in 1905. When Stalin took over Russia he inherited a country that had not only practiced antisemitism as systematic state policy from 1881 to 1917, but whose political police had deliberately fabricated the materials of antisemitism. The resumption of antisemitism in Soviet Russia from 1937 onward, culminating in the terrible years 1949–1953, was therefore not surprising.

Stalinist antisemitism had much in common with the Nazi variety. Stalin's hatred of "cosmopolitanism" ran parallel with the Nazi distinction between "culture," associated with the best qualities of the German race, and "civilization," which the Nazis associated with Jewish internationalism and the materialistic capitalism of the West. The Nazis hated big cities, huge factories, the impersonality of large-scale finance capitalism, which had no home and knew no frontiers; it "alienated" man from his own homeland. All these malign forces they attributed to the

Jews—a situation not very far from that perpetrated by Marx in 1843–1844. Indeed, the Marxist and Nazi concepts of alienation, a source of antisemitism in both, are similar—and that is hardly surprising as each had its origin in Hegel.

Hitler regarded both Marxism and capitalism as Jewish conspiracies. Had not Werner Sombart, one of the defenders of capitalism, "proved scientifically" in 1911 that the origins of capitalism were in all essentials Jewish? Sombart's book, *Die Juden und das Wirtschaftsleben*, paid generous tribute to Marx's 1844 essay, which had helped to inspire it. Yet Marx's notion that the Jewish attitude toward money was slowly infecting Christianity, then the whole of society, was akin to Hitler's nightmare of the "Jewish bacillus" getting a grip on the world, using both Bolshevism and international finance capital as its carriers. Hitler, a romantic who saw himself as an idealist and an antimaterialist, hated the capitalist system, though he was prepared to use it on his own terms, just as Lenin, then Stalin, used state capitalism. Where the two forms of antisemitism differed was in the intensity of Hitler's paranoia and the central position the Jews occupied in his thought and strategy. That was what made the Holocaust possible. In Soviet demonology, by contrast, Jewish cosmopolitanism was only one of many enemies. But even in this connection, there are signs that, from the end of 1948 onward, it had begun to obsess Stalin to the exclusion of other hostile fantasies. The "Doctors' Plot" of 1952–1953, just before his timely death, suggests that—had he lived longer—his reign too might have culminated in a general assault on Soviet Jewry.

This episode reminds us that all totalitarian systems based on conspiracy theory are prone to antisemitism, the oldest conspiracy theory of all. It is latent in their ideology and is liable to become active without warning in moments of "crisis," real or imaginary. Socialism, in both its nationalist and its Marxist-Leninist forms, cannot escape the deformation of its origins, which lie in a grotesquely oversimplified explanation of how capitalism originated and the way it functions. Societies built upon irrational premises must be expected to act irrationally when they feel threatened. So no Jewish minority can ever be wholly safe in a nondemocratic Socialist society, especially one based on Marxist dogma, which itself evolved from a primitive antisemitic model.

Equally significant is the way in which Marxist conspiracy theory lends itself to the new and virulent anti-Zionism that is the contemporary expression of antisemitic irrationality. Hatred of Zionism fits neatly into Marxist-Leninist theory at two levels. Lenin, having denied Jewish particularism, and therefore the validity of Zionism, was bound to attack it once he seized power. At that time Zionism was by far the strongest element within Russian Jewry, with 1,200 local groups totaling over 300,000 members. From September 1, 1919, onward, Lenin used the Cheka (secret police) and the Yevsektsia (the Jewish section of the propaganda department of the Communist party) to destroy Zionism systematically. Its conspiratorial object, the regime argued, was "to corrupt Jewish youth and throw them into the arms of the counterrevolutionary bourgeoisie in the interests of Anglo-French capitalism." Any Soviet Jew who asserted his or her essential Jewishness was thus a Zionist and an enemy of the state.

As Zionism was an affront to Marxist-Leninist logic, it followed that an actual Zionist state could only be an artificial creation promoted by the bourgeois powers to serve the interests of capitalism and those of its international superstructure, imperialism. At this second level, there was no difficulty in finding "evidence" for this new conspiracy theory, which might well have appealed strongly to Marx himself. For the Jews, it seemed, had a leading role in imperialism too! In 1900 the English economist J. A. Hobson published his book entitled *The War in South Africa: Its Causes and Effects*, which contained an entire chapter ("For Whom Are We Fighting?") "proving" that this imperialist war had been promoted by Jewish financial interests. Two years later he broadened his thesis in his famous work, *Imperialism: A Study*, which claimed that international finance capital was behind the drive to colonize backward people all over the world. His chapter entitled "Economic Parasites of Imperialism," the heart of his theory, contains this key passage:

> These great businesses—banking, brokering, bill discounting, loan floating, company promoting—form the central ganglion of international capitalism. United by the strongest bonds of organization, always in closest and quickest touch with one another, situated in the very heart of the business capital of every state, controlled, so far as Europe is concerned, chiefly by men of a single and peculiar race, who have behind them many centuries of financial experience, they are in a unique position to control the policy of nations. No great quick direction of capital is possible save by their consent and through their agency. Does anyone seriously suppose that a great war could be undertaken by any European state, or a great state loan subscribed, if the house of Rothschild and its connections set their face against it?

It was Hobson's book that formed the basis for Lenin's own economic theory of colonialism, set out in *Imperialism: The Highest Stage of Capitalism* (1916). This conspiracy-theory explanation of colonialism, derived from Hobson, not only became official Soviet doctrine but in time helped to shape the views of the ruling intelligentsia in large parts of what is now termed Third World. In this irrational stew, the notion of the Zionist state as an aggressive local projection of "U.S. imperialism" was a natural ingredient. Indeed, Soviet and Third World conspiracy theory coincide perfectly.

Needless to say, the historical facts of Israel's creation reveal the theory as nonsense. The only explanation they do support might be termed "accident theory." Israel climbed into existence through a fortuitous window that opened briefly in history. In terms of *realpolitik* it did not then seem in the United States' interests to promote a Zionist state, as Roosevelt in his last months was beginning to see. David Niles, FDR's pro-Zionist assistant in the White House, was probably right when he later testified: "There are serious doubts in my mind that Israel would have come into being if Roosevelt had lived." It was Harry S. Truman, with his need for Jewish swing-state votes in the forthcoming 1948 election, his distrust of those he termed "the striped-pants boys in the State Department," and above all his strong and simple sense of justice, who pushed the partition scheme through the United Nations and gave immediate *de facto* recognition to the new state. The constituent elements of "U.S. imperialism" were all hotly opposed. The State Department prophesied disaster for U.S. interests. Max Thornburg of Cal-Tex, speaking on behalf of the U.S. oil industry, claimed that Truman had "extinguished" the "moral prestige of America." Echoing the views of the armed forces, Defense Secretary James V. Forrestal denounced the Jewish lobby, which had been "permitted to influence our policy to the point where it could endanger our national security."

Even more destructive of the "imperialist" conspiracy theory of Zionism was the actual behavior of the Soviet Union. For tactical reasons, Stalin abandoned anti-Zionism, in practice though not in theory, between 1944 and the autumn of 1948. He seems to have thought that a Socialist Israel would operate decisively against British and U.S. interests in the Middle East. In any event, Russia played a part in the creation of Israel second only to that played by the United States, as Andrei Gromyko survives to testify (if he would!), for it was he, as deputy foreign minister, who cast the first major Soviet vote at the UN in favor of Israel's creation. Semyon Tsarapkin, head of the USSR's UN delegation, offered members of the Jewish Agency the toast "To the future Jewish state" before voting for partition on October 13, 1947, and in the General Assembly the entire Soviet bloc followed suit on November 29. During the spring of 1948 Soviet policy was more pro-Israel than that of the United States, and Soviet recognition of the new state, following the United States' recognition by four hours, was not just *de facto* but *de jure*. Above all, it was the Czech government, on instructions from Moscow, that made Israel's physical survival possible by defying the UN arms embargo and turning over an entire military airfield to fly arms to Tel Aviv. Five months later Stalin reversed his policy, but by then Israel was established.

These facts demolish the myth of Israel as an imperialist creation. But when have facts been allowed to interfere with conspiracy theory, especially one that reflects an underlying antisemitic pattern? By the 1970s, the historical record of Israel's birth had long been buried by the Soviet Union and its satellites, and conveniently forgotten by the Arab world. Leaders of many Third World countries, who systematically voted against Israel because its caricature fitted into their own paranoid theories of how the world works, were ignorant or uninterested. In the

West, many intellectuals had come, without much inquiry, to accept Israel's conspiratorial role as an imperialist bridgehead—for, as noted, intellectuals have a weakness for such theories.

But those Western intellectuals who embrace anti-Zionism, whether on its merits or as a substitute for an antisemitism that is now unavowable in their own societies, find themselves in strange company. I will end by giving just one suggestive example. The history of hostility to the Jews for more than two millennia is rich in episodes of human cruelty and folly, but it contains few scenes so disgraceful as that enacted at the United Nations on the occasion of the state visit by President Idi Amin of Uganda, on October 1, 1975. By that date he was already notorious as a mass murderer of conspicuous savagery; he had not only dispatched some of his victims personally, but dismembered them and preserved parts of their anatomy for future consumption—the first refrigerator-cannibal. He had nevertheless been elected president of the Organization of African Unity, and in that capacity he was invited to address the UN General Assembly. His speech was a denunciation of what he called "the Zionist-American conspiracy" against the world, and he demanded not only the expulsion of Israel from the UN but also its "extinction." This blatant call for genocide was well received by Marxist, Arab, and many other Third World delegations. The Assembly awarded him a standing ovation when he arrived, applauded him periodically throughout his speech, and again rose to its feet when he left. The next day the UN secretary general and the president of the General Assembly gave a public dinner in his honor.

That is where the ineluctable logic of radical anti-Zionism leads. As such it is firmly rooted in irrational Marxist conspiracy theory.

4
The "Jewish Question": Left-wing Anti-Zionism in Western Societies

Robert Wistrich

Ever since political Zionism first emerged on the stage of history at the end of the nineteenth century, it has had its opponents as well as its advocates on the left. In the golden era of the Second International—that is, before 1914—it was generally the Marxist as opposed to the "revisionist" wing of social democracy, especially in Central and Eastern Europe, that stood in the forefront of opposition to Zionism as a political ideology and movement. Frequently, too, it was Jewish intellectuals, especially in Eastern Europe, who were most vehement in their rejection of Zionism, branding it as a clerical, obscurantist attempt to return the Jews to the ghetto or as a design to subjugate the Jewish masses to the retrograde nationalism of the Jewish bourgeoisie. Both Jews and non-Jews in the revolutionary Marxist movement tended to see Jewish nationalism in Lenin's terms (derived from a polemic against the anti-Zionist Bund rather than against the Zionists!) as an absolutely "unscientific" and "reactionary" idea whose purpose was to divert the Jewish masses from the class struggle. As Karl Kautsky and the Austro-Marxist Otto Bauer emphasized at the turn of the century, Zionism and Jewish nationalism stood in contradiction to the only truly progressive solution of the "Jewish question"—namely, assimilation of the Jews in the classless society of the future to be created by Socialist revolution.

By seeking to revive a fossilized ghetto Judaism, the Zionists, so the argument ran, were perpetuating a reactionary caste, a relic of the Middle Ages, and creating an obstacle in the common struggle against antisemitism. The Russian Marxists Lenin, Trotsky, and Julius Martov also shared this view, as did an entire generation of internationalist revolutionaries—many of whom were, in Isaac Deutscher's phrase, "non-Jewish Jews" seeking to cast off their ethnic identity and escape into the utopia of universalist socialism. Already this first phase of Marxist anti-Zionism showed a curious characteristic that has persisted to the present day—namely, that individuals and ideological tendencies with little else in common (and sometimes even bitter enemies *within* the Left), such as the Centrist Kautsky, the reformist Social Democrat Otto Bauer, the ultraleftist Rosa Luxemburg, the Bolsheviks Lenin and Stalin, the Menshevik Martov, and the internationalist wanderer between the worlds, Trotsky, could unite on at least one issue: their opposition to Jewish nationalism.

The arguments of this classical Marxist left against Zionism are still frequently quoted in the ideological anti-Zionist literature of the contemporary left, but it is crucial to note some very important differences. In the first place, before 1914 and indeed until the post-Holocaust period and the creation of the State of Israel, the subject of Zionism never assumed *major* importance on the left. Although there are a number of basic doctrinal texts, even these possess an ad hoc character and have only in retrospect been invested with a quasisacral quality. Thus modern Soviet propaganda will endlessly refer to Lenin's so-called polemics against the "Zionists" without revealing that he barely discussed the subject and reserved most of his polemical efforts on the "Jewish question" for denouncing the Bund or condemning antisemitism. Similarly, the Western New Left as well as the Communist will resuscitate texts on the *Judenfrage* as ancient as Karl Marx's young Hegelian polemic of 1844 against Bruno Bauer to justify an entirely different political purpose in 1984—namely, the Soviet political war against "international Zionism." Neither Marx, Engels, Kautsky, Lenin, Trotsky, or Rosa Luxemburg would ever have dreamed that Zionism could become a *major world problem*, an ideological issue of the first importance for the Socialist bloc on a par with the struggle against capitalism or imperialism, or that it could become a code word for the forces of reaction in general.

For the traditional Marxist left such a proposition would have been incomprehensible, and to admit it would have implied that something had gone radically wrong with the entire Marxian view of the historical process, in which ethnic and national antagonisms are inevitably to be superseded by class polarization on a universal scale. For if one thing united traditional left-wing thinking on the Jews (in both East and West) it was the assumption that Judaism was bound to disappear according to the laws of historical development, that the final emancipation of the Jews implied the dissolution of any Jewish group identity. The total failure of this historical prognosis or prediction is, in my opinion, itself one of the reasons for the extraordinary antipathy of many Marxists toward Zionism today—for it is the State of Israel, the offspring of the Zionist movement, that more than any other factor has exposed the bankruptcy of the whole Marxian tradition of theorizing on the Jewish question.

As we have pointed out, Marxism did from the outset relate to the ideological content of Zionism but rejected it on principle as incompatible with the doctrines of proletarian internationalism. In particular, it denied that the Jews were a nation, that they had a common history, language, culture, and so on—arguments that frequently recur in the extreme-left polemics against Zionism today. But here, too, the context is very different, as are the mode of debate, the tone of the argument, and its underlying meaning or deep structure. No one familiar with the older "anti-Zionist" texts could, for example, mistake the fact that they were motivated by a pro-Jewish attitude or, rather, sympathy for the Jews as the object of persecution through the centuries; that in opposing Jewish nationalism, Socialists believed in all sincerity that they were serving the *best interests* of the Jews, whose salvation, so they thought, depended on the creation of a classless society in which all differences of race, religion, ethnicity, and caste would become irrelevant. This anti-antisemitic anti-Zionism may still exist in some quarters on the left, but it is hardly the dominant mode of discourse. For the extreme left in Western societies not only denigrates Israel and Zionism in a systematic manner, but its irrational hostility frequently spills over into contempt or antipathy for Jews and Judaism as such. True, this contemporary anti-Zionist left—whether it be orthodox Communist, Trotskyist, Maoist, gauchiste, or anarchist— will invariably claim that it is antiracist and rejects antisemitism. Yet the stereotypes of Jews that are found in the literature of the political left are extremely negative, reflecting as they do a built-in visceral hatred of Israel and Zionism. Thus the Israelis are invariably militarist, aggressive, expansionist, fascist oppressors; colonizers who ruthlessly confiscate other people's lands; blackmailers who try to silence criticism by playing on the Holocaust; and, worst of all, modern practitioners of "genocide" against the Palestinian people. Those in the Jewish Diaspora who support such devils are themselves accomplices of war criminals, aiding and abetting the oppression of defenseless people, financing and white-washing a military machine that is a threat not only to the Palestinians or the Arabs but to all of humanity and to world peace as a whole.

Nor should it be thought that this type of wild rhetoric is merely Israelophobic or that it remains at the level of an abstract "anti-Zionism" with no practical consequences or implications for the perception of Jews in general. True, the extreme left will often bracket Israel with other ultrareactionary regimes like South Africa or the fascist military junta in Chile—or, as in the past, with governments like white Rhodesia, Peron's Argentina, or the shah's Iran—and then claim that its hostility derives from the racist colonialist policies of the Israeli government. But if this were really the case, there would be no need for the far left to expend such enormous polemical energy in vilifying "Zionism" and arguing that the ideological basis of the State of Israel is *a priori* pernicious, malevolent, and inherently racist. Moreover, by insisting on dismantling the Jewish State and "de-Zionizing" Israel so that it can then be replaced by the "secular democratic state" of Palestine—one in which the Jews would at best be reduced to their traditional status under Islam (i.e., that of a "protected" minority)—the left makes itself the accomplice of a radically discriminatory, *politicidal* formula invented by the PLO. Thus on the extreme left, sanction is given to the destruction of an existing state—one that is based on the democratic will of its Jewish majority—if necessary by the use of terror and in any case by the method of armed struggle and a popular war of liberation. In these respects, the extreme left in Western societies is in fact more radical than the Soviet Union, which has been careful, even as it infects the bloodstream of its own population and that of the Third World with the antisemitic virus, to proclaim its respect for the 1948 borders of Israel.

Admittedly, the Soviet position on this issue is also ambiguous at times, yet it has never *officially* embraced the PLO thesis on the need to physically destroy the Zionist "entity." For Soviet purposes it would appear sufficient to significantly weaken Israel, to isolate it and cut it off from its Diasporic hinterland and its main protector, the United States. A completely successful Arab campaign against the Jewish State might after all have the unfortunate effect of rendering the USSR superfluous in the Middle East, given that apart from its armaments and ideological warfare against Israel it can offer little else to its client states. Not suprisingly, the position of Communists in Western societies tends to reflect this Soviet ambivalence and to be less virulent than that of the far left as a whole toward Israel. This is particularly the case given that Western Communists in general do not share the endemic antisemitism of their Soviet counterparts and, of necessity, seek to adapt to the ethos and norms of their surrounding democratic and literary environment. Not that the French or Italian or any other Western Communists are anything but militant anti-Zionists and Israelophobes, ready to denounce the new "fascism" as the occasion demands—but they are rarely to be found disseminating the occult theory of the "World Jewish Conspiracy" and other such made-in-Russia concoctions. Unlike the Soviet or East European Communists, they generally present Zionism not as the sinister manipulating force *behind* Western imperialism but rather as its agent. Nor on the whole do they characterize Israel as a "settler colonialist state" implanted as an alien entity in the heart of the Arab East—this is the militant Trotskyist theory—inasmuch as such a characterization would undermine their recognition of the Jewish State's right to exist. But if Western Communists can today sound relatively *moderate* even in their vituperative anti-Zionism, that would be a sign of just how far things have gone on the left. The origins of this development go back to the rise of a militant "gauchisme" in most Western societies in the late 1960s, the emergence of a radical generation for whom Israel and Zionism were depicted as belonging to the wave of the future. The new prophets of the left all came from the Third World—Ho Chi Minh, Che Guevara, Fidel Castro, Franz Fanon, Mao Tse-tung, and, last but not least, Yasser Arafat—a fact that has by now borne its bitter fruit. Although the fringe politics of the *Radikalinskis* and the antics of the left may at that time have seemed a marginal issue in many Western countries, "anti-Zionism" has since become an integral part of the political culture of the left *as a whole*—contaminating the mainstream Social Democratic parties, the trade unions, the liberal-left intelligentsia as well as the traditionally receptive student milieu, the Trotskyist sects, and the Communist subculture. Even beyond the organized political left, the influence of this diffuse, almost instinctive anti-Zionism reaches into related sectors like the peace movements, the women's liberation movements, black power, the ecologists, and so on. At first sight, this development may seem puzzling as well as disconcerting. Why should the Green parties or women's lib or black militants or the peaceniks care so much about the Palestinian cause or feel the need to ritually denounce the "Zionists"? Could it be that they are all puppets of the KGB, naive fools manipulated by His Master's Voice in Moscow, whose role is simply to destabilize and demoralize the Western democratic countries from within? In the East-West confrontation, anti-Zionism does undoubtedly play an important role, but is it credible that all these diverse radical groups, in the West often led by politically rather sophisticated people with minds of their own, who are far from enamored of the Soviet system, are themselves mere tools of an expansionist superpower? It would be tempting to believe as much, and it would greatly simplify our task of understanding and combatting the phenomenon, but I do not think it is really the case.

The Western left's progressive alienation from Zionism and its love affair with the Palestinians stems, I believe, from deep inner changes in its composition, character, outlook, and *modus operandi* as well as from its radically altered perception of the nature of the conflict in the Middle East. Since the stunning Israeli victory of 1967 it has gradually ceased to believe in the picture of an embattled, tiny Jewish State surrounded by bellicose enemies intent on its destruction. It has increasingly accepted the Arab view that the real confrontation is between an oppressive militarist State of Israel and the oppressed Palestinians under its occupation, deprived of national and human rights and subjected to racist discrimination. Israel, the idol of the Social Democratic left in the 1950s and early 1960s with its kibbutzim, its constructivist socialism, its secularism, and its egalitarian ethos, has for many on the left progressively turned into the nightmarish vision of a ruthless Sparta busy expropriating occupied lands, threatening its neighbors, adopting an exclusivist, theocratic tone of self-righteousness and the posture of a *Herrenvolk* vis-à-vis the Arabs under its rule. As with many caricatures, one may totally reject the hysterical exaggeration in this picture yet recognize the grain of truth without which it would be inconceivable that people who are by no means antisemites could actually come to believe in such distortions.

For it is undeniable that Israel has steadily moved to the right during the past decade at a time when the main thrust for *delegitimizing* Zionism was being developed on the international left. Equally important, the fact remains that Israel is technically an "occupying" power in an age when for states that are not superpowers, such power is bound to evoke criticism. Moreover, most of the original Socialist, pioneering ethos has withered, and in its place has come a narrow, integral nationalism with a strong religious messianism sometimes underpinning it—one that for the secularist left inside (let alone outside) Israel is difficult to digest. Furthermore, as Israel has gained in military strength and increasingly radiated an image of self-confident, coldly efficient power—not in itself guaranteed to evoke the enthusiasm of the left, especially its neutralist and pacifist wing in the West—identification has naturally tended to shift to the weaker party in the conflict, namely, to the Palestinian Arabs. That many of these people should be landless, homeless, and abandoned was already enough to win them sympathy on the left; that they are nonwhite and non-Western, technologically backward, and politically disorganized has not exactly weakened this tie of sympathy. The rise of Palestinian terror, moreover, was bound to win the applause of the new left, given its romantic cult of *guerilleros*, its attraction for direct action and political extremism, its belief in simple slogans, and its studied indifference to gradualism, old-fashioned Socialist programs, and liberal democracy. Leftist anti-Zionism over the past fifteen years has built on these affinities, which extend beyond ideology and have led to the establishment of organizational links between Palestinian and Arab terror groups from Syria, Iraq, and Libya on the one hand and militant extremists in the West on the other. It is no accident that groups like the Red Army Faction in West Germany, the Red Brigades in Italy, the IRA, and the neofascist extremists in Europe have cooperated with the PLO or Libya's Qaddafi, just as they have maintained contact with Soviet and East European security services. For this terrorist international, "anti-Zionism" is an important link in a larger pattern of seeking to undermine the very fabric of the Western democracies by a campaign of terror, intimidation, and disinformation. The fact that the object of such campaigns also include Jewish as much as Israeli institutions in the Diaspora is a reminder of the way in which the struggle to destabilize Israel requires that the position of the Jews as a whole be undermined. For extreme left anti-Zionism does not ultimately distinguish between the Israelis and "Zionist" Jewry in the Diasporic hinterland any more than do the Soviets or radical Arabs—and the weakening of the civil position of Jews who support Israel is regarded by militant groups as an important strategic task.

Does this mean that we should therefore regard the anti-Zionist attitudes and actions of the extreme left in Western society and the gradual permeation of the more moderate left by the same virus as unequivocally antisemitic in motivation and character? Has the systematic defamation of Israel and Zionism, and the turning of Israelis into "Nazis" and Palestinians into "Jews," created or invented a new form of anti-semitism? Are the dangerous new stereotypes first promoted on the left but no longer its exclusive property (e.g., those of the Imperialist, Racist, and Genocidal State of Israel) themselves the continuation in the post-Holocaust world of Hitler's legacy, or are they perhaps something different for which we have yet to find an adequate category or meaning? My own inclination would be to see this phenomenon as a continuation, albeit in a novel form, of some radical left and even Nazi traditions and, at the same time, also as a break from the mainstream of classical Marxist ideology. The internationalism of the founding fathers of Marxism is dead, and in its place have emerged all kinds of hybrid and bastard forms of national socialism, especially in the Third World. Within this pantheon, Zionism has never really found its place as a legitimate national-liberation movement, although, in theory, there are no overriding reasons that I can see for this, beyond the heavy Marxist dogma of the disappearance of the Jews and Judaism as a necessary prerequisite of human progress. The older Marxism did not, however, denounce Zionism as a colonialist movement (at least not before the 1920s); nor did it brand Zionism as racist, even though the charge was frequently made that it represented a mirror image of antisemitism. On the other hand, the newer and more eclectic offshoots of Marxism have turned not only Zionism but also Judaism into prototypes of "racism," thereby reviving in contemporary language the old radical stereotype of the bloodthirsty, tribal, Moloch-like character of the religion of Jehovah and his people. Such anti-Judaic images and stereotypes have begun to gain wider currency in circles far beyond the leftist intellectuals, and when they are picked up by the mass media—as in the wake of the Lebanon War— they inevitably inflame public opinion. This is particularly the case now that the taboos against post-Holocaust antisemitism have begun to fade and repressed passions in the collective unconscious of the West are reasserting themselves. After 1945, racism became the unpardonable sin and crime against humanity, yet this very charge is turned in a quasiracist manner against its ultimate victims by the children and grandchildren of the perpetrators, by the accomplices and bystanders in Western Christian civilization who only forty years ago were responsible for genocide against the Jewish people. The irony is compounded in that the finger is pointed in the name and on behalf of that Third World which also suffered directly in the flesh from the original sin of Western racism. The psychological ramifications and the buried guilt complexes in this complicated intellectual maneuver are mind-boggling, yet they too are part of the total gestalt of contemporary anti-Zionism in its leftist and other incarnations. The negation of Israel and the related assault on Judaism have their latent as well as their manifest content, their deep structure as well as their transparent functions and motivation. To decode their buried message must be one of the primary tasks of any analysis of contemporary anti-Zionism, of which we are only at the beginning.

Part Two

Religion and Politics

5
Radical Islam and the Arab-Israeli Conflict

Emmanuel Sivan

Introduction

However much it draws upon traditional Islamic attitudes toward the Jews, the fortunes of antisemitism in the modern Arab world have been, on the whole, closely related to the peripeties of the Arab-Israeli conflict. It is thus from this angle, as a tool for mobilizing support for the anti-Israel jihad, that the role of antisemitism in the radical Islamic movement (also termed Islamic resurgence or fundamentalism) should be discussed. This is not to say that, once instigated, antisemitism cannot acquire an autonomous existence and dynamics, or that there may not be radical circles in which hatred of the Jews preceded involvement with the political conflict.

Two hallmarks of radical Islam are relevant to this chapter. The first is the *quest for authenticity*—that is, for solutions and cures to present-day problems and maladies of the Islamic world that fit in with (though do not necessarily imitate) the traditions or essence of Muslim religion and historical experience; Islam should not be judged (nor should it be treated) by values and panaceas produced by the West. The second is the *turning inward*: The problems of contemporary Islam are mostly internal; one should thus avoid externalization of guilt and zero in on eradicating the "enemies within"—from despotic rulers to materialistic and hedonistic media.

The quest for authenticity did away with the apologetics so typical of modern Islam (especially in its reformist brand, but also in the religious establishment). It was no longer necessary to prove that Islam cherishes the same values of scientific inquiry, tolerance, democracy, and the like as those of the West. The new radicals feel no embarrassment in speaking, inter alia, of the two major cleavages of discrimination of the Islamic tradition—male/female, Muslim/non-Muslim. If they call for women to be relegated to homemaking and procreation, they also proclaim the need to put the non-Muslims "in their proper place"—that is, as second-class citizens, paying the poll tax, devoid of most political rights, and so on. Polemics against these "inferior religions" are licit for Muslims—and the radicals do indulge in them occasionally[1]—and, of course, it should be forbidden for the non-Muslims to respond in kind.

This is an ominous development, no doubt, but one that should be viewed in the proper context. The turning inward means that external problems are marginalized, and it is the challenge of the modern Arab military nation-state that looms largest in radical thought. Christians do come in for vituperation (as educators, as top civil servants, and above all for their excess of freedom, dubbed "arrogance"). Yet even they are the focus of hostility mostly in Upper Egypt (where they constitute between 28 percent and 42 percent of the population in certain counties), though rarely elsewhere in the Fertile Crescent. Local Jews are never mentioned, for they barely exist; and as for the Arab-Israeli conflict—the major source of modern antisemitism—the importance of this "external challenge" has been questioned by the radicals, as we shall presently see.

No to Jihad?

A recent memoir on life in Nasser's political jails recounts:

> In May 1967, during the crisis weeks preceding the Six Day War, the authorities tried to enlist the support of the political prisoners to the *Jihād* against Israel. Some [Muslim Brethren] inmates of the notorious Abū Za'bal prison camp resolved to voice their unreserved support and even published a wall newspaper to that effect.
>
> Yet a group of young inmates, led by Sheikh 'Ali 'Abduh Ismā'īl, argued that the State is infidel and so is whoever supports it. Israel and Nasser were both, for them, but two variations of tyranny, both totally inimical to Islam; they fight each other for wordly reasons but "in infidelity they are just one bunch." Reported to camp authorities by stoolpigeons, Ismā'īl and his followers were thrown into solitary confinement, to live on dry bread and a little water. They refused, however, to renounce their views and were later to be remanded to ordinary cells where they kept to themselves, praying in their own group, refusing to have anything to do with Muslim Brethren who aided the anti-Israel *Jihād*, and thereby establishing the first cell of the *Takfīr wa-Hijra* [the major terrorist organization of the 1970s].[2]

The frame of mind of these and other inmates is highlighted by letters sent in late May from the Military Prison by a Muslim Brother:

> There is a lot of talk about war. Yet who is it who is going to fight? Those who prostrate themselves before idols, those who worship other deities than Allah? . . . Verily God is not about to succor in battle people who have forsaken Him. . . . Can He bestow victory upon people who have been fighting Him, His religion and His true believers, massacring and torturing them, inflicting upon them imprisonment and humiliation?

. . . Don't you know, Dear Mother, that those (i.e., the Muslim Brethren) who had defeated Israel in 1948 were thrown into jail in 1955, a year before Israel attacked us, and were thrown there once again in 1966, a year prior to another eventual Israeli incursion? . . . Doesn't that indicate, Dear Mother, treason and collusion?

And in a letter to his wife:

It is inconceivable that those who abolished the religious courts [in 1956]—with the purpose that no legal recourse would be made to the *Shari'a*—that they would win this war. And do you think that those who "developed" al-Azhar into a secular type university [in 1961] in order that it deviate from its original mission and dilute the substance of its teaching, that such people could triumph? . . . Can those who massacred Muslims in Yemen by napalm bombs and poison gas . . . and allied themselves with infidel Russia . . . have the upper hand?[3]

No wonder that the June 1967 debacle was greeted in the prison camps with a mixture of shock and gloating. "This was no surprise to us," wrote one, "for how can a ruler governing his people with a whip triumph on the battlefield? . . . Dignity is trampled underfoot, hypocrisy and cowardice reign supreme." And after the demonstrations of June 9 and 10: "How shameful it is for their leader (*za'īm*) to remain in power after he had admitted his responsibility for the debacle. Why had not he prepared for that war which he said he had expected?" A third prisoner added: "Soldiers were supposed to obey orders and fight for the slogans and for the *za'īm*. . . . Yet under fire all evaporated. Neither slogans nor the *za'īm* could be of any help. The soldier remains alone and had to save his own skin."[4]

Such reactions are cast into relief when read against the commitment of the Muslim Brethren (MB) to the Palestinian cause since the 1930s, culminating in their massive participation in the 1948 war and violent opposition to the 1949 Armistice Agreement (as a result of which they were driven underground for the first time). In the mid-1950s, persecuted by Nasser, their erstwhile ally, one of the major accusations they hurled against him was that he had neglected the question of the Palestinians and was in effect preparing the terrain for a tacit rapprochement by stages with Israel.[5]

The contrast comes into an even sharper focus when set against the behavior of the MB prisoners during the Suez War. By mid-1956 the prison camp authorities were trying to brainwash the inmates and also to sow dissension in their ranks by offering parole to all those ready to sign telegrams of support for the regime. Quite a few inmates were persuaded by ideological arguments and/or attracted by the release offer. A hard core refused to sign despite all the promises, the theological admonitions by secret police "Islamic experts," the harassment, and the torture. Yet when the war broke out in October, one of the hard core reminisced: "We presented prison authorities with the request—to be transmitted to Nasser's government—to allow us to volunteer to fight the aggressors. We solemnly pledged that those of us who would survive, having done their duty on the battlefield, would go back to prison. We further suggested that a special battalion of MB prisoners would be set under special command. A list of names of volunteers was appended to the request and the whole dossier was relayed by the camp commander to the powers-that-be."[6]

In the context of this chapter, it is immaterial that the government, having for a moment accepted the request, finally rejected it. What is important is the state of mind of the prisoners two years after the onset of Nasser's crackdown upon their organization. By 1967 the picture was entirely different. Nor was the Abu Za'bal case an isolated episode; rather, it ushered in a brand new attitude among Muslim radicals toward the anti-Israel jihad predicated upon a reordering of priorities. The Islamic Liberation party (which tried to instigate a coup d'état in Egypt in 1974) would even argue that the fight for the liberation of Sinai cannot be considered a jihad, for its aim is not the establishment upon earth of a unified Muslim state—and this despite the fact that the party was led by a Palestinian, Salāh Sirrīya. Well before Sadat's peace initiative, this group and others made desertion from the "infidel" Egyptian army one of their major slogans.[7] The leader of the Takfir wa-Hijra group (1977), Shukrī Mustafā, on trial for his life, gave the following answer to the question as to what his votaries would do if the "Jewish armed forces" invaded Egypt: "If they come, our movement should not take part in battle in the ranks of the Egyptian army. Our members should rather escape to a safe place."[8]

The best exposition of this stand can be found in the book written by Aba al-Salām Faraj, the ideologue of the *Jihad Organization*, the assassins of Sadat, to be used for indoctrinating members:

> There are some who say that the *Jihād* effort should concentrate nowadays upon the liberation of Jerusalem. It is true that the Holy War is a legal precept binding upon every Muslim . . . but let us emphasize that the fight against the enemy nearest to you has precedence over the fight against the enemy further away. All the more so as the former is not only corrupted but a lackey of imperialism as well. . . . In all Muslim countries the enemy has the reins of power. The enemy is the present rulers. It is, hence, a most imperative obligation to fight these rulers. This Islamic *Jihād* requires today the blood and sweat of each Muslim.[9]

The Paradox

The preceding string of quotations may illustrate the paradox involved in the current attitudes of oppositionary Islam (especially in Egypt, the center of the Sunni world) toward the Arab-Israeli conflict. Although the radicals view the fight against Israel as jihad, they assign to it a very low priority, so much so that they even oppose many specific acts taken by the authorities to engage in action. To heap paradox on paradox, as one proceeds in the Islamic movement from the radical core to the more moderate—or reformist—periphery, the commitment to the anti-Israel Holy War grows and antisemitism became more salient and more virulent.

This phenomenon is to be explained in terms of the transformation of Muslim radical thought in the early 1960s. Under the shock of Nasserist repression, one part of the movement, led by Sayyid Qutb (then in the Cairo military jail), turned abruptly inwards. In letters smuggled out of prison to his young supporters still at large, and published in book form in 1964 (*Ma'ālim fi-l-Tarīq*), he preached a new doctrine premised on a simple diagnosis: The Islamic world has reverted to a state of *Jāhiliyya* (barbarity), much like the state of the Arabian Peninsula before Muhammad. This process, launched by the westernizers of the early nineteenth century (and having its distant origins in the moral decline of the later Muslim Middle Ages), was greatly catalyzed by the military-controlled nation-states that came to rule the Arab world since 1949. Their new gospel, nationalism (especially that of the Pan-Arab variety), was, for Qutb, distinctly secularist in content, grounded as it was in language, history, and consciousness, with no place in it for religion; and this nationalism—couched in plebeian lingo and sprinkled with references to Islam—wielded a powerful attraction upon the masses. It was about to replace religion as the primordial loyalty and thereby to bring in the secularist Trojan Horse. The reforms of the religious establishment, the cult of economic growth, and (from 1962 on) the Marxist tendencies in high places—all these, and many other pieces of evidence, were marshaled to bolster the nationalist cause.

What rendered the state even more dangerous was a monopoly of power hitherto unheard of. It enjoyed, on the one hand, a monopoly of all means of persuasion (particularly the electronic media), which now penetrated into home and family, the traditional bastions of Islam; and, on the other hand, a monopoly of all means of coercion (army, secret police, intelligence services, etc.), which the Free Officers employed with a ruthless efficiency that made Muslim activists wax nostalgic for the good old days of the monarchy.

The world of Islam, in a word, was in a state of apostasy. War to the hilt, jihad, had thus to be proclaimed against the *Jāhili* (barbarian, pagan) rulers. These rulers and their votaries were the number-one public enemy. The danger of the "New Tyranny," that "enemy within"—as the radicals call it—eclipses that of "external enemies" such as Israel, the United States, and the USSR. It is significant that the demonology of the terrorist groups of the last decade is dominated by two "apostate Muslims": Ataturk (who abolished the Caliphate) and Nasser (who established the first military nation-state).

Sayyid Qutb himself paid only scant attention to Israel, although when he did so he made ample use of his vast knowledge of the Koran to conjure up the image of an essentially depraved Judaism, an age-old enemy of Islam. All his writings on Judaism and Israel amount, however, to but one small booklet (*Our Struggle with the Jews*), assembled and published in 1970 (five years after his execution) in Jedda, Saudi Arabia. This order of priorities informed his underground activity as well. When making preparations for seizure of power (1965), Qutb opposed the suggestion of a number of operational commanders of his group to blow up major electrical power, communications, and military installations, for fear that actions of this kind might weaken Egypt vis-à-vis Israel. He finally had to give in and to agree to the plan, judged imperative to cripple the "New Tyranny," albeit in a pared-down form.[10]

The same order of priorities was adopted, as we have seen, by the numerous groups that Qutb's radicalism spawned after his martyrdom. This is all the more remarkable given that, in the generation drawn to radicalism (from the late 1960s on), the prison experience was not the formative experience known to the radicals of the early 1960s but, rather, the trauma of the 1967 debacle. It is thus that Talāl, an imprisoned terrorist of a mid-1970s group, described his conversion to an interviewer:

> Talāl recalled the deep shock which hit him when he was fifteen in the wake of the 1967 defeat. He stayed in his room for several days taken up by weeping, contemplation, meditation and sleep, neither eating nor talking to anyone. Finally his mother counseled him to pray and read the Koran. To his amazement he felt a great peacefulness settling upon him. He had read and memorized a chapter of the Koran at school, but had never had such a feeling before as if the significance of the Koranic verses were seeping through him and speaking directly of his own crisis and of the crisis of his country. He felt that he was born again, and knew that the Koran held all truth.

> Ten days after the war's end he went with his father to a political rally in a nearby town. The speaker was one of Nasser's aides. Talāl recalled how much he had loved Nasser and believed in him; yet he was struck off balance by the speaker's allegation that the Arabs had not lost the war. The argument was that as the aim of Israel and the Imperialists was to isolate Nasser or undermine his power, as long as Nasser and other "progressive" regimes prevailed, the enemy's conspiracy was a failure. Mystified by this speech, he noticed that the audience (including his father) was reacting with an enthusiastic ovation. Talāl continued to live in this state of perplexity for two years, finding refuge and a sense of release only in prayer and reading the Koran.

> This state of mind was ended during his first year at Alexandria University. One of his friends invited him after prayer in the mosque to a lecture at the University on the war against Zionism. The speaker was a bearded student from another university. Talāl was enraptured by the latter's claim that Zionism, Communism and Capitalism are the enemies of Islam and that the sole way to combat them is return to the Koran and to the Sunna. From that day he began to read about the Muslim Brethren. Soon he joined the Islamic Association on campus, thus enlisting

in the *Jihād* for the sake of Islam. Thanks to his zeal and devotion he became, within a year, one of the major leaders of the Association, whose aim was to purify the Islamic world of the corrupt regime and effect the return to the rule of the *Sharī'a*.[11]

The interview sums up the process quite neatly: from shock of defeat to doubting the leader (*za'īm*) and his regime; from the solace of religion to a more activist vision of the duties of the believer; from the *za'īm* (be he Nasser or Sadat) as the arch-devil, and thus war, to the knife against the "apostate" edifice that he created. It is no wonder that the fight against "external enemies" such as Israel will remain, for the New Radicals of the Qutb school, an ancillary task to be postponed until after power is seized and society cleansed. It is not and cannot be the end-all, even after the Peace Initiative (as the cases of Shukrī Mustafā and 'Abd al-Salām Faraj prove).

The Periphery

The dynamics are rather different in the periphery of the radical movement, led by former Muslim Brethren leaders (such as Omar al-Tilimsānī and Salāh al-'Ashmawī) who, chastised by long prison terms, opted for a reformist strategy upon their release (in 1971–1974). Their diagnosis is virtually as bleak as that of Qutb, but the conclusion they draw is diametrically opposed: Because the state is so powerful, one has to operate within the system—above all, through education and the media—and avail oneself of the relative liberalization under Sadat (e.g., access to state media and license to republish their periodicals, *al-Da'wa* and *al-I'tisām*).

In the leaders' critique of the regime's policy throughout the 1970s and early 1980s, foreign policy had pride of place, both because these leaders were reared in the long fight against British occupation (and in 1948 against Israel) and because, unlike Qutb, they thought that "external agents" of "cultural invasion" (e.g., foreign television programs and films, tourists, technical experts) are no less dangerous than the "internal agents" (e.g., Sadat, Mubarak, and their cronies and henchmen). Hence their demonology focused on four idols: Judaism, "Crusades" (i.e., Imperialism), Communism, and Secularism.[12] Israel, in this context, is part and parcel of the perennial Jewish danger depicted with a wealth of allusions to the Koran and to *Hadīth* (oral tradition), with special emphasis on Jewish inbred treachery and belligerency and occasional references to the *Protocols of the Elders of Zion*.[13]

Animosity toward Israel grew in intensity following the Peace Initiative—particularly following the signature of the Peace Treaty and, in a mounting crescendo of opposition to the normalization of relations, during the last months of the Sadat regime.[14]

Here are two sample paragraphs from this opposition activity. The first deals with the diagnosis:

How shameful is the peace produced at Camp David and the treaty with the enemy of God. We believe from the depth of our hearts that it is a false peace. The Zionist existence on the land of Muslim Palestine at the expense of the Palestinian people is totally illegitimate. It is based on usurpation and pillage. Any treaty with a usurper, therefore, is itself false. Any outcome based on falsity is itself false and must be done away with sooner or later. As the treaty is false, so are all its consequences. Normalization, therefore, is not only religiously condemned but it also entails rampant dangers to Muslim Egypt. It is a disguised Jewish invasion of the Egyptian society which hitherto was the fortress of Islam. Egypt has been the last line of defense against the three enemies of Islam: Western crusaders, Communists and Jewish Zionists.[15]

The second exposes the solution:

War is the true means laid down by God in the Koran for those whose rights, honor, or wealth having been encroached upon by an aggressor. Allah addressed the faithful "fighting is your lot despite its hardship." Muslims do not seek fighting if they can protect or restore their rights through other means. If the aggressor ceased his aggression "and opted for peace, then opt for peace and rely on God." Thus when we assert that war is the authentic means for liberating Palestine it is because for more than half a century Israel and its Western supporters have neither ceased their aggression nor showed any real inclination for peace. Israel has usurped the land of Palestine and expanded beyond. It has continued to build an awesome destructive arsenal including nuclear weapons. It has terrorized the Arabs, divided their ranks, plotted against their unity, and sapped their resources. . . . The Arabs have tried the West to see if it would help them restore their rights but to no avail. If anything, the West has persistently supported Israel with money and weapons to aggress more and expand more. There is no hope for the Arabs out of this predicament except through fighting.[16]

Amplified through the firebrand sermons of Sheikh Abd al-Hamid Kishk, the most popular preacher in Egypt today,[17] as well as by wallpapers and leaflets of the Muslim associations in the universities, this propaganda joined hands with other political elements (especially the extreme left) opposed to the peace process. The hard-core Muslim radicals, whether in their clandestine propaganda or in declarations in their trials, remained largely mute on this issue, at best mentioning it at the bottom of the lists of sins of the "New Tyrants." However, there should be no mistaking the prospects of the Israeli-Egyptian relationship once these political elements seize power.

Notes

1. Examples of such radical polemics follow: M.'I. I. al-Tahtāwī, *Al-Nasrāniyya wa-l-Islām* (Cairo, 1977); M.'A. Mansūr, *Al-Yahūd al-Maghdūb Alayhim* (Cairo, 1980); A. H. al-Saqa, *Bayān Fasād Banī Isrā'il* (Cairo, 1977); idem, *Mina-l-Furūq*

Bayna-l-Tawrāt al-Sāmiriyya wa-l-Ibrāniyya (Cairo, 1978); 'A. F. Sa'īd, *Ma'rakat al-Wujūd Bayna-l-Qur'ān wa-l-Talmūd* (Cairo, 1980); A. Jabari, *Jarimat al-Zawaj bi-ghayr al-Muslimat* (Cairo, 1980); M. Qutb, *Yahūd al-Donmeh* (Cairo, 1980).

2. S. al-Bahasnāwī, "Behind Bars," *al-'Arabi* (Kuwait), June 1982, p. 45.

3. 'A. Jirrīsha, *Fi-l-Zinzāna* (Cairo, 1979), p. 41; idem, *'Indama Yahkumu al-Tughāt* (Cairo, 1975), pp. 48–49.

4. K. al-Faramāwī, *Yawmiyyāt Sajīn fi-l-Sijn-al-Harbī* (Cairo, 1976), pp. 170, 174; 'A. al-Sīsi, *Min al-Madhbaha Ila Sahat al-Da'wa* (Cairo, 1978), p. 20; 'A. Jirrīsha, *'Indama*, pp. 50–51.

5. See *Al-Ikhwān Amām al-Mashnaqa* (Cairo, 1955).

6. See J. Rizq, *Madhbāhat al-Ikhwān fi-Limān Torra* (Cairo, 1979), p. 47; see also idem, *Madhābih al-Ikhwān fi Sujūn Nāsir* (Cairo, 1977), p. 27. Both books are based on eyewitness reports. See M. 'A. Fāyid, *Wa-bi-l-Haqq* (Cairo, 1976), pp. 118–119.

7. *Al-Ahram*, 12 July 1974; *Akhbār al-Yawm*, 31 May 1975.

8. Proceedings of the trial can be found in H. Hasan and M. 'A. 'Ali, *Muwājahat al-Fikr al-Mutatarrif fi-l-Islam* (Cairo, 1980), p. 63.

9. See Faraj's book as reproduced in *al-Ahrār* (Cairo), 14 December 1981, and in M. 'Imāra, *Al-Farida al-Gha'iba* (Cairo, 1982), p. 23.

10. Rizq, *Madhbāhat*, p. 120.

11. Sa'd al-Din Ibrahim, "Arab Social Change: Six Profiles," *Jerusalem Quarterly*, no. 23 (Spring 1982), pp. 13–23.

12. See the special section on Israel in *al-Da'wa*, October–November 1976; May, July, and October 1977; May 1980; September 1980 (editorial); *al-I'tisām*, January 1977; February–March 1981.

13. *Al-Da'wa*, December 1977; January, April, May, and June 1978; March, April 1979 (editorials).

14. See *al-Da'wa*, February through October 1978; March, April 1979; February through May 1981; *al-I'tisām*, April–May 1981.

15. *Al-I'tisām*, April–May 1981, pp. 28–29; *al-Da'wa*, May 1981, pp. 62–63.

16. Ibid.

17. See the text of one of Kishk's sermons in J. Keppel, *"Le Prophète et le Pharaon"* (Paris, 1984), ch. 5.

6

Antisemitism in the
Contemporary Arab World

Norman A. Stillman

One commonly hears in the vast corpus of propaganda and polemics that surrounds the Arab-Israeli conflict the statement made that Jews tend to be overly sensitive, seeing antisemitism around every corner and in all forms of opposition. In fact, Jews are commonly accused (even among themselves) of raising the bugaboo of antisemitism in order to silence the genuine political dissent of people who are in no way antisemitic but merely anti-Israeli, anti-Zionist, or anti-the-policies of the particular Israeli government in power.

Another oft-repeated theme in some quarters is that it is absolutely absurd to refer to any antisemitic feelings (latent or otherwise) on the part of the Arabs. After all, the argument runs, the Arabs cannot possibly be antisemitic, since they are Semites themselves.

Let us consider for a moment the words of a man who I am sure all will agree is an indubitable authority on the subject of contemporary Arab attitudes toward Jews, the chairman of the Palestine Liberation Organization, Yasser Arafat. In a 1975 *New York Times Magazine* interview with the late David Holden, Arafat was quoted as saying: "Don't forget, we and the Jews are Semites. Over the years our hearts were open, and our homes too, to the Jews, and we lived together on our land without discrimination and with love and peace."[1] Not only are Jews and Arabs fellow Semites, Arafat is saying, but they have traditionally lived together in familial harmony. There can be no antisemitism here.

Now, history—like beauty—is frequently in the eye of the beholder, and Arafat's remark concerning the fraternal past relations between Jews and Arabs is no less a gross exaggeration than the statement made by Maimonides in his *Iggeret Teman* (Epistle to the Jews of Yemen), which is often cited by revisionist historians in Israel and elsewhere as an antidote to popular notions of a medieval golden age—namely, that no nation has persecuted, debased, and humiliated the Jewish people more than the nation of Ishmael.[2] Historically, the relationship between the two peoples was neither as idyllic nor as dismal as these diametrically opposed points of view would purport.

Arafat's argument regarding the common racial bond between the two peoples is even further from the mark and, indeed, is an exercise in sophistry, for in Arab propaganda it is frequently emphasized that Jews are not really Semites, are a mongrel race, and are certainly not cousins of the Arabs.[3]

Antisemitism, of course, has nothing to do with peoples of a so-called semitic race. If there ever was an ethnic group, the Semites, they belong to prehistory and are no more. The term *semitic* was only coined in the late eighteenth century by A. L. Schlözer to describe a family of related languages that included Hebrew, Aramaic, Ethiopic, and Arabic (the others in the group were not even known at that time). During the first half of the nineteenth century, anthropologists such as Christian Lassen, Ernest Renan, and Count Gobineau, who were imbued with romantic and pseudoscientific notions of race, language, and culture, created the idea of a semitic, as distinct from an Aryan, race.[4] "Antisemitism" is of even more recent vintage and was only coined in 1879 by the German Jew-baiter Wilhelm Marr as a polite term for Jew-hatred (*Judenhass*). The expression quickly became popular in France, Germany, and Eastern Europe as a euphemism for anti-Jewish sentiments, which now had a modern racial and political rationale in addition to the age-old religious and social justifications.

Western antisemitism never concerned itself with the Arabs (even though in the anthropology of Renan and Gobineau they too were Semites), and no less sincere antisemites than the Nazi leadership felt few if any qualms about entertaining the Muftī Hājj Amīn al-Husaynī in Berlin during the war. Nevertheless, the claim that they were Semites as well provided a convenient defense in Arab polemics that their justifiable attacks upon Zionism and Jewry were in no way related to some base form of prejudice. Some Arab writers, such as Ibrahim al-Hardallo, have suggested that the term *antisemitism* was coined by the Zionists themselves and was cultivated and propagated by them for their own devious purposes.[5]

In the Arab polemical literature produced for foreign consumption (i.e., written in English and other Western languages), a careful distinction is usually made between Jews and Zionists. Arab opposition is directed only against the latter. The argument further runs that there are many good Jews who do not support the Zionist cause. Alfred Lilienthal, Elmer Berger, and the American Council for Judaism are usually cited as prime examples.

Unfortunately, the niceties of this distinction are often ignored in Arabic literature, news media, and in daily speech. *Yahūd* (Jews) and *Banū Isrā'īl* (the koranic expression for the Children of Israel) are employed interchangeably with *Sahāyana* or *Sahyūniyyūn* (Zionists) and *Isrā'īliyyūn* (Israelis and Israelites). As noted in a recent article in *al-Ahrām al-Iqrisādī*, Egypt's leading financial journal: "It is imperative not to differentiate between Jew and Israeli. To this day, I cannot fathom the reason for distinguishing this sort of classification when the Jews themselves reject it. The Jew is a Jew, unchanging over thousands of years."[6] Taking this essential identification of the Jew, both historical and contemporary, with the Israeli and with Israel, I should like to quote another statement in marked contrast to that of Arafat cited above:

> Israel has had malicious intentions since ancient times. Its objective is the destruction of all other religions. It is proven from history that they are the ones who ignited the Crusades at the time of Saladin the Ayyubid, so that that war would lead to the weakening of both Muslims and Christians. They regard the other religions as lower than their own and other peoples as inferior to their level. And on the subject of vengeance— they have a certain day on which they mix the blood of non-Jews into their bread and eat it. It happened that two years ago while I was in Paris on a visit, that the police discovered five murdered children. Their blood had been drained, and it turned out that some Jews had murdered them in order to take their blood and mix it with the bread that they eat on this day. This shows you what is the extent of their hatred and malice toward non-Jewish peoples.[7]

These remarks were made by the late King Faysal of Saudi Arabia in a 1972 interview with the Egyptian journalist Fu'ad al-Sayyid that appeared in the popular pictorial magazine *al-Musawwar*. It is highly unlikely that a statement such as this would have been made by King Faysal's father, and certainly not by his grandfather. The "Blood Libel" (a classic of Western judeophobia) is simply not one of the stock images of the Jew in traditional Islamic, Arabic society. As with much of the antisemitic imagery now current in Middle Eastern writing, the Blood Libel is of fairly recent vintage and is a European import.

This is not to imply that the premodern Arab world did not have its own indigenous store of negative attitudes vis-à-vis Jews. Due to the Prophet Muhammad's conflict with the Jewish tribes of Medina, Jews came to be denounced in the Koran as the number-one opponents of the early Muslim community along with the pagans, who had previously been the sole enemy. In Sura 5:82, for example, the Prophet is told by God: "Indeed, you will find that the most vehement of men in enmity to those who believe are the Jews and the polytheists."

In the Medinese suras of the Koran, Jews are accused of having knowingly tampered with and distorted their scriptures.[8] Their image as a perfidious and rancorous group is reinforced by assorted stories of the transgressions of the ancient Israelites, who broke the convenant, disobeyed Moses, killed prophets, and desecrated the Sabbath.[9] This depiction of the Jews as untrustworthy and malevolent was not only sanctified in holy writ but expanded and amplified in the hagiographic literature on the life of the Prophet, such as the *Sīra* of Ibn Ishāq and the *Kitāb al-Maghāzī* of al-Wāqidī, two of the earliest and most important examples of this genre. In these works, the Jews appear as villainous caricatures in a hopeless struggle against the forces of good. But, though wicked and treacherous, they never appear as terribly effectual. They possess none of the demonic qualities of the Jews in a medieval Christian passion play. Their ignominy stands in marked contrast to Muslim heroism and, in general, conforms to the koranic image of "wretchedness and baseness stamped upon them."[10]

The Koran and the early Muslim hagiographies created a derogatory Jewish stereotype that would continue through fourteen Islamic centuries in both literature and folklore. A Moroccan proverb with variants throughout North Africa warns: *"Lā tteq b-lihūdī ida slem alu yebqa arba'in 'am"* (Don't trust a Jew if he becomes a Muslim, even though he remains so for forty years).[11] Another Arabic proverb, again from Morocco, observes: *"Lihūdī ida ghashsh l-meslem ka-ikūn ferhān f-dāk l-yūm"* (When a Jew cheats a Muslim, he is happy that day).[12]

The negative image of the Jew in the traditional Muslim world was mitigated by several important factors. First among these was that although the Prophet Muhammad decided at a certain point in his career that the Jews (and later the Christians as well) had in some degree corrupted their scriptures, he never questioned the basic validity of their religion. They were to be opposed only until they submitted to Muslim rule as humble tribute bearers in accordance with the clear koranic injunction to "fight against those to whom the Scriptures were given . . . until they pay tribute out of hand and are humbled."[13] As long as they accepted a subordinate status, they were not only to be tolerated but were entitled to the protection of the Muslim commonwealth— hence their legal designation as *ahl al-dhimma,* or "protégés."[14]

There was a prescribed role for non-Muslims within the Islamic state. The legal and social disabilities it entailed was a small price to pay in a premodern society for the relative security and communal autonomy that was granted in exchange. The fact that the Jews shared their inferior status with Christians and Zoroastrians, who were far more numerous and more conspicuous in the Middle Ages, diffused some of the specifically anti-Jewish sentiments within a broader anti-non-Muslim context. There was, in effect, an essential equality among inferiors.

However, whenever Jews in the Arab world did not conform to the humble role prescribed for them—as, for example, when a Jewish individual rose to too high a level in society or became too conspicuous in government service—then all of the worst suspicions about the Jews and all the negative stereotypes were confirmed. Much of the anti-Jewish agitation that took place in Islamic history occurred at just such times and drew upon the images that had been sanctified in the Koran and in religious lore.[15]

The subterranean wellspring of generally anti-non-Muslim and spe-cifically anti-Jewish attitudes was also drawn upon in periods of great social and economic stress (a phenomenon with parallels in European history). Some of the most virulent anti-Jewish and anti-Christian literature in medieval Islam was produced during the thirteenth and fourteenth centuries, when the Muslim world was suffering from pandemics, invasions, and a precipitous economic decline. Treatises such as al-Jawbarī's *Kashf al-Asrār* (Secrets Revealed) and al-Wāsitī's *Radd 'alā Ahl al-Dhimma* (A Polemic Against the Non-Muslim Proteges) are filled with horror stories of *dhimmi* malevolence. In one anecdote, al-Wāsitī has none other than Maimonides himself admit that the blood of Gentiles is licit for Jews.[16] Religious handbooks of the period, such as Muhammad b. al-Hājj's *Madkhal al-Shar' al-Sharīf* (An Introduction to the Noble Sacred Law), echo these sentiments. The motif of the malevolent Jewish doctor became widespread in later Arabic literature.[17]

In our own day, the Arab-Israeli conflict and the stresses it has caused in some Muslim countries, along with other factors of social stress, have led to a heightened preoccupation with these traditional anti-Jewish attitudes, in addition to nontraditional attitudes imported from Europe. European antisemitic notions seem to have been first imported into the Levant by French traders and missionaries during the sixteenth and seventeenth centuries. They found an audience among the Arab Christians of Syria, with whom they maintained commercial, religious, and to some extent cultural ties. The belief that Jews kidnaped and sacrificed Christian children was current among the Christians of Aleppo in the 1750s and may already have been in circulation at the beginning of the preceding century.[18]

This particular prejudice does not seem to have had any dire consequences until the nineteenth century, when the infamous Damascus Affair occurred. This affair was touched off by the disappearance of an Italian Capuchin friar and his native assistant on February 5, 1840. The native Christians egged on by the French consul in Damascus, Ratti-Menton, who was himself a rabid antisemite, accused the Jews of having murdered the two men in order to obtain their blood for the coming Passover. A Jewish barber was arrested and tortured into "confessing" the crime. He implicated seven leading members of the community, who in turn were arrested and put to torture. Word of the trials and the confessions spread throughout the Middle East and were believed by Muslims as well as Christians.[19]

Accusations of attempted or actual ritual murders were leveled against Jews throughout the nineteenth century in Syria, Palestine, and Egypt. In 1844, Muslims in Cairo accused the Jews of murdering a Christian for his blood. In 1847, the Blood Libel was raised against the Jews by local Maronites in the Lebanese village of Dayr al-Qamar. In that same year, the Greek Orthodox in Jerusalem accused the Jews there of trying to murder a Christian child for ritual purposes. During the 1870s and 1880s, Jews were charged with the Blood Libel on several occasions in Damanhur, Egypt.[20]

Just as the French were the purveyors of traditional European antisemitic beliefs in the Levant during the first half of the nineteenth century, so it seems they were the chief disseminators of the newer, post-Enlightenment form of antisemitism during the last decades of the second half. (It should be recalled that France was the intellectual center of antisemitism at the time.) Once again, they made their inroads principally among the Levantine Christians, who not only shared the traditional Arab contempt for the Jews but also looked upon the latter, another emerging, half-emancipated group like themselves, as rivals.

The first full-length modern antisemitic works that appeared in Arabic during the 1890s were mere translations or adaptations of French tracts. For example, Najīb al-Hājj's *Fi 'l-Zawāya Khabāya aw Kashf Asrār al-Yahūd* (Clandestine Things in the Corners, or Secrets of the Jews Unmasked), published in 1893, probably in Beirut, was an adaptation of Georges Corneilhan's *Juifs et opportunistes: le judaïsme en Egypte et en Syrie.*[21]

The principal audience for these early works of antisemitic literature in Arabic was a relatively small circle of westernized Christian intellectuals in Syria and Egypt. For the Muslim majority, this sort of propaganda was still too new and too palpably foreign to be lent much, if any, credence. However, it should be noted that these early works formed the vanguard of what was to become an extensive body of literature of this genre in the twentieth century, when the general Arab attitude toward Jews underwent a radical change as a result of the clash between Arab and Jewish nationalism. Indeed, a number of these pioneer works have even been reprinted in recent years, as, for example, Habīb Fāris's *al-Dhabā'ih al-Bashariyya al-Talmūdiyya* (Talmudic Human Sacrifices), which was published in Cairo in 1890 and reprinted in 1962.[22]

Antisemitism *à la européene* began to have a wider impact in the Middle East, partly in reaction to the stresses of colonialism, nationalism, and modernization. The single most important catalyst precipitating the new antisemitism was undoubtedly the increasingly sensitive issue of Palestine. The hardening of Arab attitudes on this question became increasingly clear throughout the 1920s and 1930s. It was at this very time that the infamous *Protocols of the Elders of Zion* first made its appearance in the Arabic translation of al-Khūrī Antūn Yamīn with the title *Mu'āmarat al-Yahūd 'ala 'l-Shu'ūb* (The Conspiracy of the Jews Against the Nations). The work was already being cited in the English translation by Palestinian nationalists in the early 1920s.[23] The *Protocols* has come to enjoy an enduring popularity in the Arab world. The book has been translated into Arabic no less than nine times and has appeared in numerous editions. It is cited extensively, in works on Zionism as well as those on Jews and Judaism. The Lebanese newspaper *al-Anwār* placed the *Protocols* in the number-one position on its list of nonfiction bestsellers.[24] It has been recommended by such leading political figures as the late Presidents Nasser of Egypt and 'Ārif of Iraq, by King Faysal of Saudi Arabia, and Colonel Qaddafi of Libya. The Saudis have been particularly active in disseminating it, presenting copies to visiting foreign dignitaries and distributing it gratis through consulates and cultural missions.[25] It has spread to the far corners of the Islamic world, owing most probably to the efforts of the Saudis and Libyans, who have been generous supporters of Islamic cultural centers. As Bernard Lewis has pointed out, its authenticity has never been seriously questioned in the Arabic media.[26]

The most frequently reprinted edition of the *Protocols* is Muhammad Khalīfa al-Tūnisī's translation entitled *al-Khatar al-Yahūdī: Brūtūkūlāt Hukamā' Sahyūn* (The Jewish Menace: The Protocols of the Wise Men of Zion). This version has a scholarly introduction by Professor 'Abbās Muhammad al-'Aqqād, a prominent Egyptian intellectual and author of some sixty books.[27] Al-'Aqqād has annotated the text with a complete critical apparatus that includes copious footnotes. The back cover of the 1972 edition lists the names of bookstores in major cities from Baghdad to Casablanca, from which the book may be ordered.

As is well known, the Axis gained widespread sympathy and even support in the Arab East during World War II. The ties with the Nazis were based neither upon any deep philosophical affinities nor upon any general acceptance of National Socialist racial theories. Rather, as Bernard Lewis has pointed out, Arab support for the Nazis was predicated on the fact that the Germans were the mortal enemies of the Western powers, of Western civilization, and, ultimately, of Western values.[28] It is for the same reason that the Soviets have received such a warm welcome in the area since World War II. The close ties with the Axis helped to familiarize the educated classes with the vocabulary of modern European antisemitism, but apparently not much more. Nazi propaganda was readily available, of course. An Arabic translation of *Mein Kampf* was published in Lebanon in 1935.[29] But there does not seem to have been any great outpouring of home-grown, locally produced hate literature at this time.[30] Most of the Arabic literature that consciously imitates Nazi Jew-baiting tracts and the libels of Julius Streicher's *Der Stürmer* dates from the postwar years. One example of this type is S. Nājī's *al-Mufsidūn fī 'l-Ard, aw Jarā'im al-Yahūd al-Siyāsiyya wa'l-Ijtimā'iyya 'abr al-Ta'rīkh* (Corrupters in the Earth, or the Political and Social Crimes of the Jews Throughout History), which appeared in Damascus in 1965. Most of the material in this book seems to have been lifted verbatim from German and French antisemitic literature of the 1930s and 1940s. In addition to the usual litany of accusations against the Jews, certain Gentiles are accused of being Jewish, among them Franklin and Eleanor Roosevelt and Cordell Hull.[31]

One explanation for the relative paucity of antisemitic publications in the Arab world during the war years may be that throughout the period, Egypt was under tight British control, as were Lebanon, Syria, and Iraq under the Free French and the British after June 1941. Furthermore, most of the Arab countries still had large Jewish populations, among which Zionism had still not become a true mass movement. And most obviously, the trauma of an Arab defeat at the hands of the newly formed Jewish state in 1948 and 1949 had not yet occurred.

The birth of the State of Israel, the creation of the Palestinian refugee problem, the military defeats of 1948, 1956, and 1967, and the loss of Jerusalem—all combined to harden and embitter Arab attitudes toward Jews in general. The new bitterness was an important (albeit not the only) factor in the mass exodus of the Jews from most Arab countries. The Zionist menace became a reality in the eyes of the majority of Arabs, and the term *Zionist* took its place alongside *imperialist, colonialist,* and *racist* in the Arabic lexicon of epithets, and may even have been the most sinister of them all. It became extremely difficult, now that most of the Jews of the Middle East and North Africa had fled to Israel, for the Arabs to distinguish between Jews and Zionists, despite claims to the contrary aimed at Western audiences.

Arab culture has always been a highly verbal one, and the conflict with Israel has stimulated the growth of a significant body of writing in which there is a considerable element of antisemitism. In 1967, Yehoshafat Harkabi surveyed some one hundred and twenty Arab works on the Middle East conflict, many of which contained antisemitic material. He estimated that there were approximately three to four hundred books in Arabic on the subject at the time. When he published his dissertation as a book a year later, he had already added another thirty such works.

In 1975, I tried to arrive at some idea of contemporary attitudes toward Jews in the Arab world by surveying some of the literature that had appeared since Harkabi made his study.[32] Of the more than thirty books I studied, fifteen dealt exclusively, or at length, with Jews *qua* Jews and with the Jewish faith. In the years that followed, I have attempted to keep abreast of new publications in Arabic dealing with the Jews. Even in those books that are primarily directed against the State of Israel and political Zionism, there are frequent characterizations of Jews from the sociohistorical, psychological, or religious viewpoint. The depictions are almost unanimously negative. The writers are frequently rather eclectic, mingling traditional Christian and Islamic themes with those of post-Enlightenment antisemitism.

The most common charge leveled against the Jews as a whole is that they are racists. Racism (*al-'unsuriyya* in Arabic) and racial exclusivity (*al-'unsuriyya al-ta'assubiyya*) are described as fundamental articles of Jewish religious belief. Jewish racism is variously attributed to the Bible or the Talmud, particularly the latter.[33] The Talmud comes under greater attack for two reasons. First, there is the basic respect accorded by Islam to the Jewish and Christian scriptures, despite the belief that they have been corrupted from their pristine form. The Talmud, on the other hand, never enjoyed any such recognition as a holy book. Second, there is the deep hostility to the Talmud that has run through medieval and modern European antisemitism and has been imported into the Arab world. August Rohling's classic diatribe *Der Talmudjude* made its appearance in the Arab world in 1899, and similar works have been published in recent years—as, for example, Muhammad Sabrī's *al-Talmūd: Sharī'at al-Yahūd* (The Talmud: The Religious Law of the Jews).[34]

The deity of the Children of Israel in the Torah is described as an instigator to pillage, theft, and breach of faith.[35] The book of Joshua is often cited as proof that the Bible encourages Jewish espionage.[36] The Talmud is described as permitting Jews to lie to Gentiles, to cheat them, and to steal from them.[37] The Talmud is alleged to teach Jews that they alone are entitled to enjoy the blessings of the earth and that non-Jews are to be considered as animals who have human form only so that they may serve Jews.[38] It allows them to violate non-Jewish women.[39] It makes licit the shedding of Gentile blood.[40]

Some of this literature has a pseudo-academic flavor, as for example, Sabrī Jirjis's *al-Turāth al-Yahūdī al-Sahyūnī wa'l-Fikr al-Frūydī* (The Jewish Zionist Heritage and Freudian Thought), which purports to be a psychoanalytical study, or Hasan Zāzā and Muhammad 'Āshūr's *al-Yahūd Laysū Tujjāran bil-Nash'a* (The Jews Are Not Merchants by Origin), which is supposed to be a socioeconomic history.[41] Much of this literature, however, is reminiscent of the medieval polemics in which verses from the scriptures of one's opponent are cited to expose and confound him. That the Jews have been cursed by God is frequently stated. Muslim writers cite koranic passages and Christians the New Testament. Thus, for example, Muhammad Barāniq and Muhammad al-Mahjūb conclude their book on Muhammad and the Jews with the following pious crescendo: "Indeed they [the Jews] have rebelled against God. They betrayed the covenant of Muhammad and the Muslims. They denied God's signs and rejected the message of the Prophets and killed them wrongfully. It is no wonder then that we see them with 'baseness stamped upon them wherever they are found.'"[42]

Christian works also cite the theme of Jewish rebelliousness. Bishop Gregorius of the Coptic Church points out in his book *Isrā'īl fi 'l-Mīzān* (Israel in the Balance) that the Messiah announced God's rejection of the Jews because of their rebellion.[43] Another book put out by the Coptic Church in Egypt entitled *al-Kanīsa wa 'l-Ma'raka* (The Church and the Struggle) emphasizes again and again that the Jews were the killers of Christ and are accursed.[44] Five of the fourteen essays are by Bābā Shenūda III, the Patriarch of the Coptic Church. In a book by Kamāl Ramzī Astīnū of the Egyptian Evangelical Church entitled *Ma'nā Isrā'īl fi 'l-Kitāb al-Muqaddas* (The Meaning of Israel in the Bible), the writer cites some of the most hostile passages in the New Testament concerning Jews, such as John 8:44 ("You are of your father the Devil and willingly you carry out his wishes").[45] He goes on to declare that the Jews are "in truth the worshippers of the dollar and colonialism and are not God's chosen people."[46] He goes on to cite the *Protocols*, which he terms the secret archives of the First Zionist Congress, as calling for the elimination of all religions in general and of Christianity in particular. On the very same page, he refers to the Talmud as the holy book of Zionist Jews and says that it attacks Jesus, depicts Christians as idolaters, and calls upon Jews to destroy Christian churches.[47]

One of the most disturbing features of the antisemitism now current in the Arab world is the ubiquity of the Blood Libel among both Muslim and Christian writers. Ostensibly, scholarly treatments of Jewish faith and practice such as ʿAlī ʿAbd al-Wāhid Wāfī's *al-Yahūdiyya wa 'l-Yahūd* (Judaism and the Jews) present it matter-of-factly in the section dealing with the Purim and Passover rituals.[48] Jew-baiting tracts such as Īliyya Abu 'l-Rūs's *al-Yahūdiyya al-ʿĀlamiyya wa-Harbuha 'l-Mustamarra ʿala 'l-Masīhiyya* (World Judaism and Its Continuing War Against Christianity) dwell upon it at great length and in morbid detail.[49] Three-fourths of Muhammad Sabrī's book on the Talmud is devoted to the Damascus Affair and provides what are supposed to be detailed transcripts of the ritual murderers' confessions.[50] Hasan Zāzā in his *al-Fikr al-Dīnī al-Isrāʾīlī: Atwāruhu wa-Madhāhibuhu* (Israelite Religious Thought: Its Phases and Schools) devotes a very learned discussion to the Blood Libel, pointing out that such a practice is indeed forbidden by Jewish law although the accusation has stuck with the Jews throughout history (as the author notes, people often do what their religious teachings forbid, either out of ignorance or malice). Zāzā finally comes to the conclusion that the accusation is justified on the basis of the confessions of the accused murderers in the Damascus Affair.[51] In a wide-ranging 1973 interview on Jewish history in the Egyptian paper *Akhīr Sāʿa*, Zāzā refers to the Damascus Affair as the actual beginning of modern Zionism.[52] Mustafā al-Saʿdanī, in his *Adwāʾ ʿala 'l-Sahyūniyya* (Illuminations on Zionism), devotes more than thirty pages to the Blood Libel.[53] The well-known Egyptian female writer ʿĀʾisha ʿAbd al-Rahmān, who goes by the pen-name of Bint al-Shātiʾ, simply mentions the custom of draining children's blood for the Passover ritual in a brief paragraph in her book *Aʿdāʾ al-Bashar* (The Enemies of Mankind).[54] She also refers to Jews by such epithets as *al-marad* (sickness), *al-wabāʾ* (plague), and *al-jurthūma al-khabītha* (noxious germ).

It would seem that King Faysal's remarks (which were quoted near the beginning of this chapter) are by no means an isolated or unrepresentative phenomenon but, rather, one very much in vogue in certain intellectual circles.

Two important questions arise in dealing with this material: How wide a circulation does it in fact enjoy? Is it indicative of a new and widespread attitude toward the Jewish people? Unfortunately, we have neither the publication nor circulation statistics to answer such questions, although the appearance of the Blood Libel in the widely read magazine *al-Musawwar* (whose place in the Arab world is somewhat comparable to that of the former *Life* magazine in this country) would seem to indicate a high degree of currency. The numerous editions of the *Protocols* and the inclusion of the book on the bestsellers list in Lebanon are also indicative of some popularity.

A further question that poses itself is this: To what extent do these new antisemitic attitudes percolate down to the larger nonreading public in the Arab world? Once again, regrettably, hard-core, quantitative data is lacking. Y. Harkabi notes that "there is more crude anti-Semitism in the Voice of the Arabs and less in the Cairo stations."[55] He also mentions an increase in antisemitic propaganda just before and after the Six-Day War. To the best of my knowledge, there have been no studies of radio programming in the decade and a half since then.

There is one instance in which hard-core data are available with regard to the dissemination of the new antisemitism in the Arab East—namely, the report of a UNESCO commission of outside experts on 127 textbooks used in the United Nations Relief and Works Agency (UNRWA) camps in East and West Bank Jordan, the Gaza Strip, and Lebanon. The report was presented to the Eighty-Second Session in Paris on April 4, 1969. It has never been published, but it is available in typescript.

The commission recommended that 14 texts be withdrawn, 65 be used only after modification, and 48 of the original 127 be retained. One of the criteria upon which the commission based its recommendations was as follows:

> All terms contemptuous of a community taken as a whole should be prohibited since this, obviously intolerable in itself, can among other consequences lead to the violation of the most sacred rights of the individual. Hence, liar, cheat, usurer, idiot—terms applied to Jews in certain passages, and part of the deplorable language of international anti-semitism—cannot be tolerated.[56]

The commission further found that in the religious and historical textbooks, "an excessive importance is given to the problem of relations between the Prophet Mohammed and the Jews of Arabia, in terms tending to convince young people that the Jewish community as a whole has always been and will always be the irreconcilable enemy of the Muslim community."[57]

It would seem, then, that a whole new generation in the Arab world is being exposed to at least some aspects of the new antisemitism. The Israeli scholar Hava Lazarus-Yafeh, who made a study of the textbooks used in those areas that came under Israeli control after the 1967 war, has observed that neither hatred of Israel nor antisemitism should be regarded as central themes in these texts. She expressed the belief that there was no systematic policy either to include or exclude such material in contrast to Nazi education, for example. She also noted that even explicit anti-Israeli and anti-Jewish sentiments seemed to be "part of a general kind of 'floating hostility,' which is today especially strong in the Arab world, but seems to have existed already for a long time."[58]

With the Sadat peace initiative and the Camp David accord, there has been a considerable diminution of antisemitic propaganda on the official level emanating from Egypt. Already after the October 1973 war, there appears to have been more restraint in the antisemitic material in Egyptian textbooks.[59] However, in other Arab countries this is not the case. Even in Egypt, antisemitic literature is still widely available in the bookstores, and articles with strong antisemitic overtones have by no means disappeared from the press. For example, in a 1982 article in *al-Ahrām al-Iqtisādī*, Jews are said to have been marked through the millennia by "vileness, depravity, cunning, and contempt for all moral values."[60] The writer, Lutfī 'Abd al-'Azīm, goes on to say that "he [the Jew] consumes living flesh and drinks its blood for a few coins. The Jew, the Merchant of Venice, is no different from the blood spiller of Deir Yassin or the blood shedder of the refugee camps. These are all similar examples of the inhuman degradation."[61] Most of the articles that appeared in the Egyptian press in the wake of the Sabra and Shatila massacres were more careful to vilify Israel and Zionism, rather than Jews in general.[62]

Some Arab countries, most notably Saudi Arabia, Libya, and Iraq (until the war with Iran turned much of Iraq's attention elsewhere), actively continue to propagate antisemitism both at home and abroad. Given the deep-rooted stresses that plague the Arab world at present, there is little reason to believe that antisemitism will disappear from the scene in the foreseeable future.

Notes

1. David Holden, "Which Arafat?" *New York Times Magazine*, 23 March 1975, p. 72.

2. The passage is translated in Norman A. Stillman, *The Jews of Arab Lands: A History and Source Book* (Philadelphia, 1979), p. 241.

3. See, inter alia, Y. Harkabi, *Arab Attitudes to Israel* (Jerusalem, 1976), p. 259. Ahmad Soussé, an Iraqi Jewish convert to Islam, even argues that the ancient Israelites were Arab Semites and that the later Jews are descended from Europeans and from Khazars. See his book *The Arabs and Jews in History* (Lausanne and Baghdad, n.d.), pp. 18 and passim. Sābir 'Abd al-Rahmān Tu'ayma devotes a detailed chapter of his book, filled with anthropological data, to the contention that the Jews represent no single ethnic strain. See his *al-Yahūd bayn al-Dīn wa'l-Ta'rīkh* [The Jews Between Religion and History] (Cairo, 1972), pp. 609–624.

4. The classic work on race from this period is Joseph Arthur, comte de Gobineau, *Essai sur l'inégalité des races humaines* (Paris, 1853–1855), with an English translation by Adrian Collins, *The Inequality of Human Races* (New York, 1915). For an excellent study of Gobineau's thought, see Janine Buenzod, *La formation de la pensée de Gobineau et l'Essai sur l'inégalité des races humaines* (Paris, 1967). Another work that is filled with theories on the differences between Semites and Aryans is Ernest Renan, *Histoire générale et système comparé des langues sémitiques* (Paris, 1855).

5. Ibrahim al-Hardallo, *Antisemitism: A Changing Concept* (Khartoum, 1970), p. 9 and passim. Oddly enough, al-Hardallo identifies Marr as a Jew (ibid., p. 9).

6. 'Lutfī 'Abd al-'Azīm, "Al-'Arab wa'l-Yahūd: Man Yubīd Man?" [The Arabs and the Jews: Who Will Destroy Whom?], *al-Ahrām al-Iqtisādī*, 27 September 1982, p. 4.

7. Fu'ād al-Sayyid, "al-Malik Faysal Yatahaddath 'an," *al-Musawwar,* no. 24, 4 August 1972, p. 13.

8. See, for example, Suras 2:75 and 3:78.

9. Breaking the covenant: Sura 2:82–85; disobedience to Moses: Sura 2:51; killing the prophets: Sura 2:61; desecrating the Sabbath: Sura 2:65 and Sura 4:47 and 154.

10. Sura 2:61

11. See Norman A. Stillman, "Muslims and Jews in Morocco: Perceptions, Images, Stereotypes," in World Jewish Congress, *Muslim-Jewish Relations in North Africa,* seminar (New York, 1975), p. 13.

12. Ibid., p. 20.

13. Sura 9:29.

14. The principal discussions of the actual and legal status of the *ahl al-dhimma* in the traditional Muslim world are A. S. Tritton, *The Caliphs and Their Non-Muslim Subjects* (London, 1930; reprinted 1970); Antoine Fattal, *Le statut légal des non-musulmans en pays d'Islam* (Beirut, 1958); S. D. Goitein, *Jews and Arabs* (New York, 1970); idem, *A Mediterranean Society, II* (Berkeley and Los Angeles, 1971); Claude Cahen, "Dhimma," *Encyclopaedia of Islam,* vol. 2, new ed., pp. 227–231; and Stillman, *Jews of Arab Lands.*

15. See, for example, Stillman, *Jews of Arab Lands,* pp. 51, 59, 66, 81, 211–213, 214–216, 217–225, and 281–286.

16. The passage concerning Maimonides is translated in Stillman, *Jews of Arab Lands,* p. 276. See also p. 72 and the sources cited there.

17. See Stillman, "Muslims and Jews in Morocco," in *Muslim-Jewish Relations in North Africa,* p. 19; see also Moshe Perlmann, "Notes on the Position of Jewish Physicians in Medieval Muslim Countries," *Israel Oriental Studies* 2 (1972):316–317.

18. Alexander Russell, *The Natural History of Aleppo,* vol. 2, 2d ed. (London, 1756), p. 74. There are several examples of the Blood Libel appearing in Turkey itself in the fifteenth and sixteenth centuries, but it does not seem to have taken root there or to have spread into the Arab provinces of the Ottoman Empire. See Uriel Heyd, "Ritual Murder Accusations in 15th and 16th Century Turkey," *Sefunot* 5 (1961):137–149 (in Hebrew).

19. For an extensive bibliography on the affair, see Albert M. Hyamson, "The Damascus Affair—1840," *Transactions of the Jewish Historical Society of England* 16 (1945–1951):47–70. See also A. J. Brawer, "Damascus Affair," *Encyclopaedia Judaica* 5, cols. 1249–1252; Stillman, *Jews of Arab Lands,* pp. 105–106, 393–402; and idem, "Middle Eastern Jewry and the Beginnings of European Penetration," in M. Abitbol, ed., *World History of the Jew People,* vol. 6 (forthcoming).

20. Jacob M. Landau, *Jews in Nineteenth-Century Egypt* (New York, 1969), pp. 38–39, 182–183, 199–200, 203–204, 215–217, 298–299; idem, "Ritual Murder Accusations and Persecutions of Jews in 19th Century Egypt," *Sefunot* 5 (1961):417–460; Stillman, *Jews of Arab Lands,* pp. 426–427.

21. See Sylvia G. Haim, "Arabic Antisemitic Literature: Some Preliminary Notes," *Jewish Social Studies* 17 (1955):307.

22. Concerning this book, which apparently first appeared in serial form in the newspaper *al-Mahrūsa,* see Harkabi, *Arab Attitudes to Israel,* pp. 270–272.

23. Elyakim Rubinstein, "'The Protocols of the Elders of Zion' in the Arab-Jewish Conflict: Palestine in the Twenties," *Ha-Mizrah he-Hadash* 26, nos. 1, 2 (1976):38 (in Hebrew).

24. Harkabi, *Arab Attitudes to Israel*, p. 518.

25. Ibid., pp. 234–236; Norman A. Stillman, "New Attitudes Toward the Jew in the Arab World," *Jewish Social Studies* 37 (1975):199, notes 11, 12; Daniel Pipes, "The Politics of Muslim Anti-Semitism," *Commentary* 65 (August 1981):42.

26. See Bernard Lewis, "The Anti-Zionist Resolution," *Foreign Affairs* 55, no. 1 (October 1976):56–57. See also the ensuing exchange of correspondence in *Foreign Affairs* 55, no. 3 (April 1977):641–643. On the *Protocols* in Malaysia, see V. S. Naipaul, *Among the Believers: An Islamic Journey* (New York, 1981), pp. 270–274.

27. Concerning Professor al ʿAqqād, see Nadav Safran, "Egypt in Search of Political Community," *Harvard Middle Eastern Studies*, vol. 5 (Cambridge, Mass., 1961), pp. 135–137 and 212–226.

28. Bernard Lewis, *The Middle East and the West* (New York, 1964), pp. 67–68; and idem, "The Palestinians and the PLO: An Historical Approach," *Commentary* 59, no. 1 (1975):42.

29. Translated by Kāmil Marwa.

30. All of the antisemitic references cited by Harkabi, *Arab Attitudes to Israel*, pp. 218–303, are from works published either before 1935 (relatively few) or after 1945 (mostly from the 1950s and 1960s), with the exception of the pamphlet entitled *The Jews and Islam* published by the Palestinian Arab Council in Egypt in 1937. The only work from this period cited by Haim, "Arabic Antisemitic Literature," *Jewish Social Studies* 17 (1955):311, is Sāmī Shawkat, *Hādhihi Ahdāfunā, Man Āmana bihā fa-huwa minnā* [These Are Our Aims, Whoever Believes in Them Is One of Us] (Baghdad, 1939). With reference to this last item, it should be noted that Nazi propaganda achieved its greatest political success in Iraq, where a pro-Axis government came briefly to power in April 1941. Concerning anti-Jewish agitation in Iraq at this time, see Hayyim J. Cohen, *The Jews of the Middle East, 1860–1972* (New York, Toronto, and Jerusalem, 1973), pp. 28–32.

31. Damascus, 1965. For the Roosevelts, see p. 326; for Cordell Hull, see p. 327, where Fiorello La Guardia is also listed.

32. The results of this survey were first given as a paper at a seminar on "Third World and Other New Attitudes Toward the Jew," sponsored by the Conference on Jewish Social Studies and the Academic Committee of the World Jewish Congress at the School of International Affairs, Columbia University, on March 23, 1975, and published in *Jewish Social Studies*, 37 (1975) that same year.

33. For the Bible as a source of Jewish racism, see, for example, ʿAlī ʿAbd al-Wāhid Wāfī, *al-Yahūdiyya waʾl-Yahūd* [Judaism and the Jews] (Cairo, 1970), pp. 50–51. For the Bible and Talmud as sources, see Mustafā al-Saʿdanī, *Adwāʾ ʿala ʾl-Sahyūniyya* [Illuminations on Zionism] (Cairo, 1969), pp. 15ff and 37–58; Muhammad al-Zaʿbī, *Dafāʾin al-Nafsiyya al-Yahūdiyya* [Jewish Spiritual Treasures] (Beirut, 1968), passim; Tuʿayma, *al-Yahūd*, p. 549. For the Talmud as a source, see (in addition to the works cited in Notes 34 and 37–40 in this chapter), Soussé, *The Arabs and Jews in History*, pp. 81–83; Kamāl Ramzī Astīnū, *Maʿnā Isrāʾīl fī ʾl-Kitāb al-Muqaddas* (Cairo, 1971), p. 24, where the Talmud is called "the holy book of Zionist Jews."

34. This book is put out by the Dār al-Hilāl publishing house of Cairo, but it bears no date of publication.

35. al-Saʿdanī, *Adwāʾ ʿala ʾl-Sahyūniyya*, p. 41; Soussé, *The Arabs and Jews in History*, pp. 78–79.

36. al-Sa'danī, *Adwā' 'ala 'l-Sahyūniyya*, pp. 48–49. The book of Joshua is also frequently cited as an example of Jewish barbarity (see Harkabi, *Arab Attitudes to Israel*, p. 257).

37. Muhammad Sabrī, *al-Talmūd: Sharī'at Banī Isrā'īl* [The Talmud: The Religious Law of the Israelites] (Cairo, n.d.), p. 28; S. Nājī, *al-Mufsidūn fi 'l-Ard*, p. 110; Hasan Zāzā and Muhammad 'Āshūr, *al-Yahūd Laysū Tujjāran bil-Nash'a* [The Jews Are Not Merchants by Origin] (Cairo, 1975), p. 118; 'Abd al-Fattāh 'Abd al-Hamīd, *Yā Muslimi 'l-'Ālam Ittahidū* [O Muslims of the World Unite!] (Cairo, 1976), p. 35; Sāmī al-Ghamrāwī, *Li-Hādhā Akrah Isrā'īl* [This is Why I Hate Israel] (Cairo, 1964), pp. 49–51; Sabrī Jirjis, *al-Turāth al-Yahūdī al-Sahyūnī wa'l-Fikr al-Frūydī* (Cairo, 1970), pp. 97–99.

38. Sabrī, *al-Talmūd*, p. 31; 'Abd al-Hamīd, *Yā Muslimi 'l-'Ālam*, pp. 32–33; Jirjis, *al-Turāth al-Yahūdī*, p. 95; al-Ghamrāwī, *Li-Hādhā Akrah Isrā'īl*, p. 48; Tu'ayma, *al-Yahūd bayn al-Dīn wa'l-Ta'rīkh*, p. 550.

39. Sabrī, *al-Talmūd*, pp. 31–32; Jirjis, *al-Turāth al-Yahūdī*, pp. 96, 100–102; 'Abd al-Hamīd, *Yā Muslimi 'l-'Ālam*, p. 37.

40. Sabrī, *al-Talmūd*, p. 29; al-Sa'danī, *Adwā' 'ala 'l-Sahyūniyya*, p. 87; al-Za'bī, *Dafā'in al-Nafsiyya al-Yahūdiyya*, pp. 165–167; al-Ghamrāwī, *Li-Hādhā Akrah Isrā'īl*, pp. 53–56; Jirjis, *al-Turāth al-Yahūdī*, pp. 99–100. For other examples, see Harkabi, *Arab Attitudes to Israel*, pp. 248–249.

41. For full citations, see Note 37 in this chapter.

42. Muhammad Ahmad Barāniq and Muhammad Yūsuf al-Mahjūb, "Muhammad wa'l-Yahūd" [Muhammad and the Jews], *ma'a 'l-'Arab*, vol. 4 (Cairo, n.d.), p. 140.

43. Bishop Gregorius, *Isrā'īl fi 'l-Mīzān* (Cairo, 1973), pp. 5–9.

44. This book was edited by Victor Yūnān Nakhla and Yūsuf Khalīl Yūsuf (Cairo, 1973). The term *al-ma'raka* is invariably understood to refer to the Arab-Israeli struggle.

45. For a full citation, see Note 33.

46. Astīnū, *Ma'nā Isrā'īl*, p. 24. This phrase is a good example of *saj'*, or Arabic rhymed prose.

47. Ibid., pp. 24–25.

48. al-Wāfī, *al-Yahūdiyya wa'l-Yahūd*, pp. 40ff.

49. (Beirut, 1964), pp. 65–180.

50. Pp. 37–119.

51. (Cairo, 1971), pp. 222–227.

52. Sultān Mahmūd, "Tasāmahna ma'a Unās lā Ya'rifūn al-Tasāmuh" [We Have Been Tolerant with People Who Do Not Know Tolerance], *Akhīr Sā'a*, 14 November 1973, p. 6. I would like to express my appreciation to Professor Bernard Lewis, who was kind enough to bring this article to my attention and to provide me with a photocopy.

53. al-Sa'danī, *Adwā' 'ala 'l-Sahyūniyya*, pp. 93–126.

54. (Cairo, 1968), p. 165.

55. See Harkabi, *Arab Attitudes to Israel*, p. 228. The author also notes that "there are more anti-Semitic references in the UAR's weeklies than in the dailies."

56. UNESCO Document 82 EX/8, Annex II, p. 9, Section III, Paragraph 6.

57. Ibid., Annex I, p. 3, Section III, Paragraph (4) [sic]. The UNESCO report is discussed in a general fashion by one of the members of the commission, R. Bayly Winder, in "Adghāth Ahlām" (1969 Presidential Address, Middle East

Studies Association Annual Meeting), *Middle East Studies Association Bulletin* 4, no. 1 (1970):15–22.

58. Hava Lazarus-Yafeh, "An Inquiry into Arabic Textbooks," *Asian and African Studies* 8, no. 1 (1972):12.

59. Avner Giladi, "Israel's Image in Recent Egyptian Textbooks," *Jerusalem Quarterly* 7 (1978):96.

60. Lutfī 'Abd al-'Azīm, "al-'Arab wa 'l-Yahūd: Man Yubīd Man?" *al-Ahrām al-Iqtisādī*, 27 September 1982, p. 4.

61. Ibid.

62. The propagation of antisemitism in the West by Arab countries is usually far more subtle than at home. For a good, albeit cursory, survey, see Daniel Pipes, "The Politics of Muslim Anti-Semitism," *Commentary* 65 (August 1981):39–45. For an example of materials with antisemitic overtones disseminated by Arab sources in the West, see the pamphlet entitled *A Critical Analysis of Islamic Studies at North American Universities* (Cedar Rapids: Unity Publishing Company, 1975).

7

Arab Antisemitism in Peacetime: The Egyptian Case

Rivka Yadlin

Arab political vocabulary has undergone considerable change over the last decade, its vehemence mitigated by a pragmatic approach. Wisdom gained through bitter lessons produced the awareness that dispassionate language better suits Western tastes and is therefore more conducive to political profit. A positive rather than hostile attitude to Israel became a central pillar in the political theory of President Anwar Sadat of Egypt, pioneer and advocate of the new style. The change became particularly marked in Egypt in the late 1970s as peace with Israel eliminated the need for mobilizing militant support by fiery rhetoric. Moreover, it even became expedient at that time to promote a temperate tone in order to create a favorable climate for the shift in policy.

The prevalence of virulent anti-Jewish attitudes in post–Camp David Egypt cannot, therefore, be ascribed to government initiative, as was previously the case. In fact, it is the opposition press—such as *al Sha'b*, organ of the Socialist Action party, or the Muslim Brotherhood's *al-Da'wa*—that carries consistently antisemitic remarks, rather than the establishment's "national press." This is not to say that the scope of the message is negligible. The opposition groups, although of limited political import, are by no means marginal, both in their influence and their representation of public opinion. The Egyptian public is highly attentive to religious authority, and the Socialist Action party is led by veteran politicians, venerated for their patriotic dedication and personal contributions.

Nonofficial books, too, whether they contain antisemitic motifs or specifically focus on them, are circulating in Egyptian bookstores. Such books are being printed, reprinted, imported from other Arab countries, or translated from European languages and are well received by the public. In 1981 two books about Jews were particularly in demand: *The War of Survival Between the Quran and the Talmud* and *The Jews, Objects of God's Wrath.*[1] These and similar titles, such as *The Future of Israel Between Extermination and Dissolution* (published in Cairo in 1980) or *Oh Ye Muslims, the Jews Are Coming* (published in Cairo in 1979), are displayed on sidewalk stalls that are Cairo's year-round bookfair. The sight of these titles, or the illustrations on the covers, such as the Star of David speared on a dagger, or a monstrous octopus, convey an immediate message to hundreds of passers-by and on-the-spot readers. Finally, the mainstream "national press," although not agitating constantly, does occasionally give vent to anti-Jewish sentiments or fleetingly allude, as a matter of fact, to antisemitic themes. Such eruptions or allusions, precisely because of this press's overall concurrence with the official peacetime style, testify to the rootedness of these ideas, to the common universe of discourse that exists between writer and readers in these subjects, and to their easy availability.

Antisemitic expressions must therefore be taken as indicative of authentic public attitudes, propagated and received in broad circles—an anti-Jewish attitude commonly shared as a body of "information." These attitudes are patently political. Not only has Arab antisemitism been originally and traditionally political rather than social,[2] but contemporary contexts as well point to the same conclusion. Anti-Jewish expressions, scholarly studies not excluded, are openly instrumental, and the pertinence, more often than not, is unequivocally spelled out. The publishers of a 1981 book, *Jews—History and Doctrine*, by Dr. Kāmil Sa'fān, who is presented as a scholar in Jewish history, offer it to readers "as a service to the Arabs and their problems which has become complicated over the last forty years because of the Jews. . . . It is a basic book and every Arab must read it. You shall find in this book a lot that terrifies and a lot that is inconceivable to normal logic, but it is all facts from the life and history of the Jews."[3]

"Woe to the world if it does not take precautions against those whose history is full of rancor, envy and hatred to God, to the Prophets, and to all mankind," warns another recent book,[4] and an Islamic magazine points out the solution: "This chaos brought about by Israel (the poisoned dagger planted in the heart of the Muslim world) will cast its shadow on their [the Muslims'] life. The draining of their material and moral wealth will continue until the Muslims are able to eliminate Israel from the heart of the Muslim world."[5]

The makeup of antisemitic argumentation, too, evinces an instrumental bent, reasoning serving as the handmaiden of the a priori final conclusion. Thus Christian incriminations are wed to Muslim ones, secular to theological, universal to nationalist. In each case, whether implicit or stated, the attitude spelled out by Egyptian antisemitism is the delegitimization of Israel, the political recognition granted to it notwithstanding.

Ideologically, this brand of antisemitism is equivalent to Western anti-Zionism, inasmuch as both of them reject the state structure as a legitimate framework for Jewish existence. Egypt, however, does not share the distaste that the West has come to harbor for racial or theological reasoning. Its attitude vis-à-vis the Arab-Israel conflict is predicated on the acknowledgment of natural determinants and divine authority, and it is therefore absolute and deterministic.

Herein lies the basic difference between Western and Egyptian anti-Zionism. In Western terms, Zionism may be treated as a political idea, condemned for regional rather than inherently Jewish considerations. Alternatively, it may even be denounced for specific policies rather than for itself alone. Egyptian anti-Zionism, however, rejects the existence of Israel primarily because it is a representation of Jewish superiority. Essentially negated, Israel is not being criticized for policies that are unacceptable to Egypt as such; rather, these policies are denounced as a symptom of the odious essence of the Jewish state.

The Racial Outlook

When bluntly stated, antisemitic racialism is plainly biological: "The transference of character, or singular characteristics from generation to generation by inheritance, as in the case of the Jews, is not disputed by scholars and psychologists," writes one scholar in the course of an extensive study of koranic styles.[6] "[The Koran says]: He turned them into apes and pigs, and although there are different exegeses to this verse, it is clear that this is an allegoric way of depicting the ugliness of Jewish character . . . which, in the prevalence of its bad aspects and its extreme ugliness which sets them apart from the rest of the people, resembles these two animals which are notorious for their extreme ugliness."[7]

A Western-trained leftist academician, Hasan Hanafī, takes exception to the validity of a biological definition of Jewish character only because of the "intermingling and intermarriage of the nations."[8] Nevertheless, in spite of this reservation, he too slips easily into statements such as "their rejection of what is right is inherent, natural, and permanent."[9] He does not shun the literal treatment of the koranic reference to the transformation of the Jews and Christians into apes and pigs.[10]

The biological conception, though infrequently articulated, is often traceable as a hidden assumption in generalizing statements: "Every Jew is a sample of religious conceit, moral decadence and withdrawal,"[11] says Anīs Mansūr, prominent mainstream journalist and editor, author of numerous books on Jewish affairs, and supposedly an expert on the subject. A year after the conclusion of the Camp David peace agreement, this popular opinion leader reconfirmed his adherence to the anti-Jewish views he had expressed in all his prepeace books.[12]

The political implications of this view are often and succinctly stated. Despite a growing sophistication in Arab conceptions of Israel following the Six-Day War, expressed in the ability to differentiate between political personalities and trends, the demonic generic image of Israel still haunts the scene and affects attitudes. An editorial in the *al-Ahrām Economist*, a semi-establishment elite magazine, illustrates the generalizing outlook rooted in the racial approach, which has become rather current in the press: "There is no difference between him [Begin] and any other Israeli. . . . The only difference is that the others have a different political cunning, consisting of slyness, deceit, hiding their plotted schemes under a veil of honeyed words, until they succeed in killing their adversary."[13] No less deterministic is the other implication of the racial approach— namely, that patterns of relations with the Jews are eternally fixed, and that no basic changes in them may be projected. The lesson of history for Egyptian writers is that "Jewish strategy since early times . . . has remained unchanged,"[14] and naturally so, given that "their policy all over the world is based on their [unalterable] traits"—fanatical, rancorous, racist, hypocritical, oppressive, niggardly, egotistic, envious, and ill wishing.[15] The conclusion, perforce, is that "Israel will remain evilmeaning as long as there is one Jew on earth, comparable to some creatures, whose tail will never change its form."[16] Hence Egyptian intellectuals do not trust "the olive branch raised by the Israelis in Egypt," because they know "Jewish history and precedents all through the past and all over the world."[17]

The Theological Approach

It is only natural that the main bulk of anti-Jewish argumentation is of a theological tenor. Egyptian audiences are receptive to religious messages on any subject, and hardly any Egyptian writer may be rightly described as secular. Their argumentation is rooted in cultural convictions and endowed with unchallenged divine authority. Its negation of Jewish political existence is therefore essential and definitive.

A most flagrant Jewish trait to be presented to an Arab audience whose religiosity is all pervading is the presumed lack of any true religious feeling. In a culture where spirituality as value is paramount and morality is anchored mainly in religion, such failure is tantamount to failing humanly.

> Jews are incapable of religious faith, and distinguished by this from other races. Since religiosity is one of the primal authentic traits of mankind in all societies, therefore they are anomalous to human nature in its most important components; and little wonder that is, for the fact is that Jews are not anomalous to humanity in this trait only, but in quite a number of other aspects, which anomaly brought them to withdraw [from humanity]. . . . Religion, values and valor are of no worth, as far as the Jews are concerned; it is all trivial to them, they are ready to sell it for cheap, because they do not have any regard for religion, or covenants, honour, or chivalry, but rather for the price, no matter how insignificant it may be.[18]

Muslim scripture and the prophetic tradition, which for the most part are treated ahistorically by Egyptian writers, offer rich "evidence" of

Jewish breaches of the Covenant, murder of (their own) prophets, and corruption and twisting of their own and others' religions. Writers, whether designated as Islamic or otherwise, draw on these sources as well as on Christian and Jewish ones. To the extent that statements in these sources are isolated from their historical context, they may be, and are, applied to current issues. "The Jews are not descendants of the prophets," claims the organ of the Socialist Action party; "they are not descendants of our Lord Abraham, they are not cousins of the Muslims and they are not Semites as they claim; rather they are, as described by the Quran, murderers of the prophets, having no covenant, spreading corruption and stirring strife and war among people. . . . Jews thus were the first to introduce murder into human society, a precedent which they have preserved and inherited from generation to generation."[19]

Anīs Mansūr, a Muslim, relies on Christian history for his view that

it is inevitable that those people [in Europe] should hate the Jews because of their relation first and before everything with what happened to Christ: they have conspired against him, and tried to kill him. They are those who were blamed for crucifying him. The Christian religion believes that the Jews crucified Christ, and therefore they deserved the curses of the Christians in every prayer and remained accursed for twenty centuries. These curses were alleviated only recently in the Ecumenical conference in Rome, where the Catholics have proclaimed the exoneration of the Jews of Christ's blood; Jews, who have killed tens of prophets, who butchered little children in Europe, and in Palestine as well, to put their blood in the Passover bread, who poisoned Christian kings, who spread the plague.

The author goes on to suggest that exoneration from the blame of the crucifixion was bought by Jewish money:

Cardinal Sulayman announced . . . that he demands the Vatican issue a resolution exonerating the Jews, out of concern for Papal capital invested in America, and that he fears for Vatican capital because of the anger of the Jews in America and in [the rest of the] world. This is the real meaning of the Jewish document. It is not the Vatican's regret over what the Jews had suffered at the hands of Hitler and not an attempt to make up for Pius XII's position when the Germans occupied Italy.

In fact, the author regrets this exoneration:

The Vatican had labeled "infidel" an Italian writer who claimed that the mercy of God includes the devil as well. What will the Vatican label today him who exonerates millions of devils, millions of robbers of the land of peaceful Arabs? Judas was accused of treachery for buying Christ for a trivial sum. No doubt the fourth session of the next Ecumenical synod will exonerate Judas who sold Christ to the Jews. The Vatican has sold Christ once again to the Jews, but for a high price, the money and the indignation of the Arabs.[20]

The ostensible manifestations of religion in Israeli life are interpreted as Machiavellian manipulations. As a popular left-of-center magazine has suggested:

> The choice of Palestine by the Zionists was merely to stir Jewish sentiments and an attempt to attract them to participate in supporting a state established on a racial basis under a religious cover. They have not stopped for a minute to dwell on the religious aspect in every occasion . . . a one and only national fatherland, propagated, on a religious basis, by a people who have no relation whatsoever to religion. Not only that, they even trick their own holy book: one of the most curious things happening now in Israel is that they sell the land every six years, to outwit the holy book.[21]

Another writer points out that "although the gatherings of the Rulers of Zion are devoid of religion and its morals, after clinging to Palestine they raised the flag of religion, and donned the robe of clergy and described it as a holy war to retrieve the promised land, the land of Israel from the Euphrates to the Nile."[22]

Jewish antihumanism is the active manifestation of their alleged lack of humanity and isolation from humanity. Their "hatred and murderous activity" against "all people with no exception" is extrapolated from the notion of the Chosen People, as well as discriminating edicts in the Halacha concerning relations between Jews and Gentiles: "A careful study of the history of the Jews, both ancient and modern, will give us a true idea of their psychological make-up and the extent of their black hatred to all the nations of the world, because as they claim, they are the chosen people. . . . Their brutality in Deir Yassin and Bahr al-Baqr is a decisive proof that the Jews, worshippers of the calf, have in themselves a tremendous amount of the nature of animals."[23]

A latter-day adaptation of this historical subversion is staged in the context of current Israeli realities: "Children in the kibbutzim are raised to be unfeeling towards their parents, and freed from worrying about getting their food or studying. . . . Therefore, it is easy to focus the child's interest on the love for Israel and hate for its enemies, or hate for anybody who is not Jewish."[24] Specific descriptions of Jewish activity against humanity are presented through the myths of the blood libel and the *Protocols of the Elders of Zion*. These are quoted in detail by eminent opinion leaders, including mainstream moderates.

Another actualization of a classic theme claims that "the *Protocols of the Elders of Zion*, the secret constitution of the Jews, advises the Jews to be obstetricians, and to specialize in abortion, and in fact this is just what they did all over the world and in Egypt. The reason is that abortion is an attempt to reduce the numbers of non-Jews. They are beasts but we tend to forget!"[25]

Kamil Sa'fan's book, *Jews—History and Doctrine*, takes up in great detail the 1840 Damascus Affair, and states that "there is no doubt that many other similar cases went unnoticed by the chronicles or were so manipulated by the Jews that the friends of the victims were unaware of this."[26]

Not only are the *Protocols* widely published, circulated, and quoted, but a whole set of perceptions of the Jews is predicated on the theorems postulated in that thesis. Themes from the *Protocols* are echoed in frequent references to the presumed surreptitious Jewish existence. A series of articles run by the *al-Ahram Economist* in March–June 1981 concerning, and denigrating, Jewish economic activity in prerevolutionary Egypt resorts to terms such as "infiltration," "invading," "penetrating," "tightening their hold," "taking over" (this last was included in a title repeated three times on the cover,[27] thereby imparting a feeling of danger or alarm)—all of which imply an aggressive, unlawful attack by an unwanted element. Egyptian Jews, so it seems, were constantly attacking dangerously, while Egyptian institutions or persons were always victims who either "managed to escape" the "Jewish presence"[28] or "fell prey" to Jewish entrepreneurs.[29] The latter are alluded to as a "Jewish net" ("the role of the Jewish net in the great economic crisis in the Middle East")[30] or as "Jewish groups," thus implying a mode of operation, never bona fide or innocent, in a framework of vicious plans or plots, such as the one in which "the ultimate interests of Jewish capitalism met with the capitalist interests of imperialist countries, based on the ideology of the Zionist movement, to mobilize the Jewish masses for the services of the imperialist movement."[31]

Even the remnants of the Jewish community in Egypt, admittedly "disabled or old," are said to be "kept by the Tel Aviv Government as political spies."[32] An introduction to Kamil Sa'fān's recent exposé of Jewish history and religion asserts that "Jews are spread all over the West, yet you will not notice their existence, unless you know the *secret of their infiltration* into foci of control in all realms of life in any Western country, and from these foci of control they *spread* to other sites" (emphasis added).[33]

Jewish transgressions and subversion, which inhere in Jewish nature, are purported to be deserving of divine punishment. In this connection, the racial and theological approaches come together. "Because of their *evil characteristics* Jews were destined by *divine will* to contempt and scorn . . . lowness, misery and wrath,"[34] says one book. "God's threat to inflict suffering on the Jews is still valid doubtlessly, as long as they have this evil in them for which they deserved whatever torment and dispersion that was inflicted on them, for they have suffered in medieval and modern history various forms of humiliation, degradation, dispersion and bitter torment, the most recent of which is the extreme Nazi assault on them."[35]

An observation made by the late Mahmud Abbās al-Aqqād, venerated veteran writer and thinker, and quoted by Anīs Mansūr, has greater finality if less explicit orthodoxy: "There is no need to say perhaps, or maybe, for history is in front of us, completely clear and the end will be more violent than beginning, suffice it to read what they say about themselves in the Tora, or what the Qur'ān said, to know what their fate will be on this earth and among people."[36]

A War of Survival

Conclusions deriving from the civilizational zero-sum struggle have never been clement. In some aspects they are now perhaps even less so than ever, because of the frustration generated by a political peace that contradicts the accepted ideological maxims. Drawing on the *Protocols* and bolstered by manifestations of Israeli power, the idea has been promulgated in the 1980s that "Jewish strategy" is aiming to annihilate the Arab nation. "Those who limit the Zionist danger to this minute patch of land in Palestine or in the heart of the Middle East," says *al-Da'wa*, "are people who do not understand history, and do not know enough about the character of the Jews."[37] "It is obvious to anybody who studies history," says the *al-Ahram Economist*, "that this [occupation of the lands of Arab Palestine and the Golan Heights, desecration of the holy places in Jerusalem and occupation of Lebanon's skies] is only a stage preparing for other stages, leading to the annihilation of the Arab nation."[38]

The Arab nation is thus conceived as defending itself in a war of survival, and the contemplated (though not implemented) measures are equal to the threat—namely, annihilation, mostly political. Reversing the course of history, as well as dismantling the state of Israel, is suggested as a voluntary option for the Jews ("abandon Zionist thinking and return truthfully to the Torah, the book given to Moses in its pure form and its right Muslim principles")[39] or is otherwise projected as a process of "dissolution" in the region in which the Arabs will be instrumental.[40] Not that physical considerations are eschewed. The notion of forcible coercion of Israel has regained prominence after a few years' lull, not falling short of a feeling of nostalgia toward the "Great Hitler, the smartest of those who dealt with the problem (the human mistake called Jews) who tried to annihilate all Jews, out of mercy for humanity, since he gave up on handling this cancerous growth in the body of humanity."[41]

A more concrete version of the contemplated physical coercion is the Muslim exhortation for jihad. "No Muslim," says *al-Da'wa*, "wherever he may be, may excuse himself from carrying the Holy War against these Jews. Muslims must refer back to the Book of God and the tradition of his Prophet, of blessed memory: The hour of Resurrection will not come until you fight the Jews, and until a stone will say, Muslim, there is a Jew behind me, kill him. This is a short reference—due to shortage of space, to Israel, the biggest crime of the 14th Muslim century."[42] In a less apocalyptic vein, the same magazine propounds that "wars are natural phenomena and are necessary to defend God's religion. The attempt to avoid war with such an enemy is a policy that God rejects. Those who defend peace are losing time and swimming against the trend, the trend of human nature and the trend of God's will. There will be animosity between Arabs and Jews as long as there is life on earth. The war between us will go on until the day of resurrection."[43]

These forcible solutions, however, are assumedly known for what they are: part long-range wishful visions, mostly exhortations for a militant stance. The major bulk of the defensive thrust is aimed at what is felt (much more credibly) to be the encroaching ideational and psychological menace of Zionism. The intensity of the resistance to this dreaded "assault" and to the staggering normalization process that is viewed as its vehicle cannot be overstated. "Their scheme of ideational colonialism is of a graver nature than their usurpation of land, in which case its inhabitants might not rest until they have expelled them," says *al-Sha'b*.[44] "Proof for the fact that [Israel is a racist state] is the extent of their haste and interest in normalization of relations following the peace, so that they can quickly and immediately infuse their poison."[45] Israel should not be allowed to participate in the Cairo book fair because it "affords the Israelis a golden chance to get into the heart of the Egyptian cultural movement, and to carry on their attack on the mind of the Egyptian Man, and spread the poisons of their racist imperialist culture."[46] Nor is this anxiety limited to ideological extremists. A letter from the editor of the leading mainstream weekly *Akhbar al-Yawm* commended the *al-Ahram Economist* for standing up against the "ignorant clamouring voices, propounding the benefit which will accrue from the re-opening of the gates [for the Jews], letting them enter again our economic life, and later on infiltrate into our social, cultural and moral life."[47]

Observing this furor, one wonders what it is that is meant by "ideational assault." In sentiment and rationale this notion may be easily traced to the *Protocols'* theme of ideational disruption. Considered in detail it transpires that the perceived threat is to Muslim specificity and its pristine confidence in its faith, culture, and nationalism. The assault is presented as undermining "patriotic feeling, claiming that it is contradictory to humanity" as well as undermining religious feelings, "claiming that religion is the cause of backwardness, strife and hatred."[48] But it is not only through exposure to another agent of westernization that Islam is threatened. The ultimate danger, it would seem, inheres in understanding and accepting Zionism.

In the Muslim-Egyptian view there is a direct link between the truth of a civilization and its power ascendancy, the former expressing itself in the latter. "Might is Right" is in this context not a Machiavellian maxim but an intrinsic cultural conviction. Accordingly, Israeli military victories have been devastating in more than one way, as much as the October War has been reassuring. "The October War," noted Ibrahim al-Adawī of Cairo University, "is the victory of civilization by recourse to the sword. . . . The Arab nation, in overcoming the technological and scientific lag in the course of the October War, has crushed the challenge to her civilization."[49]

Following Sadat's peace initiative, the Arab-Israeli conflict has been recast in Egypt as a mostly cultural, rather than a military, confrontation. While facilitating the acceptance of the political peace, this notion underscored the broader dimensions of the conflict and further blurred the lines between ideational and physical losses and gains. The very admittance of Zionist positive qualities, let alone superiority, has thus become tantamount to an actual defeat of Islam.[50] Such a perspective not only aborts any attempt to establish normal relations; it also throws Egyptian attitudes into a vicious circle of anti-Jewishness and bolsters the perception of Islam and Judaism as mutually exclusive civilizations. It is not for naught that the distinctions between Zionists and Jews, traditionally flaunted in Egyptian argumentation, are currently being abandoned. Moreover, the point has been made in recent deliberations in the press that such distinctions must be reassessed if not forgone.[51] Questions pertaining to the conflict are now formulated as "whether it is Islamically lawful to make peace with the Children of Israel (i.e., the Jews)"[52] or "who will destroy whom—the Jews or the Arabs."[53]

The zero-sum conception regarding the two civilizations lends credence and depth to a parallel attitude in politics. "Who will destroy whom" is the old fatal denouement of anti-Jewishness, newly enacted on the stage of current Middle Eastern politics.

Notes

1. *al-Izā'a wal-Telephizion*, 7 February 1981.
2. See Y. Harkabi, *Arab Attitudes to Israel* (Jerusalem, 1976), p. 293.
3. Kamil Sa'fān, *al-Yahud Ta'rīkhan wa-Aqīdatan* (Cairo, 1981), cover.
4. al Sayid Rizq al-Tawīl, *Banū Isrā'īl fī al-Qur'ān* (Cairo, 1980), p. 142.
5. *al-Da'wa*, December 1980.
6. Abd al-Halīm Hafnī, *Uslūb al-Sukhriya fi al-Qur'ān al-Karīm* (Cairo, 1978), p. 249.
7. Ibid., p. 277.
8. Hasan Hanafī, "Hal Yajūzu Shar'an al-Sulh ma' Banī-Isrā'īl," *al-Yasār al-Islami* (Cairo, 1981), p. 98.
9. Ibid., p. 105
10. Ibid., pp. 123, 125.
11. Anīs Mansūr, *al-Hā'it Wal-Dumū'* (Cairo, 1979), p. 36.
12. *al-Ahrām*, 17 March 1981.
13. *al-Ahrām al-Iqtisādi*, 15 June 1981.
14. Ibid., 4 May 1981.
15. al-Ta'wīl, op. cit., p. 142.
16. *al-Da'wa*, January 1981.
17. *al-Ahram al-Iqtisādī*, 4 May 1981.
18. See Hafnī, op. cit., pp. 249–251, 255; see also *October*, 22 March 1981.

19. See *al-Sha'b,* 17 February 1981; see also ibid., March 24, 1981.
20. Mansūr, op. cit., pp. 64, 99.
21. *Roz al-Yousef,* 16 February 1981.
22. al-Tawīl, op. cit., p. 146.
23. See *al-Da'wa,* December 1980; see also Hafnī, op. cit., pp. 257–258, and Mansūr, op. cit., p. 61.
24. Mansūr, op. cit., p. 290.
25. Ibid., p. 17.
26. Sa'fān, op. cit., p. 220.
27. *al Ahrām al-Iqtisādi,* 20 April 1981.
28. Ibid.
29. Ibid., 30 March 1981.
30. Ibid., 13 April 1981.
31. Ibid., 6 April 1981.
32. Ibid., 4 May 1981.
33. See Sa'fān, op. cit., and book cover in ibid., p. 216; see also *al-Sha'b,* 10 February 1981, 17 February 1981, and 3 March 1981.
34. al-Tawīl, op. cit., pp. 65, 67.
35. Ibid., p. 145.
36. *October,* 3 May 1981.
37. *al-Da'wa,* November 1980.
38. *al-Ahrām al-Iqtisādi,* 15 June 1981.
39. See al-Tawīl, op. cit., p. 150; see also *Roz al-Yausef,* 16 February 1981.
40. See Kamāl Muhammad al-Astal, *Mustaqbal Isrā'īl bain al-Isti'sāl wal-Tazwīb* (Cairo, 1980), pp. 280–287; see also *October,* 28 December 1980.
41. See *al-Ahrār,* 12 July 1982; see also *October,* 12 April 1981.
42. *al-Da'wa,* November 1980.
43. Ibid., November 1982.
44. *al-Sha'b,* 10 February 1981.
45. Ibid., 3 March 1981.
46. Ibid., 3 February 1981.
47. *al-Ahrām al-Iqtisādī,* 4 May 1981.
48. *al-Sha'b,* 3 February 1981.
49. Ibrāhīm al-Adawī, "The Effect of the October War in Overcoming the Civilizational Lag" (mimeo), Cairo International Symposium on the October War (Cairo, 1975), pp. 4, 12, 13, 18.
50. Hanafī, op. cit., pp. 99–101.
51. *al-Ahrām al-Iqtisadi,* 27 September 1982; al-*Ahrār,* 12 July 1982.
52. Hanafī, op. cit.
53. *al-Ahrām al-Iqtisādi,* 27 September 1982.

8

Past Trials and Present Tribulations: A Muslim Fundamentalist Speaks on the Jews

Ronald L. Nettler

Anti-Jewishness was a long-established tradition in Islamic thought. It was a *central motif* that outweighed by far other, more positive Islamic attitudes on this matter. In our time, the anti-Jewishness of Muslim thinkers assumed its sharpest form yet, as Islam faced the unique challenge of Jewish statehood in the heart of Dar al-Islam. Here, for most Muslims, Israel was the contemporary revival of Muhammad's Jewish problem in Medina; and just as the Prophet had fought that battle to a victory, so must Muslims today emulate the early success. However, among Muslim thinkers were those—the fundamentalists— whose attitude toward the problem was even more thoroughgoing, those whose Jewish miseries could be even more acute.

Characterized by xenophobia in facing the challenge of Islam's decline and Western and Zionist ascendancy, and aspiring to recapitulate Islam's earliest period of success, the fundamentalists have been sensitive to Islam's Jewish problem and attentive to the lessons of Islam's sacred sources on this subject. Whether directly or indirectly, in the center or on the periphery, the Jews have often invaded the general concerns of fundamentalist intellectuals. As with most Muslims, here too Israel was the stimulus behind this interest, and it was likewise seen in the historical

This chapter is a revised and lengthened version of the author's lecture given upon receiving the first James Parkes Prize of The Hebrew University, Jerusalem (December 20, 1984). While the basic structure and main themes of the lecture remain here, much additional material by way of illustrative example and explication have been added. The International Center for the Study of Anti-Semitism at The Hebrew University, granter of the Parkes Prize, has kindly given permission to publish this version of the lecture. With the support of the International Center for the Study of Anti-Semitism, the author is engaged in a study of Muslim fundamentalist attitudes toward the Jews.

frameworks of Islam's early Jewish problem. For many fundamentalists, however, the Jewish Zionist enemy "out there" was somehow related to the internal Islamic crisis of westernization and the resultant erosion of tradition. These latter issues, though surely crucial for all of twentieth century Islam, were in fundamentalist eyes the painful razor's edge of Islam's breakdown. Fundamentalist discussions of the Jews and Israel thus often brought them into the orbit of these more general dangers. Sometimes the fundamentalists even portrayed the Jews as identical with, partners of, or related to the persons and forces responsible for the catastrophe. Using the Koran *hadīth,* and *sīra* literature as foundations, various fundamentalist writers brought the story up to date, each in his own way, in the context of Islam's modern challenges. Sayyid Qutb's essay, "Our Struggle with the Jews," was one important rendition of the tale.

The Jews in Islam's Mirror

What was this Islamic attitude described above as anti-Jewishness? Certainly it was part of Islam's general negative category of the *dhimmis,* those condescendingly protected and often humiliated Christians, Jews, and others who lived (and sometimes still live) under Islamic rule. The origins of this idea and of the erstwhile Islamic social organization derived therefrom are to be found in Islam's notion of its own spiritual finality and superiority, which the Muslims have always felt they must prove in the challenges provided them by history. For this reason, as well as for more "material" reasons, Islam needed to expand territorially and to rule over Christian and Jewish populations, to humble them, and, even in the best of circumstances, to remind them constantly of their inferiority. Through their subjugation, the *dhimmis* were transformed into the living proof of Islam's great claims for itself.

Although theological argumentation to prove Islam's superiority over non-Muslims was certainly an Islamic practice, the *fact* of Islam's rule over these people and Islam's possession of what had formerly been their territories was for Muslims the clinching proof. And for those non-Muslims whose communities and territories still lay beyond the boundaries of Islamic sovereignty—the "Realm of War," as Islam called it—they, too, would one day be part of Islam's home, the "Realm of Peace." This was Allah's plan, the full realization of which would of necessity precede the End of Days.

Certainly the Jews were a main element in this *dhimmi* idea and practice, and they, like the Christians, were *dhimmis.* But the specific attitude toward the Jews differed somewhat from that toward the Christians, and vice versa. Let us look at the Jewish difference here.

Most would agree that in Muhammad's relations with the Jews of Medina something was amiss. That "something" was the Jews' refusal (inability?) to accept Muhammad's preaching. And this in a time and at a place in which Islam's political and social destiny was beginning to be realized. No wonder, then, that in Medina the Muslims saw the Jews' stubborn resistance to Islam as a major practical problem. For in addition to being a sharp insult to Muhammad and Islam, the Jews' "theological" disagreements with the new faith were, in the Muslims' view, the foundation of an alleged Jewish tendency toward political incitement—even rebellion—against the reign of Allah's Truth. Such thinking on the part of the Muslims was quite natural in a tribal milieu where "religion" inevitably sought its political expression, and where "doctrinal" disagreements were often expressed in internecine conspiracies and even encounters in the field. For their suspected conspiracy against Islam, Muhammad dealt very severely with Medina's Jewish tribes.

Whether these Islamic allegations against the Jews were historically well founded or not is irrelevant. Islam's historical memory of these allegations has been long and strong. In the early Islamic theoretical literature on the subject, the Jews were generally portrayed as anti-Islamic provocateurs and conspirators, well after Muhammad's earlier troubles with them. This legendary tradition became firmly fixed.

The *dhimmi* status for the Jews, then, was not just their required humbling before Islam's superior truth and power, as it was for Christians and others. It was also Islam's way of containing this alleged natural Jewish predilection for harming Islam. If for medieval Christianity the Jews were a deicidic people, here for Islam they were a *potential* destroyer of creed and society—potentially so not for want of enthusiasm on their part but owing instead to Islam's successful thwarting of their "evil plans." As the Koran itself put it, "The Jews and the polytheists are the worst enemies of the Believers."

Zionism and Israel

Centuries later, with the onset of Zionism and the creation of Israel, this koranic accusation became a "proof text" that contemporary Muslim thinkers could invoke in building their response to Islam's contemporary Jewish problem of Zionist nationalism. That is, this passage associated the monotheistic Jews with the polytheistic pagans, implicitly linking the Jews with this source of the earliest animus toward Islam. However, although the pagans were defeated by Islam early on, the Jews remained a subversive threat through the centuries, controlled only by Islam's constant supervision of their activities. Then, in our time, say the Muslim writers, with Islam's catastrophic decline, Muslims had in principle and practice strayed so far from their earlier Koran-based institutions that the West and its nefarious influences could easily conquer the Muslim countries. Part of this invasion was Zionism, the Jewish "genie in the bottle," which was uncorked with Islam's loss of power.

Muslims writing since 1948, whether fundamentalist or not, usually portrayed the Jews in this hostile fashion. Here, Muhammad's past trials with the Jews, before Islam had finally put them in their proper place, provided a comfortable example by which to understand Islam's present tribulations with them. The line of reasoning was clear: The evil Jewish intent toward Islam was presumed to be natural and fixed. Muhammad suffered from it but subsequently defeated it, relegating the Jews to the status of powerlessness and inferiority. Islam's power was able to maintain this control through the centuries. But now, with Islam's decline, the Jewish head had once again been raised in rebellion against Allah's people and His Truth. Islam's power had waned, the West had entered, and control was lost. The Jewish aggression now took the form of a sovereign nation-state dedicated to defeating and subjugating all of the Islamic Middle East. The only solution was a continuous struggle—jihad—until Israel had been defeated and the Jews returned to their proper role of inferiority, submission, and humiliation. The yoke of dhimmihood would again be imposed.

The Muslim conception of the Jews associated with this historical analysis was formulated accurately and succinctly by the Egyptian writer Muhammad Abd al-Rahman Husayn: "The position of the Jews toward Islamic teachings is known: an unbroken chain of treachery and plotting. In spite of that, our leader, Muhammad, . . . opened his heart to them and forgave them many times. But soon the Jews returned to their previous ways of treachery, enmity and hatred."[1]

The Fundamentalist Difference

The militant Muslim fundamentalists in the Arab world accepted this general conception of the Jews and Israel. But their particular concerns and goals as fundamentalists led them to extend it in a certain direction. With the thesis that Islam's predicament stemmed from attrition of Islamic values and their substitution by alien Western ones and the advocacy of society's radical Islamic renewal as the solution, some fundamentalists even saw the Jews and Zionism as an *internal* presence somehow identified with the westernizing forces that were bent on corrupting Islamic traditions. Here the Jewish menace was not just Israel as a dramatically new form of the erstwhile Jewish threat to Islam, for in this view the Jews were also a symbol, and often the reality, of all that was wrong *within* the Muslim world. The Jews were both metaphor and literal instrument of the secularization that had wrecked contemporary Islam. In its most extreme versions, such as that of Sayyid Qutb, this view saw the secular nationalist leadership and intellegentsia that ruled most Muslim countries as being Jewish Zionist agents themselves, whether they knew it or not. They destroyed true Islam in their own countries at the behest of international Jewry and Zionism, the leaders of all the anti-Islam forces.

This sort of fundamentalist attitude, then, not only held that the former *dhimmi* Jews had run amok in creating their own state but maintained also that this state was only one symptom of the general damage done to Islam by the Jews and their helpers. The solution was to be found not simply, or even primarily, in jihad against Israel, although cessation of jihad and making peace would be abominations signaling Islam's ultimate ignominy. The solution lay in fundamentalism's prescription for a cure of the general Islamic malaise—that is, in reinstating the true Islam, which is not "religion" but, rather, a comprehensive system of divinely organized personal behavior, society, and polity. Central to this goal was opposition (sometimes violent) to the secularizing "Muslim" politicians and intelligentsia. Revolution might thus be sanctioned, not as the overthrowing of fellow Muslims but as the elimination of the alien (Jewish) presence. Death in such actions might be far preferable—and certainly more honorable—than so-called life under alien (Jewish) rule.

Sayyid Qutb's Essay: "Our Struggle with the Jews"

Born in the village of Qaha in Asyut province in Egypt in 1906, Sayyid Qutb became a hero and supreme guide to Muslim fundamentalists, particularly after his execution by Nasser in 1966. Known in fundamentalist circles as "al-Shahīd the Martyr," Qutb, through his written works, inspired both the Iranian students who helped bring Khomeini to power and the Egyptian groups that produced Sadat's assassins. Qutb's personality and thought exemplified the Muslim condition and spirit in the latter part of the twentieth century. In both the Muslim world and the West many have agreed with Qutb scholar Yvonne Haddad, who maintained that "few Muslim thinkers have had as significant an impact on the reformulation of contemporary Islamic thought as has Sayyid Qutb."[2]

In his clearest and most accessible statement on the Jews, his essay of the early 1950s entitled "Our Struggle with the Jews," Qutb formulated the question as Islam's eternal Jewish problem, with a special emphasis on the Jews as Islam's true internal enemy. Conceived and written after Islam's 1948 defeat, the essay revealed a particularly poignant bitterness and a deep hatred of this "worst enemy of Islam."

Qutb fashioned his doctrine of the Jews in the fundamentalist style of invoking koranic and other early sources as directives toward a revival of early Islamic forms. Inasmuch as the present corruption of Islamic values in Egypt (and, by extension, elsewhere as well) was, in Qutb's view, somehow identified with the Jewish threat to the Creed, then following koranic directives for dealing with this enemy would free the Muslim community from the Jewish threat and would be an important example of the Muslims living once more as true believers according to their own teachings. These were the same koranic teachings that enabled Muhammad to deal with Medina's Jews, whose machinations threatened to confuse the minds of the weaker Muslims and thereby to destroy Islam. The general revival of Islam was therefore conditional upon removal of the internal Jewish malignancy, whereas the struggle against the Jews could succeed only with a true Islamic renewal. In Sayyid Qutb's thought, there was no contradiction here; instead, there was a crisis whose solution would of necessity arise concomitantly from both these directions. Let us turn now to some excerpts from Qutb's essay, "Our Struggle with the Jews."[3]

PAST TRIALS

"The Worst Enemies of the Believers are the Jews and Polytheists"
(The Qur'ān)

If people would become aware of this sacred principle of historical reality which has been evident from Islam's inception [and until the present moment], then they would not hesitate to confirm that the enmity of the Jews toward the Muslims was always stronger, crueler, deeper in its persistence, and of longer duration than was the enmity of the polytheists.

The Jews confronted Islam with enmity from the moment the Islamic state was established in Medina. They plotted against the Muslim Community from the first day it became a community. The Qur'ān [in fact] contained directives and suggestions concerning this [Jewish] enmity and plot. These directives were sufficient to portray this bitter war which the Jews launched against Islam, the Messenger of Allah [Muhammad], and the Muslim Community during its long history. This is a war which has not been extinguished, even for one moment, for close on fourteen centuries, and which continues until this moment, its blaze raging in all corners of the earth. . . .

The Messenger [Muhammad] made a treaty of coexistence with the Jews when he first arrived in Medina. He called them to Islam which would have confirmed the Torah which the Jews possessed. But the Jews did not honour this pact. Rather they were in this instance as they were with every covenant they had made with their Lord or their prophets long ago. . . .

The Jews have preserved in their heart of hearts an enmity toward Islam and the Muslims from the day that Allah brought the [Arab tribes of] Aws and Khazraj together in Islam. Thus the Jews had no choice [but to oppose Islam] from the day that the leadership of the Muslim Community was established with [Muhammad] the Messenger of Allah at its head. . . .

The Jews used every weapon and all means which the scheming Jewish genius could devise, and such devices helped them from the years of [their] captivity in Babylon, their slavery in Egypt . . . and their ignominious condition under the Romans. . . . Although Islam certainly made their situation more comfortable after various peoples had got fed up with them through the course of history, the Jews from the first met Islam's offer of kindness with the ugliest plot and most painful treachery. . . .

The Jews gathered all the polytheistic forces of the Arabian peninsula against Islam and the Muslims. They began collecting together the dispersed tribes for war against the Muslim Community. . . .

But when Islam overcame the Jews with the force of Right [in the days when people were *real* Muslims], the Jews turned around and conspired against Islam in a conspiracy of calumnies against Islam's books. The only thing spared from this conspiracy was Allah's Book [the Qur'ān], which was guaranteed by His protection, glory be to Him. And they conspired against Islam with a conspiracy in the ranks of the Muslims . . . , and incitement to civil disturbances. . . . They also conspired against Islam by inciting its enemies against it throughout the world. . . .

Jews were enemies of the Muslim Community from the first day. The Jews were the ones who instigated the polytheists, made promises to them and conspired with them against the Muslim Community. The Jews were those who undertook a war of rumors, hidden conspiracy and treachery within the Muslim ranks; just as they instigated the dissemination of doubts, suspicions about Islam, and falsifications of the Muslim creed and allegations against its leadership. . . .

PRESENT TRIBULATIONS

The struggle between Islam and the Jews continues in force and will thus continue, because the Jews will be satisfied only with the destruction of this religion [Islam]. . . .

Jews in the latest era have become the chiefs of the struggle with Islam, on every foot of the face of the earth. . . . The Jews [also] utilize Christianity and idolatry in this comprehensive war. . . . The Jews are the ones who . . . make the "heroes"[4] who carry Muslim names. . . . They attack every foundation of this religion [Islam], in a Crusader-Zionist war!! How right was Allah, the most Mighty, in saying: "You will surely find the worst enemies of the Muslims to be the Jews and the polytheists."

. . . Behind the doctrine of atheistic materialism was a Jew; behind the doctrine of animalistic sexuality was a Jew; and behind the destruction of the family and the shattering of sacred relationships in society . . . was a Jew.[5]

Today, the struggle has indeed become more deeply entrenched, more intense, and more explicit; this was since the Jews came from every place and announced that they were establishing the State of Israel. Their greed now extends from afar to Jerusalem, and today they are merely steps away from it. . . . Nothing will curb their greed short of Islam's defeating them. . . .

The Jews have doggedly engaged individuals and regimes in [their] conspiracy against the Muslim Community. Hundreds, even thousands, were thereby conspiring [against Islam]. For example, there were the Orientalists and their students who now occupy high positions in the intellectual life of countries whose people say they are "Muslims"!!

The tens of personalities who have been foisted upon the Muslim Community [as conspirators against it] in the guise of "heroes" were manufactured by Zionism, in order that these "heroes" should do for the enemies of Islam what these enemies were themselves not able openly to do. . . .

Anyone who leads this Community away from its Religion and its Qur'ān can only be a Jewish agent—whether he does this wittingly or unwittingly, willingly or unwillingly. . . .

This antagonistic Jewish force threatening the Islamic world today also has a massive army of agents in the form of professors, philosophers, doctors and researchers—sometimes also writers, poets, scientists and journalists—carrying Muslim names because they are of Muslim descent!! And some of them are from the ranks of the "Muslim religious authorities"!!

This army of "learned authorities" means to break the Creed of Muslims in all ways—through research, learning, literature, science and journalism; by weakening the foundations of the Creed and weakening the Creed and the Sharī'ah in equal measure.

The Jews invent conceptions, teachings, and principles of understanding and behaving which contradict and shatter the conceptions and teachings of the [Islamic] Creed. . . . Then they decorate these contrived conceptions in a manner befitting the mutilation of the Islamic ideas and teachings. . . .

The Jews free the sensual desires from their restraints and they destroy the moral foundation on which the pure Creed rests, in order that the Creed should fall into the filth which they spread so widely on this earth. They mutilate the whole of history and falsify it, just as they falsify words!!

. . . And so they are Muslims!! Do they not carry Muslim names? Bearing these Muslim names they proclaim [their Islam] at the beginning of the day. And with these tricks they apostatize at day's end!! . . . Thus do they fulfill the ancient role of the Jews. Nothing has changed except the form and the framework of that ancient [Jewish] role. . . .

They display their Islam—you have a "proof" of this in the [Muslim] names [they carry]—at the beginning of the day, and apostatize at the end of it, so that perhaps Muslims will [under this influence] leave their religion. . . .

The agents of Zionism today are like that. . . . They agree with each other on one issue . . . , that is the destruction of this [Islamic] Creed at the first auspicious and unrepeatable opportunity. . . . This Jewish consensus [on destroying Islam] would never be found in a pact or open conference. Rather it is the [secret] agreement of one [Zionist] agent with another on the important goal, as something fundamental [and unquestioned]. . . .

This conspiracy continues uninterruptedly. The source of security and salvation from it remains in rigorous adherence to and reliance on this Preserved Book [the Qur'ān], for the guidance it provides in this fierce battle of so many centuries. . . .

The Qur'ān spoke much about its Jews and elucidated their evil psychology. It is not mere chance that the Qur'ān elaborated on this. For there is no other group whose history reveals the sort of mercilessness, [moral] shirking and ungratefulness for Divine Guidance as does this one. They had killed, butchered, and expelled many of their prophets. This is the most disgusting act that has come out of any community which had had sincere preachers of the Truth. The Jews perpetrated the worst sort of disobedience [against Allah], behaving in the most disgustingly aggressive manner. . . .

It is clear, then, that the worst enemies of this Community [Islam] are [the Jews] who lead it away from its Creed, dissuading it from taking Allah's way and path, and deceiving it about the reality of its enemies and their ultimate goals. . . .

Islam and the Jews, Today and Tomorrow

Zionism and Israel's creation were the soil in which contemporary Islamic thought on the Jews took root. Muslim writers since 1948 have usually referred to that date as the year of The Catastrophe (*al-Nakbah*). Written just subsequent to The Catastrophe—in the early 1950s—"Our Struggle with the Jews" was a pioneer in the history of that thought.

In its framework story of Islam's past trials and present tribulations with the Jews, Qutb's essay impressively adumbrated the later general themes of Muslim thinking as well as the fundamentalist line. Although Qutb's fundamentalist thesis of the Jews being—or being behind—the secularizing Muslim leaders was so thoroughgoing in its formulation, some variation on this theme was commonly to be found in many later fundamentalist writings, if not always similarly putting the finger of blame on the "Jewish identity" of the leaders. At the very least, whenever fundamentalists did write about the Jews, there was usually some allegation of connivance between Jewish forces and Arab leaders and some identification of the Jews as part (if not all) of the cause of Islam's deterioration within the Muslim countries. And sometimes Qutb's claims, in all their logical perfection, were repeated in a way of which the master himself would greatly have approved. The most dramatic recent example of this can be found in the Muslim Brothers' literary responses to Sadat's Jerusalem visit, Camp David, and the subsequent peace. Found mainly in the Brothers' two journals, *al-I'tisām* and *al-Da'wah*,[6] these writings saw the peace as part of the ancient and continuing Jewish plot to undermine Islam and its creed, for henceforth the Israeli Jews would be permitted openly to do their nefarious work in one Muslim state, Egypt, through their "diplomatic," "trade," and "cultural" representations. And it was the Egyptian "Muslim" rulers who had offered the Jews this "peace"!

Fundamentalism is today Islam's most vital and prospering branch. Throughout the Muslim world the popular fundamentalist preachers, writers, and militants have succeeded in gaining substantial support for their views and aspirations. Although this success certainly has its own internal religious and cultural logic, it is also related to the larger issue of the continuing failures of the Muslim world under its recent secular leadership. These material, social, and political failures shake the foundations and, in ways not always understood or as yet fully apparent, seem to provide impetus for the fundamentalist machine. Islam's losses to Israel serve as a pointed symbol of all the Muslim lapses, and they offer Muslims, both fundamentalists and others, a reason to rally round the flag.

We can thus expect the Muslim fundamentalist views on the Jews to become dominant. Israel's triumphant presence, Muslim's failures, and fundamentalism's rise might in fact engender a widespread revival of the earliest Muslim antipathy toward the Jews. Sayyid Qutb, for one, would have seen that as a sign of Islam's true health.

Notes

1. Muhammad Abd al-Rahman Husayn, *al-'Arab wa al-Yahūd fī al-Mādī wa al-Hādir wa al-Mustaqbal* [The Arabs and the Jews in the Past, Present and Future] (Alexandria: n.d.).

2. Yvonne Y. Haddad, "Sayyid Qutb: Ideologue of Islamic Revival," in John L. Esposito, ed., *Voices of Resurgent Islam* (New York and London, 1983), p. 67.

3. "Ma'arakatunā Ma'a al-Yahūd" [Our Struggle with the Jews]: The early textual history of this essay is somewhat vague. It was published sometime in the early 1950s, but it is not clear where. However, in 1970 the Saudi government reprinted it in a collection of Qutb's writings, and named the whole collection *Our Struggle with the Jews*. The Saudis disseminated this small volume widely in the Muslim world.

4. *Heroes* is a term often used by fundamentalists to denote secular leaders.

5. That is, Marx, Freud, and Durkheim.

6. See R. L. Nettler, "Islam vs. Israel," *Commentary* (December 1984).

9
New Testament Antisemitism: Fact or Fable?

John T. Pawlikowski

The issue of New Testament antisemitism has generated considerable scholarly research in both the Christian and Jewish communities during the course of the last decade or so. Although some consensus has developed regarding the major problems that need to be faced, we are far from consensus regarding either the causal or contemporary dimensions of these problems. If we have learned one thing from this extensive research it is that any simplistic affirmations or denials of New Testament antisemitism should be discarded out of hand. The question is highly complex. In saying this I am not trying to whitewash the historical record. On many occasions Christians clearly used New Testament texts as a pretext for the persecution and slaughter of the Jewish people. But this historical fact does not necessarily mean that the churches were correctly interpreting their biblical canon. Contemporary concern about the abiding presence of antisemitism in our society, including its ecclesiastical realms, must never deter us from sound scholarship on the subject.

Here I shall attempt to present a brief overview of some of the critical questions surrounding possible New Testament antisemitism. It will not be possible to engage in detailed exegesis of all the relevant New Testaments texts. It is my hope, however, to introduce the basic parameters of the discussions as they have been defined by a multiplicity of scholars in recent years.

Probably no other Christian accusation with a seeming New Testament basis against the Jewish people has been responsible for more Jewish suffering throughout history than the charge of deicide. Simply put, this was the accusation that the Jewish community of Jesus' time, in its blindness and spiritual haughtiness, put to death the very Son of God. This claim laid the groundwork for a highly developed theology within Christianity claiming that Jews, for the remainder of human history, were to be subjected to continual suffering and to live in a state of perpetual wandering without a homeland as a punishment for this monumental crime. Without doubt this accusation played a major role

107

in the acceptance by so many Christians of the Nazi "final solution" of the "Jewish problem." While not the primary cause of this genocidal attack, it did provide an indispensable seedbed for its popular acceptance.[1]

The Christian churches have moved a long way toward eliminating the deicide charge from their teaching and liturgy—surely the greatest single advance in Christian-Jewish relations since the declaration of the Second Vatican Council and similar statements from leading Protestant denominations. But this does not mean that the accusation is now history, for the more traditional beliefs regarding responsibility for the crucifixion of Jesus continue to linger in popular culture (both secular and religious) and in piety.

New Testament scholars are virtually unanimous in agreeing that the death of Jesus was instigated by the Roman imperial government as a political execution. Although there may well have been some collaboration by the priestly elite of the Jerusalem Temple in this effort, it must be remembered that this priestly elite was not held in high favor by many Jews of the period, as research into Jewish materials from the period has clearly uncovered. In one of the few areas of widespread scholarly consensus with regard to New Testament antisemitism, primary responsibility for Jesus' death has been assigned to the Roman government.

Oscar Cullmann is but one of many prominent New Testament scholars who have pinpointed Roman rather than Jewish guilt in the execution of Jesus. In his study of Jesus' relationship to the revolutionary movements of his time, Cullmann concluded that Jesus was a prisoner of the Romans, arrested by a cohort in the Garden of Gethsemane on Pilate's orders. The actual trial of Jesus was in the hands of Pilate—hence clearly a political trial: "Thus Jesus suffered the Roman death penalty, crucifixion, and the inscription, the 'titulus,' above the cross named as his crime the Zealotist attempt of having strived for kingly rule in Israel, a country still administered by the Romans."[2] This same position has been unqualifiedly stated by the Catholic exegete Bruce Vawter: "The Gospels represent the Crucifixion as a Roman execution precipitated at the initiative and with the complicity of some highly placed Jews, chiefly of the high priestly, Sadducean element." Theological motivations, Vawter goes on to say, were primary in the narratives of Jesus' death. Hence the actual details have "to be reconstructed rather than read from them. There seems to be no doubt that Jewish responsibility has been heightened at the expense of the Roman."[3]

If the churches are once and for all to eliminate the antisemitic potential inherent in the crucifixion narrative, they will have to develop among their members a much better understanding of the Second Temple Judaism period. This period, in which Jesus was born and ministered, was one marked by tremendous upheaval in Judaism. Certainly legalism and corruption were to be found, especially within segments of the high priestly elite in Jerusalem. But these distortions of authentic Judaism were being denounced by new movements within the community such as Pharisaism. Though Jesus' stance was unique in a number of crucial theological areas, his personal critique of the spiritual/political leadership of his time was shared by many of his Jewish brothers and sisters. It was this criticism that brought him to death on Calvary.

The real picture surrounding the events of the crucifixion, then, is not Jesus as an isolated prophet but rather Jesus standing in concert with the progressive movements in Judaism, such as the Pharisees, against the small group of Jews who were collaborators with the oppressive Roman authorities. Until we reassociate Jesus with the wider Jewish struggle of the period against spiritual and political oppression, the crucifixion narrative will continue to carry the seeds of antisemitism despite the official condemnations of the deicide charge. Most Christians still view the situation as Jesus and themselves in opposition to the totality of the Jewish community when they read the accounts of the passion. In actual fact, however, the passion story, apart from its later theological interpretations, should serve as a source of unity between Jews and Christians, not as a source of the division and hostility we have witnessed for centuries.

The Jewish historian Ellis Rivkin made this point as clearly as anyone. Rivkin says that the question of "Who crucified Jesus?" needs to be rephrased as "What crucified Jesus?" As he sees it, Jesus died a victim of Roman imperial policy, of a type of regime "which, throughout history, is forever crucifying those who would bring human freedom, insight, or a new way of looking at man's relationship to man." If any Jews collaborated with the Romans in this venture, then they too deserve condemnation. However, the masses of Jews who felt so stifled under Roman domination that they were to stage an outright revolt against its tyrannical authority a few years later cannot be blamed for the death of Jesus. Rather, insists Rivkin, "in the crucifixion their own plight of helplessness, humiliation and subjection was clearly written on the cross itself. By nailing to the cross one who claimed to be the messiah to free human beings, Rome and its collaborators indicated their attitude toward human freedom."[4]

Making the connection between the suffering and death of Jesus and the suffering being endured by the Jewish people in Roman-controlled Palestine should become one of the most important emphases of the Church's proclamation of the crucifixion narrative, if we wish to finally undercut its antisemitic potential. The deicide charge will not completely be laid to rest until such a perspective becomes widespread within the Christian community. The problem, however, is that such a perspective is not easily developed from a simple reliance on the gospel texts dealing with the crucifixion and death of Jesus. Hence utilization of additional background material from modern scholarship on the Second Temple period is vital if the historical situation is ever to be understood. Recent research surrounding the deicide charge does give us hope that the New Testament is not as inherently antisemitic as some have claimed.

Consideration of the historic deicide charge provides an entry into the broader issue of New Testament antisemitism as a whole. Is the New Testament's overall portrayal of Jesus' relationship with the Jewish community of his time to be classified as antisemitic? Several contemporary scholars have taken up this question over the last decade or so. Gregory Baum, Bruce Vawter, Jules Isaac, Samuel Sandmel, Paul Kirsch, Joseph Grassi, John Dominic Crossan, and John Townsend are but a few of those who have involved themselves in the debate. The most provocative challenge to usual Christian thinking on this question is Rosemary Ruether's controversial volume *Faith and Fratricide: The Theological Roots of Anti-Semitism.*[5] Her contention is that the theological statement about Christ developed by the New Testament to interpret the meaning of Jesus' suffering and death are in fact anti-Judaic at their core. This is especially the case with the gospel of John. For Ruether, to use an oft-quoted phrase of hers, "anti-Judaism is the left hand of Christology."

Before examining Ruether's claims in further detail, we may find it useful to look at the general approach of earlier Christian scholars. Although differing on some specific points, the vast majority of pre-Ruether discussions of the subject of New Testament antisemitism concluded that it was devoid of any real antisemitic outlook. Rather, the opposition to the Jews evident in the Christian Scriptures was seen as arising from five factors: (1) concrete hostility between Jews and Christians in their early contest for converts; (2) fear of the Roman authorities, which resulted in a downplaying of imperial responsibility for the death of Jesus at the expense of Jewish culpability; (3) total misunderstanding of the so-called Judaizers denounced in the later Pauline epistles such as Galatians; (4) failure on the part of the later Christian community to recognize many of the supposedly anti-Jewish passages as merely a continuation of Jewish prophetic language intended primarily for members of the apostolic community rather than a judgment upon Judaism; and (5) disputes about Jewish law that were raging within Judaism itself at the time of the Church's birth and became incorporated into the New Testament.

Gregory Baum's volume *Is the New Testament Anti-Semitic?*[6] was typical of the usual Christian approach. Its general conclusion was that any anti-Jewish trends that arose in Christian history were the product of post-biblical distortion, in no direct way reflective of actual New Testament teaching. Baum basically explained any apparently hostile comments toward Jews and Judaism according to three ground rules. In the first place, there were passages addressed specifically to the Jewish community of Jerusalem to which Jesus belonged. These passages were aimed at the unfaithful members of the community. Those who ignored Jesus' preaching were perceived as being under divine judgment. It was only later generations that misguidedly turned these statements into generalized Christian indictments of the Jewish people as a whole.

Baum's second interpretative principle argued that many of the statements in the New Testament that attribute blindness and hardness of heart to the Jews should be considered prophetic declarations made by Christians belonging to the people of Israel in the hope of touching the hearts of their Jewish brothers and sisters and converting them to the Christian faith. In this perspective, such derogatory passages were not intended as descriptions of the entirety of first-century Judaism. Rather, they should be seen as exhortatory sermons, partly prophetic and partly polemical, uttered by people who still regarded themselves as loyal members of the Israelite people and whose goal was to lead their compatriots to the acceptance of the gospel message. Such passages, Baum maintained, acquired their antisemitic overtones only when they fell into the hands of Gentile Christians who used them to judge Jewish religion as a whole.

Third, Baum proposed that many sections of the New Testament in which a negative portrait is presented of the scribes and Pharisees as well as other opponents of Jesus never meant to offer an historically accurate account of these groups. They aimed instead at exposing the deformations and pathologies that threaten religious expression in all ages and at initiating the Christian Church itself into a spirit of critical self-examination. Jesus' conflict with various Jewish factions in his own time became symbolic for the New Testament writers of the perpetual conflict between authentic and inauthentic religion within Christianity. It was the unwillingness on the part of Christians to acknowledge this fact and to arrive at critical self-knowledge that led to the projection of this criticism onto the entire Jewish community. In so doing, the Church attempted to avoid the judgment of the gospel on its own life and practice.

Baum subsequently modified his position. In his introduction to Ruether's *Faith and Fratricide*, he rejects his earlier defense of the New Testament with regard to the roots of antisemitism. (We shall come back to his current position later on in this chapter.)

The rather classic defense of the epistles and gospels offered by Baum in his initial consideration of the question was repeated in large measure in the writings of Bruce Vawter. In order to properly interpret the New Testament on the question of antisemitism, Vawter insists that we need to begin with the assumption that the gospels and epistles were marked by a fundamentally polemical goal. Hence they sometimes tend to be oversimplified and one-sided, easily open to current misinterpretation. Historically, Vawter understands the following factors as having contributed to New Testament tone-setting with respect to Jews and Judaism: (1) Jewish hostility toward the new Christian community of the first century, a hostility that was part of a mutual enmity; (2) the tendency of the biblical authors to write in absolute terms (this is the case, he believes, with some of the references to "the Jews" who, particularly in John, became representatives of the unbelieving generation that confronted Jesus and the early Church); and (3) the apocalyptic tone of New Testament thought, which pitted the forces of good against the powers of evil in uncompromising language that condemned without qualification all those who refused to accept Jesus' message (new Israel versus old Israel). One might add here a point that Vawter himself does not make: From the Qumran literature we now know that such language was fairly commonplace in Jesus' time.

Vawter thus recognizes a certain unquestionable hostility toward Jews in the New Testament. But it was only later Christian generations, reading the epistles and gospels uncritically, who constructed the popular forms of Christian antisemitism that were never intended by the New Testament authors. As Vawter sees it, the gospels did not represent Jesus as rejected by the Jews of his time nor as handed over by them to the Roman authorities for execution. "On the contrary," he says, "without exception they record his enormous popularity with 'the people' or 'the crowds' both in Galilee and in Judea, and they portray the circumstances of the crucifixion as precipitated by a small and desperate cabal of men who had to do their work covertly for fear of arousing against themselves a general rebellion of their own people. The anti-Jewish hostility of the Gospels, in other words, is selective."[7]

Vawter seconds the position of Oscar Cullmann regarding primary Roman responsibility for the execution of Jesus. While he feels that there was complicity in this act by certain members of the Sadducean priestly elite, he points to the evaluation of this group offered by the noted Jewish historian Heinrich Graetz, who described the Temple in Jesus' time as having been directed by people whose chief hallmarks were avarice and greed for power.[8]

Vawter, likewise, is of the opinion that Jewish responsibility for the death of Jesus was heightened by some of the gospel writers at the expense of Roman culpability in order to lessen the threat of imperial harassment of the early Christian community. In particular, Vawter insists, the image of Pontius Pilate has been cleaned up in Matthew, Mark, and Luke based on what we know about him from other historical sources. The lone exception to this trend is the gospel of John, in which Pilate is definitely grouped with the evil and unbelieving multitudes who shun the truth of the gospel.

Another explanation of supposed New Testament antisemitism along the same lines is found in the earlier writings of the prominent Johannine scholar Raymond Brown. In his introduction to the Anchor Bible translation of the fourth gospel, Brown discusses the evangelist's use of the term *the Jews*, which has been frequently pointed to as an example of gospel antisemitism. His research shows that John employs this term some seventy times in his gospel. Yet, says Brown, in only a few instances is the term used as a designation for the real, historical Jewish community of the period. In great part John uses *the Jews* as a technical title. It symbolizes all those people who are opposed to the teaching of Jesus and refuse to accept him as Lord. And in view of the context in which Brown understands the fourth gospel to have been written, he interprets this as referring to those men and women who opposed Christianity in the late first century, wherever they might have lived:

> It is quite clear that in many instances the term "the Jews" has nothing to do with ethnic, geographical, or religious differentiation. People who are ethnically, religiously and even geographically Jews . . . are distinguished from the Jews. For instance, in John 9:22 the parents of the blind man, obviously Jews themselves, are said to "fear the Jews."[9]

Thus, as originally analyzed by Brown, *the Jews* in John constitute a theological category, symbolizing any person, Christian or non-Christian, Jewish or pagan, who would reject with full knowledge the news of salvation through Christ. In sum, Brown states without equivocation his overall assessment of John: "John is not anti-Semitic; the evangelist is condemning not race or people but opposition to Jesus."[10]

We shall subsequently see that like Gregory Baum, Brown has modified his position to some degree regarding the antisemitic factor in John. Before that, however, it would be useful to look briefly at explanations dealing with Pauline attitudes toward the Jewish people, since up to this point we have focused almost exclusively on the gospels. On the one hand, an epistle like Romans is frequently appealed to by those advocating improved Christian-Jewish relations today as a good starting-point for a New Christian theology of the synagogue. On the other hand, many of Paul's remarks about the Torah seem to some to bespeak a deep hostility to Jewish law that serves as the very basis for the traditionally damaging contrast between Judaism and Christianity as religions of law and of love, respectively. And the almost vitriolic denunciations of the so-called Judaizers in Galatians further complicate the image of the Pauline school regarding Judaism.

Several Christian exegetes who have been active in the Christian-Jewish dialogue have come to the defense of the Pauline writings on the question of their antisemitic bias. Markus Barth feels that much of the blame for unwarranted distortions of Judaism supposedly developed out of teachings found in the epistles is in fact due to inaccurate interpretations of the Pauline message by later scholars. These Pauline interpreters depicted him as a rugged individualist who opted for a religion of mystical experience, ethical quietism, psychic introversion, and almost satanic overestimation of sin in resolute opposition to a Jewish or Judeo-Christian religion of tradition, discipline, group responsibility, and ethical commitment. Barth insists that such an outlook fails to do full justice to Pauline thought. Paul did not merely abandon priestly sacrifice and circumcision. Rather, he magnified both by showing what good resulted for all people by the one sacrifice made on the cross. Not the destruction but the renewal of the Israel of God was his goal. "Just as Moses offered his life to God," said Barth, "to make, if possible, atonement for his people," so Paul writes, "For I could wish that I myself were accursed and cut off from Christ for the sake of my brethren, my kinsmen by race" (Exodus 32:32; Romans 9:3).[11] A man who writes in this manner, Barth felt, can hardly be termed an antisemite.

Barth places Paul squarely in the tradition of the biblical prophets who frequently chose to address harsh and challenging words to their own people. But this does not prove that Paul hated or despised Jews any more than Jeremiah:

> When Paul posits a spiritual temple as over against the building of stone; when he calls for circumcision of the heart, not of the flesh only; when he puts righteousness and love, brotherliness and humility, full obedience and faith above all virtues and accomplishments claimed by some of his contemporaries, then he wages a typically Jewish war.[12]

According to Barth's understanding of Pauline thought, Israel continues to give honor and glory to God even after the resurrection of Christ. Israel's task remains to give witness to God's existence, covenant, and blessing among the Gentiles. Paul sees a continuing Jewish mission to the nations. And for that reason, Barth insists that any Christian attempts to proselytize Jews are repugnant to the very heart of the Pauline message. For Barth, the full idea of salvation in the Pauline body of literature still retains its basic Jewish social character. Salvation is something that will be realized at the end of history when church and synagogue are finally reconciled.[13]

With respect to the problem of the people usually referred to as Judaizers in Galatians, Barth makes the point that they were most likely born not Jews but Gentile Christians. Otherwise they would not have isolated circumcision from the other 612 commandments of the Torah and considered it as a substitute for observing the entire Law. Moreover, if they had been Jewish Christians, they would have been circumcized at birth. But the epistle indicates that they were only in the process of accepting circumcision. Paul's venom is thus directed against ritualistic, pagan-born distorters of the gospel message, not against Jews or Jewish Christians. His condemnation of them sprang as much from his own "liberal" understanding of Judaism as from his acceptance of the teachings of Jesus. Paul's line of argument in this regard parallels to some degree the rabbinic teaching of the period, which held, for example, that the Adamite and Noahite commandments need not be fully imposed upon Gentiles for them to attain participation in the coming final kingdom.

Barth warns, as a result of his research into the question of the opponents of the Pauline message in Galatians, that it is misleading to refer to them as Judaizers. This label has an antisemitic ring to it and suggests that Jewish-born Christians were forcing upon free Gentile Christians some unnecessary or even harmful components of their Jewish heritage. Historically this simply was not the case.

Another New Testament scholar who has looked extensively at the issue of the Jews in Pauline theology is Krister Stendahl. In an essay that has now become something of a classic, Stendahl argues in a vein similar to that of Barth. He believes that what he terms a "Western introspective mentality" has been imposed on the writings of Paul by his interpreters in Western Christianity, especially those related to the Protestant tradition. Stendahl is quite convinced that such an interpretation fundamentally disfigures Paul's real teaching and intensifies the Jewish-Christian tension:

> Paul's statements about "justification by faith" have been hailed as the answer to the problem which faces the ruthlessly honest man in his practice of introspection. Especially in Protestant Christianity—which, however, at this point has its roots in Augustine and in the piety of the Middle Ages—the Pauline awareness of sin has been interpreted in the light of Luther's struggle with his conscience. But it is exactly at that point that we can discern the most drastic difference between Luther and Paul, between the sixteenth and the first century, and perhaps between Eastern and Western Christianity.[14]

Luther's struggle with his own conscience read in the framework of late medieval piety led him to interpret Pauline statements as answers to the quest for assurance about personal salvation out of a common human predicament. And Luther's own struggle became a model for the way many subsequent Christians conceived of the Pauline debate with the Jewish tradition. Paul, however, was not concerned primarily with the personal struggle as Stendahl sees it, but with the possibility for Gentiles to be included in the messianic community.

With respect to the famous chapters in Romans (9–11) where Paul offers theological reflections on the Jewish-Christian relationship, Stendahl believes Paul intended to attack directly what he perceived as unwarranted feelings of superiority on the part of Gentile Christians over the people of Israel. The mysterious coexistence Paul posits between Jews and Christians is designed to counter the spiritually haughty attitude he picked up among Roman Christians. It may not be coincidental in Stendahl's eyes that throughout four pages in the Greek text (10:17 to the end of chapter 11) we do not find even a single mention of Christ. And the doxology concluding this section is the only Pauline one that refrains from a Christological emphasis. The dominant motif here, Stendahl, observes is "God language":

> Now if this language usage is conscious it is interesting; if it is unconscious it is even more interesting. Nobody could ever claim that Paul did not have the guts to wave the Christ flag, that he would fall short of evangelistic zeal and zest. Whatever flaws there are in the great apostle, this is not one of them. That is why this absence of Christ language, this changing of thinking into God language, is so striking. Paul is actually teaching a mysterious coexistence.[15]

In light of this understanding of Romans 9–11, it is impossible in Stendahl's judgment to accuse Paul of antisemitism. Although he may have been guilty of minor indiscretions at times regarding Jews, his major theological reflection on the Church's link with Judaism reveals a love and respect so profound that it completely wipes out the validity of any other comments he might have made during his missionary career.

Having examined representative arguments for the claim that the New Testament is not basically antisemitic, we need to look now at the counterarguments. As indicated earlier, probably no thesis advocating that the roots of traditional antisemitism lie in the New Testament itself has received as much attention as that put forward by Rosemary Ruether. In *Faith and Fratricide* she tries to demonstrate that the term *Jews*, as used in the gospels, Acts, and the Pauline writings, signifies the Jewish religious community. As a result, the word *Jews* took on the role of a hostile symbol for all those men and women who dared to resist and reject the gospel teaching. She finds that the book of Acts utilizes the term in this hostile sense some forty-five times, while the term *a Jew*, *Jews*, or *Jewish* is applied to Christians on less than ten occasions. On the grounds of her extensive research Ruether has become convinced that "Judaism, represented by its dominant religious consciousness, was hopelessly apostate and represented a heritage of apostasy which merited its rejection as the true guardian of the vineyard of Israel and the election of the Gentiles instead."[16] She attributes this perspective not to Gentile converts but to alienated and angry Jewish sectarians who were certain they possessed the true interpretation of the Scriptures and were the cornerstone of God's people, but who experienced rejection and rebuff at every turn from the synagogue leadership.

Ruether also stresses the shifting of blame in the gospels for the deaths of Jesus and his disciples from the Roman political leadership to the Jewish religious authorities. The usual explanation for this, the need to avoid harassment from the Romans after the death of Jesus in order to carry on the mission to the Gentiles, she finds rather unconvincing. The full nature of the shift must be clearly understood: It was not merely from Roman to Jewish authority, but from *political* to *religious* authority. The gospel writers, in her view, felt it important to cast the blame for the deaths of Jesus and his disciples not merely upon the Jewish political hierarchy of the day, but specifically upon the head of the Jewish *religious* tradition and its authority. Thus the shift seems to have arisen not simply from the desire to ensure the success of the campaign for Gentile converts, but from the wish to engage in a polemic toward the Jewish religious tradition itself: "The idea that the religious authority of 'apostate Israel' has 'always' killed the prophets, and, therefore, culminates its own heritage of apostasy by killing the great messianic prophet, totally governs the entire story line of all the Gospels."[17]

Ruether also takes issue with benign interpretations of Paul on the Jewish question. She is especially critical of those contemporary ecumenists who look positively toward Romans 9–11. They have the right intentions but are guilty of deceptive exegesis. As she sees it, the "mystery" relationship between Christians and Jews advocated by Paul in no way suggests an ongoing validity for the Jewish covenant as an instrument of salvation in its own right. Paul admits only one authentic covenant of salvation:

> For Paul, there is, and has always been, only one true covenant of salvation. This is the covenant of the promise, given *apart from the Law*, to Abraham and now manifest in those who believe in Abraham's spiritual son, Christ. The people of the Mosaic covenant do not now and never have had any way of salvation through the Torah itself. God never intended to save his people through the Law.[18]

According to Ruether, Paul recognized that Jews would refuse to enter this new community of Israel or accept it as the spiritual lineage of the promise given to Abraham for the foreseeable future. But this hardening of Jewish hearts would ultimately change. God did not "cast off his people" in the sense that he intended to lead them into the Church at the end of time. For Ruether, then, the fact that Paul proclaims the "mystery" of Israel does little to allow a place for the ongoing authenticity of the Mosaic covenant as such or to make room for any spiritual relation to God through Judaism. "In this sense," she says, "he enunciates a doctrine of the rejection of the Jews (rejection of Judaism as the proper religious community of God's people) in the most radical form, seeing it as rejected not only now, through the rejection of Christ, but from the beginning."[19] The ultimate aim of Paul's "mystery theology" of Judaism is not to grant any permanent validity to Judaism but only to guarantee the ultimate vindication of Christianity.

Even though she offers strong critiques of the synoptic gospels, Acts, and Paul for their anti-Judaic orientation, Ruether reserves her most stringent attack for the gospel of John. In the fourth gospel the "unbelief of the Jews" is related to a deep theological mystery. John depicts "the Jews" as the very incarnation of the false, apostate principle of the fallen world, alienated from its authentic existence in God. They typify the totally carnal person who knows nothing of the spiritual realm. They are totally time-bound in their existence, unable to recognize, like the spiritual brothers and sisters of Jesus, the *kairos* of the Christ Event (John 7:6). Their instinctive reaction to the revelation of the spiritual Son of God is to murder him, for they are aware that his coming has unmasked their false way of living: "In this murderousness they manifest their true principle of existence. They show that they are 'not of God, but of the Devil,' who was a liar and a murderer from the beginning. . . ."[20]

Ruether clearly divorces herself from those "apologists" in Christian circles who claim that the division John forges between the "sons of light" and "the sons of darkness" is mere allegory, which the fourth gospel never meant to apply in a literal way to Christians and Jews.

Her contention is that John turned a realistic inner spiritual conflict within humankind—the person in God versus the person alienated from God—into a division between two differing faith postures (i.e., Christianity and Judaism). In so doing, John gave the ultimate theological form to the diabolizing of "the Jews," which served as the primary source of all future forms of antisemitism in Christian history. Hence the roots of the Church's antisemitic tradition stretch back into the New Testament itself, to the Christology of John in particular. The Christian community, understanding the Scriptures Christologically, alone shares in the life of the Father. The Jewish community, which interprets the Scriptures as a testimony to an ongoing covenant with Abraham and Moses, are "the children of the Devil" who have never known Christ or his Father. The remedy for antisemitism is crystal-clear for Ruether: "There is no way to rid Christianity of its anti-Judaism, which constantly takes social expression in anti-Semitism, without grappling finally with its Christological hermeneutic itself."[21]

As might be expected, Ruether's radical critique of the New Testament as the source of antisemitism has drawn several responses from Christian scholars. In the first place, she has persuaded Gregory Baum to draw away from the arguments he made in his volume discussed earlier. In an introductory essay in *Faith and Fratricide*, he states unequivocally that Ruether's book has convinced him he must now change his mind on the subject of New Testament antisemitism. He is now convinced, through Ruether's analysis, that Paul, for example, never had any intention whatsoever of acknowledging the Jewish religion as a way of grace. In the Pauline perspective Israel had gone blind. It now represented death and spiritual slavery. Yet God did not totally abandon the Jews. Their election remained not as a source of grace in the present time but as a divine promise of the eventual conversion of the Jews at the conclusion of human history and their absorption into Christianity, the one true Israel. In this connection, Baum writes:

> All attempts of Christian theologians to derive a most positive conclusion from Paul's teaching in Romans 9–11 (and I have done this as much as others) are grounded in wishful thinking. What Paul and the entire Christian tradition taught is unmistakably negative: the religion of Israel is now superseded, the Torah abrogated, the promises fulfilled in the Christian church, the Jews struck with blindness, and whatever remains of the election to Israel rests as a burden upon them in the present age.[22]

Baum insists that if the Church is really serious about ridding itself of the anti-Jewish bias built into its teaching, a few marginal changes will not do. Rather, a thorough cleansing of the tradition is required. And that will inevitably involve an examination and reinterpretation of the Christ Event itself. Nothing else will do.

Though not writing directly in response to Ruether, the Christian scholar from Israel, Joseph Stiassny, confirms at least some of Ruether's points regarding the fourth gospel. Stiassny distinguishes sharply between comments against the Jews in the synoptic gospels and in John. The former he views as essentially "in-house" comments, common to both the Jewish prophetic tradition and to the warring parties within Second Temple Judaism. But by the time John came on the scene, the situation had profoundly changed. At the time of the final editing of the fourth gospel, church and synagogue had become radically separate entities. Christianity's rupture from Judaism had been finalized. Unlike Paul and the synoptic writers, John's attitude toward the Jews was not missionary but apologetic and polemical. It was intended to counter Jewish propaganda and to undergird Christian claims. In Stiassny's eyes, John employed the expression *the Jews* to indicate that the Jewish people of his day were the spiritual descendants of the Jewish authorities who showed hostility to Jesus during his ministry. The refusal of the Jews to believe became for John the symbol of all men and women everywhere who fail to accept the gospel message.[23]

Raymond Brown also modified his position on the absence of antisemitism in John, which he articulated in his Anchor Bible commentary. His change of viewpoint is not nearly as dramatic as that of Gregory Baum. But there appears to be a significant switch in his thought in several more recent pieces, particularly in his contribution to *Worship* magazine[24] in 1975 and in comments in his volume *The Community of the Beloved Disciple*.

In the former article, where his comments on antisemitism in John are somewhat parenthetical and hence not fully developed, Brown indicated his conviction that by deliberately using the term *the Jews* (where other gospel writers refer to the Jewish authorities or various Second Temple Jewish parties) John meant to extend to the synagogue of his own day the blame that an earlier tradition had pinned on the authorities. Although John was not the first to engage in such extension, he is the most insistent New Testament author in this regard. Brown explains this process in John as owing to the persecution that Christians were experiencing in his time at the hands of the synagogue authorities. Jews who professed Jesus to be the Messiah had now been officially expelled from Judaism, thus making them vulnerable to Roman investigation and punishment. Jews were tolerated by Rome—but who were these Christians whom the Jews disclaimed?

Brown goes on to say that this teaching of John about the Jews, which resulted from the historical conflict between church and synagogue in his day, can no longer be taught as authentic doctrine by contemporary Christianity. Christians today must come to see that such teachings, while a realistic part of the biblical heritage, are no longer valid belief. In *The Community of the Beloved Disciple*, this point is made with even greater firmness: "It would be incredible for a twentieth-century Christian to share or justify the Johannine contention that 'the Jews' are the children of the Devil, an affirmation which is placed on the lips of Jesus

(8:44)."[25] He definitely feels a more radical solution is needed for the anti-Judaic material in the fourth gospel than merely softening the translation to "Judeans" or "Judaists," or offering the explanation that John often uses the term *the Jews* when the context implies that the chief priests alone were the culprits. Though Brown would shy away from the radical theological surgery suggested by Ruether as a corrective for the New Testament view of Jews and Judaism, he does advocate the need for significant change. The problem is that he stops short of presenting any overall approach to the issue. He likewise fails to deal adequately with the radical implications of his argument that significant parts of the Johannine theology of Judaism are no longer a valid teaching for today's Church.

Negative reactions to *Faith and Fratricide* have come from several Christians long associated with the Jewish-Christian dialogue. John Oesterreicher of the Institute of Judeo-Christian Studies at Seton Hall University has taken strong exception to Ruether's thesis. In an institute paper entitled "the Anatomy of Contempt," he rejects her basic contentions about the antisemitic roots in the epistles and gospels and seemingly accuses her of undermining authentic Christian faith through this claim. He cites the Jewish scholar Leo Baeck's much more sympathetic treatment of Paul on the Jewish question. He criticizes her generally for a failure to understand the rabbinic style of interpretation, which Oesterreicher feels had a great impact on the mode of Pauline argumentation. With regard to her charge against the fourth gospel, he claims that no competent New Testament scholar in the present day "thinks that 'the Jews' in St. John's gospel are the empirical Jews, the historical Jewish community, the people in the villages and towns of the land of Abraham and his descendants. All sound interpreters agree that in the instances that seem to degrade Jews, 'the Jews' is a theological cipher or symbol for a world that denies itself to Jesus."[26]

Several other critics of Ruether's thesis are much more sympathetic than Oesterreicher to the basic goals of *Faith and Fratricide*. This is certainly true of the contributors to the volume of criticism on *Faith and Fratricide* edited by Alan Davies.[27] It is also true of an article coauthored by Thomas A. Indinopulos and Roy Brown Ward. They do not quarrel with Ruether's proposition that the foundations for anti-Judaic thought were planted in the New Testament. Certainly, they argue, Matthew's gospel represents a genuine hardening of attitudes toward Jews articulated in such themes as the rejection of the "sons of the kingdom" (i.e., the Jews), whom God will cast into the outer darkness. Likewise, they are willing to grant that in the fourth gospel John moves the "crime of the Jews" very close to what eventually takes shape as the charge of deicide. But the appearance of certain forms of anti-Judaic thought in portions of the New Testament does not automatically justify the Ruetherian contention that anti-Judaism is of necessity the left hand of Christology.

Indinopulos and Ward are especially troubled by the position taken by Ruether with respect to Pauline theology. It is difficult for them to comprehend how she can arrive at the conclusion that, in Paul, Judaism is not an ongoing covenant of salvation in which authentic worship makes possible a genuine relationship with God. As they see Paul, he characterizes only Gentiles, not Jews, as those who "knew not God." In fact, Paul himself boasts of his Jewishness. He never argues that Judaism represents false worship of God, but only that a new righteousness has been revealed (Romans 1:17; 3:21; 10:3) that has brought about a new phase in the history of salvation. His adherence to this new revelation does not lead him to deny the holiness of the law (Romans 7:12) nor the election of the Jews (Romans 11:28). These authors find it difficult to understand how Paul can be considered any more anti-Judaic than other Jewish sectarian groups of the period such as Qumran, who joined Paul in believing that something new was taking place in history under divine guidance. Unlike the Qumran sectarians who anticipated the destruction of mainstream Judaism (which they considered in a state of apostasy), Paul expressed hope for the ultimate salvation of all Israel (Romans 11:26).[28]

An increasingly common approach to the problem of anti-Judaism in John revolves around the distinctions among several textual layers in the gospel. J. Louis Martyn has been a principal exponent of this viewpoint in his writings.[29] It has also been put forth as a missing dimension in Ruether's analysis (and is hence a weakness in her position) by the New Testament scholar John Townsend in his contribution to the Davies volume mentioned earlier.

A closer look at the fourth gospel, especially its handling of the trial of Jesus, will result in a much subtler understanding of John's claimed antisemitism according to Townsend. In some respects, he sees John as less anti-Jewish than the synoptics, a point Ruether fails to recognize. John, for example, plays down the religious charge of blasphemy found in the other gospels. For him the antagonism of the Jewish establishment against Jesus was primarily rooted in a fear that his preaching would disrupt political relations with the Romans. According to Townsend, John stresses the Roman involvment in the arrest of Jesus and makes no mention of any deal between Judas and the Temple leadership. On this point he concludes that

> according to John, Jewish authorities were responsible for arresting Jesus, but these authorities had acted under Roman pressure and had carried out the action with a band of Roman soldiers. Of the four evangelists, John alone was unwilling to shift responsibility for the arrest from Roman to Jew, even though failure to do so implied that Rome considered Jesus dangerous and invited Roman persecution of his followers.[30]

Townsend goes on to say that the Johannine trial narrative deemphasizes the Jewish proceedings in connection with the trial and sentencing of Jesus. Other evangelists described the primary charge against Jesus as strictly a crime against Jewish law, but John focused on the political aspects "by making the Jewish proceedings quite informal with no mention of the accusations against Jesus. The evangelist has featured the importance of the Roman trial in which the charge was a political crime against Rome."[31] Townsend's interpretation, were it to achieve scholarly consensus, would make our task of Jewish-Christian reconciliation easier. But problems would still persist. For even Townsend does not deny the clear anti-Judaism present in John, including the passion narratives. He is merely arguing that such anti-Judaism is not the full story. In short, John contains an uneasy mixture of anti-Jewish and pro-Jewish materials that hang together in considerable tension. Townsend would be the first to admit that the anti-Jewish, not the pro-Jewish, dimensions tend to be highlighted in Christian celebration and preaching.

A final approach to the question of New Testament antisemitism is represented in the writings of Malcolm Lowe. In an indirect response to a Ruetherian-type analysis he argues that the problem, at least with respect to the use of the term *the Jews*, is largely a question of mistranslation, not one of endemic antisemitism. Although he acknowledges that the term *hoi Ioudaioi* refers on a few occasions to "Jews in general," its basic usage is geographical. It pertains to "the Judeans" (on occasion even more restrictedly to the Judean authorities) in contradistinction to the Galileans. Lowe believes this is especially true of John, where the term is so prominent. If we wish to solve the problem of the New Testament as the basis for later (and continuing) anti-Judaic outlooks in Christianity, we must consciously attend to retranslation of this term:

> rendering "hoi Ioudaioi" as "the Jews" is not only incorrect . . . but also pernicious. As long as the mistranslation continues, generations will continue to read that "the Jews" had Jesus killed and . . . to infer that they declared themselves and their descendants responsible. Thus this philological error of the Palestinian use of "Ioudaios" to distinguish Judeans from Galileans, etc., with its wider meanings in the diaspora has provided, in practically all modern translations of the gospels, a constant excuse for anti-semitism whose further existence cannot be permitted.[32]

This position, as advocated by Lowe, has been rejected by a number of other scholars including Raymond Brown.

We have now seen several divergent approaches to the problem of New Testament antisemitism. All have been taken by scholars highly conscious of the history of Jewish persecution by Christians and keenly intent on terminating this history once and for all. Their lack of agreement, however, is evidence that the issue will remain a hotly contested one for some time to come. No total resolution lies in sight. Nonetheless, some tentative conclusions are possible.

1. It is clear that, if read with some sophistication, the gospels present a case for basic Roman responsibility for the death of Jesus. On this point, Ruether's contention about the deliberate shifting of blame to Jewish religious authorities is not that strong. There was some attempt to whitewash Roman guilt, at least in the synoptics. But there is no clear evidence, contrary to Ruether, that the primary motivation here was theological rather than political. Hence sufficient background information should provide the Christian believer with a fairly accurate understanding of the situation. The problem remains, however, as to how this background information is to be made available. So many Christians read the gospels without such information. How are they to come to know what scholars like Brown and Vawter insist upon— namely, that an accurate understanding of the New Testament cannot be gained from the pure text? The grasp of the constructive dimensions of Second Temple Judaism remains minimal in the churches. Jesus is still largely perceived as a "loner" in his gospel challenge. Until Jesus is consciously reintegrated into the Jewish community of his day in a positive way, the crucifixion narratives will remain a rich source for popular antisemitic attitudes in our day.

2. Ruether exaggerates Pauline anti-Judaism. He shows a greater love and respect for the continuing validity of Jewish religion that she is willing to grant. Nonetheless, I think she and Gregory Baum are correct when they criticize the uncritical overuse of Romans 9–11. This section of the epistle ends on a conversionalist note that I personally find unacceptable in light of what we have come to know about Judaism and by virtue of the Jewish experience of the Nazi Holocaust. Stendahl is too optimistic in his interpretation of Paul's intentions with regard to Judaism, despite his positive contribution to the dialogue on the question. What we can say is that Romans 9–11 undercuts any attempt to totally invalidate the meaningfulness and beauty of the Jewish covenant. But we cannot stop here. We need to see Romans 9–11 as a challenge for further theological development, not as an end point. Unless a Christian is willing to admit the principle of continuing development of the religious tradition that can go beyond mere biblical formulations, I do not believe the problem of the antisemitic potential of the New Testament can ultimately be resolved. We must be prepared to build a new model of the Jewish-Christian relationship that allows meaningful theological space for Judaism, and serves as the basis for discarding the kind of teachings that Raymond Brown has argued are no longer tenable as Christian faith proclamation. Otherwise, we face the prospect of continuing antisemitism within the churches.[33]

3. There appears to be a growing consensus within the sphere of recent Johannine studies that at least some parts of the fourth gospel do indeed intend to condemn the specific Jewish community of its day. This development contradicts the assertions of people like John Oester-reicher. Coupled with the growing admission of deliberate denigration

of Judaism is the increased realization that the basic substrate of John to which the anti-Judaic sections were appended at a rather late date in the composition process reveals strongly pro-Judaic tendencies. Although this latter discovery complicates the discussion of antisemitism and hence calls for a modification of Ruether's thesis, it does not remove the fact that significant parts of John come very close to what we mean by modern antisemitism—class hostility toward the Jewish people because of a sinister identification between them and the "demonic" forces of darkness. The attempts by some Christian commentators to gloss over this reality by arguing that "Jews are merely the symbol of evil everywhere" falls down, for John, on both scholarly and moral grounds. The only solution to this situation is the one suggested by Raymond Brown: We can no longer consider these sections as authentic Christian teachings. Getting this approach accepted in large parts of the Christian world, however, remains a very formidable task.

The issue of the antisemitism of John is far from a settled question. It poses problems that the more internal Jewish battles found in the synoptics do not. I am convinced that it is possible to present Johannine Christology without of necessity denigrating Judaism. In fact, I believe that the Johannine "Word made flesh" Christology provides the best possibility (along with the later Pauline Christology) for creating ongoing theological space for Judaism because it is not so directly tied to the "fulfillment of Messianic prophecies" model that so dominates the synoptics. But this thesis will still take considerable study and reflection on the part of Christian scholars. The question before us on a pastoral level is how to introduce the subtle distinctions regarding the John/Jewish question that scholars like John Townsend are beginning to make, especially in the presentation of the passion narratives. We in the churches need to face this situation squarely. Townsend himself has offered one possible solution: In association with the Israel Study Group of Christian Scholars, he has published an interpretative text of the passion for liturgical use during Holy Week.[34] Another option might be to return to the old Catholic practice of insisting on footnotes in biblical translations.

4. The denunciation of the Pharisees, so common to the synoptic gospels, is an issue on which Ruether's research is very vulnerable. This is surprising because she has shown on occasion, including in *Faith and Fratricide*, some acquaintance with current investigations on Pharisaism. But she never really relates this research to the problem of New Testament antisemitism.

A considerable amount of the hostility toward the Pharisees in the New Testament may in fact be explained by inter-Pharisaic contestation. Ruether gives too little due to this possibility.

5. The attacks against the so-called Judaizers can be disposed of rather easily on scholarly grounds. But to do so does not solve the pastoral problem. These people were simply not representative of the

Jewish mainstream. Many Jews of the time would have objected to their rigidity in Torah interpretation as strongly as did Paul. It is also likely that they were not even Jewish by birth. Yet when these passages are read without explanation, the average Christian may take them as condemnations of Judaism as a whole. Here again we run into the problem of background material that remains unsolved on the popular level.

6. Attention needs to be given to the letter to the Hebrews whose anti-Judaic language (especially in chapters 7–10, where a definite "superiority" ethos is present relative to church/synagogue) has been little explored thus far. While certainly not as influential as Pauline and gospel thought in the formation of Christian consciousness, Hebrews carries a destructive potential that should not be ignored in any overall attempt to eradicate New Testament–based antisemitic attitudes within the Church.[35]

I would now like to raise one final point. Throughout this essay the terms *antisemitic* and *anti-Judaic* have been used as virtual synonyms. A debate has ensued as to whether such usage is too loose and further intensifies the problem at hand. Edward Flannery raised this issue in a 1973 essay in the *Journal of Ecumenical Studies*.[36] While recognizing that no overly tight distinction can be drawn between New Testament hostility to Jews and Judaism and subsequent antisemitic attitudes in the society as a whole, we may still find it useful to discuss the distinction at least in scholarly circles. Samuel Sandmel also endorsed the distinction, at least to the point of considering the term *antisemitic* inappropriate as a label for the New Testament because of its modern origins.[37]

I would agree that we need to continue discussion of the distinction in scholarly circles at least, whatever the slim possibilities of introducing the distinction in popular language. With the very likely exception of sections of John, New Testament hostility toward Jews and Judaism was not characterized by the hatred, even unto death, that has been central to so many modern expressions of antisemitism. The New Testament basically was not embryonic Nazism, whatever may have happened in later Christian interpretations of the gospels and epistles. This needs to be made clear, and the distinction proposed by Flannery helps to do this up to a point. The one area in which the distinction might let the Church off the hook too easily concerns the "Jews as darkness and evil" passages of the fourth gospel. As Janis Leibig has correctly (if a bit too globally) suggested, "The Fourth Gospel far exceeds Flannery's definition of 'anti-Judaism.' It is neither 'bereft of hatred or stereotyping of Jews' nor are its polemics 'fair and irenic.'"[38] Pursuing the discussion, however, helps to make clear that the question of New Testament antisemitism, whether in John or elsewhere, cannot be answered with a simple "yes" or "no." Unnuanced accusations against the Christian Scriptures as antisemitic are in a scholarly sense unsound and prejudicial in reverse.

Notes

1. See John T. Pawlikowski, *The Challenge of the Holocaust for Christian Theology*, revised edition (New York: Anti-Defamation League, 1982).

2. Oscar Cullmann, *Jesus and the Revolutionaries* (New York: Harper & Row, 1970).

3. Bruce Vawter, "Are the Gospels Anti-Semitic?" *Journal of Ecumenical Studies* 5 (Summer 1968):486.

4. Ellis Rivkin, "The Parting of the Ways," in Lily Edelman, ed., *Face to Face: A Primer in Dialogue* (Washington, D.C.: B'nai B'rith Adult Education, 1967), p. 37.

5. Rosemary Ruether, *Faith and Fratricide: The Theological Roots of Anti-Semitism* (New York: Seabury Press, 1974).

6. Gregory Baum, *Is the New Testament Anti-Semitic?* (Glen Rock, N.J.: Paulist Press, 1965). This is a revised edition of an earlier work by Baum entitled *The Jews and the Gospel* (Westminster, Md.: Newman, 1961).

7. Vawter, "Are the Gospels Anti-Semitic?" p. 481.

8. See Heinrich Graetz, *History of the Jews, II* (Philadelphia: Jewish Publication Society, 1941), p. 237.

9. Raymond Brown, *The Gospel According to John*, vols. 29 and 29A (Garden City, N.Y.: Doubleday, 1966), p. LXXI.

10. Ibid.

11. Markus Barth, *Israel and the Church* (Richmond, Va.: John Knox Press, 1969), p. 68.

12. Ibid.

13. See Markus Barth, "Jews and Gentiles: The Social Character of Justification in Paul," *Journal of Ecumenical Studies* 5 (Spring 1968):241–267.

14. Krister Stendahl, "The Apostle Paul and the Introspective Conscience of the West," *Harvard Theological Review* 56 (July 1963):200.

15. Krister Stendahl, "Saint Paul and the Jews," *Engage/Social Action* 3 (December 1976):22.

16. Ruether, *Faith and Fratricide*, p. 94.

17. Ibid., p. 89.

18. Ibid., p. 106.

19. Ibid., p. 107.

20. Ibid., p. 113.

21. Ibid., p. 166.

22. Ibid., p. 6.

23. See Joseph Stiassny, "Development of the Christians' Self-Understanding in the Second Part of the First Century," *Immanuel* 1 (Summer 1972):32–34.

24. Raymond Brown, "The Passion According to John: Chapters 18 and 19," *Worship* 49 (March 1975):130–131.

25. Raymond Brown, *The Community of the Beloved Disciple* (New York: Paulist Press, 1979), pp. 41–42.

26. John Oesterreicher, *The Anatomy of Contempt* (South Orange, N.J.: Seton Hall University, Institute of Judeo-Christian Studies, 1975), p. 4.

27. Alan Davies, ed., *Antisemitism and the Foundations of Christianity* (New York: Paulist Press, 1979).

28. Thomas A. Indinopulos and Roy Brown Ward, "Is Christianity Inherently Anti-Semitic? A Critical Review of Rosemary Ruether's 'Faith and Fratricide,'" *Journal of the American Academy of Religion* 45 (June 1977):193–214.

29. See J. Louis Martyn, *The Gospel of John in Christian History* (New York: Paulist Press, 1979) and Martyn, *History and Theology in the Fourth Gospel* (Nashville, Tenn.: Abingdon, 1979). For a condensation of Martyn's position as well as a comprehensive overview of recent works on antisemitism in John, see Janis E. Leibig, "John and 'the Jews': Theological Antisemitism in the Fourth Gospel," *Journal of Ecumenical Studies* 20 (Spring 1983):209–234.

30. John Townsend, "The Gospel of John and the Jews," in Davies, ed., *Antisemitism*, p. 77.

31. Ibid.

32. Malcolm Lowe, "Who Were the Ioudaioi?" *Novum Testamentum* 18 (1976):130.

33. I have attempted to begin this process in my volume *Christ In Light of the Christian-Jewish Dialogue* (Ramsey, N.J.: Paulist, 1982). See also Paul Van Buren, *Discerning The Way* (New York: Seabury, 1980).

34. John Townsend, "A Liturgical Interpretation of Our Lord's Passion in Narrative Form," Israel Study Group Occasional Papers 1 (New York: National Conference of Christians and Jews, 1977).

35. J. Warren Jacobs, "A Look at Anti-Judaic Language in Hebrews," *Response* (January 1983):28–29.

36. Samuel Sandmel, "Anti-Judaism and Anti-Semitism: A Necessary Distinction," *Journal of Ecumenical Studies* 10 (1973):581–588.

37. See Samuel Sandmel, *Anti-Semitism in the New Testament?* (Philadelphia: Fortress Press, 1978).

38. See Leibig, "John and 'the Jews,'" p. 226.

10
The German Churches and the Jewish People Since 1945

John S. Conway

In May 1945 Germany was physically ruined and morally humiliated. The dreams of world hegemony under the charismatic leadership of Adolf Hitler had been shattered with the defeat and occupation of Germany by four foreign armies. Within a few weeks the world was shocked to learn the details of the horrors and cruelties discovered in the newly liberated concentration camps such as Dachau and Bergen-Belsen. A wave of moral revulsion swept around the globe as the extent of Nazi bestiality was revealed, surpassing even the most exaggerated wartime atrocity stories. As for the Germans themselves, they were obliged to recognize what up to then only the most sensitive consciences had realized: that Nazi totalitarian rule had led to the total discrediting of Germany's proud history.

The German churches were no less implicated in this spiritual debacle than other segments of the population. The overwhelming majority of German church people had enthusiastically welcomed the Nazi rise to power, seeing in Adolf Hitler the protector of Germany's national interests and their savior against Bolshevism. Even when, in 1934, a significant minority in the Protestant churches, namely the Confessing Church, had realized the misleading heretical tendencies of Nazi ideology, they were careful to stress their national loyalties and had shown themselves ready to endorse the course of Nazi aggression abroad. Yet, despite their tactical compliance with the Nazi state, these church leaders were eventually brought to see the insidious dangers of the Nazi demands for total control. Their opposition to these claims resulted in their reluctant involvement in one part of the so-called resistance movement and led a few, such as Father Alfred Delp and Dietrich Bonhoeffer, to active struggle against the regime and to eventual martyrdom for their beliefs.

Nevertheless, the defeat of the Nazi regime in 1945 did not lead immediately to any great wave of sympathy for its principal victims, the Jews. In part, this was because the main centers for the elimination of the Jews, such as the extermination camps of Auschwitz, Treblinka,

Chelmo, Belzec, and Maidanek, had been destroyed by the retreating Germans and lay in the inaccessible territory of reborn Poland. In part, it was because the full details of the whole grisly process, from segregation, to ghettoization, to enforced deportation, to mass annihilation, became known only item by item, so that it was several years, for example, before the pivotal role of Auschwitz in the destruction of European Jewry was fully realized.[1] In part, it was also because the significance and meaning of the Holocaust for the whole of European and indeed world history has been still more gradually recognized.[2] Particularly among Germans there was a widespread reluctance to examine the implications of their own involvement in the Nazi crimes, which led to a general political amnesia to cover over what become known as the *unbewältigte Vergangenheit* (unmastered past). In part, however, it was also a fact that the traditional mentalities of antisemitism, whether latent or overt, still dominated people's thinking, despite the traumatic evidence of how much suffering and death had been inflicted on one-third of the total world Jewish population. Almost two decades were to pass before the situation changed.

But from the 1960s onward, due at least in part to what Yehuda Bauer has called the Jewish emergence from powerlessness[3] and the rebirth of the State of Israel, new attempts to assess the Holocaust in its political, theological, and metahistorical dimensions have been undertaken, together with an ongoing analysis of the causes, impact, and effects of antisemitism.

In the dark days of 1945, at least one segment of the German churches recognized the need to come to terms with the traumatic events of the recent past. The remaining leaders of the Confessing Church, both those who had survived the Nazi onslaught through tactical accommodations and those like Martin Niemöller, who spent eight years in concentration camps, saw the need to issue a statement disassociating their churches from the Nazi past and yet also recognizing their own complicity. The result was the notable Stuttgart Declaration of Guilt of October 1945.[4] But, in fact, no direct reference at all was included in this document to the widespread failure of the German churches to support the Jews in their hour of need or to withstand the spread of antisemitism. The ensuing controversy within the German Evangelical churches over this ethical demand for an acknowledgment of guilt, even in this most general form, showed how reluctant the majority of church people were to alter their perspectives.

With renewed vigor and courage, Martin Niemöller set out on a campaign to convince his fellow church people that Christ alone was the Lord of the Church and no one else; that the Church must live as the servant of others, not just for itself; and that guilt must be faced because only thereby could forgiveness and a new beginning take place. But by 1947 he noted with resignation: "I have spent two years in doing nothing but preaching on Stuttgart and the Declaration of Guilt—alas, without success."[5] The majority of his ecclesiastical colleagues, like the majority of his compatriots, preferred to banish the memory of their failings during the Nazi years and instead harped on their alleged humiliations and sufferings under the occupation regimes, the denazification and reparations, the shortages of food and shelter, and, above all, their fears for the future of their society in face of the threat of Soviet communism.

In such a climate of opinion, it was hardly surprising that little incentive existed to examine in detail the contribution of the churches to the Nazi excesses in persecuting and annihilating Europe's Jews. Not until 1950 did the Synod of the Evangelical Church, meeting in Berlin-Weissensee, feel it necessary to apply the Confession of Guilt in the Stuttgart Declaration clearly and explicitly to the treatment of the Jews. "Through neglect and silence we have become accomplices in the outrages that have been perpetrated by representatives of our people upon the Jews. . . . We beseech all Christians to renounce every kind of anti-semitism, and earnestly oppose it, if it be stirred up anew, and to encounter both Jews and Jewish Christians in a brotherly spirit."[6] This belated statement at last recognized that when radical antisemitism was propagated through the land, the German churches did not show the strength to resist, largely because any true understanding of Israel in the parishes had been supplanted and extinguished.

But many more years were to elapse before church people began to realize that what was required was much farther-reaching than merely an acknowledgment of the deficiencies of their humanitarian feelings. In the years immediately after 1945, despite the accumulating evidence of the atrocities inflicted on the Jewish people, there was virtually no reflection by Christian theologians on the contribution of Christian negative stereotypes about Judaism, which had so much assisted, or at least failed to prevent, the Nazi agitation and propaganda. Instead, there was a bland assumption that, as far as the churches were concerned, the Nazi era constituted only an unfortunate episode, a so-called *Betriebsunfall* (occupational accident). As far as the Jews were concerned, especially in the circles connected with missionary work, there was often the assumption that the task of Christian witness and mission toward the Jews could now be resumed where it had broken off. Insofar as Christians had failed in their duty, this should have been an incentive for redoubled effort. Christians owed the Jews, after all their sufferings, the best they had to offer, namely the good news of the Gospel of Christ. Only His acceptance by the Jews would put the relations of Christians and Jews in order. The efforts to revive the Christian mission to the Jews were based on a continuity of traditional theological doctrines: Judaism had failed to recognize its Messiah and, by putting Him to death, had forfeited their election as God's Chosen People. The Church had superseded the Jews, and it now called for the renewed recognition that the true destiny of the Jews lay in their conversion. To be sure, the methods to be employed had to be those of love, not hatred. Nazi antisemitism and all its pernicious practices were to be opposed, but largely because they had proved to be barriers rather than avenues toward the goal of bringing the Jews to recognize the Lordship of Christ.

Such traditional teachings continued to be maintained in the authoritative statements of leading scholars in both the German Catholic and Evangelical churches. For example, Martin Noth, the prominent Old Testament scholar in Heidelberg, stated his view in 1958 that with the exile into Babylon and the destruction of the temple in A.D. 70, "Israel thereby ceased to exist, and the history of Israel came to an end."[7] Or, as Michael Schmaus, a leading Catholic theologian declared in 1959: "Israel is obsolete and its existence meaningless. Its only eschatological hope is redemption by Christ. . . . Israel can neither live nor die, only wait, blinded and hardened."[8]

The ambivalences of the postwar years in the German churches can be clearly perceived in these utterances. Even in the above-cited Evangelical Synod declaration of 1950 and the preceding Darmstadt Declaration of the surviving anti-Nazi Confessing Church leaders, issued in 1948, these traditional Christian anti-Judaic teachings were reproduced, and the justification for the Christian mission to the Jews was again proclaimed. The acknowledgment of the churches' sins of omission and silence during the Nazi years was thus only a partial admission of failure. The need for a more fundamental theological reorientation, leading to an abandonment of such "triumphalist" overtones, and particularly to the elimination of the traditional "teaching of contempt," was recognized only slowly and reluctantly in the subsequent decades.

It was not until the much-publicized trial of Adolf Eichmann in 1960–1961 that new initiatives came to fruition. By this time, not only had the awareness of the enormity of Nazi crimes become general, but the state of Israel had established itself as a redoubtable haven for Jews from all parts of the world. The West German chancellor, Konrad Adenauer, had led his compatriots to accept the principle of reparations—reparations not only for the surviving victims of the Holocaust but for the new State of Israel as well. Significantly, too, there were important developments in the theological field. On the one hand, the nineteenth-century missionary impulse, with its exclusivist view of the uniqueness of Christian salvation, had ebbed away in most western European countries, to be replaced by a more open and ecumenical stance toward other religions, including Judaism. On the other hand, the teachings of the prominent Swiss theologian, Karl Barth, who was revered as the mentor of the Confessing Church during the Church Struggle, challenged the hitherto prevalent view of the relationship between Judaism and Christianity.[9] In place of the assertion that God had abandoned Israel because of its disloyalty and rejection of its Messiah, Barth stressed the continuity and interrelationship of God's chosen people, linked together in an indissoluble bond. Equally significant, this theology repudiated the traditional accusation of deicide—the view that the Jews were guilty of the crucifixion of Jesus—surely the most pernicious (if popular) example of anti-Judaism in the churches, and one that was still heard as a justification for the Nazi persecution during those terrible years among both Catholics and Protestants in Germany.

In 1961, on the occasion of the major Evangelical Church rally in Berlin, a new section was added to discuss Christian-Jewish relations, which found very wide support. In the subsequent years, this *Arbeitsgemeinschaft Juden und Christen* has undertaken a large-scale educational activity among church people and published a notable series of volumes, the first of which was appropriately entitled *Der Ungekündigte Bund* (The Indissoluble Bond).[10] At the later biennial rallies, prominent Jewish speakers, such as Shalom Ben-Chorin, Pinchas Lapide, Edna Brocke, and Rabbis R. R. Geis and N. O. Levinson, sounded the call for a change in Christian teachings and Christian action toward the Jewish people.[11]

At the same time, further initiatives were taken in the German churches to give concrete expression to this new climate of opinion. The German equivalent of the Peace Corps, known as *Aktion Sühnezeichen*, founded by one of the leading laymen in the Church Struggle, sought to mobilize young Germans to undertake practical tasks of reparation, including service in Israel. Despite very natural hesitations on the part of their hosts, one may suggest that this program has had a positive effect. Likewise, courses for German theologians in Jerusalem and participation in an ongoing series of conferences and seminars at Israeli-based institutions have strengthened the awareness and understanding of the Jewish heritage.[12] One of the more interesting experiments has been the founding of a Christian *moshav* (collective smallholders' agricultural settlement) in northern Israel, Nes Ammin.[13] First established by a Dutch advocate of Christian-Jewish reconciliation, this now-flourishing center, which also produces roses for the European winter market, has received strong support, financially and in numbers of volunteers, from West Germany. A similar development can be seen in the work of the only Protestant order of nuns, the Mary Sisters of Darmstadt, whose redoubtable founder, Mother Basilea Schlink, established the order in 1947 with the explicit desire to express repentance for the sins of the Nazis and reconciliation with the victims.[14]

Although less prominent, the Catholic Church in Germany has also experienced similar reassessments. Particularly notable has been the pioneering work of such people as Fraulein Gertrud Luckner, who was herself imprisoned in Ravensbrück concentration camp for her efforts to assist Jewish people during the war. Since the late 1940s she had edited and published almost singlehandedly the *Freiburger Rundbriefe*, an annual publication containing all manner of material relating to the Christian-Jewish dialogue, which must be considered an indispensable reference source on this topic.[15] It should be noted that these efforts were undertaken before the well-known reassessments of the Second Vatican Council, which have also been reflected in the subsequent declarations by the German Catholic bishops.[16]

The impact of these efforts was undeniable. For instance, on the occasion of the June 1967 Six-Day War, a widespread wave of sympathy for Israel could be noted. I was myself present at a moving interfaith service held in the ruins of the Kaiser Wilhelm Gedächtnis Church in West Berlin, when Protestants, Catholics, and Jews prayed together for the peace of Jerusalem.

During the 1970s it was recognized in the Evangelical churches that these efforts needed to be consolidated and given official status as part of the Church's teaching. A special commission was appointed on the national level, which in turn produced a study book surveying the whole range of questions to be tackled.[17] Because this commission was broadly based and took soundings throughout the Church membership, its findings were rather cautious.

One branch of the Evangelical Church, however, that of the Rhineland, was determined to press the matter further. The result of the Rhineland Synod's own deliberations was the publication and acceptance in early 1980 of the highly significant Resolution on the Renewal of the Relationship between Christians and Jews, which has been described by our distinguished colleague from Philadelphia, Franklin Littell, as "without question the most impressive accomplishment to date of any official Church body, going far beyond previous landmarks in the re-thinking of Christian-Jewish relations."[18]

In view of its importance, here are some of the highlights. In its opening paragraph, the Synod took issue with all those who wanted to forget the Church's complicity in the Nazi period, and explicitly sought to remedy the deficiencies of the 1945 Stuttgart Declaration by stating: "Stricken, we confess the co-responsibility and guilt of German Christendom for the Holocaust." In its accompanying explanation of this statement the words of Dietrich Bonhoeffer, written already in 1940, were quoted with approval: "The Church confesses that she has witnessed the lawless application of brutal force, the physical and spiritual suffering of countless innocent people, oppression, hatred and murder, and that she has not raised her voice on behalf of the victims and has not found ways to hasten to their aid. She is guilty of the deaths of the weakest and most defenceless brothers of Jesus Christ."[19]

The Synod next declared: "We believe in the permanent election of the Jewish people as the people of God and understand that through Jesus Christ the Church is taken into Covenant of God with his people." This clear repudiation of the traditional supersessionist theory, by which God's Covenant with Israel was held to have been transferred to the Church, was elaborated in a later paragraph, as follows:

> We want to perceive the unbreakable connection of the New Testament with the Old Testament in a new way and to learn to understand the

> relationship of the "old" and "new" from the standpoint of the promise:
> as a result of the promise, as fulfilment of the promise, as confirmation
> of the promise. "New" means therefore no replacement of the "old."
> Hence we deny that the people Israel has been rejected by God or that
> it has been superseded by the Church.

Two highly significant conclusions were drawn from this insight. In the
first place, the Synod gave explicit and positive recognition to the
theological significance of the State of Israel: "The continuing existence
of the Jewish people, its return to the Land of Promise, and also the
creation of the State of Israel, are signs of the faithfulness of God toward
His people." Second, and equally controversial, was the conclusion
drawn about the pursuit of Christian missions to the Jews. The Synod
declared: "We believe that in their calling Jews and Christians are always
witnesses of God in the presence of the world and before each other.
Therefore, we are convinced that the Church may not express its witness
toward the Jewish people as it does its mission to the peoples of the
world."

It is clear that the impulse and theological thinking behind this
remarkable resolution were derived from the thought of those theologians
whose consciences were particularly sensitive to the lessons of the
Church Struggle and the Holocaust. They were considerably influenced
by the writings of such North American scholars as Rosemary Ruether,
Paul van Buren, Franklin Littell, Roy Eckardt, and Gregory Baum.
Another notable influence was the 1970 Declaration of the Dutch
Reformed Church formally renouncing its sponsorship of Hebrew-Chris-
tian missions. Nor should the contribution of such Catholic scholars as
Clemens Thoma, now of Luzern, be forgotten. In turn, the writings of
the leading Rhineland scholars, such as Bertold Klappert, Heinz Kremers,
and Eberhard Bethge, have had a significant impact on such international
discussions as those conducted under the auspices of the World Council
of Churches in Geneva, resulting in theological reflections that carry
forward much of the Germans' thinking into a wider field and form a
Protestant equivalent to the Roman Catholic 1975 "Guidelines and
Suggestions for Implementing the Conciliar Declaration Nostra Aetate."
The commentaries written since the acceptance of the Rhineland Synod's
Resolution by German theologians have also sought to spell out in more
detail the basis upon which this new understanding of Christian-Jewish
relations can proceed.[20]

It was only natural that such a sweeping renunciation of previous
and inherited theological positions should have aroused opposition. Most
prominent among these opponents were the group of well-known
Evangelical theologians from the University of Bonn (i.e., from the home
university of the Rhineland Synod).[21] In the first place, these scholars
attacked the use by the proponents of the Synod Declaration of contemporary events as the source of theological truth. They rejected the
view that the awfulness of the Holocaust, and the German guilt for its

perpetration, necessitated a totally new view of Christian teachings. The finger of God was not, they believed, to be discerned in contemporary history, neither in the national renewal of Germany under Hitler in 1933 nor in the "miraculous" return of the Jews to the land of Israel. More specifically, the Bonn professors, with astonishing disregard for the massive evidence of Christian complicity, denied any Christian responsibility for the Holocaust: "The national socialist ideology was just as clearly un-Christian and anti-Christian as it was anti-Judaic."

In particular, the Bonn professors disagreed with the rejection of the missionary imperative toward the Jews, which they believed to be still valid. The Jews, they affirmed, could not be regarded differently from all other peoples, since a special status for any ethnic group or race was foreign to the Christian message of salvation for all. "It is quite possible to admire and respect the Jews, and to approve and support the State of Israel, without trying to give these sympathies a 'heilsgeschichtliche' significance, and without giving up or relativising those Christian essentials which separate Christians from Jews."[22]

This criticism found broad acceptance among those sections of the German churches who were still unwilling to draw theological conclusions from the events of the Nazi years or to admit that, after Auschwitz, many traditional perspectives were simply no longer tenable.[23] This unwillingness can be seen in the refusal to grant any theological significance to the rebirth of the State of Israel, which is to be treated as simply a political event like that of any other newly independent nation, for any such admission would be obliged to reject the longstanding view that the Jews had lost their special status as chosen people or that the Church was now the true Israel. It would also mean a rethinking of the concept of the "Promised Land," which had long been spiritualized and divorced from the territory of Palestine. Above all, a concrete confrontation with the Holocaust would mean that the Church, which for so many centuries had fostered the cultural myth about the Jews as Christ-killers, must now meet itself as Jew-killers. It is hardly surprising that many shied away from such a traumatic encounter.

In response, the proponents of the Rhineland Synod's Declaration have been encouraged by the growing awareness and support of their position among a wide variety of church people in the Western world. Although it would be true to say that the German Catholic community has been slow to respond to the Vatican's initiatives in Christian-Jewish relations, here too there have been encouraging signs. The biblical renewal in Catholic thinking has challenged, though not replaced, the former stereotypes that dismissed Judaism as a religion of Law in contrast to the Christian gospel of Love, or relegated the Old Testament as an outdated collection of myths and stories of a primitive tribe. Today, as the Swiss theologian Marcus Barth reminds us, "every page of the New Testament has a quotation or concept from the Old Testament, not merely as timeless symbols or apologetic proof from prophecy, but because they saw their good news as the continuation and coronation of God's history with Israel. The Old Testament is cited in the New Testament as an invitation to listen to the dialogue between God and Israel and to join in it."[24] Or as the American theologian Paul van Buren expressed it: "The Bible reminds us that we are not the first to be called."[25]

These insights, and similar revisions to the inherited prejudices against such Jewish groups as the Pharisees, owe much to the fact that in recent years German theologians, such as those who wrote the Rhineland Declaration, have begun to study the biblical texts in cooperation with Jewish scholars in joint seminars and conferences. No longer are Christians content to speak about the Jews; rather, they speak with them. The enrichment that has followed has undoubtedly been of great value, even though virtually no attention has as yet been paid in Christian circles to the abundant theological life within Judaism over the last two thousand years.

The reasons for such neglect are readily apparent. According to the Canadian scholar Gregory Baum:

> As long as the Christian Church regards itself as the successor of Israel, as the new people of God, and proclaims Jesus as the mediator without whom there is no salvation, there is no theological space left for other religions, and especially the Jewish religion. The central Christian affirmation on these lines negates the possibility of a living Judaism. According to this exposition the religion of Israel has been superseded, the Torah abrogated, its promises fulfilled in the Christian Church, and the Jews struck with blindness.[26]

The presuppositions of the Bonn professors and many similar statements by more conservative German church people are striking evidence that such views are still current in the German churches, leaving no theological space for modern Judaism.

The two most controversial issues, at least for the generality of German church people, remain the question of Christian missions and the attitude to be adopted toward the State of Israel. The categorical statements on these issues as expressed by the Rhineland Synod have yet to find widespread agreement. On the one hand, the rapid changes in attitudes toward the missionary movement in general have been complemented by the fact that in Germany itself there are hardly any Jews left. This discussion has therefore been more theoretical than practicable. But, at least, it has provided an opportunity for a rethinking of the traditional Christian teachings and for the abandonment of the dangerous affirmation of superiority, or of nationalistic cultural identity with Protestantism, which played so fatal a role in earlier years. On the other hand, there is still a marked reluctance to adopt the more positive stance of solidarity between Christians and Jews that the Rhineland Synod called for. As earlier noted, the initiative of the Dutch Reformed Church was significant.

As early as 1949 the Dutch Church resolved to replace its active mission to the Jews with a commission for dialogue with the people of Israel. The memory of the common sufferings at the hands of the Nazis was undoubtedly one of the principal factors. Other church bodies were more cautious, though certainly more positive than in earlier years. For example, the Faith and Order Commission of the World Council of Churches in 1967 stated that "the Church and the Jewish People can be thought of as forming the one people of God and the attitude to the Jews should be different from that to other non-believers. We reject proselytising in the sense of the corruption of witness, in cajolery, undue pressure or intimidation or improper words."[27] Likewise, in Germany the Council of the Evangelical Church declared in 1975 that

> both Christians and Jews must give witness to their own faith. . . . But meetings on this basis can only achieve success if they take place in a conscientious awareness of the long and painful history of mutual relations. . . . Even today missionary practices exist which give Jews justified cause for suspicion. Such practices are decidely rejected by the Church. . . . However, such misuse does not release the Christians from an authentic endeavour to render account according to the Gospels. Faith must not remain silent.[28]

In its most recent statement, the World Council of Churches balanced carefully between the call to witness and the desire to avoid the mistakes of the past:

> There are Christians who view a mission to the Jews as having a very special salvific significance, and those who believe the conversion of the Jews to be the eschatological event that will climax the history of the world. There are those who would place no special emphasis on a mission to the Jews, but would include them in the one mission to all those who have not accepted Christ as their Saviour. There are those who believe that a mission to the Jews is not part of an authentic Christian witness, since the Jewish people finds its fulfilment in the faithfulness to God's covenant of old.[29]

On the one hand, "Christians are called to witness to their faith in word and deed. The Church has a mission and it cannot be otherwise. The mission is not one of choice." On the other hand, "Christians have often distorted their witness by coercive proselytism—conscious and unconscious, overt and subtle. . . . Steps towards assuring non-coercive practices are of the highest importance. In dialogue ways should be found for the exchange of concerns, perceptions, and safeguards in these matters."

It is clear that the majority of theologians are not yet ready to make exceptions, even for the Jewish people, to the dominical commandment: "Go ye into all the world and make disciples of all nations" (Matthew 28:19), nor to be persuaded by Paul van Buren's argument that, in this context, the word *nations* refers to foreigners (i.e., Gentiles). It is also clear that most church people are insufficiently aware that, to many Jews, dialogue presents itself only as a more sophisticated and indirect form of mission.[30] The long sad history of conversion attempts still throws its shadow. Furthermore, it is necessary to note the suspicion, or at least the skepticism, directed against Jewish scholars who attempted to conduct dialogue with Christians in Germany, such as Franz Rosenzweig during World War I, Leo Baeck and Martin Buber during the 1920s and 1930s, Jules Isaac during the 1940s and 1950s, and more recent advocates such as Shalom Ben-Chorin and Pinchas Lapide. Nevertheless, it is undoubtedly true that, through these efforts, the German churches have been obliged to rethink, at least in part, their traditional attitudes toward Judaism.

For some, such as the proponents of the Rhineland Synod Declaration, the results have been disappointing. No other German Evangelical church has as yet followed the Rhineland Church's example. But the reasons for this hiatus are probably attributable less to theological obscurantism than to the wider context in which these discussions and controversies have taken place. Particularly in Germany, but not only there, the general attitudes of church people have been far more affected by the political developments of recent years, especially those concerning the secular course of events in the Middle East.

During the 1960s, as earlier noted, there was a widespread growth of sympathy amongst Germans toward the state of Israel, which peaked, in my estimation, in 1967. After the Six-Day War, which many Jews saw as a devastating threat to the very existence of the new state, great disappointment was expressed at the lack of explicit support by the Christian churches. In some quarters, it was even felt that this would mean the end of the dialogue.[31] The subsequent disillusionment was only strengthened by the appearance and growth of a substantial body of opinion in the German churches, which sympathized with the plight of the Palestinian Arabs. In part, this was reflected in a significant generation gap, whereby the older survivors of the Nazi era, conscious of their passivity during the Holocaust, were confronted by a younger generation who sought to make concrete what they believed were the lessons of the German Church Struggle—namely, the need to declare Christian solidarity with the poor and oppressed. After 1967, and still more after 1973, these sympathies came to be identified with the cause of self-determination for the Palestinian Arabs.

It is hardly surprising that certain Jewish spokesmen should fear that the adoption of any "anti-Zionist" stance by some Christian circles might signify a disguised renewal of the antisemitism of the past or indicate how quickly the fact that the Holocaust perpetrated by the Germans was being forgotten or suppressed.[32] Likewise, even though both the German Evangelical Church and the World Council of Churches have repeatedly called for the recognition and achievement of secure and defensible borders for the State of Israel, doubt still remains about the validity of these pronouncements. Would Christians be prepared to back up such declarations if Israel's future as a political entity were once again in danger? How far have such statements found real acceptance in the ranks of the average church person? In view of the increased and vocal support given to the Palestinians, would Christians be ready to follow their leaders in affirming Israel's continued right to exist? The wide variety of opinions voiced in church circles, in both Germany and elsewhere, have not reduced the misgivings of Jewish observers. They have undoubtedly served to increase misunderstandings and thereby have made more difficult the task of fostering Christian-Jewish relations.

The recent heart-searching and tension within the ranks of the German churches was particularly marked in 1982 on the occasion of the crisis in Lebanon, the intervention of the Israeli defense forces, and the subsequent bloodshed and turmoil in that unhappy land. It is notable that, among the many condemnations by leading world church people of the "invasion of Lebanon," the official German statement avoided any such terminology. Instead, Bishop D. Eduard Lohse, the president of the Council of the Evangelical Church on Germany, presumably in an attempt to be "even-handed," limited himself to noting that

> the new toll of blood . . . hitting Lebanese and Palestinians alike, increases the hatred between the political opponents and makes peace efforts in the Near East even more difficult. In this atmosphere of extremely sharp divergences, neither the legitimate aspiration of Israel to recognised, safe borders, nor the right of the Palestinians to self-determination in their own homeland can be realised. In the common hope for peace, I am calling the Evangelical Christians of our country to intercede for Lebanon and its inhabitants, as well as to help actively to alleviate suffering.[33]

By contrast, the National Assembly of the Delegates of the Student Christian Movement in the Federal Republic of Germany had no hesitation in declaring: "With anger and sorrow we are thinking of this war of Israel against the liberation movement of the Palestinians, with whom we declare our solidarity by our work."[34] A year later, at the Sixth Assembly of the World Council of Churches, meeting in Vancouver, Canada, anti-Israel feeling was still running strongly. In its Statement on the Middle East, the assembly not only called for "greater awareness among the churches about the urgency and justice of the Palestinian cause," but it even sought "to remind Christians in the Western world to recognise that their guilt over the fate of the Jews in their countries may have influenced their views of the conflict in the Middle East and has often led to uncritical support of the policies of the State of Israel, thereby ignoring the plight of the Palestinian people and their rights."[35] It is not known whether any of the German church people present on this occasion protested against this interpretation of the legacy of the Holocaust.

In these circumstances, the German church leaders are facing countervailing pressures that have only increased their sense of ambivalence and confusion. This conflict of loyalties has created a dilemma that is most sharply felt among those who have genuinely sought to learn the lessons of the Church Struggle and the Holocaust. The German church leaders are now having to recognize the perils of whether to speak or not to speak. Open support of one side or the other invites criticism and condemnation, and may lead to exploitation for political reasons. But silence is equally open to misrepresentation. If the church leaders try to avoid taking sides and speak only of the need for peace and the alleviation of suffering, as did Bishop Lohse, they inevitably remind some critical observers of a similar "neutrality" adopted toward the policies of the Nazis, and of the Christian failure to act concretely to avert the Holocaust in time. The moral dilemma of being unable to conceive, let alone to commend, any policy or solution that might bring both peace and justice to all the participants in an apparently unresolvable situation now impels the churches to keep silent.[36] It is these pressures of conflicting obligations, rather than any resurgence of antisemitism, that have led to a more far-reaching reserve. What cannot be ignored, however, is the danger that these politically inspired polarizations may be reflected in the other areas of Christian-Jewish dialogue, hence putting into jeopardy the achievements of recent decades.

In the nearly forty years since the overthrow of Nazism, possibly the most significant development in the Christian churches has been the recognition that the events of the Holocaust, and in Israel since 1945, are of concern not just to the Jewish people but to Christians as well. The credibility of the churches was thrown in doubt because of their acts of omission during the Nazi era. It can be regained only through an abandonment of previously held stereotypes and a determination to engage in the learning process now begun in the German churches. No longer can Christians repristinate the age-old arguments of theological anti-Judaic bigotry; no longer can they lend their support to the more modern racist antisemitism or to political anti-Zionism. Rather, Christians and Jews are called as a common witness to discern the way forward for both communities of faith. At a time when the values that both have inherited are being radically challenged or distorted, this will call for both sensitivity and faithfulness. The German churches, some with enthusiasm, some with reluctance, are now embarked on this path. We shall follow their endeavors with watchfulness and also, I hope, with sympathy, in the years ahead.

Notes

1. This can be seen by the relatively minor attention given to the crimes perpetrated in Auschwitz at the Nuremberg Trials of 1946–1947. The use of Auschwitz as the symbol for the whole Holocaust came into use only in the mid-1950s.

2. Lucy Dawidowicz, in her recent book *The Holocaust and the Historians* (Cambridge, Mass., 1981), has clearly if polemically outlined what she considers to be the deliberate suppression of the significance of the Holocaust by the world academic profession. The general failure to grant the priority of antisemitism in the formation of Nazi policy and practice is still a matter of heated debate.

3. Yehuda Bauer, *The Jewish Emergence from Powerlessness* (Toronto, 1979).

4. For a full analysis of this significant statement, see M. Greschat, ed., *Die Schuld der Kirche. Dokumente und Reflexionen zum Stuttgarter Schulderklärung vom 18/19 Oktober 1945* (Munich, 1982).

5. Ibid., p. 311.

6. *Kirchliches Jahrbuch 1950* (Gütersloh, 1951), pp. 5–6.

7. Quoted in C. Thoma, *A Christian Theology of Judaism* (New York, 1980), p. 31.

8. Quoted in C. Klein, *Anti-Judaism in Christian Theology* (London, 1978), p. 32.

9. See B. Klappert, *Israel und die Kirche. Erwägungen zur Israellehre Karl Barths*, Theologische Existenz heute, no. 207 (Munich, 1980); Eberhard Busch, *Juden und Christen im Schatten des Dritten Reiches, Ansätze zu einen Kritik des Antisemitismus in der Zeit der Bekennenden Kirche*, Theologische Existenz heute, no. 205 (Munich, 1979).

10. D. Goldschmidt and H. J. Kraus, eds., *Der Ungekündigte Bund. Neue Begegnungen von Juden und Christliche Gemeinde* (Stuttgart, 1962).

11. See, for example, H. Gollwitzer and E. Sterling, eds., *Das Gespaltene Gottesvolk* (Stuttgart, 1966); *Wegweisung: Jüdische und christliche Bibelarbeiten und Vorträge. 17 Deutscher Evangelischer Kirchentag, Berlin 1977*, Veröffentlichungen aus dem Institut Kirche und Judentum, no. 8 (Berlin, 1978); *Glaube und Hoffnung nach Auschwitz, Jüdische-Christliche Dialoge, Vorträge, Diskussionen 1980*, Veroffentlichungen, no. 12 (Berlin, 1980).

12. See, for example, the conference report entitled *Christianity and Judaism Under the Impact of National Socialism*, international symposium held at the Hebrew University, Jerusalem 1982 (Jerusalem: Historical Society of Israel, 1983).

13. See S. Schoon and Heinz Kremers, *Nes Ammin. Ein christliches Experiment in Israel* (Naukirchen, 1978).

14. See M. Basilea Schlink, *For Jerusalem's Sake I Will Not Rest* (Darmstadt, 1969).

15. *Freiburger Rundbriefe: Beiträge zur christliche-jüdischen Begegnung*, vols. 1–34 (Freiburg, 1949–1982).

16. See, for example, "Für ein neues Verhältnis zur Glaubensgeschichte des jüdischen Volkes," Erklärung der gemeinsamen Synode der Bistümer in der Bunderrepublik Deutschland vom 22 November 1975 (Declaration of November 22, 1975, of the joint synod of the dioceses in the Federal Republic of Germany), reprinted in G. B. Ginzel, ed., *Auschwitz als Herausforderung für Juden und Christen* (Heidelberg, 1980), pp. 312–314; see also "Uber das Verhältnis der Kirche zum Judentum," reprinted in *Freiburger Rundbrief*, vol. 32 (Freiburg, 1980), p. 7–15.

17. R. Rendtorff, *Arbeitsbuch Christen und Juden. Zur Studie des Rates der Evangelischen Kirche in Deutschland* (Gütersloh, 1979).

18. *Zur Erneuerung des Verhältnisses von Christen und Juden. Handreichung für Mitglieder der Landessynode, der Kreissynoden, und der Presbyterien in der Evangelischen Kirche im Rheinland* (Mühlheim, 1980) [the English translation is in *The Church and the Jewish People*, newsletter of the World Council of Churches,

no. 1 (Geneva 1980), p. 20–22]; Frank Littell, "A Milestone in Post-Holocaust Church Thinking," *Christian News from Israel* 27, no. 3 (1980):113–116.

19. D. Bonhoeffer, *Ethics* [English translation] (London, 1955), p. 50.

20. B. Kappert and H. Starck, eds., *Umkehr und Erneuerung, Erläuterungen zum Synodalbeschluss der Rheinischen Landessynode 1980* (Neukirchen, 1980); P. von der Osten-Sacken, *Grundzüge einer Theologie im christlich jüdischen Gespräch*, Abhandlungen zum christlich-jüdischen Dialog, no. 12 (Munich, 1982).

21. See, for example, the "Erwägungen zur kirchlichen Handreichung zur Erneuerung des Verhältnisses von Christen und Juden" [Declaration of Thirteen Theology Professors of the University of Bonn], reprinted in *Evangelischer Pressedienst*, no. 412/80 (Frankfurt/Main, September 1980).

22. Ibid.

23. See the extensive arguments in Ginzel, ed., *Auschwitz als Herausforderung*, and R. Rendtorff and E. Stagemann, *Auschwitz-Krise der Christlichen Theologie*, Abhandungen zum christlich-jüdischen Dialog, Band 10 (Munich, 1980).

24. M. Barth, *Jesus the Jew* (Atlanta, 1978), p. 24.

25. P. Van Buren, *Discerning the Way* (New York, 1980), p. 156.

26. G. Baum, in introduction to R. Ruether, *Faith and Fratricide: The Theological Roots of Anti-Semitism* (New York, 1974), pp. 5–6.

27. Quoted in H. Cronen, *Stepping Stones to Further Jewish-Christian Relations* (London, 1977), pp. 81–82.

28. Ibid., pp. 147–148.

29. "Ecumenical Considerations on Jewish-Christian Dialogue," *Current Dialogue*, no. 4 (Winter 1982-1983):11–12.

30. See Rendtorff, *Arbeitsbuch Christen und Juden*, p. 256.

31. See G. Seltzer and M. L. Stackhouse, eds., *The Death of Dialogue and Beyond* (New York, 1969).

32. Klappert and Starck, *Umkehr und Erneuerung*, p. 250.

33. World Council of Churches, *Invasion of Lebanon: Christian Response in Face of the Threat to Lebanese and Palestinian Existence* (Geneva, 1982), p. 34.

34. Ibid., p. 22.

35. World Council of Churches, *International Affairs at the Sixth Assembly, World Council of Churches,* (Geneva, 1983–1984), p. 28.

36. For a trenchant view of the situation in Israel outlining many of these dilemmas for the Christian conscience, written by a distinguished Anglican bishop, see K. Cragg, *This Year in Jerusalem* (London, 1982).

Part Three

Israel and Zionism

11

Is Anti-Zionism a New Form
of Antisemitism?

Dan V. Segre

In the great political and ideological debate waged around the Palestine question and the State of Israel there exists a fundamental cleavage of opinion on the nature and role of Zionism. For one side, Zionism is a progressive, democratic, liberal, secular liberation movement of the Jewish people, a successful reaction to oppression and colonialism, a nation-building effort inspired by the lofty ideals of prophetic messianism, and a precise political and historical phenomenon concerning only the revival of the Jewish people after a long period of dispersion and unmatched suffering. For the other side, or sides—which with overlapping variations include not only the Arabs and the Communist world but parts of the right and left Western intellectual and political estalishments, vast sections of the Third World leadership, and last but not least, a considerable number of Jews, liberal and orthodox—Zionism is the incarnation of total evil.

The recurring feature of this Manichean phenomenon among those who view Zionism as political, social, and religious satanism is the polarization, accumulation, and worldwide extension of the negative perception of the Jewish national movement. By *polarization* I mean the lack of gradualism in the hostility to Zionism. For those who oppose it, Zionism is not a bad political phenomenon; it is a cancerous growth, a monster. The ongoing state of war with the Arabs does not imply— as it does for other states—a situation of military occupation so much as one of automatic colonial racism, while the occasional victims of clashes between Arab civilians and Israeli forces (less than 500 in seventeen years of military occupation) represent a permanent "holocaust." The war in Lebanon has raised the negative eschatological dimension of Zionism to such a height that there seems to be no space for rational discussion. Every event seems to belong either to Hitler or to the Messiah—with nothing in between—when the tables are turned against the Zionists.

By *accumulation* I mean the process by which opposing, reciprocally exclusive elements are constantly being joined together in order to condemn Zionism and its supporters. They are at one and the same time Marxists and capitalists, weak and powerful, internationalists and nationalists, cowards and warlords, atheists and theocrats, Westerners and non-Westerners, racists and cosmopolitans, stooges of U.S. imperialism and bosses of the White House. Like the stereotype of the Jew under Nazi and Stalinist regimes, Zionists have ceased to be human beings. They have assumed mythological satanic roles and become symbols of the "other," the enemy, the carrier of all sins (Madaule, 1983).

By *worldwide extension* I mean the geographical diffusion of the image of Zionism as total evil, beyond the geographical area of the original conflict between Jewish and Arab nationalisms. When the radio of the Soviet Mongolian Republic accuses the Chinese of being Zionists, it obviously does not mean to tell the Chinese that they are Jewish. In the same way, when a French Communist automobile shop steward denounces a competing Socialist automobile workshop as "a band of Fascists and Zionists" (*Le Monde*, 13 August, 1983), he obviously does not intend to imply that the workers on the other side, many of them Muslims from North Africa, have become Israelis. In this propaganda context the word *Zionism* has lost all rational connotation with history and geography and assumed an autonomous derogatory meaning of its own. In the minds of those who use it in this sense, Zionism has a generalized aggressive meaning, supposedly understandable to all people, a universal derogatory value that, like the idea of God, transcends both time and space. By comparison, emotionally loaded political terms such as Fascism and Communism, Nazism and Imperialism, sound old-fashioned.

The current Israeli or pro-Zionist explanation of this extraordinary phenomenon is that anti-Zionism is just another metamorphosis of antisemitism and should be treated and fought against as such. This explanation is certainly valid for the Christian world—which of course includes most of the Communist world—because of the love/hate relationship of the churches with the Jews. For the Islamic world, in which the Arab-Israeli fight has for the last thirty years symbolized the historical conflict with the West, the antisemitic explanation is less valid. For people as different as the Zambians and the Vietnamese it simply makes no sense. Even if the Palestine conflict and its centrality in the mass media is taken into consideration, it does not justify the new, almost magic use of the word.

It therefore seems to me necessary to look elsewhere for at least part of the explanation of the anti-Zionist phenomenon. I submit that, grafted onto the old antisemitic root and the much publicized political, religious, and emotional drama of the Arab-Israeli conflict, there flourishes an element of fear that Zionism elicits in modern political society. It is a fear connected with the crisis of the idea of the national and transnational state, which has legitimized most of the contemporary international system. Originally developed in the West, this idea is becoming increasingly unadapted to the rest of the world.

Israel, of course, is not the only exception to the ideologically founded political system. Pakistan, for instance, is a "national" state built on and legitimized by a religious idea, originally promoted, as in the case of Zionism, by secular leaders such as Jinnah, and like the state of Israel, increasingly moving toward theocracy.

As for the transnational idea, Zionism stands halfway between a purely religious, anti-ideological state like the Vatican and a purely ideological, antireligious state like the Soviet Union. Neither, incidentally, has ever accepted Zionism. To this day the Vatican refuses, for political and theological reasons, to recognize the State of Israel.[1] The Soviet Union, on the other hand, for tactical reasons supported the partition of Palestine in 1947 and recognized the State of Israel, although it broke off relations in 1953 and again in 1967. But from the very beginning the Soviet state has strongly opposed Zionism and made anti-Zionism a permanent feature of Communist ideology and propaganda. The efforts displayed by the Soviet Union since 1975 to condemn Zionism as a racist movement at the UN are by no means due to political expediency: They are part and parcel of a deep-rooted ideological hostility to a political phenomenon that looks to them like a dangerous deviation from and a challenge to the modern political international system. In this sense, Zionism represents to the Soviet regime a problem paradoxically not very different from that of Iran under Khomeini, with its violent antisecularism and its relations with the Shi'ite diaspora outside Iran, the USSR included. Students of the nationality problem in the Soviet Union (Monteil, 1952; Bennigsen, 1975; Carrère d'Encausse, 1966) have stressed the vital importance attributed by the Soviets to the ideological war against all types of cultural and political trends among peoples in the Soviet empire whose affiliations or centers of identity reside outside the Communist sphere of influence and more specifically outside that of the USSR multinational system.

Commenting on the role of the Soviets in the promotion of the official denunciation of Zionism by the UN General Assembly in November 1975, Bernard Lewis (1976) noted the small ideological interest shown by the Arabs in their fight against Zionism compared with the enormous ideological efforts of anti-Zionism made by the USSR since the beginning of the Soviet regime. "For the Arabs the conflict over the Palestine question long antedates any interest on their part in Zionism. The extensive literature produced in the late 19th century until the period following World War II shows a remarkable lack of concern with Zionist theory and doctrine," the Palestine conflict being perceived by the Arabs essentially as the battle of two peoples for the possession of the same territory. In the Soviet Union, on the contrary, the fight against Zionism as an ideology preceded and followed the creation of the State of Israel and developed its logic independently of it. More specifically, in the technical vocabulary of Soviet vituperation, "the term racist is applied to nationalist movements linking the non-Slavic peoples of the Soviet Union with their kin elsewhere. . . . The charge of racism is often brought against such movements and its extension to Zionism—a kind of pan-Judaism with a *focus*, in Israel—is a development of its use against pan-Turkish and pan-Iranian movements" (Lewis 1976).

In all these cases, the importance of the enemy is weighed not in terms of its material strength but in terms of the possible disruptive ideological value for the transnational Soviet regime. The state created by the Zionist movement claims to be a national, secular state. Why should it in particular be chosen by its enemies to symbolize total evil? Granted all the direct and indirect factors composing the Middle East conflict, there seems to be some very particular cause for this selective hate: the enigma of Jewish existence. This enigma has much in common with the enigma that lies at the root of modern antisemitism and leads many people to see anti-Zionism as an extension of antisemitism, a perception I consider incorrect.

Hebrew University political sociologist Jacob Katz (1979) has shown how modern hostility toward the Jews (i.e., the particular form of hate for which Wilhelm Marr invented the term *antisemitism* in 1879) was not the cause of Zionism as is usually claimed but "rather modern antisemitism was itself a reaction to Jewish proto-nationalism." Katz cites the antisemitic writings of Bruno Bauer, Richard Wagner, and Schopenhauer against the inexplicable strength of the separate Jewish identity. This strength perturbed most of the antisemites because both Jewish and Christian traditions had once accounted for the phenomenon of Judaism and for its dispersion as divinely sanctioned. Once the Jewish question "became divested of this shielding interpretation by the growth of rationalism and historical criticism, Jewish existence turned into enigma."

I submit that this enigma—transferred from the individual to the political plane—is one of the new causes of worldwide hostility to Zionism. As in the case of the emancipated Jew, Israel seems to its enemies to be "divesting" itself from the "shielding interpretation" of the ideological rationale of secular nationalism to which Zionism claims to adhere. Israel, of course, meets some of the criteria by which modern nationalism defines the nation. On the one hand, Jews have in common customs, religious laws, and communal institutions. At least in the stereotyped image of both their enemies and their admirers, they appear to be a people with a strong common identity. But this identity is not only enigmatic but also disturbing and confusing. On the other hand, Jews do not have a common land of residence, do not share common historical experiences, do not speak the same language, do not even today have a common religion, inasmuch as the difference between an Orthodox Jew and a liberal Jew is greater than that between a Catholic and a Protestant. Nothing is more significant of the Zionist political enigma than the fact that a Jew cannot yet be officially defined as such in the only existing secular state of the Jews. Jewish nationalism, even in classic Zionism, does not retain the characteristics that seem to be typical and ever present (Berlin, 1979) in all types of nationalism—for instance, the belief in the overriding need to belong to a nation, which is certainly not that of the open, sacred elite promoted by Judaism, and the belief that the pattern of life of a society is similar to that of a biological organism, a similitude that finds no support in rabbinic tradition. The Talmud is extremely suspicious of all organic wholes and stresses the importance of education and discipline as against abstract ideas in the formation of the Jewish collective identity (Steinsaltz, 1976).

Another characteristic of nationalism is the belief in the value of our own, simply because it is ours—a concept diametrically opposed to the Jewish right of sacred use (not possession) of all goods, including the Promised Land. And, finally, there is the belief in the supremacy of the national claim when faced with contenders for authority and loyalty. On this last criterion of nationalism, the cleavage between Jewish and other nationalisms could not be more evident. Zionism never renounced the belief in the generality of moral values, in the validity of objective and eternal laws and rules that apply everywhere at all times to all men—a universalism advocated by the leaders of both the French and Jewish Enlightenments, out of which stemmed the principal impulse for the revival of modern political Judaism.[2]

The enigma of Jewish nationalism thus touches upon a fundamental issue of contemporary nationalism. It represents an ideologically and historically heretical position that neither a specific nationalism movement (such as Arabism) nor a universal secular "church" (like communism) can easily accept. To critics, Zionism looks like something straddling over two opposing concepts of society: one in which people realize themselves in the selective particularistic morality of étatism and socialism, and the other in which they realize themselves in the universal, unchanging morality of a transcendental scheme camouflaged by Jewish étatism or socialism. This conflict, which in a sense revives the uniqueness of Jewish destiny among the new nations of the Third World, can have (or at least looks as though it has) a direct relation to a central political problem of our time—the inability of ideological regimes to cope with the centrifugal process of separatist groups, whose identity is founded on nonideological principles such as religion, kinship, economic particularism, tabooism, or mafia solidarity. Biafra, Kurdistan, Southern Sudan, Bangladesh, Eritrea, Corsica, Ireland, Montenegro, and Sicily are cases in point. They are all linked in one way or another by one common feature: The process—called "decolonization" in new states and "decentralization" in old ones—can no longer be stopped by political ideology, especially when it takes place in multi-ethnic countries with territories arbitrarily carved out by foreign powers. As for the Soviet colonial empire, it is difficult to believe that it will escape the fate of other colonial systems simply because Marxists believe that colonialism is a capitalist sin and that transnational communism has solved the nationality problem. Obviously it has not—and the fact that Zionism is both a religious and a hybrid national movement makes it particularly irksome to the Soviet regime. Those who still believe that contemporary Soviet anti-Zionism is a phenomenon dictated mainly by circumstantial considerations linked with Soviet interests in the Arab world would do well to read the official protocols of the trials of Rudolf Slansky and other Jewish Communist leaders in Prague in 1952. Slansky has since been rehabilitated, but the accusation against Zionism as a world conspiracy stands as strong as ever.

Anti-Zionism might, however, not have been so virulent had its challenge—real or imaginery—to the ideologically based states not coincided with the crisis of national and transnational institutions on the one hand, and with the explosion of the postindustrial, science-based technological revolution on the other.

Political scientists are becoming increasingly aware of the changes in economic and military power that allow a country to emerge not because of its natural resources or its population but because of its ability to exploit new technological breakthroughs. Here again the Zionist experience is for many people a reason and a justification for blind hostility—and this by virtue of two major causes: the change brought into political geography by the information revolution, and the advantages offered in the postindustrial era by cultural marginalism to Diasporas with strong identity links.

It was, I believe, Lenin who said that communism was a combination of socialism and electricity. The question today concerns the opposite: Can communism or any other form of centralized ideological political existence survive while science and technology are putting so much destructive power into the hands of separatist groups, and information (the French word, *informatique*, is better) is radically transforming relationships among men?

Obviously the mere fact that a state is big, populous, and rich in raw materials is no longer a guarantee of political strength. Japan, which was once defined as a "museum of raw materials" because all its natural resources could be contained within a museum, has become a major power *because* it is poor in natural resources (Cleveland and Abdel Rahman, 1981). Similar examples are Singapore, Southern Korea, and Israel.[3] It is true, of course, that while new centrifugal forces are operating in contemporary political society, others are still working in the opposite, centripetal direction. For instance, it has been noted (Ben-Dor, 1983) that in the Middle East the weakening of the pan-Arab nationalist ideology has coincided with the consolidation of "national" states with centralized regimes. Even in multi-ethnic countries such as Iraq, Kenya, or the Ivory Coast, there is a new feeling of collective identity overlapping the various tribal identities of minorities indiscriminately lumped together by colonial powers. But such a unifying process, far from contributing to the stability of the ideologically based national or transnational centralizing regimes, only increases their political and social problems.

Consider, for instance, what information does to political geography. Well back in the 1960s it had already become clear that the African businessperson or politician who could afford to travel by plane or use an air conditioner lived in a totally different world from the local farmer who, during the rainy season, say, could not even reach the nearest market place. Today, the individual who possesses an electronic means of communication can be in closer contact with a partner a thousand miles away than with somebody in the same region. This communications revolution, over which central governments are increasingly losing control, gives to once dispersed Diasporas a new dimension of operational unity. Khomeini ran the first successful political revolution by electronic proxy from a village in France, thousands of miles away from Iran. One does not have to relate to that dramatic example to understand the new power of dispersed minorities or terrorist groups. In many cases, this power is increased manifold by the cultural marginalism of politically motivated groups.

Psychologists and sociologists have long since recognized the sharpening of talents that marginal situations give to enterprising individuals. When one looks at the millennia-old, coordinated dispersion of the Jewish people, the very phenomenon that Jacob Katz (1979) shows to be one of the main causes of the fearful reaction of modern antisemitism to the Jewish enigma, it is easy to understand why in our postindustrial society the association of Jewish cultural marginalism with transnational Diaspora conditions and with the emergence of such a "hybrid" national state as Israel provokes strong, irrational, negative reactions. Whether Zionism will eventually have an impact on the political aspirations of active or dormant dispersed minorities such as the Armenians, the Kurds, the Copts, the Chinese, the Ibo, or the Parsi is a matter of pure speculation. It has already affected the Palestinians, who certainly owe their international influence to their cultural marginalism, their dispersion, and the intelligent use of technological resources. Paradoxically, they are increasingly becoming Arab "Zionists" with some of the negative connotations (for the Arab states) attributed by anti-Zionist propaganda to the Jews. This is a natural result of the prolonged conflict and coexistence of the two peoples in the same physical and political territory.

But why should the leaders of national and transnational states, especially those who know so little about Judaism and Jewish history, take a light view of the Israeli precedent and believe that it will remain restricted *only* to the Jewish case? Although many people with mystical expectations of the Zionist experiment may feel frustrated by its "parochial" behavior (to the point of turning against it, as many Jews and non-Jews have done), it would be naive to think that others who are sensitive to the crisis of the centralized ideological regime should not come to believe in the worldwide "conspiracy of Zionism."

At least part of the violence, the incongruity, the new eschatological nature of anti-Zionism, stems from such a perception. Indeed, for those who fear the consequences of the momentous changes taking place in modern society, the temptation is great to switch the *symptoms* of change for the *cause* of unwanted change, and to equate the former with evil. In this sense, there exists a clear parallelism between anti-Zionism and antisemitism, insofar as Judaism and Zionism act as indicators of the social, moral, and political crises of their environment. But Judaism and Zionism are by no means the only objects of vulgar, instinctive reactions on the part of those for whom breaking the thermometer appears to be a means of curing the fever: The persecution of Indians in Africa, of the Bahai in Iran, of the Armenians in Turkey, all have points in common with the persecution of Jews. Yet here again the message of Zionism may have a different significance, independent of its direct or indirect political impact.

For early promoters of Africanism such as Edward Blyden, Marcus Garvey, or W. E. Burghardt Du Bois (Blyden, 1873, 1898; Cronon, 1964; Du Bois, 1947), Zionism had been seen as an inspiration for the liberation of the blacks. Even for later black political writers, Zionism was not simply an imitation of European nationalism (Fanon, 1970) insofar as it was concerned with human dignity and cultural self-assertion as much as, if not more than, with political independence. The fact that sovereignty has often been attained without a concurrent process of cultural de-colonization has plunged many Third World societies into a crisis of identity that explodes in all sorts of radicalism. The crisis of identity of the Jews, who in very great numbers abandoned their traditional values in favor of those of the Western society from which Zionism drew its inspiration, took place—and is still developing—in historical circumstances totally different from those experienced by African peoples.

I have, however, tried to show (Segre, 1980) that psychologically there exist some interesting similitudes between the Jews and the Africans to the extent that both groups have experienced a crisis of self-confidence owing to the breakup of a traditional way of life that served as the sole consistent matrix of group identity. This raises the question, seldom asked by students of Israeli politics, of how culturally colonized the State of Israel is. But it also raises the question, uneasily touched upon even by African scholars unfriendly to Zionism (Mazrui, 1969), of the direct or indirect impact that the emergence of such a modern and at the same time culturally colonized polity as Israel can have on the intellectual elites of the Third World, particularly in connection with the problem of legitimacy of power (Ekeh, 1975). Both societies—the Jewish and the African—have to face similar dilemmas. One is how to graft foreign culture and modernization onto an ancient, indigenous, non-Western root. Another is how to act and react in situations in which the search for a collective identity clashes with the desire and the need for change, both of which call for a growing acceptance of alien cultures.

A third dilemma is how to shake off stereotypes created by hostile environments that have made it difficult for both groups to regard themselves objectively—"to deal with illusions born of the accusations of others and through self rejection, just as myths were created to counter the accusations" (Memmi, 1971).

Just as archeology in Palestine is never simply archeology, given that the simple uncovering of the past is inevitably accompanied by anticipation, however fearful, of some unknown future, so the emergence of the Jewish State on the political map of the world represents something more encompassing, potentially promising, and awe inspiring than the appearance of just another state.

It is therefore understandable, if by no means justifiable, that such a hybrid nationalism should raise such strong reactions. The identification of Zionism with total contemporary political evil, no less than that of the Jew of the past with moral and social satanism, is therefore a part of a psychological mechanism that draws its neurotic energy from primeval fears and its logic from the need to exorcise developmental situations with which no rational ideology or power structure seems able to cope.

The historical, emotional connection of Zionism with antisemitism and the involvement of the Jews in the long and much publicized Middle East crisis serve as a propellant of anti-Zionism, but they do not wholly explain its nature. Anti-Zionism, therefore, is not a simple extension and dramatization of old-new antisemitism. The two have common roots, but anti-Zionism possesses a logic of its own, a logic that has inspired a worldwide campaign of hate against 4 million Jews who have created a state on a territory smaller than the island of Sicily—the reason being that, in spite of its declared restricted national aims, this state represents something both different from all other ideological national states and far more significant than it claims to be.

Churchill once said that the creation of the State of Israel would in time be considered the major historical event of the twentieth century. He may well have been more correct in that assessment than most Zionists today are prepared to admit.

Notes

1. When Theodor Herzl visited Pope Pius X in 1904, he was met by theological hostility because the Holy See found it difficult to conceive of the return of the Jews to Palestine or to accept that, if such an event were to take place, it should be carried out by secular liberal Jews. As late as 1922, Cardinal Gasparri, the Vatican secretary of state, said to Weizmann that he feared The Hebrew University—not the Zionist agricultural pioneering work (*Encyclopedia Judaica*, pp. 76–77).

2. This paradox, by the way, explains why the PLO has put so much effort into denying the existence of a Jewish nation and into making a distinction between Jews, whom they claim to respect, and Zionists whom—as the embodiment of evil—they pretend to fight in the name of world justice and for

the benefit of humanity as a whole. Incidentally, the position of some extreme orthodox Jews is not very different ideologically.

3. Israel, which in the 1950s probably led the world in solar energy research, lost its lead in 1967, as soon as it captured Sinai with its oil wells. One of the most backward branches of Israeli industry today is construction, in which the widespread employment of Arab labor has hampered mechanization and modernization.

References

Ben-Dor, Gabriel, 1983. *State and Conflict in the Middle East.* New York.

Bennigsen, Alexandre A., 1975. "The Crisis of the Turkic National Epics 1951–1952: Local Nationalism or Internationalism?" *Canadian Slavonic Papers* 17, nos. 2–3: 433–474.

Berlin, Isaiah, 1979. *Against the Current, Nationalism, Past Neglect and Present Power.* London. Pp. 333–335.

Blyden, Edward W., 1873. *From West Africa to Palestine.* London.

————, 1898. *The Jewish Question.* Liverpool.

Du Bois, W. E. Burghardt, 1947. *The World and Africa.* New York.

————, 1972. In H. L. Moon, ed., *The Emerging Thought of W.E.B. DuBois.* New York.

d'Encausse, H. Carrère, 1966. *Réforme et révolution chez les Musulmans de l'empire russe.* Paris.

Cleveland, Harlan, and I. H. Abdel Rahman, 1981. "Dynamism and Development." In *World Development*, vol. 8. Pp. 275–290.

Cronon, Edmund D., 1964. *Black Moses, The Story of Marcus Garvey and the Universal Negro Improvement Association.* Madison.

Ekeh, Peter P., 1975. "Colonization and the Two Publics in Africa." *Comparative Studies in Sociology and History*, no. 1. Pp. 91–112.

Encyclopedia Judaica, vol. 16. 1972. Jerusalem. Pp. 76–77.

Fanon, Frantz, 1970. *Towards the African Revolution.* London. Pp. 41–45.

Katz, Jacob, 1979. "Zionism vs. Anti-Semitism." *Commentary* 67, no. 4 (April): 46–52.

Lewis, Bernard, 1976. "The Anti-Zionist Resolution." *Foreign Affairs* 55, no. 1:54–64.

Madaule, Jacques, 1983. *Israël et le Poids de l'Election.* Paris.

Mazrui, Ali A., 1969. *Towards a Pax Africana—A Study of Ideology and Ambition.* London. P. 11.

Memmi, Albert, 1971. *Dominated Man.* Boston. P. 15.

Monteil, Vincent, 1952. "Essai sur l'Islam en URSS." *Revue des Etudes Islamiques.* Pp. 107–125.

Segre, Dan, 1980. *A Crisis of Identity: Israel and Zionism.* New York.

Steinsaltz, Adin, 1976. *The Essential Talmud.* London.

12

Anti-Zionism—A Global Phenomenon

Nathan Glazer

In early 1984, the bookstores in Cambridge, Massachusetts, were featuring displays of books on the war and the continuing crisis in Lebanon: There had been a number of books published simultaneously and it was a good moment for them to make such a display. The display would not have made any friend of Israel or of Zionism happy. The books on the war in Lebanon were all hostile to Israel. Some were by well-known foreign correspondents with established newspapers. Some were from well-known antagonists of Israel, publishing with small publishers, but nevertheless with considerable influence (for example, Noam Chomsky). There was the report of an international commission highly critical of Israel headed by Sean McBride. (One book available at the time was a demonstration—from an American writer, not from a Soviet or Arab one—of the close links between Zionism and Nazism.) One noticed two books from authors with Arab names—one translated from the German. Even the one book from an Israeli source was the report of the Kahan Commission on the massacres in the Beirut Palestinian refugee camps.

It was clear that the friend of Israel could not find much in the bookstores of Cambridge, in the country with the largest number of Jews and the most solid supporter of Israel, to defend Israel's actions in Lebanon. The interpretations ranged from the only slightly neutral and hostile to the most extreme hostility. The only views available from Israel reflected internal criticism. One had to conclude that for the ordinary literate American, the balance of available material on Israel and the Zionist movement had shifted radically from the fare that was available up until the 1970s or so.

One still finds more sympathy for Israel and Zionism in the United States than in any other country. Not long ago, an Italian-American

This paper was presented to the Centre for Contemporary Studies' symposium *Anti-Semitism and Anti-Zionism: The Link*, held at the Royal Society of Arts in London in June 1984. It was subsequently published in the record of proceedings and is reproduced here by kind permission of CCS.

who had lived in Italy for a long time and who directed a conference centre for an American foundation asked me why everyone he knew was against Zionism, and why most of his friends thought it was a form of fascism, and was it so? One had to take a long breath before one could answer such a question. The more interesting question is, how has it come about that in a country without any major tradition of antisemitism, which we would all take to be friendlier to Jews than Germany, perhaps France, whose Jewish community was more closely integrated with the national experience than that of perhaps any other West European nation, such a question can be asked?

Anti-Israelism

In order to explain why such a question can be asked, we have to make some distinctions. We deal not only, I would argue, with two different if closely linked phenomena when we deal with antisemitism and anti-Zionism, but also with two other phenomena, anti-Israelism and anti-Israeli-governmentism. (One can no longer say anti-Beginism.) There are good reasons why so many Jews feel that an attack on Zionism is not simply an attack on one political movement of the Jewish people— a movement which, we may recall, was probably in a minority among Jews until the early 1940s. It is more than understandable that we see it as a reflection of the age-old hostility against the Jews in the Christian and the Muslim world. There seems such a strong element of ignorance, of malevolence, of sheer malice in the attack on Zionism that it is hard to see in it any part of legitimate political opposition to a political movement. It is also understandable—though I would argue with somewhat less justification—that we would see attacks on Israel as reflecting this age-old anti-Jewish feeling. Few of us would see attacks on the Israeli government of the moment as necessarily reflecting antisemitism— though once again any attack on it may exhibit aspects that would lead us to suspect that. But I do think all these forms of antagonism are different, and each has to be analysed in its own terms.

Zionism as an Agent

Let us explore another hypothesis: that the special situation of the state of Israel and the policies of its government arouse a hostility that is widespread, that finds some support in antisemitism, but that are perhaps now themselves a main support of antisemitism.

In this sequence of antisemitism, Zionism, Israel, and the government of Israel, Zionism stands as a mysterious middle element. If it is the existence of the state of Israel and its policies that arouse hostility, why do we find a worldwide attack on Zionism? Is this not merely a concealed form of simple antisemitism? Antisemitism having been given a bad name (though not everywhere in the world) by Hitler, Jew-hatred no longer expresses itself in the form of attacks on the Jewish religion or race, so much as in attacks on a political philosophy and movement that is clearly Jewish, and whose history and significance most people are unaware of. There is also the fortuitous accident that "Zionism" bears the same name for the Jews as we find in "the elders of Zion," who, in a notorious forgery, it was claimed, were plotting to control the world, and whose "protocols" still circulate widely in Arab countries. Mysterious Zionism thus serves to direct the age-old hostility against the Jews to the same people, under a slightly different rubric.

But now to our problem. It is not only the enemies of Jews and Israel who have turned Zionism into a mystery; it is the history of the Jewish people themselves that has made the term mysterious because the creation of the State of Israel left the Zionist movement without an obvious and easily explainable function.

For Jews and Zionists, this was only a problem. For non-Jews, it was not a problem but a confusion, or truly something of a mystery.

The Zionist movement was created, existed to build a national home for the homeless and widely persecuted Jewish people in Palestine. While the Zionist movement struggled, it was scarcely necessary for antisemites to raise the spectre of Zionism to arouse fear and hatred of Jews. The Jewish presence, in those countries where antisemitism was strong, was the spur to antisemitism: A movement to create a national home for Jews in a distant country hardly mattered in making friends or enemies for Jews in Western Europe or the United States, though it mattered greatly in the Arab world.

The creation of the Jewish state, as all were aware at the time, raised a problem for Zionism. What was a movement to create a national home for the Jewish people in Israel when that home already existed? Was its purpose to encourage all possible Jews to move there? Was its purpose simply to support the new state of Israel in whatever tasks it undertook? To help defend it against a ring of enemies? Who would now run the Zionist movement? The Jews in the Diaspora? In Israel? The government of Israel? There was always the possibility and indeed the reality of conflict between the movement and the state. These were problems for the Jewish people, and they were in fact resolved, if not to the satisfaction of all. The state now had the power, and held clearly the upper hand.

The movement continued to exist: It was an adjunct to the state. It mobilised the Jews of the world to support the state. The philosophy itself of Zionism became irrelevant. The Zionist movement simply became the form (and only one form) in which Jews around the world, but primarily in the Western world, where they were both numerous and free, supported the state of Israel. In that there was no mystery—nor should there have been any.

But history insists on placing the Jews in exceptional positions, whatever the strength of their desire to "normalise" their position in the world—and Zionism was pre-eminently a movement to "normalise" the Jewish position, to give them a state, a normal occupational distribution, secular laws, and everything all other peoples had.

The astounding success of Zionism in truly creating a national home, embodied in a small but powerful state, did not normalise the position of the Jewish people. It could not, because it is not, in the eyes of much of the world, a "normal" state. There are three major reasons.

The Zionist State as "Suspect"

The first was that the state was established under conditions of unremitting hostility, now sustained for more than 35 years. Israel is a country permanently surrounded by enemies. Its supporters—the Jews of the rest of the world—must expect to draw upon themselves the hostility of its enemies. And they do. Other states have enemies too, other wars have festered, cold or hot, for many decades (consider Kashmir, and India and Pakistan), but the situation of the Jewish state is unique in the *number* of its enemies, and in its inability, except for the exceptional case of Egypt, to moderate their hostility in any way.

A second reason Israel failed to become "normal" was that it was denied legitimacy by much of the world. The state was given an immediate international legitimacy by the recognition of the super powers and the major nations of Europe. It was provided with a remarkably effective army through the resources of the small Jewish community of Palestine, assisted by contributions from Jews in the United States and other countries, by states who found it for a while in their interest to support or sell arms to Israel, and finally by the United States. But despite the substantial degree of legality, of legitimacy and this *de facto* power, it is still unrecognized as legitimate by all its neighbours but one. These neighbours are linked to all the countries of the Arab world, all the countries of the Muslim world, to the "third world" of states emerging from European colonialism. All have been pulled into the denial of legitimacy of Israel. Unimportant as the recognition of Israel by a host of minor powers may be, in practical terms, it is [in a] unique and anomalous position: Only South Africa is in the same position.

The third reason the state failed to still doubts as to its normality is its special relationship to the Jewish people, particularly as mediated through the Jewish religion. It is this that gives the only colour of plausibility to the equation "Zionism is racism." To deal with it one not only has to understand Zionism, but Judaism; and not only understand Zionism and Judaism, but also the politics of the Jewish people and the state of Israel. So equipped, one knows that the charge that Zionism is racism is an outrageous lie. But there is a tiny node of meaning wrapped up in the "Zionism is racism" equation. The node is the fact that Israel, because it was established under the ideology of Zionism, as a home for the Jewish people, must be a home for all the Jewish people; because of its internal politics (and possibly not only because of that) it must accept the Orthodox religious definition of "who is a Jew," and must consider such questions as, are Indian Jews of the oldest Indian Jewish communities, are Falashas, are American blacks who claim to be converted, truly Jews? The issue is not racism but as a result of this chain of religious, historical and political circumstances, Zionism, overwhelmingly a *secular* movement for the *national liberation* of Jews, can be attacked as racist.

Zionism, Racism, and National Liberation

One wonders why it is Israel, Zionism, and the Jew should be made to bear this cross. The situation is not unique. Can one be a Christian and a Saudi? I believe not.

But there is a reason for it that has nothing to do with religion: It is that discrimination on grounds of *race*—descent—is the only form of discrimination that the entire world is ready to condemn. A state can torture its political enemies, religious minorities, the rich or the poor, and manage to escape without the world's opprobrium; not so if the line is drawn on *racial* grounds. The once dominant white race condemns such behaviour; so do the formerly subordinate races.

Would the situation be any different if the definition of Jew used by the state of Israel in implementing its law of return were one that was purely secular? But the question answers itself almost as soon as it is asked. There is no usable definition of the Jews aside from the religious one that defines a Jew by birth, and by conversion. The only alternative available is the truly racial definition of the Nazis—that was secular, and ignored rabbinic authority. The secular definition of Western societies—"one looked upon as a Jew and who considers himself a Jew"—would not serve. It would arouse the outrage of the powerful Orthodox minority, would cut a two-thousand-year chain of history that defines who are these people who claim their ancient land. The religious definition that prevails in Israel and is used to police those who want to enter the State and join the people creates enormous difficulties for Israelis themselves, and for many Jews wanting to settle in Israel. It is hardly surprising that it would not be easy to explain, and that Israel's enemies would seize upon it. To believe that they would really 'know' that Zionism is not racism, and Jews are not racist, would be to give them too much credit in understanding the complexities of Jewish history, Judaism, Zionism and Israel.

But the entire discussion is beside the point. Israel was established to become a *Jewish* national home. Even the binationalists were not thinking of a merged or integrated society of Jew and Arab. That was not the hope of Judah Magnes, or of the Hashomer Hatzair. Binationalism was a *political* solution—it assumed each community would live separately, apart. For the Jews, that was the reason they were coming to Palestine—so they could live in a society in which they were not a minority. For the Arabs the question did not arise: They were the original settlers, they saw no need, at the least, to merge with or integrate with the newcomers.

In Israel we have a society in which integration is not the ideal, in which a people who once permanently lived as an endangered minority now wish to become a majority—more than a majority, they hope for a state only for Jews, free of non-Jews. *That* is the idea. Leave aside, then, the religious definition of Jew with its odd insistence on birth as the legitimating sign. How could a community trying to create itself in the midst of another people as a majority have escaped the charge of racism?

Zionists, Israelis, Jews—and I—argue it is not like that at all; Zionism is a liberal and progressive nationalist movement. Its forebears are those who created the unity of Italy and Germany, the freedom of Czechoslovakia, Hungary, Finland. But these fortunate 19th and early 20th century nationalists did not have to decide *who* was an Italian, or a Finn, or a Czech, or a Slovak, or how to concentrate them in a country of their own—the answers were given by history; the nations already existed as massive concentrations of people on a common soil, with a common language, a common history (even if it had to be created), and often a common religion. But the Zionists had to create such a majority and concentration in a country which was already inhabited by another people.

Liberal and progressive and democratic intentions were undermined by reality. Since there was war, it was imprudent to allow Arabs to serve in the army. It was imprudent to allow them sensitive positions in administration. The way they taught their children had to be checked— one would not want them to be taught hatred of Jews. Areas of exclusive Arab settlement had to be policed, controlled, administered. How could one avoid the charge of racism? And the strain of long decades of intense preparation for war, repeated wars, inevitably produced its racist sentiments, incidents, attitudes. In a democratic society which had been so widely admired, these made news. The miracles of the desert reclaimed, the collective colony flourishing, the making of a people out of a hundred ethnic groups, became old hat. That Jews were becoming anti-Arab and exclusively nationalist *was* news. It is the case that a democratic society does not produce good propaganda for itself.

Antisemitism and Anti-Zionism?

The charge that Zionism is racism arises because the state of Israel is surrounded by enemies who of course use every weapon to attack it, and one of the most effective in the current climate is the charge of racism. There is also a peculiarity we have explored that permits the charge to be made.

Now we have to explore, however, the question with which we began. Has antisemitism transmuted itself into anti-Zionism, which is legitimated by the formal actions of a hundred states and the United Nations? To some modest measure. But let us limit the degree to which we accept this idea. The fact is most of those hundred states that follow the Arab lines have no Jews at all in them. Many of those that do are not marked by antisemitism at all (consider India, where there has never been any prejudice against Jews). Some states simply go along because of Arab money, or because of loyalty to the varied groups of third world states in the United Nations, or because of Muslim minorities that would make trouble if they did not, or for other reasons that have nothing to do with antisemitism.

The Muslim nations, one must say, are truly anti-Jewish, for the most part. Islam believes the existence of the Jewish state is a terrible affront to the expected worldwide victory of the true faith. Arabs and Muslims are anti-Israel and anti-Jewish. And they borrow and distribute anti-semitic literature from Europe (such as the *Protocols of the Elders of Zion*) to express their anti-Jewishness, and to try to show [that] the small state they cannot overcome is in some way bolstered by powerful and malevolent forces. However we interpret the connections between the anti-Israelism, anti-Jewishness, or antisemitism of Arab and Muslim states, they have become places in which Jews cannot live with any dignity or safety. By now, hardly any do.

The common view that anti-Zionism is a cover for antisemitism seems to make the most sense in a Christian (or ex-Christian world). I include Russia and Eastern Europe in the category. We find an endemic popular antisemitism in Eastern Europe. On the other hand, I find it doubtful that this endemic antisemitism needs any cover in the form of anti-Zionism.

The Jews of Eastern Europe were hated before they became Zionists. Indeed, that is why they became Zionists. Anti-Zionism in Eastern Europe, or more specifically in the Soviet Union, is rather the ideology of the government, with which it tries to court popularity with Arab, Muslim, and other third world states, and with its own people. The Communist government can cynically claim to be maintaining its early opposition to antisemitism while reassuring its people it is really antisemitic at heart; otherwise, why the antisemitic words and images in the attack on Zionism? There are differences between the antisemitic people and anti-Zionist government: Russian antisemites would prefer to see the Jews leave rather than—as the government does—keep them in Russia.

Does the fierce anti-Zionism of the government reflect antisemitism among the high officialdom too? Probably, but does it matter? Its anti-Zionism or antisemitism is based on the decision that the Soviet interest would be best advanced by alliance with the Arab and Muslim world and the third world. By now, too, there is often legitimate suspicion of Jewish loyalty to the Soviet Union. But why should Jews be loyal when they are portrayed as murderous Hitlerites, blood-suckers, exploiters?

In Soviet Russia, anti-Zionism has become the official name of a full-fledged state antisemitism.

In Western Europe, I believe, anti-Zionism is most widely spread and most honestly believed in. This is owing to the strength of sympathy for third world countries among the young and on the left. Israel is engaged in permanent war against a ring of third world states, a war in the course of which many Arabs have left or been forced out. For Western leftists, Israel is too strong, too victorious, too Western, and looks too much like their own colonisers of the past, who have now been fully rejected, to attract the sympathy or understanding of Western leftists. Israel is in fact a state created by Europeans, in a country inhabited by non-Europeans, and one in which the European element holds the upper hand. It is very hard to explain to young people and leftists why Israel is different from a colonising Britain, France, Holland, Belgium, Germany, Italy, etc. It looks too much alike. It is true that in the aftermath of the Holocaust, and while Israel was still small, weak, poor, and was taking in the Holocaust survivors and the persecuted Jews of Arab countries, a different view of Israel prevailed on the left. But all this has changed: Israel has won too many wars, and has fought a major war, that was not instigated by immediate fear of destruction. It is less and less inclined to return majority Arab areas, and seems prepared to govern them forever, or even to expel the inhabitants. Under the circumstances, it is hardly likely one will find much sympathy for Israel on the left, and one does not.

On the right, and in government circles, such issues as concern for exports, for oil supplies, for friendly third world trading partners and buyers of military goods, will always ensure considerable support for Arabs. Is this antisemitism? For the most part, no. It is self-interest on the right, it is ideology on the left. It is hard to counter either.

We come to the United States. Is anti-Zionism a cover for antisemitism? I think not. There has been a lot of antisemitism in the United States in the past. There is much less now. There used to be overwhelming sympathy for Israel in the United States in the past. There is less now. Understandably, Israel fights wars that American policy makers think it should not, gets more than $2 billion of aid a year, has an enormously effective lobby which frustrates policy makers and angers elected officials who will, nevertheless, not go against it. On the popular level, there is also a modest weakening of support for Israel, again understandable. The fact is Israel is too strong, and comes across badly on television. Even when a bus is hijacked, the pictures shown on American television are [of] the houses of the hijackers being blown up and their mothers and aunts grieving over the ruins. There are no television men on hijacked buses showing the terror of the passengers. If Israel were weaker, or appeared weaker, it would have more sympathy. Does it want to be, or appear weaker?

But this is anti-Israelism, not anti-Zionism or antisemitism. I do not believe there is a wide underground stream of antisemitism in the United States ready to be tapped.

Anti-Israeli-Governmentalism

Which brings me to the last of the four antis, anti-Israeli-governmentalism. Unfortunately for euphony, we cannot say anti-Beginism. This is strong in the United States. It was not only a media problem, in that Sadat came across better than Begin. It was also a matter of policies. Begin insisted on planting settlements in the midst of Arabs. He presided over a war that was initiated on planting settlements in the midst of Arabs. He presided over a war that was initiated by no apparent threat to Israel's security. He dismissed American government efforts to bring peace to the Middle East. His successors do the same. The issue is policies, not personality, though personality did not help.

Conclusion

With our four antis, we deal with a complex phenomenon, or a group of phenomena. But in dealing with them, let us not take the easy explanation that Jews are permanently threatened by the world simply because they *are* Jews, and that anti-Zionism is its current form, succeeding attacks on Jewish religion and on Jewish race with attacks on the Jewish state and all who support it. The fact is that the policies of Israel's government are not fore-ordained, but are forged by a democratic polity trying to meet the problems of a difficult and hostile world. In adopting those policies, it makes enemies. Perhaps one of the reasons that the United States and Americans are still most sympathetic to Israel, and Israel's dilemma, is that they have one of their own: They too are forced to use power in what they conceive of as the national interest and the interest of the democratic world, and find less sympathy in making their difficult choices than they would like.

13
Zionism as Racism: A Semantic Analysis

Arthur Hertzberg

Since the early years of the nineteenth century, first in Europe and then in Africa and Asia, national liberation movements have arisen to drive out foreign or colonial rulers in the name of the right of self-determination of nations. These revolutionaries have spoken for peoples resident in their lands. Inasmuch as very few regions contain only one people or one tribe, new nations have often been faced by revolts by minorities demanding their own self-realization. Such minorities have usually spoken, in their turn, for their right to rule in their own province. When faced by such conflicts, new states have often become even more oppressive then their former masters. It has thus remained true that, since the beginning of nationalism as a political force, the base for political aspiration has been the territory. Claimants to independent national identities have put forward their particular and unique associations with their lands and cultures as the claim of the nation to have its own sovereign political institutions.

Zionism as a national movement is the striking exception to this rule. Here the process has been reversed. Toward the end of the nineteenth century, when Zionism began in earnest, the Jewish population in the land of the ancestors was less than 10 percent; Jews had not been in the Holy Land in any great numbers for at least twelve or thirteen centuries. The national language, Hebrew, was still alive, universal among Jews as the language of prayer, of learned books, and even of some business correspondence, especially between Ashkenazim and Sephardim. It had long, however, ceased to be the common tongue of all Jews in daily usage. Zionism drew upon religion and historical memory to assert a claim to return to the land and to reestablish there the full national life and identity that the centuries of "exile" had interrupted.

Many writers and polemicists, Jews and non-Jews alike, expressed doubts from the very beginnings of Zionism as to whether it could qualify as a valid national movement. The fair-minded among these critics were willing to acknowledge that there was something unique in the Jewish memory of and passion for the Holy Land, the land of their biblical ancestors; but most of these critics suggested that there were ways other than Zionism of translating these memories into modern politics. Ethical universalists suggested that the biblical message itself had been broadened by the prophets to separate the religion proclaimed at Sinai from any rootedness in a specific people and territory. Jewish revolutionaries who were influenced by Karl Marx were mostly antinationalist, particularly in relation to Jewish nationalism; they argued that the victory of the proletariat was the great hope for humanity and that such a victory would end antisemitism forever. Some Marxists, Jewish and non-Jewish alike, even reinterpreted the Bible as a record of class struggle and defined the prophets as the advocates of the dispossessed; they were leaders of lower-class protest against the rich, and they were, thus, forerunners of those who in the modern age would finally effect the triumph of a just social order. For most of the nineteenth century, these ideas were more powerful than Jewish nationalism.

Modern Zionism existed, by theory very nearly full-blown by the 1830s, very near the dawn of nationalism in Europe as a revolutionary force, but it lay dormant for a half century. During the middle decades of the nineteenth century, it was still widely believed in Europe, and especially by Jews, that Western liberalism was on the rise and that it would eventually reach even czarist Russia. The Jews would ultimately achieve equal rights in law and equal treatment in society everywhere, and thus the question of Jewish nationalism, which posited the return of many, or even most, Jews to the land of Israel, seemed simply a theoretical dream. Zionist nationalism became a serious political option and necessity, at least in some views, as a result of a rising antisemitism in Europe in the last decades of the nineteenth century. Its most virulent form, including large-scale pogroms, was native to czarist Russia, but it existed everywhere in one form or another and with renewed vigor in Western and Central Europe. In France, groups that hated the results of the French Revolution expressed themselves in the antisemitic incitements of the Dreyfus Affair. In Germany, Richard Wagner gave currency to Aryan racialist doctrines, which were soon expressed in politics by the pan-German movement. In Austria, Karl Lueger led an antisemitic party to repeated victories in Vienna before and after the turn of the century. In Hungary and Bohemia, there were blood libel accusations, revivals of the ancient canard that Jews slaughtered Christian children before Passover in order to use their blood in the baking of matzoh.

Many Jews wanted to believe that even these attacks were a last gasp of dying Jew-hatred, but some, such as Leon Pinsker in Russia in 1882 and Theodor Herzl in Paris and Vienna in 1895, decided that the renewed antisemitism was not a passing phenomenon. This hatred had declared Jews to be aliens in Europe; it had asserted that Jews were members of an alien people that was not assimilable. At this point in

Jewish and European history, when masses of Jews, in the hundreds of thousands, were fleeing from Eastern Europe in search of a new life, the Zionists put on the political agenda a new answer to the question, How can a permanent ending of the tension between the Jewish minority and the various Gentile majorities among which it lived be realized?

In the 1880s and 1890s the justification for Zionist nationalism changed, at the very moment at which Zionism became a political force. It once was the plea to Jews to go and labor for their national liberation and equality, just as the other nations in the world (e.g., Greeks, Italians, and Hungarians) were doing. Under the impact of antisemitism, Zionism was much more concerned with the uniquely troubled relationship between Jews and Gentiles. The formula that created the modern Zionist movement was ultimately defined by Theodor Herzl. He did not merely appeal to the Jews to cease being a minority and to become a "normal" nation. He addressed himself to the powers of the world, to persuade them that it was in their interest to help found a Jewish state. Thus the nations would solve a problem of their own; they would end the turmoil caused within their own borders by negative encounters between Jews and non-Jews. The founding of a Jewish state would be an act of redress to Jews for their many centuries of living as a minority. Herzl asserted that whatever discomfort such a creation might cause the local Arabs of Palestine would be more than counterbalanced by the good that an advanced Western society, the Jews, would bring to the entire region. He emphasized, of course, that the Jewish State would conform to the highest standards of morality in its treatment of non-Jews within its borders.

In the language of our own day, Herzl's Zionism was a plea for "affirmative action." He was himself, culturally and religiously, a highly assimilated Jew. There is nothing in his writings of the pathos and passion of a deep relationship to the Jewish past. The "Jewish problem" for him was exclusion of Jews by the Gentile majority, and he wanted to correct it once and for all through Zionism. He knew that it would take unusual effort, which would be attended by temporary injury and dislocation of Jews and of some non-Jews, including Arabs. Once this act of state building was completed, normalcy would prevail and the relationship among all the peoples involved would proceed along common norms. It would require no special consideration for anyone, and any lingering persistent tension would vanish.

This view of Zionism was held in the next generation by Vladimir Jabotinski. He knew that the creation of a Jewish state in Palestine would cause some discomfort to the Arab inhabitants of the land. Jabotinski had much less hope than Herzl that Arabs would easily accommodate themselves to the new reality, and he even proposed population transfer, with Jewish help, for those Arabs who did not want to remain in a Jewish state; but Jabotinski insisted, as Herzl had, that those who did remain would be treated as equal citizens. Zionism was a moral imperative for Jabotinski because, as he asserted, without at least one Jewish state—and only one was possible or desirable—the existence of the Jewish people in the modern era was severely endangered; on the other hand, the loss by the Arab people of some thousands of square miles of territory, and even some places that it had held dear, would not in any serious sense endanger the continuity or vitality of Arab nationalism and religion. Jabotinski argued before the Peel Commission in the British House of Lords in 1936 that the failure to achieve a Jewish state might be the end of the Jews; therefore, whatever had to be done to safeguard the continuity of Jews and their culture was morally justifiable, provided that maximum care was taken to limit the injury that this might cause to other interests.

The case for Zionism as defined by Herzl and his followers made it possible for the movement to enter the arena of international politics. To be sure, Herzl's formulation was not universally accepted, even by Zionists—at least not in its pure, theoretical form. In logic, Herzlian Zionism could have accepted any territory that might be made available to Jews. It need not necessarily have centered all the attention of the movement on the regaining of the ancestral land of Palestine. In his essay *The Jewish State*, Herzl himself suggested an unpopulated stretch of Argentina, and he was willing, in 1903, to accept the British offer of possible Jewish settlement in Uganda, at least as a temporary solution to the vast needs of the Jews under persecution in the Russian Empire. The majority of Herzl's followers did not, however, allow him to take so purely rational and formal an approach. To them Zionism meant Zion, and no place else. Unlike Herzl, even the most secular Jews among the majority of the Zionists had cultural and emotional roots in the Jewish tradition and historic experience; only the emotions about "the return to Zion" could arouse their deepest and most fervent energies.

In a very interesting way, these nonrational facts themselves became part of the national demand that Zionism posed to the world as part of its plea for "affirmative action." The cultural Zionists, those for whom the national endeavor was more than merely a solution to the problem of antisemitism or a regularization of the political status of Jews in the world, analyzed the internal situation of Jewish culture and tradition and came to quite pessimistic conclusions. These required radical action to save Judaism—however that might be defined—for the future, not only for Jews but also for the world. This argument was made primarily by a Jewish intellectual Asher Ginsberg, who wrote under the pen name of Ahad Ha-Am. The essence of his argument was that Jews, like all Western people, were now living in a postreligious age. The function that religion had once performed, to encase and preserve the existence of Jewish spiritual teaching in a scattered Diaspora, it could no longer discharge in an age of growing disbelief. Hence a new center of Jewish energy was required, one in which the majority culture was Hebraic. In such a center, the Jewish spirit would survive, in contemporary redefinition. Ahad Ha-Am even believed that this center would provide a new spiritual content and energy for the Diaspora. It is not necessary to analyze Ahad Ha-Am's theories or to measure them against the evolving reality of Zionism and Israel. It is enough for our present purposes to note that the conception of the renewed Jewish settlement in Israel as critical to the revitalization of Judaism and to its preservation (even as Zionists differed about their definitions of Judaism) became central, early on, to Zionist argument.

The basic contention of cultural Zionism is thus, in its own way, a plea for "affirmative action": If the world wants the Jewish experience not to vanish or, at best, not to be distorted, there must somewhere be a place where that experience does not always exist under the pressure of some other culture, in an endless majority/minority situation. The interest of the world as a whole in the preservation of one of its major traditions, the spiritual heritage of the Jews, requires an unprecedented act of one-time favoritism. All the other major traditions were entering the twentieth century in places where each had a normal home—that is, where the majority lived within the culture and had only to face the task of adaptation to modernity. Only the Jews had no such center; only the Jews lived always under the pressure of another, the majority, culture. Therefore, it could justly be maintained that it was not only in the Jewish interest but also in that of the world at large that such a Jewish national home should exist.

In November 1917, the British government issued the Balfour Declaration, which ranged the greatest power of the day, the leader of the soon-to-be-victorious allies, on the side of Zionism. In its very language, the Balfour Declaration was an act of redress, of affirmative action. The British cabinet that decided on this pro-Zionist action accepted the idea that a nonresident people, the Jews (they were then perhaps 10 percent of the population of Palestine) had larger rights in the land than the resident Arabs, because the Jews, scattered around the world, had a national need to return to the land of Israel. On the other hand, the Balfour Declaration set the pattern for the affirmative action declarations, foreign and domestic, that were to follow in years to come and on other shores. The declaration also tried to limit the hurt such an action might cause to those who were affected by it; it specified that the rights of the Arab inhabitants of the land were to be respected. In fact, a balance between these two clauses of the Balfour Declaration has not yet been found, either in law or in politics or in military fact. Those who have fought against this action have used every means from armed struggle, including terrorism, to intellectual defamation in an effort to destroy the Jewish state.

The assertion that "Zionism is racism" is the newest, and most flagrant, attack. This defamatory slogan is being used by Arabs, who have been joined by anti-Western forces in the Soviet Bloc and in large parts of the Third World. Jews have been so angered by this canard that any form of criticism of Israeli policy, even when uttered by proven friends and sometimes even when stated by Jews, has become, among some Jews, the subject of another equation: that all criticism of Israel is defined as antisemitism and that it is therefore, willy-nilly, in league with the canard "Zionism is racism." It is true, unfortunately, that much of the criticism of Israel masks a wish that the State of Israel should not exist at all. Nonetheless, it is a self-defeating exaggeration to equate all criticism of Israel's policies with antisemitism and with at least tacit approval of the big lie that "Zionism is racism." There is a legitimate argument within Israel, in the Jewish world as a whole, and among the friends of Israel as to whether annexation policies on the West Bank are in the best interests of Israel, of peace in the Middle East, and of sound future relationships between Jews and Arabs. Ronald Reagan and François Mitterrand are not enemies of Israel; they are both opposed to the annexationist policies in which the right wing in Israel fervently believes. It is not an assault on Israel to question some of its policies, out of identification with moderate or even left-wing opinions in Israel's political spectrum, as traducers of Zion. The Jewish people have enough enemies without adding to their number those who are critical friends.

More fundamental still is the definition of a correct Jewish and pro-Zionist attitude, both in theory and in practice, toward those who have seized upon the "Zionism is racism" slogan and are using it in political battle with the State of Israel and its friends. It is an ironic, even tragic, paradox that most of these hostile forces are themselves making claims on the world in this century in accents comparable to those of Zionism. The moral demand for special consideration, for major acts of redress for past wrongs for which present generations are expected to pay, are made far more insistently by various forces of the Third World than the Zionists have ever dared to claim. No one seriously believes that the bulk of the Third World countries will ever repay the vast loans, which amount by now to many tens of billions of dollars, that they have taken from governments and banks in the West. This transfer of capital is justified by the argument that these countries were colonized and exploited by their Western masters in previous centuries and that the money (which will probably never be repaid) is a form of recompense for past wrongs.

To the degree to which such a claim can be sustained, a claim based on the memory of injustice inflicted on a helpless people by a foreign oppressor, the Jews are actually the prime example. The "colonialist" attack on the Jews was different only in geography from those experienced—and remembered—by the Third World. The Roman conquerors of Judea in the first century enslaved and exiled most of its Jewish population. After that, the Jewish Diaspora has existed until recent generations under exploitative laws. Jews have been excluded from most economic pursuits, taxed much more heavily than anyone else, and often victimized by pogroms, or worse. The only strikingly comparable situation is that of American blacks, who were victims of slavery in a country to which they have been dragged by force. American blacks insist, quite correctly, that their experience is at one with the pain inflicted by colonialism on resident peoples all over Africa, Latin America, and much of Asia. The Zionist passion of Jews for self-determination and for dignity as a people is thus a prime example of recoil from colonialism, from the almost unique colonial relationships through the ages between Gentile majorities and a Jewish minority, who were persecuted everywhere. What follows from these reflections is the proposition that those who make the case for special consideration for the Third World, in the name of anticolonialism, cannot defend the principles that justify their demands without accepting Zionism. "Zionism is racism" is thus intellectually a fraudulent assertion. It can be understood only as a political tactic, and a very nasty one at that, in the Jewish-Arab confrontation.

From the Zionist point of view, there are essentially two options. One is to presume that all of those countries and forces that now mouth this terrible slogan are irredeemable, that empires of evil must be confronted and brought to their knees. The trouble with this construction is that the United States, the most powerful nation in the world, has finally discovered that even it cannot afford a solidly united bloc of enemies that include the Soviet Union and its satellites as well as the Third World. U.S. policy has begun to move, again, in the direction of moderating conflicts and of trying to increase the shades of difference among various parts of the Soviet Bloc (and even among various factions within the Soviet Union) and among the great varieties of countries and opinions that belong to the Third World. Even when the world appears to be Manichean, when large blocs seem to be arrayed against Zionism, it is in the Jewish interest that the ice be frozen, patiently, at least in part. World Jewry cannot afford to unite its enemies further by using only the tactic of unceasing counterattack. It will work for Jews even less well than it has for Americans.

This policy is necessary even in relation to the Soviet Union. It is true, of course, that Moscow is today, and has been for too many years, a center of hostility to Zionism and, all too often, of the most brazen antisemitism. These expressions are to be condemned, and the actions based on them must be fought in every forum. Nonetheless, it is necessary to remember that this is not the only possible version of a Soviet relationship to Jews and to Zionism. During World War II, the Soviet Union saved tens of thousands of Jews from Eastern Poland, under their control from 1939 to 1941, as these Jews fled before the advancing Nazis. Andrei Gromyko's speech in the United Nations in 1947 on behalf of the creation of a Jewish state (without the Soviet votes in the United Nations, the creation of Israel could not have happened) is one of the most Zionist among international documents. Since 1948, the negative comments and actions have been far more prominent than the supportive gestures, but it has remained a fact of Soviet policy, even at the most hostile moments, that the existence of the State of Israel has never been called into question. Jewish policy should be based on the attempt to strengthen within the Soviet Union those forces that want a moderate policy toward Israel and a reasonable friendship with world Jewry, based on the end of repression of the aspirations of some Jews to emigrate and of others to continue to live openly and creatively as Jews within the Soviet Union.

"Zionism is racism" is an unforgivable attack upon a movement that asked special consideration in order to help a people with unique troubles find a way of righting itself. Most of those who attack Zionism are undermining their own legitimacy, for such are the very claims they have been advancing in their own interest. Those who would defend Zionism must not presume that the present confrontation is necessarily eternal. It is our task to help reason and moderation prevail, especially among those who are hostile. Jews should remember the Talmudic dictum: "Who is a hero? He who makes of his enemy a friend."

14

Is There a New Antisemitism?

Michael R. Marrus

History is supposed to teach Jews important lessons. Among these the most commonly cited is that antisemitism is an unbroken historical stream, forever present, albeit varying its guises and intensity over time. From this Jews are supposed to arm themselves with pessimism, to presume the worst when non-Jews address issues of Jewish concern. Recently, as many have argued in this mode, antisemitism is heating up again. Jews remain the principal focus of attention, but the declared target is the State of Israel, which has become "the collective Jew among the nations." Persistently emphasized by those who describe this phenomenon is the direct line of continuity linking attacks upon Israeli positions and the ancient current of anti-Jewish sentiment and ideology.

This vision draws more upon old habits of thought than upon sound judgment. Antisemitism persists, of course, but it is hardly the most virulent or significant form of prejudice, racism, or xenophobia in the West, and there are even signs that it has been steadily declining since the end of World War II. Anti-Israel feeling certainly exists, much of it based upon distorted media presentation and ingrained Western susceptibilities to any manner of nonsense about societies and conflicts foreign to Western experience. But evidence suggests that antisemitism is not normally behind such evaluation, however unjust, inaccurate, or ill-conceived.

Antisemitism and Anti-Zionism

Brooding upon the increasingly hostile international climate for Israel in 1976, the late Jacob Talmon, a distinguished Israeli historian, published an article headlined "The New Antisemitism."[1] Talmon looked back on a year of mounting anti-Israel propaganda orchestrated internationally. In July 1975 the UN International Women's Year Conference in Mexico City resolved to see the elimination of Zionism, together with such other great evils in the world as "colonialism, neo-colonialism, imperialism, foreign domination and occupation, apartheid, and racial discrimination." In November, the UN General Assembly followed suit, declaring Zionism to be "a form of racialism and racial discrimination" and Israel to be "the racist regime in occupied Palestine."

With due qualification, including a nervous reference to extremists in his own society, Talmon ascribed the unprecedented intensity of this attack in Western countries to the centuries-old heritage of anti-Judaism. "Throughout the ages, the Christian-Jewish relationship has been beset by a profound neurosis. The peculiar, indeed unique, concatenation of historical circumstances never ceased to feed the conflict of feelings in the Christian psyche toward the Jew: awe, sense of obligation, resentful hatred, contempt, guilt. The gentiles were thus conditioned to react to the stimuli that the Jew projected with an intensity out of all proportion." Since Israel was "the sole heir and repository of the destroyed Jewish civilization," decimated during the Holocaust, it had become the object of the newest campaign to eliminate the Jews. At bottom, then, remained the old conflict between the antisemites and the Jewish right to survive on a basis of genuine equality. Fueling this quarrel, moreover, was the demonic energy that antisemitism had displayed in times past. "At the end of the road," Talmon pointedly told his readers, "is Auschwitz."

Since Talmon, the claim has been made repeatedly that the worldwide campaign against the Jewish state derives largely from antisemitism. Elaborating, the Israeli political scientist Shlomo Avineri sees behind much anti-Israel propaganda an effort to delegitimize the Jewish state. And this, argued Avineri, former director-general of the Israeli Foreign Ministry, was the link to traditional antisemitism.[2] Since Israel has increasingly come to represent the broadest common denominator for Jewish self-consciousness in the world, and perhaps the sole basis for Jewish self-definition, serious attacks threaten the legitimacy of a distinct Jewish existence today. Joining the old and the new antisemitism was the repudiation of a separate, self-defining, independent Jewish peoplehood.

Such notions rest upon a theory of antisemitic persistence—an idea often disputed by students of antisemitism today. While accepting that anti-Jewish attitudes are frequently conditioned by old traditions of hostility toward Jews in the Christian West, some historians emphasize discontinuities—the way that antisemitism can wax and wane, can emerge in some historical contexts and disappear in others. All this suggests the need for a closer look at the phenomenon. It seems to me that arguments for a "new antisemitism" propose two rather different links to antisemitic tradition: The first has to do with the form and content of anti-Israel positions; the second treats the motivation of such attacks.

The eminent Irish critic Conor Cruise O'Brien commented in the autumn of 1983 on the particularly unbalanced reporting of Israeli actions during the war in Lebanon—descriptions that ignored Syrian depredations and the brutality of the previous Palestine Liberation Organization (PLO) occupation, which recklessly inflated numbers of civilian casualties and held the Jewish state to high standards of behavior nowhere observed in Middle Eastern conflicts. The clue of malevolence, O'Brien suggested, was the gratuitous comparison of Israelis to Nazis— a smear so odious, he suggested, as to be an obvious indicator of deeply felt prejudice. In fairness, O'Brien did *not* see antisemitism on the rise; but he did report widely diminished inhibitions against antisemitism, the progressive social acceptability of anti-Jewishness. Moreover, he saw anti-Zionism as a cover for new forms of the old disease, admittedly a judgment that did not apply in all cases. The unmistakable sign was the smear of Hitlerism.[3]

Yet a chronicling of the misuse of Nazi references to demonstrate a new antisemitism, as so many have done, is unconvincing. Every era operates in the shadow of its historical past, and it is inevitable that the great reference points of our own time—particularly Hitler and the Nazi genocide against Jews—will be used and misused to describe what people think and feel about momentous political upheavals. As so often in the past, Menachem Begin set the tone, publicly imagining himself before Beirut in the summer of 1982, for example, about to destroy "Hitler" in his "bunker deep beneath the surface" in "Berlin." During that war, as the tone of political debate coarsened in Israel, pro-Begin Likud attacks on the Israeli opposition were replete with portentious accusations: Jewish critics of the war, wrote Nathan Brun in *Yediot Ahronoth*, were "poisoning our wells," a hoary antisemitic charge. A board member of the Broadcasting Association referred in the same tabloid to Peace Now campaigners against Begin as calling for "Putsch Now." And in a particularly monstrous formulation one contributor compared the murdered peace demonstrator Emil Grunzweig to Horst Wessel, the Nazi victim of the Communists whom Hitler and Goebbels turned into a martyr of the movement.[4]

To a lesser degree, Israeli opponents of their government also use the linguistic debris of fascism and Nazism to vent anger and frustration. Speaking of West Bank settlement before Begin, referred to as the "creation of facts," Talmon himself likened that notion to Mussolini's *sacro egoismo*, doomed to disaster like the predatory designs of the Duce.[5] In the *New York Times* Amos Elon spoke recently of the failure of the "new order" that Begin and General Sharon attempted to create in Lebanon,[6] and in *Ha'aretz* he described Israeli settlement on the West Bank as creating a democracy of *Herrenvolk*.[7] Labor parliamentarian Shevah Weiss referred to "a neo-fascistic lynch atmosphere" inspired by the government, and others have characterized the colonizing zeal of the Likud as inspired by an ideology of "blood and soil"—distinctly reminiscent of the folkish origins of Nazism.[8]

On the walls of Tel Aviv and Jerusalem it is possible to find crudely sprayed swastikas, supposedly emblems of lower-class Sephardic militancy or ultra-Orthodox protests against the Israeli police. Not long ago youthful vandals from a poor neighborhood rampaged in a posh Tel

Aviv suburb, leaving graffiti saying "Ashkenazi" written to stress the last syllable "nazi." In these and related manifestations, form reveals little about content except perhaps to suggest a lack of balance, hardly in itself an indicator of antisemitism.

Antisemitism and the Media

Media distortions of Israel often deserve to be called antisemitic, some insist, because the double standard upon which they are often based is so reminiscent of how antisemites stigmatized Jews in the past. "Historically," wrote Norman Podhoretz in his widely discussed *Commentary* article "J'Accuse," published in September 1982, "antisemitism has taken the form of labeling certain vices and failings as specifically Jewish when they are in fact common to all humanity: Jews are greedy, Jews are tricky, Jews are clannish—as though Jews were uniquely or disproportionately guilty of all those sins." Criticisms informed by such a double standard should be deemed antisemitic, he insisted, no matter who made them.

Doubtless *some* anti-Israel coverage fits this indictment. But it seems to me extraordinarily short-sighted and blindered to neglect other factors that shape collective judgements. Consider television. Students of that medium tell us repeatedly how TV news thrives upon disaster and craves the juxtaposition of heroes and villains. In the nightly melodrama presented as reality, writes critic Mark Crispin Miller, "there are no issues, and only two sides: the bullies and the little guys." Television, he goes on, "will only champion those groups whom it can sentimentalize."[9]

For many years Israel was the beneficiary of this predisposition. Championed in popular fiction, celebrated as a model society of pioneering *chaluzim*, Israel was seen in the West scarcely without a blemish—a super-clean image now resented by many Israelis of Sephardic origin who are only just beginning to feel that their problems are being properly aired. Justly portrayed as an underdog internationally, Israel had a remarkably good press.

Now that the tables have turned and the Israelis cannot be so readily idealized, the course of media reporting sometimes runs against the Jewish state. But does it make sense to ascribe this shift to antisemitism? Numerous writers have told us that Jews can be tolerated only as victims, never as conquerors. Yet television journalism has its own casting criteria for the two sides in any conflict that have to do with such myths. The parts of hero and villain are assigned not according to national or religious background, but rather according to what can be credibly sold to an audience. In Lebanon, the images could hardly have been more stark: a modern, mechanized army, tens of thousands of men, including air and sea power, deployed against a screen of hopelessly outclassed and outgunned guerrillas and laying siege to a helpless capital.

Rushing headlong to their daily deadlines, reporters with only the vaguest idea of historical context concocted their "stories" in a way that doubtless seemed consistent with television's continuing saga. Predictably, the cameras pictured the Jews in a poor light. Calling this process antisemitism, as did Norman Podhoretz, illuminates nothing; seeing those responsible as prejudiced bigots only contributes a new layer of distortion to an already obscured reality.

In his scathing critique of the press coverage of the Lebanese war, *New Republic* editor Martin Peretz offered a more balanced explanation, one that did not fall back upon antisemitism as the root of the trouble. For Peretz the failure was, more simply, a lapse of professionalism under circumstances inevitably more damaging to the Israeli side:

> The media, fast-paced for multiple deadlines—early edition, late edition, morning news, 7 o'clock news, 11 o'clock news—are always after new vivid images of conflict, violent if possible, even if they beg, unrequited, for explanation. Why would anyone be interested in buildings that have remained standing or in bodies that have remained whole? The standing order for the armies of the fourth estate is for "good copy." Journalists have a professional interest—and it is a vocational hazard for their thinking—in broken necks and amputated limbs, the equivalent of fires and armed robberies on the local news.[10]

Under pressure, the complexities of the Lebanese imbroglio proved far too taxing to pursue, and too time-consuming to report. For journalists bred on Watergate, and with an international vision colored by Vietnam, the war was yet another round in a familiar drama. Israeli leaders, in this case, played the parts of both the stonewalling Richard Nixon and the warlike Lyndon Johnson—a combination for which there was ample enough evidence, even without inaccuracies, though this characterization represented only part of the truth.

Antisemitism and the Rhetoric of the Holocaust

Analysts of a "new antisemitism" frequently advise that its propaganda is exceptionally subtle or clever. By this they mean that its real objectives are carefully disguised. Aiming at Jews, new-style antisemites cannot be open about their targets because traditional anti-Jewish ideology is so largely discredited in much of the post-Holocaust world. Israel has been chosen as the butt of the antisemitic image-maker, because the Jewish state can be vilified with relative impunity, and through Israel the Jewish people can be discredited and defamed. The public in Western countries is ready for this campaign, it is further suggested, because residual guilt built up by the Holocaust can now be discharged with little cost, and there are signs of mounting popular antipathy toward Jews.

The problem with this formulation is that the anti-Jewish core upon which it depends has thus far escaped detection. No one has proven that there ever existed much "guilt" in the West for actions taken or not taken during the Holocaust, and the evidence about a rising tide of popular antisemitism seems to me utterly unconvincing.

The hypothesis about post-Holocaust guilt is extremely speculative and probably cannot ever be tested scientifically. I know it is very persuasive in some quarters, and I have even seen Jewish audiences rise spontaneously to applaud particularly eloquent expressions of the idea. Nevertheless, it would pay to temper this theory with a simple demographic fact: Most people alive in North America and Europe were born considerably after World War II; for them, the notion of some sort of personal or inherited responsibility for what happened to Jews forty years ago seems inherently absurd. My students at the University of Toronto mentally file Hitler and World War II with Napoleon or Karl Marx—important landmarks of the past, but seldom part of their personal or family histories. For most, the Holocaust occurred further back in their sense of time than many of us like to imagine. It was not their parents who were making decisions during the war years, but their *grandparents* or even their *great-grandparents*.

Seeing things in this perspective prompts a reflection upon the political uses of guilt and the unexpected results it may provoke. For years, Israeli spokesmen, usually in genuine rage and sorrow at the crimes committed against Jews in the Hitler period, encouraged Western leaders to proclaim a kind of expiation for past sins by supporting the Jewish state. Along with this disposition, whether conscious or not, went an accusation against non-Jewish statesmen: You are guilty, either for what you did or did not do; it is incumbent upon you to prove to us that you have changed. Accompanying this charge went the implicit claim that Jews were, as Leonard Fine has put it, "a people with an especially refined moral sensibility." Only the leaders of such a people could presume thus to address Western spokesmen—and only such a claim for moral distinction could justify the charge flung in the face of the world.

No one more thoroughly personifies this tendency than Menachem Begin, much of whose family was murdered in the Holocaust. In May 1981 the issue became a matter of wide public discussion in Israel when Begin personally attacked German Chancellor Helmut Schmidt, whose crimes in the Nazi era seem no more than to have been ensnared in a totalitarian system in which he served as a junior anti-aircraft officer near Berlin. Abba Eban recently decried the implications of this style of diplomacy: "Under Mr. Begin, Israeli relations with other countries have ceased to be regarded as similar to other international relations, whether concerning cooperation, opposition and even confrontation. With Mr. Begin and his cohorts, every foe becomes a 'Nazi,' every blow becomes an 'Auschwitz.'"[11]

However understandable and common in societies that have been deeply wronged, such accusations prompt unease and irritation, and eventually hostility and anger. What else could one expect from an audience who does not generally, or could not possibly, feel guilty? As time passes, and as the Holocaust recedes into the historical past, reactions to this perceived attitude on the part of some Jews or their leaders are bound to become more harsh. In the time since the Israeli invasion of Lebanon, there has been evidence of resentment against this rhetoric of actual or implicit accusation. Justifying Israeli actions, General Sharon inflamed such responses by continually declaring that no one could teach the Jews lessons in morality and that the Jews could instruct others in that domain. Many who so eagerly broadcast evidence of Israeli wrongdoing, whether accurate or not, seem to have been driven by a desire to turn upon such pretentions, to show that Jewish hands could also sink into the dirt.

It is clear that the reserves of moral pressure drawn upon by Israeli politicians for almost four decades are now coming to an end. "That account is being closed," Abba Eban reflected at the height of the Lebanese War. "Perhaps it is for the best. It is about time that we stood on our own feet and not on those of the six million of our dead."

Recent Trends in Antisemitism

Meanwhile, however, a fund of anti-Israeli sentiment has been created, with perceptible anti-Jewish overtones. Is this configuration the "new antisemitism" that many seek to explain? If so, its origins and character differ strikingly from earlier anti-Jewish ideologies, and I question whether this emotional spasm warrants the term *antisemitism*. Indeed, the answers to this question are highly conjectural and are likely to remain so. What can be said with greater assurance, however, is that popular antisemitism of the old-fashioned variety—dislike of Jews and of whatever they may do or say simply because they are Jews—seems largely on the decline in Western countries.

Since the 1930s, pollsters have sounded public opinion in order to gauge the strength of anti-Jewish sentiment in Western countries. Although particular surveys can be criticized for one shortcoming or another, there is a sufficient number of such polls to make reasonably firm judgments. The results seem plain: Antisemitism peaked in many countries just after the war against Hitler, and thereafter, levels have dropped steadily. In recent years any number of surveys have shown Jews to be near the bottom of lists of those groups seen to have too much power or influence. Evaluating a very considerable literature on this theme, Milton Himmelfarb of the American Jewish Committee recently reported: "We keep hearing about rising antisemitic feeling, but the polls have not found it. We kept hearing about it during the Arab oil embargo following the Yom Kippur War of 1973, and then too the polls did not find it. In retrospect we can see that the polls were a better guide than the stories."[12] Writing in the Jewish periodical

Midstream in February 1983, Earl Raab concurred: "There has been a steadily decreasing proportion of Americans who believe that Jews are more dishonest than other people, that Jews are more sinister or distasteful. . . . As far as negative stereotypes are concerned, Jews have apparently reached a state of parity with other white ethnic groups—all of which are in a more favored position than blacks or Asians."[13]

Even in France, with its reputation for antisemitism, and in which many North American writers have been confused by recent terrorist attacks, the polls have told a similar story: Popular hostility toward Jews has declined steadily and regularly since the end of the 1940s. On a day-to-day basis there is vastly more prejudice and discrimination against alien workers—mainly North African Muslims—than against Jews.[14] Much the same can be said of countries like West Germany and Switzerland, which have large numbers of foreigners and are experiencing economic difficulties. If there is a search for scapegoats and a mounting tide of racism in such places, the perpetrators are certainly not singling out Jews.

The objection has been raised that people do not tell the truth when polled about Jews because antisemitism is so discredited in the West. Yet such inhibitions do not seem to have significantly obscured American antiblack sentiment, which has been discredited in the United States (at least to some degree) in the past twenty years. Moreover, even if true, this critique suggests a real measure of progress toward the elimination of antisemitism; surely one step along that road has been the rendering of such sentiments as nonrespectable. More important, it has been said that surveys turn attention away from small antisemitic minorities, whose activity may dangerously increase despite an apparent lack of mass following. But the *results* of such surveys suggest that even the committed, fanatical fringe is shrinking. According to Raab, "the survey results are convincing that the percentage of hard-core antisemites has continued to diminish in this country, as has the percentage of soft-core antisemites. It would be foolish to ignore the evidence on this score, even though in this case some would like to kill the messenger when he brings the good news."[15]

To counter these findings, some have presented statistics illustrating a growing number of anti-Jewish "incidents," which may include anything from antisemitic graffiti to a terrorist bombing.[16] Whatever problems may exist with respect to public opinion surveys, however, these pale in significance beside the difficulties in measuring such supposed anti-Jewish acts and in assessing their significance. The obvious challenge is the consistent defining and reporting of these events—something hardly ever achieved anywhere with scientific accuracy. Milton Elerin, a veteran investigator of such trends, revealed recently in *Reform Judaism* that a close study failed to indicate a reliable trend:

As we probed this phenomenon further, we discovered a corresponding increase in all forms of juvenile vandalism attributable to a variety of societal factors. Nuns are being raped, clergymen assaulted, and Christian churches vandalized. Most antisemitic incidents solved by arrest were committed by teenagers and were often the result of peer pressure to engage in destructive behavior. It is important to note that not a single incident resulted from organized hate group members. In some cases, there was an antisemitic motivation, but in the majority of cases the synagogue was simply a target of opportunity.[17]

Moreover, even when these measurements are used to indicate antisemitic trends, there are admissions now of a downward turn, suggesting that the vandals may be looking for newer targets.[18]

Needless to say, Jews have earned the right to be pessimistic despite the weight of empirical evidence. Antisemitism has been extremely volatile in the past, and it could well be so again in the future. Antisemitism can arise when least expected, and it thrives upon indifference—of which there is more than enough in Western societies. Anti-Jewish ideology is not quite ready for the dustbin of history. Yet it is incumbent upon analysts not to be swept away with the notion of a new antisemitism, as I fear many have become, simply because it seems preferable to sound a warning rather than to encourage complacency.

The antisemitism that persists in Western societies is not new, and it continues to feed from traditional roots. It is largely on the decline, so far as we can tell. The anti-Israel sentiment that has arisen in recent years does possess a sense of novelty, and it is, indeed, linked to some factors utterly extraneous to the conflict in the Middle East. It is conditioned by the structure of the electronic and print media, as well as by the particular rhetoric of some Jewish leaders. It is sometimes unfair, exaggerated, and defamatory. But it is neither generally antisemitic nor illuminated by that term.

Notes

1. Jacob Talmon, "The New Antisemitism," *New Republic*, 18 September 1976.

2. See, for example, Avineri's contribution to the symposium "Antisemitism Today," *Patterns of Prejudice* 16 (October 1982):4–5; and *A Symposium on Antisemitism and Anti-Zionism* (Jerusalem: Van Leer Institute, 1983), pp. 2–8.

3. See "Antisemitism Today," pp. 42–43.

4. *Yediot Ahronoth*, 25 June 1982, 2 July 1982, 5 October 1982, and 14 February 1982.

5. Jacob Talmon, "Is Force the Answer to Everything?" in *Dispersion and Unity* (Jerusalem, 1970), quoted in Howard M. Sachar, *A History of Israel* (New York, 1976), p. 713.

6. See Elon's favorable review of Jacobo Timmerman's *The Longest War* in the *New York Times Book Review*, 12 December 1982, p. 31.

7. Amos Elon, *Ha'aretz*, 4 February 1983.

8. Shevah Weiss, *Davar*, 11 February 1983; Shlomo Ben-Ami, *Hotam*, 18 February 1983.

9. Mark C. Miller, "How TV Covers War," *New Republic*, 29 November 1982.

10. Martin Peretz, "Lebanon Eyewitness," *New Republic*, 2 August 1982.

11. Abba Eban, *Yediot Ahronoth*, 16 July 1982.

12. Milton Himmelfarb, "Antisemitism Here and Now," paper delivered at the University of Southern California, April 23, 1983.

13. Earl Raab, "Anti-Semitism in the 1980s," *Midstream* 29 (February 1983):1.

14. I have surveyed this issue in "Are the French Antisemitic? Evidence in the 1980s," *Jerusalem Quarterly*, no. 32 (Summer 1984):81–97.

15. Raab, "Antisemitism," p. 12.

16. See, for example, League for Human Rights, *The Review of Anti-Semitism in Canada 1982* (1983) and the reckless conclusions apparently drawn from this report by the national chairman of B'nai B'rith's sponsoring organization: "Canadian Anti-Semitism Worsening, Study Finds," *Globe and Mail*, 9 June 1983. The idea that antisemitism is "worsening" in Canada, stemming from the sixty-three incidents noted in 1982, is entirely unwarranted. There was no audit of incidents for 1981 or any previous year. There was no measure of related forms of vandalism. The other means to measure antisemitism in the League of Rights report, an "analysis" of Canadian news coverage of the Middle East that sees some people wanting "to bring about a new Holocaust for the Jews," is utterly fanciful.

17. Milton Elerin, "How Secure Are America's Jews?" *Reform Judaism*, Winter 1983.

18. See Anti-Defamation League of B'nai B'rith, *1982 Audit of Antisemitic Incidents* (New York, 1983).

Part Four

Discrimination:
Action and Expression

15
Soviet Antisemitism and Its Perception by Soviet Jews

Zvi Gitelman

The Soviet Union, which has the third largest Jewish population in the world, has come to be perceived by many as the most antisemitic country in the world, aside from some Arab states. It is alleged that the Soviet government not only promotes domestic antisemitism but also "exports" it by way of propaganda aimed at non-Soviet people. The late Reuben Ainsztein asserted that "antisemites in the Party and their allies in the Russian New Right are openly proposing to make it the official ideology of the Soviet Union. Already it is the official doctrine of the Soviet armed forces, despite the opposition of some of their wartime leaders."[1] Yet, in contrast to the Nazis, Soviet spokespersons consistently maintain not only that the USSR opposes antisemitism, but that it hardly exists there. The chair of the recently formed Anti-Zionist Committee of Soviet Society, the Jewish Colonel-General David Dragunsky, stated at a press conference on June 6, 1983: "It is well known that Soviet people resolutely condemn all forms of chauvinism [and] nationalism, [and] are against nationalistic expressions such as antisemitism or Zionism. . . . The myth about the existence of a so-called 'Jewish problem' in the USSR is exploited, as is known, in order to strengthen the standard thesis, . . . one of the pillars of Zionism, about 'eternal antisemitism.'"[2] Another participant in the conference, Professor of Jurisprudence S. L. Zivs, complained that "Zionist propaganda tries to portray as antisemitism every critique of either the ideology or the political practice of Zionism."[3] Whereas Soviet spokespersons link Zionism and antisemitism as two sides of the same chauvinist coin, many Western commentators link Soviet *anti*-Zionism with antisemitism, arguing that the former is frequently a mask and a vehicle for the latter. William Korey, commenting on the proliferation of extremely harsh Soviet attacks on Zionism in the 1970s, argues that "the distinction between Jew and Zionist became almost completely blurred as the campaign progressed and central elements of Jewish tradition were portrayed as the root of the Zionist evil."[4]

185

This chapter traces the development of official Soviet attitudes toward both antisemitism and Zionism and attempts to explain their evolution. It can be shown that there is no single, monolithic Soviet opinion on the linkage between Zionism and Jews or Judaism, although in recent years the bulk of Soviet publications have indeed blurred the distinction between Jews and Zionists, and, in effect, attacked both with great ferocity. Moreover, it will be argued, whatever may be the intent of the Soviet authorities, the effects of their propaganda and their policies are quite clear: There is convincing empirical evidence that Soviet Jews perceive governmental and popular attitudes as antisemitic.

Soviet Attitudes in Historical Perspective

The first Soviet authority to link antisemitism and Zionism was, of course, V. I. Lenin himself. In the course of his struggle against the Bund, the Jewish Socialist movement that was anti-Zionist but advocated some autonomy for the Jewish proletariat (Plekhanov mocked the Bundists as "Zionists afraid of sea-sickness"), Lenin acknowledged that "the Jewish workers, as a disfranchised nationality, not only suffer general economic and political oppression, but they also suffer under the yoke which deprives them of elementary civic rights."[5] But he rejected the idea that Jews constitute a nation as "untenable scientifically" and "reactionary politically": "The idea of a Jewish 'nationality' is definitely reactionary not only when expounded by its consistent advocates (the Zionists), but likewise on the lips of those who try to combine it with the ideas of Social-Democracy (the Bundists). The idea of a Jewish nationality runs counter to the interests of the Jewish proletariat, for it fosters among them, directly or indirectly, a spirit hostile to assimilation, the spirit of the 'ghetto.'"[6]

Lenin condemned pogroms and took care to spread this condemnation to the masses by means of gramophone records in 1919, but he pointed out that, like other peoples, Jews were divided into workers and capitalists, and insisted that the latter must be opposed. But he stressed that "among the Jews there are working people, and they form the majority. They are our brothers . . . [and] they are our comrades in the struggle for socialism. . . . Shame on those who foment hatred toward the Jews, who foment hatred toward other nations."[7] It should be remembered that these statements were made at a time when pogroms were very popular, especially in the Ukraine, and when the White foes of Bolshevism made ample use of antisemitism in an attempt to win over the masses. Thus, Lenin, who sincerely saw the solution to the "Jewish problem" as assimilation into the new Socialist society, did not hesitate to take a principled stand against antisemitism at a time when it might not have been politically prudent to do so. Official policy and popular sentiment, reinforced by the teachings of the Russian Orthodox Church, had combined to make antisemitism a pervasive reality of Jewish life in the czarist empire, and Lenin seemed committed to changing this as part of the revolutionary remaking of society.

When considering the question of antisemitism today, one must be aware of the continuities between the czarist and Soviet periods.[8] In both eras the Jews have been legally identified as Jews, and this identification has prevented them from disappearing into the larger mass of the Russian population. Of course, during the Soviet period the law has never singled out the Jews for discriminatory treatment, as it did under the czars. On the contrary, especially in the earlier years of the Bolshevik regime, explicit legal provisions were made to condemn and punish instances of antisemitism. Observance and implementation of the law may be quite another matter, but the legal status of the Jews has changed dramatically for the better since 1917. The power and influence of the Church have been broken, and it can no longer use its doctrinal base as a platform from which to launch attacks on the Jews. In terms of their legal status Jews are no longer *inorodtsy* (aliens to whom special laws apply), and yet they are perceived as aliens by significant elements in the Soviet population. Popular stereotypes of the Jews no doubt persist, although they may be less widespread than they once were. As late as the 1970s there were cases of blood libel in the USSR, but these were undoubtedly exceptional occurrences.

Antisemitism has evolved through the interaction of events, official policies, and changes within the Jewish population itself. It is not a phenomenon that appears suddenly, but rather one that feeds on the past, taking on new forms in response to new realities. Therefore, any discussion of antisemitism in the USSR today must be preceded by a brief overview of the evolution of the problem in its Soviet context.

The Course of Antisemitism in the Soviet Union

The fall of the czarist regime in February–March 1917 ended official discrimination against Jews and other non-Russian nationalities, for one of the early acts of the Provisional Government was to declare the equality of the peoples and religions inhabiting the former Russian Empire. At one stroke the Pale of Settlement was abolished, and the legal disabilities endured by the Jews were done away with. Naturally, it was not as simple a matter to change the popular sentiment and belief, but Jews could now move freely throughout the country—or beyond it—and they could also enter professions and occupations hitherto barred to them. The new system also allowed the development of Jewish political, cultural, and social organizations, and in 1917 there was a tremendous flurry of communal activity among the Jews, who had set about planning their individual and collective lives in the new society in which they would enjoy equal rights. When the Bolsheviks took power in the fall of 1917, they reaffirmed the principle of national equality and their actions seemed to support their words. At the same time, the liberal and Socialist opponents of the Bolsheviks were quickly rendered politically impotent, while a full-scale civil war broke out between the Bolsheviks and the supporters of the old regime. For the Jews and others, this war crystallized the choices confronting them as non-Russian peoples. The White forces explicitly proclaimed that their fight to restore czarism involved also a restoration of the status quo ante vis-à-vis the nationalities. They fought for a Russian-dominated autocracy in which non-Russians would be legally and socially subordinate. Such proclamations were backed up by mass murders of Jews in a wave of pograms far worse than those experienced in the late nineteenth century. Other opponents of the new regime, such as various anarchist bands and Ukrainian nationalists, also pogromized the Jewish population, whereas the Bolsheviks continued to stand on a platform of national equality. The Red Army, with but few exceptions, not only refrained from attacks on Jews but succeeded in recruiting large numbers of non-Socialist (even Orthodox and Zionist) Jews, who saw it as a vehicle for Jewish self-defense and revenge against the White armies.[9] The civil war taught the Jews that there were grounds for hoping that the new regime would succeed in eliminating antisemitism as a government policy, and some may have believed that in time it would disappear as a social phenomenon as well.

It became clear that whatever the attitude of the regime, the age-old attitudes of the population would not be easily changed. The Soviet press in the 1920s brought ample evidence that antisemitism was still very much alive. What was new was the condemnation by the same press of anti-Jewish attitudes and actions. Moreover, the immediate catalysts of anti-Jewish expressions were different from what they had been in the past, although the traditional "reasons" for antisemitism persisted as well. The new themes sounded by antisemites included the argument that, under the New Economic Policy (1921–1928), the Jews had gone back to their old exploitative ways and were getting rich at the expense of the simple folk; that the Jews had made the revolution and were now enjoying its fruits (given that they held many important posts in the party and the state); that the Jews were "invading" or "overrunning" places in which they had not been seen before (e.g., Moscow and Leningrad); that the Jews were getting the soft jobs in the Soviet economy and avoiding the difficult ones; and that they were getting free land and depriving the peasantry of its land. These themes reflected the difficulty experienced by the population in adjusting to the changed status of the Jews. That a Jew should hold a government position, own land, or live in the capital city was very rare under the czars, and the new realities simply did not fit the image of Jews that most people held. White Russian propaganda had explained the revolution as an atheistic-Jewish plot, as the work of the Antichrist, and the prominence of Jews in the new regime seemed to confirm this interpretation, particularly when the regime moved forcefully against the established church and against religion in general (including, of course, the Jewish religion). The Jews themselves were pleasantly surprised at their newfound opportunities. For example, they jokingly referred to the VUTSIK (All-Union Central Executive Committee) as being an abbreviation for *vu tsen idn komandeven*—"where ten Jews give the orders." Non-Jews were highly conscious of the political power wielded by Jewish individuals and found it hard to adjust to this new reality. Since the Jews could not own land under the czars, settlement of Jews on land, such as occurred in Belorussia, the Ukraine, the Crimea, and the Far East in the 1920s, aroused similar wonder and resentment. Peasants felt that Jews were receiving land that might otherwise have been theirs, although in no instance was there expropriation of lands already in use, and much of the land assigned to Jewish colonization existed in remote areas or was otherwise unattractive to the peasantry. The Jews no longer "knew their place" and began to appear in cities and in professions in which they had been totally unknown before 1917. For the first time the Jews became the direct competitors of the non-Jews, who had hitherto been given the exclusive right to a vocation or profession. As Solomon Schwarz wrote, "The antisemitic wave of the mid-1920's did not originate in the villages. . . . Antisemitism originated to a large extent among dispossessed urban groups, people, that is, whose families, having lost their middle class independence, saw themselves reduced to working for a wage or salary in factories and offices."[10]

Soviet newspapers reported antisemitic moods and incidents among the factory workers, many of whom had just migrated from the countryside and had carried with them traditional peasant attitudes and values. Non-Jews attempting to enter the professions found themselves in competition with Jews, previously excluded from the professions, or very much limited within them. In a society undergoing fundamental restructuring, with the Jews largely benefiting from that process, there were many reasons for resentments, and these sometimes were expressed in antisemitic forms. Aside from the charges of land grabbing and of Jewish domination of the government, the other expressions of resentment against Jews can at present still be heard in the USSR. What underlies these attitudes is the refusal to see the Jew as anything but alien, someone different and strange who can adopt Russian culture and even create Russian culture but who will never become part of the Russian people. No matter how long an individual Jew and his or her ancestors may have lived in what is now the USSR, some will regard them not merely as outsiders, but as intruders who have no business being where they are.

Reports of antisemitism published in the Soviet press were part of a unique and noteworthy attempt by the government to combat this social problem. Never before in Russian history—and never subsequently—has a government made such an effort to uproot and stamp out antisemitism. About fifty Russian-language pamphlets and books of a frankly propagandistic and hortatory nature were published in the late 1920s and early 1930s, and an equal number of more scholarly and descriptive works all dealt with antisemitism.[11] Organized workers' trips to Jewish agricultural colonies were also arranged in order to enable non-Jewish proletarians to see for themselves that Jews had become a productive element and were doing their share in "Socialist construction." Beyond this, not much was done in the way of campaigning against antisemitism, and there seem to have been few instances of judicial prosecution for antisemitic offenses, although the fact that such behavior was illegal was rather widely publicized. Furthermore, the propaganda program tailed off and essentially ended by 1934; only one sixteen-page pamphlet linking fascism with antisemitism was published after that date. (It is significant that this pamphlet, written by Academician Struve, was published in 1941, only after the Nazi-Soviet alliance had broken down.) In view of the limited time span and the superficiality of the campaign against antisemitism, one may question whether it had any real impact on attitudes in the short run; it certainly had almost no effect in the long run. Nevertheless, its significance lies not so much in its actual accomplishments as in the fact that it set a standard by which subsequent government activity (and inactivity) could be judged. The campaign against antisemitism demonstrated that the Soviet regime was perfectly capable of discussing the issue openly, of admitting the existence of antisemitism not only among "backward elements" but even among the favored working class, and that there were certain measures the government could take in dealing with this problem. Since 1934 no similar effort has been made in the USSR. In recent years, only passing references to antisemitism have been made by top leaders: once by former Premier Kosygin in 1965, and once by Leonid Brezhnev at the 26th Party Congress in 1981. On the other hand, the volume of anti-Zionist literature has grown tremendously. Several anti-Zionist tracts have been issued in editions numbering 100,000, and the press is full of articles on the subject.

While the campaign against antisemitism was going on, the parallel but much more vigorous campaign against Zionism was mounted. Led largely by the Jewish sections of the Communist party (*Evsektsii*), the campaign was launched in the early 1920s, and it used propaganda, coercion, and attempts to provide alternatives to Zionist dreams. Many anti-Zionist tracts were published, lectures given, and meetings held. Zionists were arrested, "deported to Palestine," or exiled to Siberia. Agricultural settlement of Jews in the USSR was hailed, in the words of one Jewish peasant woman, as "Eretz Yisrael in our own land." The Leninist critique of Zionism was expanded upon and linked to the Jewish clericals and their bourgeois sponsors. Zionist "exclusivism" was condemned ("racism" was not yet a popular term). This campaign was part of the "struggle on two fronts—against antisemitism and against Jewish nationalism."

But there are two crucial differences between the campaigns of the 1920s and those of today. First, the anti-Zionist campaign, as well as the campaign against the Jewish religion, was carried out largely by Jews—members of the *Evsektsii*. Moreover, as the propaganda was predominantly in Yiddish, especially the antireligious material, the campaigns remained, to a considerable extent, internal Jewish affairs. Today, the anti-Zionist and anti-Judaism campaigns are carried out overwhelmingly in Russian, Ukrainian, Moldavian, and other languages accessible to the entire population, with consequences that will be explored later in this chapter. Second, there really was a "struggle on two fronts," even though the struggle against antisemitism was weaker. Today, despite the ritualistic formula of combating both Zionism and antisemitism, nothing concrete is done in regard to the latter. In fact, a plausible case can be made that, at a minimum, Soviet policies allow for the growth of antisemitism or are themselves directly antisemitic.

Although we do not know with any certainty why the campaign against antisemitism was ended, we do know that there was a fundamental shift in Soviet nationality policy as a whole. In the previous decade the emphasis had been on combating "Great Russian chauvinism," protecting minority rights, and encouraging non-Russian cultures, whereas in the 1930s, a period of collectivization and of five-year plans, the emphasis was focused on the dangers of "petit bourgeois nationalism" (i.e., nationalism of the non-Russian peoples) and on the common Socialist content of all the cultures of all the peoples of the USSR, thereby deemphasizing the "national forms" of those cultures that differentiated them from each other. There were indications that antisemitism was now becoming acceptable even at the highest echelons of the party and state. During the Great Purge, the most prominent of the Old Bolsheviks were eliminated, and attention was frequently drawn to their Jewish origins. Because the campaign against antisemitism had been halted, Soviet citizens realized that it was no longer unacceptable to indulge one's prejudices. In the tense atmosphere of the purges and at a time when large numbers of peasants, driven off the farms by collectivization and attracted to newly available industrial jobs, were flowing into the cities, some of the social tensions found expression in interethnic hostilities, including antisemitism. Whereas an earlier generation of Soviet leaders had attempted to confront and combat antisemitic sentiments among the population, the Stalinist leadership seemed willing to countenance such feelings and make its peace with them. Thus, when the Soviets took control of the Western Ukraine, West Belorussia, and the Baltic states in 1939–1940, few Jews were appointed to official posts, despite their prominence in the previously illegal Communist parties in those regions. They were told informally that since the local populations would resent such appointments as the creation of Jewish mastery over Gentiles, the authorities could not politically afford such actions. Concessions were also made to the Nazis, with whom the Soviets had signed a nonaggression pact in 1939; one such concession was the removal of the Jew Maxim Litvinoff from the post of foreign minister. The number of Jews in prominent political positions declined, although it is impossible to say with certainty how much this was due to antisemitism as opposed to other factors.

World War II exacerbated popular antisemitism and confirmed a growing reluctance on the part of the regime to acknowledge the problem and do something about it. Nazi propaganda, which blamed all the sufferings of the Soviet peoples on the Jews, had its effect, and since the Nazis played on the Jewish theme so extensively, some Soviet citizens concluded that were it not for the existence of the Jews the USSR would not have been involved in the war. Great resentment was aroused by the appearance of Jewish refugees and evacuated officials in Soviet Central Asia and other areas. The idea that the "Jews had fought the war in Tashkent" was widely entertained in the USSR, despite the outstanding war record compiled by Jewish military men and women. There were serious tensions even in the partisan movement. Not only did Soviet authorities try to prevent the formation of separate Jewish units, but Jewish partisan units often found themselves in serious conflict with other units, and some partisan units simply refused to accept Jews.

Before the war, the Soviets did not inform their population of the special role occupied by the Jews in Nazi ideology, and they kept Jews and non-Jews alike ignorant of the special fate meted out to Jews by the Nazis. As a consequence, many Jews were left unprepared for the actions taken against them by the invaders. All during the war the Soviet government consistently refused to bring to light the special Jewish fate and insisted on maintaining the position that all Soviet citizens were suffering equally under the Nazi yoke. This has remained Soviet policy to the present day.

The Harvard Project on the Soviet Social System extensively interviewed 329 ex-Soviet citizens living in the West in 1950–1951, all of whom had left the USSR during or after the war. William Korey, who analyzed these interviews, concluded that about three-quarters of the respondents stereotyped Jews in one way or another.

> Of the total number of respondents, approximately 60 percent held negative stereotypes of Jews, although a number of these, at the very same time, also held positive stereotypes. Approximately 10 percent of the respondents expressed a violent hostility to Jews. . . . In addition to those who expressed blatant antisemitic sentiments, approximately 25 percent of the respondents revealed various shadings of strongly hostile attitudes toward Jews. . . . The most frequently expressed stereotype was that the Jews were the most privileged and favored group in Soviet society. Of the total number who expressed hostile attitudes, approximately 70 percent stated that a characteristic feature of Soviet society was the "favored" position of Jews.[12]

The sufferings of the Jews in the war, to the extent that they became known to the Soviet citizenry, may have aroused sympathy among some, but they failed to promote a rethinking of basic attitudes toward Jews.

Many years before, Maxim Gorky had pointed out that "the Jews are defenseless, and this is especially dangerous for them in the conditions of Russian life. Dostoyevsky, who knew the Russian soul so well, pointed out repeatedly that defenselessness arouses in it a sensuous inclination to cruelty and crime."[13]

At no time in Soviet history was antisemitism so widespread, so blatant, and so officially condoned as in the years following the war, especially between 1948 and 1952. In 1948 all Jewish cultural institutions were shut down and the outstanding figures of Yiddish culture were arrested. This was a period when Russian chauvinism and anti-Westernism reached a new peak, and all contacts with the West or interest in Western culture were considered subversive. A campaign against "rootless cosmopolitans" was launched specifically against Jews, the main propaganda line being that Jews were an alien people of dubious loyalty with far too many connections abroad. Openly expressed sympathy on the part of the Soviet Jews for the newly created State of Israel was taken as further proof that Soviet Jews constituted a potentially dangerous fifth column, ready to strike at the Soviet regime on behalf of Western imperialism. By 1952 this campaign had resulted in the physical elimination of the leading lights of Jewish literature and in the sinister "Doctors' Plot" in which Jewish doctors were accused of trying to murder high Soviet officials through medical malpractice. The Doctors' Plot was probably a prelude to a larger political purge that never came off owing to Stalin's death in March 1953, but its immediate effect was to terrorize the Jews into believing that a massive purge, perhaps wholesale deportation, was in store for them. The atmosphere created by the authorities (Stalin's own daughter has testified that Stalin was himself antisemitic) signaled the Soviet people that antisemitism was not only permissible but perhaps even required of good citizens committed to following the party line. Jews were purged from educational, scientific, and industrial establishments, often because it was thought dangerous to have too many Jews on one's staff, and they disappeared from the foreign service, the foreign trade apparatus, and other sensitive posts. Day-to-day relationships between Jews and non-Jews became filled with tension, mutual suspicion, and fear. After the "Doctors' Plot" was announced, some people refused to be treated by Jewish doctors in the polyclinics. It is no wonder that this period came to be known among Soviet Jews as "the black years."[14]

The death of Stalin brought about the renunciation of the Doctors' Plot and the cessation of the anti-Jewish campaign, but there was no attempt to revive the dissolved cultural institutions, although the individual victims of the purges were later "rehabilitated." As in so many other ways, the legacy of Stalin clearly was only partially repudiated, leaving ambiguous the entire question of official and popular attitudes toward the Jews.

Contemporary Soviet Policies

Despite all the twists and turns of Soviet foreign and domestic policies under Khrushchev, Brezhnev, and Andropov, there has been a fundamental continuity in Jewish policy since the death of Stalin. The more irrational excesses have been curbed, and Jews have found it easier to gain higher education or even the right to emigrate at certain times during the last three decades. Sometimes an anti-Zionist campaign is intense; at other times it is relatively muted. But three policies have remained in place. First, Jews have been effectively barred from higher-level positions in the party, the state, the administration of academia, the foreign service and the foreign trade apparatus, the secret police, and the armed forces. And ever since emigration gained significant proportions in 1971, Jews have also been restricted from "sensitive" fields to a greater degree than before and their admissions to higher education have declined precipitously. Thus, no effort has been made to restore Jews to the places of prominence they once occupied; in fact, the trend has been to squeeze them out.

The second constant of Soviet policy is abstention from any efforts against antisemitism. Rather than try to cure this social disease, the Soviet authorities have permitted publication of tracts so blatantly antisemitic that they have aroused publicly expressed protests on the part of otherwise entirely conformist Soviet personalities who are disturbed by the "inaccuracies," "distortions," or "careless formulations" that even they have discerned in official mass propaganda. On rare occasions, the outcry at home and abroad is sufficient to cause a partial "retreat," as when Trofim Kichko's notorious *Judaism Without Embellishment* was withdrawn from circulation—but two years later its author was given high honors and restored to his position as a favored propagandist.

Third, there has been no significant improvement in the status of Jewish culture. Not a single Jewish school of any kind exists anywhere in the country; the number of synagogues and clergymen keeps shrinking; no Jewish culture in the Russian language is allowed to develop. The monthly *Sovetish haimland*, begun in 1961, continues to appear in a small edition (7,000 in number), and courses for Yiddish writers have been established at a prestigious institute. But when Yiddish language electives were proposed for high schools in Birobidzhan, where less than 10 percent of the population is Jewish, no textbooks were available. Hebrew, now of greater interest to the younger generation than Yiddish, cannot be studied legally, except by non-Jews in a few specialized faculties of higher education.

Another policy directed against the Jews—though, like the others, not articulated in public policy pronouncements—is the restriction of the entry of Jews to higher education. Since the 1971–1972 academic year, the number of Jewish students in higher education has fallen by more than 40 percent. A similar decline has taken place in the number of Jewish graduate students and in the number of Jews in Moscow's higher educational institutions, generally considered the most prestigious in the country.[15] Such a consistent and strong trend can only be the result of a central policy decision. The timing of the decision, made during the same period in which emigration assumed a mass character, leads us to suspect the rationale for it: If Jews are going to emigrate, why give them the benefit of a Soviet higher education? Why should the Socialist fatherland prepare cadres for neofascist Israel or the imperialist United States? All Jews have become potential émigrés and disloyal elements, and must be treated as such. Restricting the entry of Jews into higher education closes the last channel of social mobility left to them. As mentioned earlier, they have long been excluded from the upper political and cultural echelons, but higher education at one time gave them the opportunity to make reasonable scientific and professional careers. Now that the prospects for such careers have dimmed,[16] many Jews see no future for themselves or their children in the USSR, and this perception has become a major push for emigration in recent years.

Thus far we have discussed the policies that are clearly directed against Jews. But there are other policies whose antisemitic effects may not have been intended as such. For example, the campaign against Judaism should not, in theory, affect the large numbers of Soviet Jews inasmuch as they are not at all religious. Yet, just as in the case of Muslims who no longer adhere to Islam, the Soviet public identifies Jews with their historical religion. This tendency is especially strong with regard to Judaism because it is a religion uniquely associated with the Jewish people, unlike Christianity or Islam, which are "universal" religions practiced by many nations and ethnic groups. Thus attacks on Judaism are perceived as attacks on Jews. Moreover, linkages are often made between Zionism and Judaism, although some of the most determined opponents of Zionism are the most fanatic religionists. In one recent commentary it was alleged that the "ideological sources of Zionist gangsterism originate in the scrolls of the Torah," which, in turn, was described as a "textbook unsurpassed for betrayal, perfidy, and moral dissoluteness."[17] Soviet authors differ on the nature of the links between Judaism and Zionism, but the majority see an intimate connection between them.[18] Religious Jews who may have no desire to emigrate to Israel are tarred with the brush of Zionism, even while secular Zionists are linked to Judaism. Jews who are neither religious nor Zionists are stigmatized by association with both.

Another policy with antisemitic consequences, stronger than the ones flowing from anti-Judaism propaganda, is the shrill, almost hysterical anti-Zionism that has emanated from the USSR since 1967. Content analysis of the Soviet press shows that it was only after this date that Zionism reemerged as a major topic of official discussion.[19] In the last twenty years, more than seventy books and pamphlets condemning Zionism have been published, several in editions numbering over 100,000, in addition to writings on Israel, Judaism, and other themes that are almost invariably tied into Zionism. The post-1967 anti-Zionist propaganda connects Zionism to fascism, racism, an international anti-Communist conspiracy, and Judaism. Zionism is portrayed as a racist ideology preaching the superiority of Jews to all other peoples. Some argue that it is a variant of fascism. Indeed, as one publication put it, "Many facts have convincingly demonstrated the fascist nature of the ideology and policies of Zionism. Fascism is disgusting in any of its guises. Its Zionist version is no better than the Hitlerite one."[20] More and more frequently one finds the assertion that the Zionists collaborated with the Nazis.[21] However odious this claim may be, it is calculated to clarify for Soviet readers just what this Zionism is all about and to link it in their minds to the greatest evil their country has experienced. By associating Zionism with fascism and Nazism, it is transformed from an esoteric doctrine of a far-off people to a hateful ideology tied to the most repugnant people of this century, who caused the loss of 20 million Soviet lives.

But if the Soviet propagandists succeed in arousing strong feelings against Zionism, it becomes crucial to know whether and in what ways Zionism is associated with Jews. For if it is, then Jews are associated with Nazis, not necessarily as victims but as supporters of the same kind of racism and politics that led to the death of 20 million Soviet people in 1941–1945. Even a casual glance at anti-Zionist propaganda will reveal that Jews and Zionists are very closely associated. When Zionism's alleged aim of world domination is discussed, distinctions between Jews and Zionists are erased. Hence non-Zionist and even anti-Zionist organizations (the Bund, Agudat Yisrael, Hebrew Immigrant Aid Society), theorists (Simon Dubnow, Henri Bergson, Hermann Cohen), and non-Zionist reformist Communists (František Kriegel, Eduard Goldstücker) are all brought under the rubric of "Zionists." Yet, at the same time, the Soviets rail against the Zionist "myth" of the "unity of the Jewish people," for there are anti-Zionist Jews as well as Zionists. But the vituperative attacks on Zionists and the clear association of Zionists and Jews have even aroused protest by some Soviet commentators, some of them "active fighters against Zionism" themselves. It has been claimed that "even in the United States the great majority of Jews are Jews, not Zionists," thus implying that this was certainly the case in the USSR. Some Soviet authors and academics have objected to terms such as *Zionist capital* and *international Zionist conspiracy* as counterproductive from a propaganda point of view.[22] Even the author of an article charging Zionism as being "in the service of imperialism and reaction" has asserted that in a book entitled *Zionism—The Tool of Imperialism*, the authors "unmask Zionist propaganda which attempts to . . . identify the concepts of Jew, practising Jew, and Zionist. However, the authors themselves manifest some carelessness in terminology, calling Zionist and Judaic (*iudaistskie*) organizations Jewish."[23] Yeshayahu Nir, while studying Soviet caricatures that surfaced in the press between 1967 and 1973, observed that in those depicting the Arab-Israeli conflict, "some caricaturists clearly avoided making use of the Jewish stereotype; others used it explicitly. Some papers do not publish such figures; others do, often." Thus, in *Izvestiia* only 20 percent of the caricatures used recognizably Jewish features, but in the newspaper *Gudok* half the caricatures did so.[24]

Whatever the intentions of the policymakers and propagandists, the crucial question for us is how their policies and propaganda are perceived. What matters in the daily lives of ordinary citizens is how they are regarded by the regime and by their fellow citizens. It is the interpretation of Soviet policies and the reception given to propaganda that will affect their social and psychological position.

Perception of Antisemitism in the USSR

Soviet leaders rank their achievements in inter-nationality relations with the greatest accomplishments of their system. Leonid Brezhnev proudly claimed that the achievements of "Leninist nationality policy . . . can truly be put on the same level with achievements in the construction of a new society in the USSR such as industrialization, collectivization, the cultural revolution."[25] On the sixtieth anniversary of the October Revolution, the Central Committee of the party declared: "Factual equality of all nations and nationalities in all spheres of . . . society has been assured . . . and genuine brotherhood of the people of labor, independent of nationality, has become established, a brotherhood welded by a community of fundamental interests, goals, and Marxist-Leninist ideology."[26] However, it is acknowledged that progress toward the goal of amalgamation (*sliianie*) of the peoples is slow, and that not "all questions of nationality relations have been solved. . . . The degree of development of such a large multinational state as ours gives rise to many problems which demand the Party's close attention."[27]

Such assertions can be tested empirically, not in the USSR where official dogma and political sensitivities severely restrict research on interethnic relations[28] but among those who have lived recently in the USSR. True, information provided by émigrés may be biased and unrepresentative of the total population from which they emerged. But because the likelihood of being able to do fieldwork on ethnic questions within the USSR is next to nothing, a second-best strategy should be followed, especially since the assumption of émigré bias may well be exaggerated. In any case, for some research purposes political bias and demographic unrepresentativeness are largely irrelevant. It should be pointed out that the emigration is demographically unrepresentative not because only Jews, Armenians, and Germans have chosen to leave the country, but because Soviet policy has made it possible for only those groups to leave. Therefore, the ethnic imbalance of the emigration is as much a product of Soviet emigration policy as it is of special feelings of alienation on the part of those who have left.

Second, when questioned about their reasons for leaving the USSR, the members of our sample, to be described below, cited a wide variety of reasons, many of them having nothing to do with alienation from the system. Thus, 23 percent gave as their primary reason for leaving the fact that they had relatives abroad, or that they were following—often reluctantly—spouses, parents, or children who had decided to emigrate. Another 23 percent cited their desire to live among people of their own ethnic group, and nearly a fifth gave such varied answers as to defy coding under common rubrics (e.g., "Soviet life has become boring"; "My sister in Israel fell ill, and I felt I had to come and help her"; "Everyone was going, so we went too."). Only 15 percent cited "political reasons" or "hatred of the Soviet system" as their primary reason for emigrating. In the absence of reliable data on the attitudes of the Soviet population toward the system, it cannot be assumed that the émigrés are significantly more hostile. Moreover, it is reasonable to assume that ethnic attitudes are not peculiar to émigrés but quite widespread in society, and that opinions of the émigrés might be representative in *direction* if not in *intensity*. We may assume that any biases present in the sample as a whole are distributed fairly uniformly across population subgroups. Therefore, any differences observed across subgroups are similar to those characterizing those same groups within the Soviet population. This means that relationships among variables—the relationship, say, between education and ethnic prejudice—are likely to be brought out in our sample and are also likely to be present within the Soviet population, though perhaps in different degrees of intensity.[29]

A group of 1,161 ex-Soviet citizens who had left the USSR in 1977–1980 were interviewed during 1980–1981 in Israel (n = 590), the Federal Republic of Germany (n = 100), and the United States (n = 471). Six hundred women and 561 men were interviewed, the youngest being 22 and half the sample having been born in the 1930s and 1940s. Nearly half the respondents had received higher education (the immigrations to Israel and the United States have consistently revealed about 40 percent with such education). Seventy-seven percent, or 889 people, had been registered as Jews on their internal Soviet passports; 129 were registered as Russians; 98 as Germans; 18 as Ukrainians; and 27 were of other nationalities. The areas in which the respondents had lived most of their lives are as follows: RSFSR, 330; Ukraine, 247; Moldavia, 210; Baltic, 174; Georgia, 120; Central Asia, 165. Men and women are quite evenly distributed in the age and regional categories, but men dominate the blue-collar professions and females the white-collar ones, despite very similar educational levels (48 percent of the men and 46 percent of the women have higher education). Educational levels are highest among those from the RSFSR, and from the ethnic groups,

TABLE 15.1
Relationships Between Pairs of Nationalities in the USSR*

Lithuanians and Latvians	Best
Russians and Belorussions	
Jews and Moldavians	↓
Russians and Uzbeks	
Russians and Ukrainians	
Russians and Estonians	
Georgians and Armenians	
Jews and Russians	
Jews and Ukrainians	Worst

*As 59 percent of the respondents did not characterize Russian-Kazakh relations, we have eliminated this pair from the table.

among the Russians (69 percent of the former and 72 percent of the latter have had higher education). The lowest educational levels are found among people from Central Asia (18 percent with higher education) and from Moldavia (23 percent). Those from Moldavia also had the lowest income of the European groups, and the Central Asians had the lowest income of any group.

These people were interviewed in Russian or Georgian by native speakers. Despite the fact that the interview lasted between two and three hours, remarkably few declined to be interviewed.

Our respondents took a substantially different view of inter-nationality relations from the official one expressed by Brezhnev and the Central Committee. When asked "In your opinion, to what extent does 'friendship of the peoples' (*druzhba narodov*) exist in the USSR?" more than half of all respondents answered "hardly at all" and three-quarters fell into the two categories of "to a small extent" or "hardly at all." These feelings were especially strong among the Europeans, although even among Georgians and Central Asians a majority took a negative view. Jews from the RSFSR had the most negative evaluation, and there was not much difference among the other Europeans. The entire sample was asked to characterize the relationships among ten pairs of nationalities. In order to test the degree to which the respondents paid serious attention to the questions and were willing to differentiate among inter-nationality relations, we included pairs of nationalities between whom tensions are widely reported and those between whom there are few difficulties. Summarizing the answers given to all the questions by all the respondents (including non-Jews), we found the following results (Table 15.1).

In order to test the salience of problematic ethnic relations, respondents were asked to identify those nationalities that would be involved in such relations. The question was left open, and up to four replies were coded. The following are the frequencies with which the poor relationships

TABLE 15.2
Frequency of Antisemitic Encounter, by Republic (in percentages)

	RSFSR	Ukraine	Baltic	Moldavia	Georgia	Central Asia
Often	33.2	38.0	26.8	25.2	6.3	13.1
Sometimes	40.4	31.9	36.9	37.4	20.5	34.3
Rarely	21.2	16.9	22.3	18.3	30.4	31.3
Never	4.1	12.7	11.5	18.3	40.2	19.2
Don't know, No answer	1.0	0.5	2.5	0.9	2.7	2.0

were mentioned by the entire sample: Balts and Russians, 495; Armenians and Georgians, 389; Jews and Ukrainians, 362; and Jews and Russians, 318. When analyzed by ethnicity of the respondents, it turned out that Jews and Russians had very similar views, except that the Russians mentioned the Ukrainian-Russian as problematic significantly more often. (Germans have a quite different order, reflecting their own experiences. Their most frequent response is that "relations among all nationalities are bad," and they also identify Russian-Asian relations as poor, which is explained by the fact that many Germans spent long periods in Central Asia.) Both Russians and Jews mentioned Jewish-Ukrainian relations third in order of frequency, and for both this is the pair mentioned second most frequently (Jews mentioned Jewish-Russian relations most frequently, and Russians mentioned Armenian-Georgian relations). Taking the first four pairs mentioned, irrespective of order, we find Jews mentioning most frequently the following pairs: Armenian-Georgian (34.4 percent of Jews mentioned this pair at some point or other); Jewish-Ukrainian (33.2 percent); Jewish-Russian (29.6 percent); and Russian-Baltic (29.4 percent).

Moving from generalized images to personal experiences, we asked whether respondents "personally experienced antisemitism in the Soviet Union." Among all Jews in the sample, 60.7 percent reported encounters with antisemitism often (26.5 percent) or sometimes (34.2 percent), and only 15.5 percent said they had had no experiences at all with antisemitism. The responses by republic are presented in Table 15.2. The most frequent antisemitic encounters were reported by people from the Ukraine. But when the first two response categories were combined, there was little difference between the RSFSR and the Ukraine. Nor was there that great a difference between these two republics and the other European republics of the Baltic and Moldavia. The sharpest difference, of course, was that between European republics and Georgia–Central Asia, where the incidence of reported antisemitism is dramatically lower.

TABLE 15.3
Frequency of Antisemitic Encounter, by Education (in percentages)

	Elementary education	Secondary	Higher
Often	18.7	20.4	34.2
Sometimes	30.9	33.4	35.9
Rarely	28.8	21.9	20.4
Never	20.1	22.2	8.5
Don't know, No answer	1.4	2.1	1.0

It is striking that there were no consistent differences by age in perceptions of antisemitism. Whether one came to maturity in the "black years," during the pogrom period, or at more benign times makes no difference as far as perceptions of antisemitism are concerned. This and other analyses[30] lead us to suspect that either each generation has had its own experiences with antisemitism or that a folklore of antisemitic experiences is being handed down from generation to generation—or both. There is also no relationship between the strength of one's Jewish background and upbringing and perceptions of antisemitism, nor are the more religious inclined to see more antisemitism than the others. However, there is some tendency for men to report more frequent encounters with antisemitism than women. Since the educational levels of the two sexes are almost the same but their occupational distribution is different, we can only speculate that men may be encountering more antisemitism in their vocational lives, especially those who have ambitions to reach positions of leadership and responsibility, positions not often gained by Soviet women. Artists, scientists, economists, and engineers report the most frequent encounters with antisemitism, whereas clerks (mostly women), students, and low-level medical personnel report the least frequent. Blue-collar workers, teachers, and some types of low level–collar workers fall in between these two groups.

In view of the occupational distribution noted, it is not surprising to find that there is a positive correlation between education and frequency of encounters with antisemitism. This can be observed in Table 15.3. These relationships hold true in all the republics from which the respondents came. Since admission to higher education and job assignment after graduation have been—and are—problematic for Soviet Jews, we can understand the relationship between education and perceptions of antisemitism. There may well be less discrimination against Jews employed in lower-level and less desirable jobs. Moreover, more educated people are more likely to be aware of the Soviet propaganda directed against Judaism, Zionism, and, by implication, Jews. They are more likely to pick up the nuances of Soviet messages that carry antisemitic overtones, and to contrast the lofty ideals of "friendship of the peoples" with the social and political realities they observe daily.

The same reasoning may explain the astounding finding that former members of the Communist party, presumably well integrated into the "establishment" and accepting its myths, report more frequent encounters with antisemitism than the sample as a whole. Thus, 30.4 percent of the former party members report encountering antisemitism "often" and 41.1 percent say "sometimes." Perhaps they are more aware of the realities of Soviet decisionmaking, of the attitudes of the "leading circles," and of the rationales of various policies. It seems that the higher one goes in Soviet society, the more one encounters antisemitism—or at least perceives its existence.

These findings on perceptions of antisemitism are quite similar to the results from other surveys that addressed the same issue in a variety of ways. In four surveys encompassing in all about 3,200 recent Jewish émigrés from the USSR, about three-quarters of the respondents claimed frequent or occasional personal encounters with antisemitism in the USSR. One-third to one-half of those interviewed said that they had experienced antisemitism "often." The surveys included interviews in 1972 in Israel with 148 male immigrants from the Soviet Union who had had at least a high school education;[31] interviews in 1976 in Detroit with 132 recent arrivals from the USSR; a 1973 survey in Israel among 2,527 immigrants from the USSR (of whom 447 had been active in the Jewish national movement there); and a 1976–1977 survey comparing over 300 émigrés in Rome (bound mainly for the United States), with more than 200 Israel immigrants having similar demographic characteristics.[32] In those surveys, too, there was a tendency for men to report more frequent encounters with antisemitism than females did, and the regional variations are similar to those reported here.

Conclusion

Jews from the Soviet Union, especially those from European republics, perceive antisemitism as quite pervasive. They do not accept the official image of a society in which "fraternity of nationalities" is characteristic and where antisemitism has been largely wiped out. Instead, they see themselves as the victims of ethnic discrimination and social opprobrium. Any analysis of Soviet publications—and they are all officially sanctioned—makes it clear that these perceptions are genuine and undoubtedly justified. Most of the words and many of the deeds of Soviet officialdom are perceived as directed against Jews at home and abroad. If Soviet authorities continue to invoke the ritual formula of a "struggle against Zionism and against antisemitism," their actions indicate that they are committed only to a struggle against the former.

In a larger sense this uneven "struggle," a kind of "selective Leninism," is symbolic of the changes that have taken place in the nature of the

Soviet regime. In Lenin's day the system was a genuinely revolutionary and substantially idealistic one, seeking not only to completely overhaul the political and economic structure, but also to renovate culture, change people's attitudes, values, and beliefs, and overcome "bourgeois prejudices." The Bolsheviks were revolutionaries committed to making a better world as they conceived it. Their present-day successors are conservatives, and even reactionaries. Their aim is not to remake society but to preserve it as is. They struggle to strengthen the existing order, thereby preserving their own rewards from it. Far from talking about the "withering away of the state," they are concerned with increasing its power and that of those who administer it, a vast army of bureaucrats and politicians who have established not a dictatorship *of* the proletariat but one *over* it, as many Marxist critics of the USSR have pointed out.

A subtle shift has occurred in the basis of the USSR's political legitimacy. World War II, representing the heroic struggle for the state and the system, is replacing the revolution, representing universal and radical ideals, as the "golden age" and the legitimizing myth. The revolution was supposed to be worldwide and to create wholly new values and modes of social organization. The war was fought to preserve an established state and to defend a particular territory. All the films, books, lectures, and other media devoted to arousing patriotic feelings connected with the war indicate the importance that this event has assumed in justifying the entire present order.

As long as this trend away from universals and idealism continues, policy toward Jews will not change for the better. If Soviet policy is now more pragmatic, designed to strengthen the status quo and the power of those who maintain and nurture it, and if it is useful and even beneficial to the regime to pursue antisemitic courses, it will continue to do so. For the Jews, the only option—not always available—will be to "vote with their feet" against a system they helped to found and to build, but one that has betrayed them along with other people and many of its original ideals.

Notes

1. Reuben Ainsztein, "The Soviet Union Today: Anti-Semitism Institutionalized," *New Statesman*, 15 December 1978 (also in the *Jerusalem Post Magazine*, 29 December 1978).

2. David Dragunsky, quoted in "Prese-Konferents funm antitsienistishen komitet fun der Sovetisher gezelshaftlikhkeit," *Sovetish haimland*, no. 8 (1983):103–104.

3. S. L. Zivs, quoted in ibid., p. 108.

4. William Korey, "Anti-Zionism in the USSR," *Problems of Communism* 27, no. 6 (November-December 1978):65.

5. V. I. Lenin, "To the Jewish Workers" (1905), *Collected Works*, vol. 8 (Moscow: Foreign Languages Publishing House, 1962), p. 495.

6. V. I. Lenin, "The Position of the Bund in the Party" (1903), *Collected Works*, vol. 7, pp. 100–101.

7. V. I. Lenin, "Anti-Jewish Pogroms" (1919), *Collected Works*, vol. 29, pp. 252–253.

8. The following section draws heavily on Zvi Gitelman, *Anti-Semitism in the USSR: Sources, Types, Consequences* (New York: Synagogue Council of America, 1974), pp. 9–20.

9. For details, see Zvi Gitelman, *Jewish Nationality and Soviet Politics* (Princeton, N.J.: Princeton University Press, 1972), pp. 159–167.

10. Solomon Schwarz, *The Jews in the Soviet Union* (Syracuse, N.Y.: Syracuse University Press, 1951), p. 250.

11. Based on titles listed in Mordechai Altschuler, ed., *Russian Publications on Jews and Judaism in the Soviet Union, 1917–1967* (Jerusalem: Society for Research on Jewish Communities and the Historical Society of Israel, 1970), pp. 51–66.

12. William Korey, *The Soviet Cage: Anti-Semitism in Russia* (New York: Viking, 1973), pp. 5–6.

13. Maxim Gorky et al., *The Shield* (New York: Alfred A. Knopf, 1917), p. 15.

14. See Yehoshua A. Gilboa, *The Black Years of Soviet Jewry* (Boston: Little, Brown, 1971).

15. For All-Union data, see Central Statistical Administration under the USSR Council of Ministers, *Narodnoe obrazovanie, nauka, i kultura v SSSR: Statisticheskii sbornik* (Moscow: Statistika, 1977), p. 313. For Moscow data, see Statistical Administration of Moscow City, *Moskva v. tsifrakh 1917–1977 gg.* (Moscow: Statistika, 1977), p. 144.

16. Official Soviet spokesmen deny that there is discrimination against Jews in higher education, citing the large number of Jews with such education. One spokesman asserts that "there is no discrimination and can be none," and mentions the names of Jews who held high academic posts—in the 1920s and 1930s! See M. I. Kabatchnik, *Sovetish haimland*, no. 8 (1983), p. 107. Of course, the large (but declining) role of Jews in higher education and in scholarship is due to their influx into higher education at a time when ethnicity was not much of a bar to admission.

17. Vladimir Begun, *Vtorzhenie bez oruzhiia* (Moscow: Molodaya gvardiya, 1977), quoted in Korey, "Anti-Zionism in the USSR," *Problems of Communism*, p. 64.

18. For a discussion of three Soviet positions on this question, see Zvi Gitelman, "Moscow and the Soviet Jews: A Parting of the Ways," *Problems of Communism* 29, no. 1 (January-February, 1980):27–28.

19. See ibid., pp. 25–29, especially Table 1 on p. 26.

20. *Nash otvet klevetnikam* (Kharkov, 1976). Ironically, this pamphlet is an "answer to those who slander the USSR" as antisemitic.

21. For twenty-three different citations from the Soviet press in 1975–1978 making this claim, see Institute of Jewish Affairs, *Soviet Antisemitic Propaganda* (London, 1978), pp. 67–76. See also the charges against the Zionist "Palestine Office" in prewar Berlin, made by Iu. A. Kolesnikov, in *Sovetish haimland*, no. 8 (1983), p. 109.

22. See "Protocols of the Anti-Zionist Elders," a report by E. L. Sol'mar on a meeting at the Institute of Oriental Studies of the USSR Academy of Sciences, February 1976. Published in *Evreiskii samizdat* 16 (1977):128–144.

23. A. Teplitskii, "Na sluzhbe imperialism i reaktsii," *Aziia i Afrika segodniia*, no. 7 (July 1977):63.

24. Yeshayahu Nir, *The Israeli-Arab Conflict in Soviet Caricatures 1967–1973* (Tel Aviv: Tcherikover, 1976), pp. 78–79.

25. L. I. Brezhnev, *Leninskom Kursom*, vol. 4 (Moscow: Gospolitizdat, 1975), p. 50.

26. Quoted in M. I. Kulichenko, "Sotsial'no-ekonomicheskie osnovy vzaimovliianiia i vzaimoobogashcheniia natsional'nykh kul'tur v usloviakh razvitogo sotsializma," *Voprosy istorii*, no. 5 (1977), translated in *Soviet Law and Government* 17, no. 1 (Summer 1978):53–54.

27. See Brezhnev's report to the 26th Party Congress, *Pravda*, 24 February 1981.

28. In recent years, some interesting Soviet empirical research has been done on ethnic relations, but the raw data are unavailable to foreigners and we lack complete information on the methods and contents of these studies. Some examples are V. K. Bondarchik, ed., *Etnicheskie protsessy i obraz zhizni (na materialakh issledovaniia naseleniia gorodov BSSR* (Minsk: Nauka i technika, 1980); Iu. V. Arutunian, *Opyt etnosotsiologicheskogo issledovaniia obraza zhizni* (Moscow: Nauka, 1980); A. M. Lisetskii, *Voprosy natsional'noi politiki KPSS v usloviakh razvitogo sotsializma (na materialakh Moldavskoi SSR)* (Kishinev, 1977); L. M. Drobizheva, "Sblizhenie kultur i mezhnatsional'nye otnosheniia v SSSR," *Sovietskaia etnografiia*, no. 6 (1977); and Iu. V. Arutunian, "Sotsial'no-kulturnye aspekty razvitiia sblizheniia natsii v SSSR," *Sovetskaia etnografiia*, no. 3 (1972).

29. Still the best discussion of émigré research and controlling the effects of sample bias is Alex Inkeles and Raymond Bauer, *The Soviet Citizen* (Cambridge, Mass.: Harvard University Press, 1961), ch. 2.

30. See Zvi Gitelman, "Contemporary Jewish Perceptions of Ukrainians: Some Empirical Observations," paper presented at the McMaster Conference on Jewish-Ukrainian Relations in Historical Perspective, McMaster University (Hamilton, Ontario), October 19, 1983.

31. For details, see Zvi Gitelman, *Becoming Israelis: Political Resocialization of Soviet and American Immigrants* (New York: Praeger Publishers, 1982).

32. For the Detroit data, see Zvi Gitelman, "Recent Emigres and the Soviet Political System: A Pilot Study in Detroit," *Slavic and Soviet Series* (Tel Aviv University) 2, no. 2 (Autumn 1977). The other data are from the as-yet-unpublished findings of the Project on Rebirth of Jewish National Consciousness in the USSR, at the Center for Research and Documentation of East European Jewry, The Hebrew University, Jerusalem; and the final survey was taken by Elazar Leshem (see his "The 'Drop-Out' Phenomenon Among Soviet Jews: Main Findings and Recommendations," Jerusalem, Center for Research and Documentation on East European Jewry, The Hebrew University, mimeo).

16

Economic Boycott and Discrimination

Terence Prittie

There is an unfortunate tendency, where the Arab-Israeli dispute is concerned, to consign its different facets to compartments, each of them supposedly totally detached from all others. Thus the press of the outside world, listening with less than half an ear to anti-Israeli propaganda, has been ready to accept that "anti-Zionism" has really nothing to do with antisemitism. Anti-Zionism, one is then told by Arab propagandists, is not even a rejection of the State of Israel; it is a rejection of its "imperialist," "expansionist," maybe even "fascist" connotations. And so it has nothing to do with antisemitism, which has to be a European invention and a European disgrace. One is even informed, absurdly, that Arabs could not possibly be antisemitic—because they, too, are "Semites"! Any child knows there has never been an antisemitic campaign against the Arabs.

In the same way Arabs, and their friends, will explain that the economic war waged against Israel, the Jewish state, has nothing to do with anti-Jewish sentiments. Yet this economic war takes the form of an Arab trade boycott, directed with malice and muddlement, against Israel's trade with the outside world and involving the affairs of countries that have no part whatever in the Arab-Israeli dispute. The *form* of this boycott is not a guarded mystery; it is directed against Israel and its people, against Jews and anybody else in the outside world who support Israel in any way or who merely trade with Israel, against Jews *simply because they are Jews*, who in turn can conveniently be labeled as enemies. Are this boycott and this economic war against Israel, then, not anti-Jewish? The question deserves investigation.

The first relevant reflection is that both boycott and all-out economic war started long before the State of Israel came into being, during the period of the British Mandate in Palestine. The operative call for the boycott of all Jewish businesses in Palestine came in 1922 from the Fifth Arab Congress, meeting in Nablus. In 1929 the assistance of women, who were generally ignored, was invoked; the First Palestine Women's Congress asked "every Arab to buy nothing from the Jews but land, and to sell them everything but land." Demands for the economic and trade boycott of Jews were made in 1931 and 1933, and in 1936 they were given the seal of the Islamic faith—Haj Amin al-Husseini, the Grand Mufti and religious leader of all Palestinian Arabs, proclaimed a total and permanent boycott of all Jewish goods and all Jewish shops and other places of work.

Some day there may be a historical study in depth of the links between what the Mufti was doing in Palestine and what Hitler was doing in Germany at the same time. The Nazi boycott of German Jewry began on April 1, 1933. Jews in general were to be depicted as social outcasts. In particular, the Jews were to be hit "where it hurt most," in their pockets—a phrase used only a few years later by a respected and otherwise respectable British general, Sir Evelyn Barker. All Jewish shops and businesses in Germany were picketed by Nazi stormtroopers. Their banners announced "Germans, defend yourselves! Don't buy from Jews!" The Nazis called off the boycott after twenty-four hours, chiefly because of its adverse effect on opinion abroad. It is strange to reflect that the Arab boycott of Israel and the Jews has been going on, in one form or another, for nearly sixty years and that "opinion abroad" has shown a truly amazing readiness to "live with it" and to offer next to no protest. The 1930s were supposedly a "silly" era of irresponsibility. What, then, of today?

One fact, at least, needs to be underlined. The Arab and Nazi boycotts of the Jews were exactly similar in nature and in purpose. What the Arabs had tried to do in the 1920s was emulated by the Nazis in the 1930s; and what the Nazis did then, and later, served as a model for the full-scale Arab trade boycott of Israel, which was launched the very moment that Israeli statehood was proclaimed in May 1948. By then, total economic war against the Jews of Palestine was already three years old; on December 2, 1945, the Council of the Arab League announced that "Jewish products and manufactured goods shall be considered undesirable to Arab countries." All Arabs were instructed not to deal in "Zionist" produce. The words *Jewish* and *Zionist* were, in effect, interchangeable. They have been ever since.

There is nothing odd about this. By 1948 it was quite plain to those who framed Arab policies and directed Arab actions that a great majority of Jews supported the creation of the State of Israel. To suggest that this "Zionist state" was supported only by a minority of cranks and fanatics was nonsensical. It therefore should have been equally plain that anti-Zionism's sole special trademark was its denial of the right of Jews to have a state of their own—even though the Jews had been carefully creating the sinews of a state for at least half a century. Again, there is nothing surprising about this Arab brand of anti-Zionism; for thirteen centuries the Jews who lived in the Arab world had been categorized as *dhimmis*, the "protected ones," second-class citizens who had been periodically demeaned, discriminated against, or even violently persecuted. A *Jewish* state, in a part of the Arab world and against

Arab wishes, was a deadly insult to Islam. Here, then, is the essential root of Arab refusal to accept the State of Israel down to this very day.

Economic boycott was a weapon of total war against not only the State of Israel but also against its Jewish citizens who had dared to cast off the sackcloth of second-class citizens of the Arab world, and against all other Jews who gave material aid. The mechanics of this boycott can be dealt with briefly. All frontiers were closed against Israel, as was the Suez Canal to Israeli shipping. A state of total war against Israel was proclaimed by all the states of the Arab League, and they undertook to establish their own boycott offices, with a Central Boycott Office in Damascus. Where possible, international waterways (specifically, the Straits of Tiran and the Gulf of Aqaba) were barred against ships bringing goods to Israel.

Early on, boycott regulations made it clear that Jews did not need to be distinguished from Zionists, or the reverse. Thus a British company was required to declare that "the company is not a *Jewish* company not controlled by *Jews* or Zionists, and that it has no relations with Israel." This demand came from an allegedly "moderate" Arab government, that of Saudi Arabia. And in 1955 a Dutch firm received the following questionnaire from the Central Boycott Office:

> Do you have any *Jewish* employees in your company, if yes, how many and what are the positions held by them?
>
> Are there any *Jews* in your board of directors as members?
>
> Is any of your managers or branch managers a *Jew*?
>
> Is any of the persons authorised to sign on behalf of your company a *Jew*?
>
> What is the number of *Jewish* labourers in your factories or offices?

It was clearly not regarded as necessary to ask whether such Jews were Zionists; it was important only that they were Jews. Maybe there is nothing indelibly antisemitic in asking who is a Jew, but in instances like this was the implicit Arab recognition that Jews were enemies, because they were virtually certain to support the State of Israel. The distinction between economic and racial discrimination at this stage becomes blurred; indeed, they appear to be of the same genus, perhaps twins. Antisemitism and anti-Zionism merge.

Protagonists of the Arab cause in Britain have steadfastly insisted that economic sanctions against Israel cannot possibly be classified as racist. They were given the lie in the notorious "Mancroft case" in 1963. Lord Mancroft belonged to Britain's "upper crust" and was educated at Winchester and Oxford; as a former junior Minister turned businessman, he had not paraded himself as a Zionist, but he never failed to show friendly feelings toward Israel. He had been four years a member of the board of the Norwich Union Insurance Company when the Arab

League brought pressure to bear on his company to force him to resign from the board. Unbelievably, the company complied—and the case remains unique in Britain up to this day. Amazing, too, was the fact that the subsequent storm of criticism had next to no result, save that the Norwich Union invited Lord Mancroft to rejoin its board and he, with dignity, declined. Lord Mancroft was a director of Great Universal Stores, which had contributed to Jewish and Israeli charities. This, in Arab eyes, may have been a crime. What is relevant is that the Arab League and its boycott offices were able to endanger, and indeed damage, the career in commerce of a respected and reliable member of the Jewish community in Britain.

The Arabs continue to maintain that economics have nothing to do with politics, and that Arab economic measures against Israel have nothing to do with racism. One can readily admit that there are Arabs in positions of power who believe this most sincerely. Perhaps, then, the basic document of the Arab Trade Boycott deserves examination in order to dispel their illusions. This basic document was drawn up in Damascus. On its first page it lays down that boycott action should be taken against "natural persons having Zionist sympathies." A blanket-phrase such as "Zionist sympathies" can be held to cover anyone who accepts the State of Israel. Boycott action is also extended to institutions or companies that are "pro-Zionist"; again, this can be interpreted as including any company that trades with Israel or any institution with relations with Israel.

There is a special provision prohibiting any Jew who has left his or her home in an Arab state from residing in another Arab state, or even from entering it. Companies in which more than 50 percent of the capital is in the hands of "pro-Zionists" are automatically to be blacklisted. Ever and again the phrase "pro-Zionist" occurs, but it is left to boycott offices to determine who comes under this heading.

It can at once be seen that the Central Boycott Office in Damascus was careful not to use the word *Jew* in any context that might imply antisemitic bias. But the individual boycott offices in the countries of the Arab League, and the governments of those countries, have made it perfectly plain that *pro-Zionist* is no more than a euphemism for *Jew*. Thus only last year the Syrian Ministry of Defense demanded that "suspected persons, particularly *Jews*" should be debarred from participation in a proposed contract with the Sybron Corporation of Rochester in the state of New York. Similar demands were made to the Buck Engineering Company of Farmingdale, New Jersey, and to the Central Scientific Company of Chicago. Moreover, Iraq has for years past been issuing confidential documents in which it is explained that foreign companies will be blacklisted if it is found that they contain "any person who is Zionist or a *Jew*." And Malaysia, which, being a predominantly Muslim country, has been drawn into the orbit of the Arab Boycott, has issued a formal governmental statement that no official department or statutory body has any links with *Jewish* or Israeli enterprises.

Last year Saudi Arabia was demanding a "solemn declaration" that any firm exporting goods to it "is not a *Jewish* company nor controlled by Jews." Ten years ago, indeed, Saudi Arabia gave more striking evidence of the antisemitism underlying its political as well as economic actions. Sir Horace Phillips was appointed Britain's ambassador to Jeddah. He was initially accepted by the Saudi government, until it became known that he was a Jew. His credentials were at once withdrawn. As it happened, Sir Horace had spent most of his diplomatic career in Islamic countries, could speak perfect Arabic, and had mastered a number of dialects. But the British government had to accept the humiliating outcome of the affair.

Saudi Arabia, again, demanded the screening out of Jewish applicants for jobs in Bendix-Siyanco of Columbia (Maryland) in 1975, forced a North Carolina building contractor to bring no Jewish employees to the country, and broke off negotiations with a Chicago firm of architects because it was not prepared to say that it was not partly Jewish-owned.

Kuwait, like a number of other Arab countries, had made a habit of denying entry of Jews and had made this practice effective by demanding the production by all visiting businessmen of Christian baptismal certificates.

There is, of course, nothing surprising about this anti-Jewish discrimination. The great and thriving Jewish communities in the Arab world have virtually vanished. The few struggling survivors in countries like Syria and Iraq are subjected to intermittent harassment and persecution. Even a "moderate" Arab country such as Jordan has made its position plain. Its territory was designated after World War I as a part of the Jewish "homeland" in which Jews, under British protection, were to be encouraged to settle. When Jordan became a semi-independent emirate in 1923 all Jewish settlement was ended; the country became "Judenrein." One hates to have to say it, but in this respect—and in this respect only—King Hussein's Jordan has followed the precepts of Hitler, whereas Syria and Iraq have adopted those of King Pharoah and Stalin, by retaining and in effect imprisoning Jews who can be used as hostages or as objects of incitement to racial hatred.

The Arabs' economic war against the Jews is not circumscribed by the borders of the Arab world. The operations of the boycott are, of course, carried on in all countries that trade with Israel, even in those that have diplomatic relations with Arab states but not with Israel. There is no space here to detail these operations, which involve threats and blackmail, constant interference in the economic affairs of other countries carried out on their soil, and a formidable waste of time. The Arabs would maintain that there is nothing antisemitic about these activities, which are ostensibly directed only against the State of Israel.

Thus the Arabs would seek to justify the campaign to boycott Israeli produce in Britain, which was launched in November 1982 with the help of groups like the Trade Union Friends of Palestine, the Labour

Committee on Palestine, and the Labour Friends of Palestine. The campaign, which has concentrated its attention to a large extent on Jaffa oranges, has been singularly ineffective. Attempted picketing of Jewish-owned stores has broken down and British customers have continued to buy the oranges that they like best. Among the most freely spending patrons of these Jewish stores, it may be noted, are Arab visitors to Britain.

But the boycott has, inevitably, encouraged cases of antisemitic discrimination. That of Lord Mancroft is not isolated. Gulf Oil, for instance, withdrew promotion promised to the non-Jewish Mrs. Saul Friedberger, after she had married her Jewish husband. Britain's Race Relations Board secured cash compensation for her, believed to be about £23,000 ($34,500), but she did not get the job.

Another case concerned a young Israeli architect, Uri, whose British employers took on a major job for Arab customers in 1975. Uri was moved out of the company's head office to a suburban office where his presence would not embarrass his British employers or offend their Arab visitors. Uri's family name was not disclosed, for the obvious reason that he did not wish to prejudice his future terms of employment. In the case of a Mr. Richard Herman, dismissed by his employers, Murray Ward and Partners, allegedly because of an Abu Dhabi requirement not to employ Jews, it was thought advisable to take a more public stance. It paid off, for he found another job—ironically, with a company that also did business with Arab countries.

Sometimes antisemitism involves nothing more damaging than a brash and ill-considered statement, as when a British firm that had been in the habit of selling bandages to the Shaare Zedek Hospital in Jerusalem suspended deliveries—presumably under Arab pressure—in November 1982. Its general manager, when asked why this had been done, answered that it was because "as far as I am concerned, Israel does not exist."

A case that came right out into the open was that of a young solicitor, Anthony Simmons, who in September 1980 was served notice of dismissal by one of Britain's biggest property companies, MEPC. He had acted as legal adviser to this firm for several years and as assistant secretary from April 1973 onward, dealing with conveyancing, landlord and tenant problems, and such financial matters as negotiation of loans and preparation of the necessary legal documents. He was, in fact, a trusted and long-serving member of his firm. In his view, no adequate reasons were given for his dismissal. He believed it was because he was a Jew, for at the time MEPC was negotiating two 8.25 percent and 8.75 percent convertible bond issues largely underwritten by the Kuwait International Investment Company. Simmons, indeed, attended the initial meeting between MEPC and underwriters Morgan Grenfell. The latter expressed the opinion that *so far* there had been no objection by the Kuwaitis to the participation of Mr. Simmons. Nonetheless, he was dropped from the negotiations. At the same time, MEPC decided to exclude Jewish banks from the bond issues—presumably at Kuwait's request.

The firm protested that it "had no racial employment policy" but Simmons took his case to an Industrial Tribunal in the summer of 1981. The tribunal found that he had been unfairly dismissed and that MEPC had "unlawfully discriminated against the applicant because of his race" (one member of the tribunal dissented on this latter point). The tribunal noted that "the Arab countries most prominent in exercising the Boycott were Syria, Iraq, Libya and Kuwait" and that "the Boycott was exercised not only against Zionists but against Jewish firms and individual Jewish employers." In addition, "it was exercised in an arbitrary manner, depending on how anxious these Arab countries and firms were to do business."

The Simmons case was only the tip of an iceberg. I have come across other cases of the same kind, but they have not been publicized—for this reason only: because the persons discriminated against have not wanted publicity, because they might still be able to keep their jobs, because they were offered financial compensation and did not want to endanger its payment, or because they felt that exposure of their cases would prejudice their chances of finding another job.

The antisemitic aspect of the Arab-Israeli dispute as a whole, is a mainly grey area. Is anything "proved" by Saudi Arabia's refusal to allow the United States to station Jewish servicemen at their base in Dhahran; by Saudi King Faisal's personal distribution of viciously, even pornographically, antisemitic literature to visiting journalists; by the demand of Libya's Qaddafi that the Jewish editor of the Italian newspaper *La Stampa* should be sacked; by King Faisal's designation of the Jews as "the infidels who are the authors of all evil in the world"; by Bahrain's periodic refusal to let Jews into the country; by the pogroms that have taken place in Libya, Iraq, and elsewhere in the Arab world? The connection between economic boycott and antisemitism will remain largely undocumented but it undoubtedly exists.

Returning briefly, now, to the matter of "compartmenting" both of the Arab-Israeli dispute and of different aspects of antisemitism, we may note that behind and beyond all of these aspects is a traditional, *instinctive* brand of antisemitism that is rarely mentioned because it is supposed to be semidefunct or innocuous. This sort of antisemitism may well have played a part in the deliberations of the ultrarespectable directors of the Norwich Union Insurance Company, when they reached the decision to request the resignation of their Jewish colleague Lord Mancroft, or of the board of the MEPC property company, which effectively sacked its tried and trusted legal adviser.

Traditional, instinctive antisemitism keeps cropping up in Britain. Thus, as previously noted, one finds General Sir Evelyn Barker, who, upon hearing of the blowing up of the King David Hotel in Jerusalem, issued an order-of-the-day in which he adjured his officers and men "to hit the Jews where it hurts them most, in their pockets." One finds the far more esteemed Field-Marshal Lord Montgomery opining, in

1948, that "now the Arabs will hit those Jews for six"—in baseball terms, hammering them for a "homer." One cannot miss the note of instinctive glee in this typically terse statement.

When a certain British peer of the Realm was convicted of fraud, British newspapers headlined the event with *"Jewish* peer found guilty," and the like. No harm was meant, perhaps—but supposing that he had merely "belonged" in Birmingham, or Glasgow, or even Northern Ireland? That, somehow, would have been less interesting, or less significant. It would not have been mentioned. Where this particular British peer was concerned, a conversation with an old friend may have been relevant. We discussed the case, and he added: "But what would you expect of a Jew!"

There is a school of thought that supposes that these somewhat febrile manifestations of antisemitism do not matter. Unfortunately, people talk to people and the contagion spreads, or at least persists. Perhaps it seems far-fetched to relate economic boycott with traditional, instinctive antisemitism. Not so: Economic boycott feeds off and exploits this sort of antisemitism. Economic boycott may look like a mere pimple; the virus remains.

17

Antisemitism and the Law: Effects and Options for Action

Stephen J. Roth

In this chapter I deal with the legal aspects of current antisemitism, focusing on two issues: first, on the legal *effects* of current antisemitism; and second, on the possibilities of legal *action* to fight it. At the end, I also deal with some basic questions relating to the justification of this fight by law.

Legal Effects of Antisemitism

Perhaps the most obvious, and certainly the most measurable, manifestation of antisemitism, as we have known it for centuries, has been the denial to Jews of equality with other human beings, a discriminatory curtailment of their rights in various, and sometimes all, aspects of human life and society. Some forms of such discrimination were beyond the reach of the law (e.g., private or social ostracism of Jews by Gentiles), but in many instances the discrimination actually expressed itself in legal measures—though not always overtly. In most cases it was de facto, though probably laid down in unpublished administrative instructions. Other cases were those based on decisions of professional bodies, university senates, and trade associations, which, although not being "law" in the proper sense, created legal effects, almost by delegated authority.

The most frequent areas of anti-Jewish discrimination have been the denial of political rights, such as the right to citizenship or to suffrage; denial of cultural rights, particularly the *numerus clausus* (quotas) and sometimes even *numerus nullus* (no admission) restrictions in admission to higher education; denial of economic rights like nonadmission to independent occupations, whether in trade or in the professions, especially where these were dependent on governmental licenses, and exclusion from certain types of employment particularly in the civil service; and special discriminatory levies and taxes. These are only the more modern forms of discrimination, characteristic roughly of the nineteenth and twentieth centuries up to the advent of Hitler. The discrimination was often directed against Jews as a group, affecting their collective rights as a religious, linguistic, ethnic, national, or cultural entity. Not only were Jews placed in a disadvantaged position as a minority, they were treated worse than other minorities or "groups." This kind of legal discrimination exists in only two areas—in the Soviet Union and in Arab and Muslim countries—and both cases are *sui generis.*

The Soviet Union establishes in its constitution the equality of all its citizens. This is always correctly cited by Soviet spokespersons when the charge of antisemitism is made against the USSR, and in fact one cannot find a single norm in the vast corpus of All-Union legislation and the legislation of the fifteen Soviet republics that contains discrimination against Jews. Discrimination arises in the implementation of the laws and in administrative measures, both general and individual. Implementation is quite arbitrary and often contrary to the letter of the law. This is a general feature of the Soviet system, not specially limited to the problem of Jews. However, where arbitrariness rules, prejudices, ideological beliefs, and unannounced policies can easily prevail—and Soviet Jews are special targets and victims of all three. Expressed in another way, the Jews in the USSR are equal in law but unequal in lawlessness.

The discrimination against Soviet Jews is well known and needs only brief mention. They are denied equal facilities with those available to other religious denominations and to other national minorities—the two forms in which Jews as an entity are recognized in the USSR. Individual discrimination was less noticeable for a long time. Jews succeeded in achieving high positions in political, economic, and particularly academic life. In the last three decades or so, this has gradually changed: first in the Communist party and governmental positions, including the diplomatic service, and, more recently, extending to employment, job promotion, and admission to higher education, with special emphasis on certain better universities and on certain disciplines such as mathematics. There are no overt legal norms underpinning this discrimination, but a number of recent studies have supplied convincing evidence of its existence. Concrete figures are available about the decline in the numbers of Jews in the party, in the highest organs of the state and the party, in local soviets, among scientific workers, and so on. Suffice it to give here one statistical fact: In the academic year 1980–1981, the number of Jewish undergraduate students was around 50,000 to 55,000, which is about half of what it was ten years earlier (105,800 in 1970–1971). The size of the total Jewish community dropped in this period through natural decline and emigration by at most 18 percent. The great divergence can thus be attributed only to discrimination. It should be noted, however, that the treatment of Jews in regard to emigration would not fall under the heading of "discrimination," since the right to leave the country does not exist in practice in the Soviet Union. Moreover, the Soviet Union's discrimination against its Jewish population is not fully emulated by the Socialist countries of the Soviet bloc. It appeared in Poland in 1968 on a large scale, but very little is noticeable in Hungary, for instance.

Discrimination by Arab and Muslim countries is different from the aforementioned cases, and—again, this should be emphasized—in no way uniform or even present in all the countries. Such discrimination as exists is directed either against the country's Jewish population, as in Syria, where from time to time it reaches a degree of virtual persecution, or against Jews outside the country, as in the denial of entry visas to foreign Jews or the inclusion in the Arab boycott against Israel not only of firms trading with Israel but even of those with Jewish ownership or Jews in the management. In other instances, the relegation of Jews to a minority status *de jure*, as in Iran, creates a discrimination in comparison with the Muslim population, but this discrimination is applied to all minorities and not specifically to Jews.

As with the Soviet Union, the case of the Arab and Muslim countries is also *sui generis*, though for different reasons. There, the discrimination is a combination of religious prejudices and a reflection of the Arab-Israel conflict. On the other hand, in Western countries, where the majority of Jews outside Israel live, and even in the non-Muslim Third World countries, legal discrimination against Jews is almost nonexistent. Jews enjoy full rights and they are free to reach, and do reach, the highest echelons in politics, culture, and economic life. There is no government and no political party of any significance in opposition (the small neo-Nazi parties, unrepresented in any parliament of the world, can safely be ignored) that would advocate the curtailment of the rights of the Jews or include this demand in their political platform. Indeed, such a proposition would be more of an electoral liability than an asset. On the contrary, we have reached a stage where positions achieved by Jews appear threatened by "positive discrimination" (i.e., preferential action and/or quotas) in favor of other disadvantaged minorities, but such positive discrimination is not antisemitic by any stretch of the imagination—whatever its actual effect on Jews may be.

The general nondiscriminatory policies of democratic societies are somewhat threatened by the Arab boycott against firms with Jewish ownership or management. Although the discrimination is of Arab making, the Western countries seem to overlook that in their weakness in resisting the boycott, for economic reasons, they permit an extraterritorial reach of Arab laws into their own countries that undermines one of the pillars of their democratic systems—namely, the equality of all citizens.

One exception to the overall satisfactory position in the West occurs in countries that do not follow democratic principles: the discriminatory treatment of Jews, especially Jewish prisoners, which occasionally occurs in oppressive clean-up operations by military regimes against their opposition. There is evidence that in Argentina, for instance, Jewish

prisoners have fared much worse at the hands of military authorities—
another example of the case involving the Soviet Union (though appearing
at the other extreme of the political spectrum): the danger to Jews of
lawlessness. In law, Jews have remained equals even in the military
dictatorships.

This is not to say that no antisemitism currently exists in Western
countries. On the contrary, it is present in many forms and degrees,
varying in time and place. Discrimination against Jews (albeit de facto
and unadmitted) even exists in some occupations, certainly in some
large firms, and in some aspects of social life in many countries, but
it is not "legalized" or legitimized by law in any way.

Legal Action Against Antisemitism

Is the nonlegalized antisemitism illegal, then? It does not follow. A
large range of human activities is neither sanctioned by law nor forbidden
by law; in other words, it is regulated neither in a positive permissive
way nor in a negative prohibitive way. But many of what we call
antisemitic activities are illegal—and, in my view, many more could
and should be made illegal.

To best understand this subject, we will find it useful to break down
antisemitic activities into their main categories and to distinguish, first,
between domestic law and international law, and second, between the
position *de lege lata*, as the law now stands, and *de lege ferenda*, as to
what future legislation would be possible and desirable.

Discrimination Against Jews

Not only is legalized discrimination against Jews nonexistent outside
the Arab or Muslim world, but the principle of nondiscrimination is
firmly upheld in international law, given its incorporation into all postwar
international instruments relating to human rights in the broadest sense
of the term. The grounds on which discrimination is forbidden generally
include the following categories relevant from the Jewish point of view:
religion, race, and national origin. In one important instance, the International Convention on the Elimination of All Forms of Racial
Discrimination (1965), "religion" is omitted but "ethnic origin" and
"descent" are included.

Several such international instruments have made it incumbent on
the state parties to introduce laws in their countries that would give
domestic legal effect to their commitment under international law. As
a result, most countries have adopted laws against discrimination, and
this principle is frequently entrenched in their constitutions.

There are two shortcomings that should be mentioned in a situation
that is otherwise generally satisfactory. The first relates to the grounds
on which protection is offered against discrimination. As mentioned
before, the 1965 UN convention omitted "religion" from the protected

categories because this convention is specifically designed to deal with the problem of racism. In 1962, when in reaction to the 1959 worldwide campaign of Swastika-daubing the drafting of this convention was considered at the UN, the proposal was made to adopt a parallel convention on discrimination on the grounds of religion (as well as the freedom of religion in general), but until today, some twenty-six years later, the United Nations has not yet succeeded in agreeing on such a convention on religion; only in 1981 did the UN General Assembly get so far as to adopt a Declaration on the Elimination of All Forms of Intolerance and of Discrimination Based on Religion or Belief. However, a declaration is not a legally binding instrument, and thus no country is obliged, on the strength of it, to enact corresponding domestic laws. A declaration is a symptomatic reflection of the relative importance that the United Nations today, given the atheistic Communist countries on the one hand and the African countries that regard racism as the principle political issue on the other, attaches to the problems of race and religion.

Yet the Convention Against Racial Discrimination is the most widely ratified UN instrument in the human rights field. Many of the domestic laws adopted in its implementation therefore also omitted the category of religion from the grounds on which they guarantee protection against discrimination (and against group hatred, a subject to be discussed later). Fortunately, however, the convention included instead two other criteria (not appearing in the other human rights instruments)—namely, "ethnic origin" and "descent." Nevertheless, in the case of Jews the most obvious and unequivocal notion is religion, whereas "race" and "ethnic origin" are often contested and "descent" is very vague (some believe it was meant to refer to "caste"). Doubts have therefore arisen as to the extent that domestic laws adopted by way of implementing the convention actually cover Jews. The question was recently considered, directly or indirectly, by the courts in various countries, not necessarily in cases involving Jews, but certainly in cases requiring definition of the above-mentioned categories. A court of appeal judgment in New Zealand (1979) and a judgment by the House of Lords with respect to England (1983) defined "ethnic group" in a manner that laid emphasis on the historical and cultural content of ethnicity rather than on a purely biological meaning of the term. In the construction of these judgments, the category of ethnic group would undoubtedly apply to Jews. But in the United States, for instance, where, in the absence of newer statutes protecting against discrimination on grounds of creed, action must still be based on legislation enacted in the aftermath of the Civil War (notably the Civil Rights Act of 1866), problems have arisen. That act, which now appears on the statute book as Section 1981 of 42 USC, merely guarantees equality with "white citizens." Some courts have therefore ruled that persons who are not members of a racial group distinct from "whites" cannot benefit from the act; but other judgments have been more positive.

The second shortcoming relates to the area of discrimination prohibited by the domestic laws. It varies from country to country and is nowhere all-embracing. In connection with the Arab boycott problem, discrimination in trade is prohibited only in the supply of goods (and usually only in places open to the public) but not in the purchase of goods (with respect to choosing one's supplier)—probably because the first is a public function, whereas the second is not. (An exception is the French Law of 1972 on the Fight Against Racism.)

Incitement to Group Hatred

The most prevalent form of antisemitism today is antisemitic propaganda. Both in international law and in the legislation of many individual countries, advocacy of or incitement to national, racial, or religious hatred is outlawed. There are also provisions of a positive nature that demand education "to promote understanding, tolerance and friendship among all nations, racial and religious groups," to use the terminology of the Universal Declaration of Human Rights. However, several countries—among them the United States—though willing to adopt legislation against discrimination, are rejecting the notion of curbing by law the advocacy of or incitement to hatred on racial or religious grounds. The objection is based on the libertarian argument that such curbs would interfere with the freedom of speech or expression.

In countries that have adopted legislation against incitement to group hatred, two kinds of problems emerge nevertheless. The first is the one already mentioned under the heading of "discrimination"—namely, that the Convention Against Racial Discrimination does not cover "religion" and, as a result, many national laws also omit the category of religion. Thus created for Jews is the ambiguous position described earlier. Although this omission of religion is of less significance on the subject of discrimination—given that anti-Jewish discrimination is no longer the decisive form of antisemitism—it is of very considerable import in regard to the virulent form of Jew-hatred propaganda.

The second problem relates to the restrictions that various countries in their domestic laws have attached to the principle of outlawing propaganda for group hatred. These restrictions primarily include the following: (1) The prohibition of incitement to hatred is often limited to acts that lead to, or are likely to cause, further consequences, variably defined as "violence," "public disorder," and "breach of peace." Thus the stirring up of hatred, in itself, is not an offense under such laws. (2) The laws, which often are not satisfied with the objective test of whether hatred (or its consequences) were engendered, also introduce the subjective element of the motive or intent of the hate-monger. (3) The offending pronouncements are often qualified. It is not enough that they cause hatred; they must also be "threatening," "abusive," "insulting," and so on. (4) Procedural restrictions, such as limiting prosecution to, or making prosecution dependent on, the decision of a state authority, often arise.

Curbing Nazi, Fascist, Racist Organizations and Their Activities

This issue of propaganda is in some ways related to the problem of incitement to group hatred, given that the most important activity of neo-Nazi, fascist, and racist organizations is their propaganda—and in the context of the problem of antisemitism we are concerned, of course, with their anti-Jewish propaganda. Curbing, or possibly prohibiting, the organizations per se, or banning their publications, would have a preventive effect as well as an impact not only on hate-mongering but on other activities as well in which such organizations have frequently engaged, particularly vandalism, violence, and terrorism.

As in the case of outlawing expressions that constitute incitement to hatred, we also face the objection that such curbing or banning might conflict with the freedom of association, assembly, or the press. And probably because a restriction of such freedoms is desired for preventive purposes, international law is weaker on this subject than on the others treated so far. Of all universal and regional instruments, only the Convention Against Racial Discrimination contains a provision outlawing racist organizations, and only a few countries have introduced domestic laws against such discrimination. However, the multilateral treaties relating to the settlement of issues arising out of World War II—notably the 1947 Peace Treaties with Bulgaria, Finland, Hungary, Italy, and Romania; the 1952 Conventions between the United States, the United Kingdom, France, and the Federal German Republic (indirectly, by upholding the Control Council legislation); and the 1955 State Treaty with Austria—contain specific clauses prohibiting the reestablishment of Nazi or fascist organizations. A special area in the constitutions is the ban on Nazi or fascist insignia, memorabilia, gramophone records of songs and speeches, and so on. Some of the domestic laws also deal with these problems, as well as the problems of paramilitary organizations, the wearing of uniforms, and political marches, which are often used for neo-Nazi and fascist purposes.

Violence, Vandalism, Terrorism

In the last few years, anti-Jewish violence, vandalism, and acts of terror have been among the most frequent—and the most dangerous—manifestations of antisemitism. The awareness in the United States that a great deal of such vandalism originates from racial or religious bigotry has induced a number of state and local legislatures to take new legislative initiatives specifically directed toward this problem. According to a report of the U.S. Commission on Civil Rights (January 1983), thirteen states have passed a total of eighteen bills on the subject.

On the issue of terrorism there is a large body of international legal instruments (also covering such problems as hijacking and hostage-taking) and a great number of corresponding domestic measures, but the issue has in no way been satisfactorily solved. Extradition of terrorists is often thwarted by the misguided concept that terrorist acts are not simply crimes but political moves exempted from extradition rules and offering a right of asylum to the perpetrators. Still beyond universal acceptance is the principle that if extradition is denied, the country apprehending the terrorist is obliged to try him or her for the crime (*aut dedere aut punire*). The worst practice of all is the simple expulsion of the terrorist to his or her homeland, even when that home country may be in sympathy with the terrorist act committed (as in the case of many Arab terrorists).

Anti-Zionism

In the foregoing we have dealt with the legal fight against such traditional forms of antisemitism as discrimination, racist propaganda, and so on (only "terrorism," given the manner in which it has been experienced recently, may be a manifestation of the "new antisemitism"). Obviously it is easier to find or suggest remedies for an old, familiar phenomenon than for an entirely new one. In fact, in approaching the issue of anti-Zionism, one must first determine the extent to which it overlaps with antisemitism. There is little doubt, for instance, that much of what appears in the USSR under the cover of anti-Zionism is regarded by most Jews (and probably by most objective observers) as antisemitic. The neo-Nazi press, too, often publishes anti-Zionist articles whose general anti-Jewish tendencies (and motivations) can hardly be doubted. In between these two extremes we find similar aberrations in the Western democracies as well.

Of course, whenever antisemitic anti-Zionism (and by using this qualification I indicate that I, for one, do not regard the two terms as being necessarily synonymous) takes one of the forms prohibited by law (e.g., incitement to racial hatred, violence, terrorism), the regulations relating to such manifestations as those outlined earlier would apply. There are, in fact, legal precedents in which the defense of anti-Zionism could not prevail against the charge of incitement to racial hatred. The best-known such case was tried in Paris in 1973, in which Robert Legagneux, the director of the Soviet Embassy Newsletter, was found guilty of defamation and "incitement to discrimination, hatred or racial violence" because of a nefarious anti-Zionist article under the title "*L'École de l'Obscurantisme*," which appeared in that publication. But there have also been cases with contrary results, as, for instance, in a judgment by a court in Aalborg, Denmark (1981), which was upheld even on appeal.

The dilemma thus arises when the antisemitic nature of anti-Zionist expressions is not manifestly clear. It is difficult to see how in such situations "anti-Zionism" could be made a criminal offense or a subject for any other legal action. Therefore, protection against anti-Zionism will have to be sought through political rather than legal means. Certainly, it would be idle to expect the international community to accomplish anything in this direction in international law. The best known expression of the United Nations on Zionism, the 1975 General Assembly Resolution equating Zionism with racism, is, after all, one of the most notorious expressions of anti-Zionism.

It should be noted, however, that because of the controversial nature of this UN resolution and because General Assembly resolution (fortunately, in this instance) do not create law, none of the UN member states that otherwise prohibit racist organizations have curbed Zionist activities in their countries on account of the resolution. In those countries in which Zionism is illegal, such as the Communist and Muslim countries, this was the case long before 1975. The only practical effect of the resolution was noticeable on the campus level, particularly in Britain, where the exclusion of Jewish student unions has been attempted by other student groups on the grounds of the Jewish unions' "Zionist racism."

Denial of the Facts of the Holocaust

One of the most pernicious new forms of antisemitism is the denial of the facts of the Holocaust by so-called revisionist historians and neo-Nazis (the two are often identical). Their allegations that no systematic extermination of Jews occurred, that there were no gas chambers, and that 6 million Jews did not perish, propagated in an atmosphere of increased anti-Jewish activity, has become one of the most significant weapons in the neo-Nazi arsenal. If the crimes of the Nazis can be wiped off the record of history, if the Nazi regime can be whitewashed and made to appear as admittedly somewhat disciplinarian and tough on law and order but basically harmless and more efficient than our allegedly lax Western democracies with their growing disorder, their crimes, violence, and riots, then the neo-Nazis would have won a great victory. The system advocated by them would also look harmless and acceptable, and the ideological resistance to it, largely based on awareness of the horrors of the past, would be undermined—particularly among younger people who have no personal experience of Nazi rule.

The distortion of historical evidence and, even more so, of historical crimes is abhorrent to all fair-minded people. In the case of the Holocaust, it must be regarded as a crime in the *moral* sense because it is offensive to the survivors of the Holocaust and indeed to all Jews and other groups whose members were victims of the Nazis. It is also a crime *politically*, because of the aid it gives to the neo-Nazi movements. However, this is far from being a crime in the *legal* sense. Indeed, it is not easy to make the negation of the Holocaust, even if it entails fabrication and falsehood, a punishable offense. Apart from the objection of curbing the freedom of expression and thought, which could be raised in this context as well, there is a more fundamental objection: Establishment of historical truth, or protection of the truth, is not the business of the law. In most instances, the denial of the facts of the Holocaust is accompanied by the allegation that the whole matter is an invention, a "hoax" (the best known "revisionist" book by the American Arthur R. Butz is entitled "The Hoax of the 20th Century") that was faked by Jews or Zionists for ulterior motives to extort money from Germany for reparations and to gain sympathy from the world for a Jewish State.

These slurs, which present Jews as the perpetrators of a despicable swindle, could, if believed, bring them into disrepute and expose them to contempt and hatred. There can be no doubt, therefore, that these defamations represent an incitement to hatred of the Jews. As the seventeenth *Chambre Correctionelle* of Paris put it in their verdict of July 3, 1981, convicting the notorious French Professor Robert Faurisson of defamation and incitement to racial hatred: "In accusing the Jews publicly of being guilty through cupidity of a particularly odious lie and of a gigantic swindle . . . Robert Faurisson could not be unaware that his words would arouse in his very large audience feelings of contempt, of hatred and of violence towards the Jews in France." Thus, in such instances, the provisions on incitement to racial hatred outlined earlier would become applicable. But it should be clear that in this event it is not the *denial* of the Holocaust but the *concomitant allegation* of a "Jewish swindle" that is the basis of the legal action.

In only one case has a court ever set itself up as the guardian of historical truth. In another French trial, not of a criminal but of a civil nature, the same Professor Faurisson was sued by LICRA, by the *Mouvement contre le racisme, l'antisémitisme et pour la paix* (MRAP), as well as by six other organizations representing members of the resistance and survivors of deportation or their families, for having failed, in a felonious manner, to discharge the responsibilities incumbent upon him as a historian to provide objective informaiton and not to omit essential facts in his treatment of the Holocaust. This was based on Article 1382 of the French Civil Code, which deals with torts or quasi-torts (*délits et quasi-délits*) and on the fact that, by his negligence, Faurisson caused "moral prejudice" and damaged the people represented by the plaintiff organizations. The *Tribunal de Grand Instance* (Paris), in its judgment of July 8, 1981, found for the plaintiffs and declared Faurisson liable to pay damages.

However, if one considers the matter more thoroughly, it will be realized that the denial of the facts of the Holocaust is not simply a denial of historical *facts* or *truth*, but the denial of *crimes*. This could much more easily be the concern of legal action. There are, in fact, provisions in various countries about the treatment of crimes after their commission, such as the prohibition against *glorification* of certain crimes (in the Federal German Republic [FRG] and Norway), against publicly *praising* them (in Italy), even against mere *approval* of certain crimes (in Denmark and the FRG). The Penal Code of Federal Germany, under certain conditions, even outlaws "*making them appear harmless.*" Following this line, the Social Democratic party (SPD) in the FRG, while in government (but able to present it to Parliament only after it lost office), prepared an amendment to the Criminal Code that would have made the *denial* or the *"making appear harmless"* of "an act of genocide committed during the National Socialist regime" a punishable offense. The proposal was rejected by the *Bundesrat* on October 29, 1982, the official reason being that the offense was not defined with the precision required in criminal law. However, the SPD announced that it will reintroduce the amendment in a revised form.

It appears, therefore, that it is not entirely impossible to deal with the denial of the Holocaust through the law. It would in many respects be a *novum*, but new problems require innovative legal actions. However, at present, no legal instruments are available against this new form of antisemitism.

To sum up the question of possible legal action against antisemitism, one could say that (1) there are a number of manifestations of antisemitism against which legal action is not only feasible, but international instruments and domestic laws in many countries are actually in existence and can serve as the basis for practical steps. (2) The international instruments, however, bind only those states that have ratified them. It would be important, therefore, to secure their ratification also by those states that have so far failed to adhere to these instruments. It is particularly regrettable that the United States has until now refused to ratify the two most important instruments in the field of human rights— namely, the International Covenant on Civil and Political Rights and the Convention on the Elimination of All Forms of Racial Discrimination. (3) Where domestic laws in this field are not yet in existence, their enactment should be sought by action on the national level. (4) Various existing domestic laws contain restrictive clauses that strongly undermine their effectiveness. This situation should be remedied as far as possible.

Justification of the Legal Fight Against Antisemitism

Two points of principle should be considered in connection with the entire complex of the legal fight against antisemitism. They are really in the nature of *questions préalables*. First, is it justified, for the sake of fighting antisemitism, to advocate legal measures that would amount to the restriction of some basic rights and freedoms, like the freedom of expression, thought, association, or assembly? The question is a serious one, the more so as it is usually raised by people and politicians who are entirely friendly to the fight against antisemitism. The issues raised in this question dominated the political thinking before the rise of Nazism, and they have since then appeared more cogent. In the face of a major onslaught on democracy, the defense and pristine preservation of democratic values seemed to be the principal demand of the hour. However, having seen how certain liberties can be misused with the most horrendous consequences, such as those suffered during the Hitler era and the Holocaust, we must also see that the matter requires rethinking.

Human rights and freedoms must be established and upheld because they are inalienable to the members of the human family and are inherent in human dignity. But no rights or freedoms must be allowed to be used at the expense of the rights and freedoms of others; or, to use the words of Article 30 of the Universal Declaration of Human Rights, none of the rights listed in the Declaration implies "the right to engage in any activity or to perform any act aimed at the destruction of the rights and freedoms set forth herein."

In other words, no rights are absolute. They are limited by the rights of others and by the just demands of society. This is true of human rights as well. In the language of one of the Human Rights Covenants, such rights can be limited by law "for the purpose of promoting the general welfare in a democratic society" (International Covenant on Economic, Social, and Cultural Rights, Article 4) or, as the American Convention on Human Rights puts it, "by the just demands of the general welfare, in a democratic society" (Article 32).

Freedom of expression (which is the issue in regard to the most important legal measure in the fight against antisemitism—namely, the curb on hate propaganda), offers, for instance, no protection against obscenity, blasphemy (in countries where this crime is recognized), defamation, incitement to engage in unlawful action, or "inciting or 'fighting' words—those which by their very utterance inflict injury or tend to incite an immediate breach of the peace" (U.S. Supreme Court in *Chaplinsky* v. *New Hampshire*, 315 US 568 [1942]). Obviously such limitations must have good reasons, and one must always deeply regard the importance of fundamental rights and freedom. A great American judge, Oliver Wendell Holmes, proposed the "clear and present danger" test for the right to restrict basic liberties—whether that danger "will bring about the substantive evils that Congress has a right to prevent" (*Schenck* v. *United States*, 249 US.47 [1919]).

The "clear and present danger" test may still serve us well. But in the light of the experience of Nazism and the Holocaust, we must realize that the danger is already present when the evil forces are still in their early stages. We need not—indeed, we *must* not—wait until their activities have attained their intended results. The activities themselves, and the organizations created to foster them, are a danger. This may not have been so visible in 1919; it became obvious in 1939, and it must be palpably self-evident in 1983.

The international community has shown that it has learned this lesson. It is on that basis that it adopted the restrictive clauses in the various human rights instruments against advocacy of and incitement to group hatred, against the existence of racist organizations, and so on. Some individual countries have thus far failed to follow this path. The current reemergence of antisemitism may be a suitable reason for them to reconsider their position.

The second threshold question is this: Can the legal fight actually be effective against a disease that has deep-rooted national, racial, social, and psychological causes? Is not the cure to be sought more in education and enlightenment? The truth is that there is no dichotomy between law and education in the fight against antisemitism. Not only are both necessary and complementary, but the law is itself one of the most powerful weapons of education. By establishing norms of behavior, it creates patterns of behavior. By prohibiting certain actions, legislators, elected representatives of the public, indicate to the public that they find these actions wrong—and thereby educate the public to recognize and be aware of the wrong. It is symptomatic of this educational role of the law that UNESCO, the international agency destined to promote education, science, and culture, emphasized in its 1978 Declaration on Race and Racial Prejudice (Article 7) that *"law is one of the principal means* of ensuring equality in dignity and rights among individuals" (emphasis added).

18
Stealing the Holocaust

Edward Alexander

Sie werden es von uns wieder stehlen.
—Martin Buber (commenting
on the Hebrew Bible in the
context of a discussion of
the Holocaust)

From 1933 to 1945 the National Socialist regime of Germany carried out policies of discrimination, oppression, and murder that resulted in the destruction of around 5.8 million Jews. The Jews held a unique position in the Nazi world because they alone, among all the peoples subject to German rule, had been marked for total destruction—not for anything they had done or failed to do but because they had been born of three Jewish grandparents.[1] Their guilt lay exclusively in having been born. Although only Jews could be guilty of being Jewish, the centrality of the Jews in the mental and political universe of the Nazis established a universal principle that involved every single person in German-ruled Europe: In order to be granted the fundamental human right, the right to live, you had to prove that you were *not* a Jew.

The anti-Jewish policies of the Nazis, which ultimately resulted in the loss to world Jewry of one-third of its population, were the direct result of the ideology of antisemitism. This would hardly seem worth mentioning were it not for the fact that several highly influential modern thinkers have alleged that antisemitism is one of the greatest pieces of good fortune to have befallen the Jewish people. The Jean-Paul Sartre–Georges Friedmann version of this thesis holds that antisemitism produced Jewish consciousness, Jewish persistence, the perseverance of Jewish existence. This perverse theory fails to explain why other peoples in the ancient Near East who also suffered banishment and persecution interpreted their misfortunes as proof of the inefficacy of their national god and prudently surrendered their religious practices, whereas the Jews, faced in exile by the same persecution, kept theirs. Unless Georges Friedmann had run into a Jebusite, a Girgashite, or a Hittite in the streets of Paris, he ought to have been asking what inner impulse kept the Jews loyal to their god and destiny *despite* persecution instead of assuming that they did so *because* of persecution.

The second version of the thesis is that the State of Israel came into existence as the result of the Holocaust and the ensuing bad conscience of the West. The most recent version of this may be found in the allegation of the *Washington Post*'s Pulitzer Prize–winning reporter, Loren Jenkins, who imputes the "culture of violence" in Lebanon to "Western guilt over the murder and torment of the Jewish people." Of course, nothing could be further from the truth. The Jewish communities annihilated by the Nazis were the most Zionistic in the world, and, as Hillel Halkin has remarked, they could have done far more for the Zionist cause as live immigrants to Palestine than they were ever able to do as dead martyrs used to prick the conscience of the West. The British, who then ruled Palestine, were so unimpressed with "the murder and torment of the Jewish people" that they continued, for several years after it ended in 1945, to prevent Jewish immigration and to strangle the state. It was not antisemitism but the Jews themselves who broke open the gates of Palestine for the survivors of the Holocaust.

Use of the term *Holocaust* in English began sometime between 1957 and 1959, in order to express the then-widespread feeling that what had happened to the Jews during World War II was unique or unprecedented, as indeed it was. It has often been pointed out that the Nazis also killed, through starvation and brutality, not less than two and a half million Soviet prisoners of war, murdered many thousands of the Polish intelligentsia during the first year of occupation of Poland, and killed tens of thousands of other Poles as real or alleged resistors. They also destroyed whole Polish villages, massacred the Czech intelligentsia, and destroyed thousands of Russian and Ukrainian peasants during German occupation of those areas. But, as Yehuda Bauer has pointed out, the purpose of these policies was to denationalize the Eastern European nations and to absorb into the Germanic race those people who were what the Nazis considered to be of "Nordic" blood, to murder the intelligentsia, destroy all cultural life, and to turn the rest of the people into a mass of slave laborers in the international Nazi regime. This was a policy of selective murder intended to destroy these nations as nations but to keep most of their members alive as a working force for the Third Reich. This is distinctly different from the planned murder of every one of the members of a community. Bauer demonstrates that, contrary to legend, there never was a Nazi policy to apply the measures used against the Jews to other national communities.[2] Thus the term *Holocaust* came into use to describe the uniquely terrible fate that had befallen the Jews of Europe: They had become the first and thus far the only, though not necessarily the last, people to be singled out for complete physical annihilation.

The uniqueness of Jewish suffering and of the Jewish catastrophe during World War II had no sooner been defined than it was called into question, by Jews as well as by Christians. We need hardly be surprised by this. The fact and the idea of suffering are central in Christianity, whose ethical values are based upon the idea of a community of suffering. Many Christians also believe that, as Mary Ann Evans (later known as George Eliot) wrote in 1848, "Everything specifically Jewish is of a low grade." Yet here was a Jewish claim to a specific suffering that was of the "highest," the most distinguished grade imaginable. Among the Jews, too, large numbers of "universalists" kicked resolutely against the notion of a distinctively Jewish catastrophe. They believed that the enormity of the Holocaust could be recognized by the world at large only if it were universalized, if its victims were recast as "human beings" rather than as Jews. This is not the place to dilate upon either the self-abasement or the mental poverty inherent in such efforts. Cynthia Ozick has remarked, with characteristic shrewdness, that universalism is the ultimate Jewish parochialism. The supposed distinction between being human and being Jewish is one that has plagued Jewish existence at least since the time it was formulated in Y. L. Gordon's assimilationist slogan: "Be a man outside and a Jew at home." The German Nazis may be said to have brought this distinction to its full flowering by decreeing that the Jews were not human at all, so that in order to be granted the right to live, you had, under Nazi rule, to prove that you were *not* a Jew.

One of the earliest and—because it became the occasion of a sensational lawsuit—most notorious attempts to steal from the Jewish victims of the Holocaust precisely that for which they were victimized was the 1955 dramatization of *The Diary of Anne Frank* by Francis and Albert Hackett. Bruno Bettelheim, in *The Informed Heart*, probably goes too far in charging that Anne Frank's story itself gained wide acclaim because "it denies implicitly that Auschwitz ever existed. If all men are good, there never was an Auschwitz." What is certain is that the play, written under the guidance of Lillian Hellman, expunged all of Anne's references to her hopes for survival in a Jewish homeland and changed Anne's particular allusions to her Jewish identity and Jewish hopes to a blurred, amorphous universalism. One example should suffice to illustrate the general pattern. In the *Diary* Anne wrote: "Who has made us Jews different from all other people? Who has allowed us to suffer so terribly up till now? . . . If we bear all this suffering and if there are still Jews left, when it is over, then Jews, instead of being doomed, will be held up as an example. . . . We can never become just Netherlanders, or just English, or just representatives of any other country for that matter; we will always remain Jews." In the stage version, this is reduced to the following piece of imbecility; "We are not the only people that've had to suffer . . . sometimes one race, sometimes another."[3]

This distortion may have helped at the box office, and it thereby made Anne Frank's name known around the world. But for every lie, a price must eventually be paid (though not, it must be added, always by the liars). In recent years, the International Youth Center of the Anne Frank house in Amsterdam was for a time used as a PLO "Information" Center, in which Anne's suffering was made prelude to what was called "the Auschwitz" of the Arab refugee camps. By this obscene travesty, the wheel comes full circle. The young girl who suffered, and who knew that she suffered, because she was a Jew, is first misrepresented as a universalist embodiment of the indiscriminate suffering of "sometimes one race, sometimes another" and then appropriated by a vast propaganda machine as the symbol of the very organization that in Article 20 of its 1968 Constitution denies the existence of Jewish peoplehood, in Article 22 labels Zionism "Fascist and Nazi," and publicly commits itself "to liquidate the Zionist entity politically, economically, militarily, culturally, and ideologically."

Cut free from her Jewish moorings, improperly understood by her own people, Anne Frank has become available for appropriation by those who have a sounder appreciation of the worth of moral capital and know how to lay claim to sovereignty over it when the question of sovereignty has been left open. The PLO is not the only organization that has sought to annex Anne for its own purposes. Some organs of the Catholic Church in Latin America have begun to suggest the suitability of Anne Frank for sainthood in the Roman Church. Educational publications of the Catholic Church in Argentina began in 1975 subtly to link Anne's fate with the Catholic martyrs over the centuries, without bothering to mention either that she was Jewish or that the death she suffered was part of a vast destruction process aimed directly at Jews.[4] This was perhaps a merely parochial phenomenon of the Church's missionary effort among Jews in Argentina. Yet who can be sure, now that Pope John Paul II has celebrated a mass at Auschwitz, that even this ultimate Jewish abattoir may not be in the process of becoming a Christian holy place? "Sie werden es von uns wieder stehlen" (They are going to steal it from us again) Martin Buber had predicted.

The process that I call stealing the Holocaust began with small acts of (usually innocent) distortion. Who does not recall the inflamed rhetoric of the American civil-rights movement of the 1960s with its references to the curtailment of free lunch programs in Harlem as genocide, or its casual descriptions of Watts as a concentration camp and of the ordinary black neighborhood anywhere as a ghetto? Not all of the orators who used this language could have been unmindful of its flagrant dishonesty, could have been wholly ignorant of the fact that no place in New York or Los Angeles or Chicago in 1960 was even remotely like Buchenwald in 1938 or Warsaw in 1942 or Auschwitz in 1944. But why fuss about precision of language or intellectual delicacy when the exigencies of radical politics make it convenient to reduce Jews from the status of human beings to that of metaphors for other people's sufferings? The only problem was that the people who were incessantly told that *they* were the new Jews, that *they* lived in ghettos and concentration camps, that *they* were victims of genocide, began to look about them to decide who the Nazis were in this situation. And, not surprisingly, they chose for *this* role the Jews themselves—that is, the white people whom they saw and dealt with and received help from most frequently. In the 1960s it became routine for black demagogues in New York to charge Jewish teachers with the "cultural genocide" of their black pupils. As if by some law of physics or conservation of energy, the instant that another group becomes "the Jews," the Jews themselves become the Nazis.

But all this was an amateurish rehearsal for what was to come. The most determined, sustained, and dangerous attempt to steal the Holocaust was begun by the Soviet Union and the Arab world after the 1967 Middle East War, and is now one of the most lethal weapons deployed against the land of Israel and the people of Israel. After the Six-Day War, cartoons were published depicting Moshe Dayan as Field Marshal Rommel, with swastikas on his uniform. These cartoons appeared not only in the Soviet Union and the Arab countries but in the journals of American civil-rights organizations like the ironically named Student Non-Violent Coordinating Committee. Before the Six-Day War, when the Straits of Tiran were closed and Arab armies were advancing toward its borders and Nasser and Shukairy were promising to turn the Mediterranean red with Jewish blood, Israel was the recipient of a good deal of cheap sympathy. But after the war, Israel discovered that the price it would have to pay for winning a war that, if lost, would have meant its destruction was the nearly universal loss of the sympathy the Jews had been collecting since 1945 when discovery of the Holocaust became general. All those statesmen and journalists whose eloquence had for twenty-two years gushed forth on the subject of the dead Jews and of their vanished civilization now fulminated with rage and resentment against a people and a state that preferred life to death and even to the rhapsodic eulogies that might be bestowed on dead Jewish martyrs and the glory that was Israel.[5]

Since 1967 this rage and resentment against the Jews for refusing to be passive victims have expressed themselves mainly in the depiction of Israelis as Nazis and Palestinian Arabs as Jews. In the 1970s UNESCO condemned Israel's archaeological digs in Jerusalem as "crimes against culture," a charge intended, as Norman Podhoretz pointed out, "to conjure up the burning of books by the Nazis."[6] The Soviet ambassador to the UN accused Israelis of "racial genocide," and the Committee on the Inalienable Rights of the Palestinian People (which in UN parlance means only Arabs, never Jews) compared the "sealing of a part of the city of Nablus" to "the ghettos and concentration camps erected by the Hitlerites in several cities of Europe." The members of this UN committee had learned their techniques from the slogan-makers of the American civil-rights movement, who spoke of Harlem as if it were Auschwitz.

The triumphant stroke in the campaign to steal the Holocaust from the Jews by inverting the roles of the victim and the predator was the

Soviet-inspired "Zionism is racism" resolution of 1975. For nearly a century, the word *racism* was in Europe virtually synonymous with antisemitism, with Jew-hatred. For the Soviets to have foisted upon the United Nations a resolution saying that Israel, the last coherent center of the historic Jewish civilization destroyed by the Nazis, is itself the sole inheritor of Nazism was to have made the public memory of the Holocaust into a potent instrument for the destruction of the Jewish people. For Jew-haters everywhere, this monstrous inversion has been meat and drink, a seminal idea whose fruitfulness burgeons in new forms every day. The student bodies in twelve British universities were inspired by it to pass "Zionism-Racism" resolutions that were used to ban Jewish student organizations. At Bristol University, for example, a Reform rabbi who was scheduled to speak on "Jewish Ethics" was prevented from doing so because it was suspected he would utter "Zionist" (i.e., "racist") sentiments. Fidel Castro, in speeches before the Third World conference in Havana and at the United Nations in 1979, described Israelis as the Nazis of our time, monsters who had driven the modern Jews (otherwise known as Arabs) off their land, committed genocide, and so forth. Vanessa Redgrave, a PLO activist, went out of her way to portray a Jewish victim of the "original" Holocaust, as it were, in order to drive home the intended equation between the Jewish victims of Hitler and the Palestinian Arab victims of the Israelis. And in a "debate" with Fania Fenelon, the survivor whom she portrayed, she claimed that she could hardly be an antisemite because the Palestinians are "semites." (This vulgar retort, which appears about once a week in papers like *Le Monde*, plays on the ignorance of those who have forgotten that the word *antisemitism* was created as a euphemism for Jew-hatred, and that antisemites hate Jews, not "semites.")

Stealing the Holocaust became central in the ideology of the most militant and aggressive of anti-Israel groups, particularly the American Friends Service Committee (AFSC).[7] This wealthiest and most politically active corporate component of the Religious Society of Friends, better known as Quakers, has since 1967 consistently sought to portray Israelis as the new Nazis and Palestinian Arabs as their "Jewish" victims. In November 1976 its New England branch announced: "Now Israelis are making Jews out of Palestinians. In the Palestinians I recognize my Jews." This was the theme repeated *ad nauseam* by speakers at the Friends' February 1977 conference on "New Imperatives for Israeli-Palestinian Peace" in Washington, D.C. The executive secretary of the AFSC, Louis Schneider, told the audience of his "thoughts" on a 1976 visit to Israel, thoughts that coincided with the Jews' observance of the thirty-fourth anniversary of the Warsaw Ghetto uprising: "It was deeply saddening to have been in Israel during the season when Jews were celebrating one of their own struggles from tyranny . . . and the Arab minority in Israel were heard voicing their own aspirations for freedom during their demonstrations against Israeli control." This implied equation between Israelis in Judea and Nazis in Warsaw set the tone for the whole meeting and was made explicit by many subsequent orators, including I. F. Stone and an Arab American who said, to thunderous applause, that Israel had created a Palestinian Auschwitz at Tel Zaatar. The PLO representative who, in laying his wreath at the Warsaw Ghetto commemoration of 1983, said that "the Palestinian people are the victims of the new Nazism" had gone to school with the American Friends Service Committee. For these people, as for the Russians and Arabs in the UN, the disgusting practice of riding on the coattails of the Jewish experience of discrimination, exile, oppression, and murder has become more than a means of collecting sympathy and expressing hatred; it has acquired the stature of a moral idea.

Anti-Israel journalists soon developed a standard formula for exploiting the Holocaust. A few examples from the late 1970s through 1980 should suffice to identify the pattern. Nick Thimmesch, the *Los Angeles Times* syndicate's tireless journalistic warrior against Israel, declared on October 6, 1977, that Menachem Begin's statements about the right of Jews to live in Judea were "the language of Hitler." The *Christian Science Monitor* began a four-part series (June 1979) on "The Struggle for Palestine" by referring to the Palestinian Arabs as "the Jews of the Arab world." It further asserted that they are living in "Diaspora," that they long for restoration to Jerusalem, indeed that they are the latest Zionists. Doug Marlette, syndicated by the Knight News Service, reported (October 21, 1979) how the eyes of Palestinian Arab refugees always looked out at him from under the photos in Yad Vashem of Jewish children being marched into gas chambers. Jonathan Randal disclosed to readers of the *Washington Post Service* (March 5, 1980) that Palestinian Arabs were living "in diaspora" or else in Lebanese camps that they thought were replicas of Dachau and Auschwitz. Five days later the novelist John Updike not only endorsed the view that "the Palestinians are Jews" but had the colossal gall to ask the readers of the *New Yorker* (March 10, 1980) to join him in bemoaning the "fact" that this is "a perspective seldom found in American newspapers." Is it possible that Updike reads no American newspapers except the *Jewish Week*?

Exactly a year before Updike complained of the paucity of metaphorical Jews, his *New Yorker* colleague George Steiner had published in the *Kenyon Review* a novella about Hitler entitled *The Portage to San Cristobal of A.H.*, which ought to have satisfied even the most voracious appetite for gross historical inaccuracies and licentious equations such as those made between Nazism and both Torah and Zionism. The latter are concentrated in Hitler's final monologue. In a controversy with Martin Gilbert in 1982 over the stage version of *Portage*, Steiner explained that he left this monologue unanswered because he did not wish to descend to the level of "didactic Shavian debate" but, rather, aspired to the sublime detachment of Milton from his brilliant Satan or Dostoevsky from his Grand Inquisitor, and hoped to keep faith with the literary principles of Henry James and Jean-Paul Sartre, who liked to speak of a sacred pact that prohibited writers from assuming any moral responsibility toward their readers.

This is the merest nonsense. If Blake and Shelley believed (mistakenly) that Milton was of Satan's party, it was certainly not because of any reservation Milton felt about confuting the devil. Satan's great speeches and moments are largely confined to the first two books of *Paradise Lost*, after which he not only declines in stature but is "answered" by several thousand lines of angelic verse. The real problem is not just that Steiner's loyalty to a minor literary tradition (one without value for Jane Austen, Thackeray, or Dickens among others) is much greater than his loyalty to the Jewish people, but the horrifying fact that, as he admits in a rare moment of candor, he is "not sure that A.H. can be answered." In other words, Steiner cannot, for all his erudition, give the lie to any of the following assumptions and assertions of his play's hero: The Nazi idea of the master race chosen (by itself) to impose its law upon inferior races is identical to the Jewish (and Christian) idea of a people chosen by God to receive His law; the Nazi idea is also like the Zionist idea (even though the Zionists explicitly rejected chosenness for "normality"); the state of Israel was created *because* of the Holocaust (and not *in spite of* the murder of millions of the most Zionistic Jews in the world); Israel's sense of its beleaguered condition grows out of its birth in the Holocaust (and not out of brooding over such minor annoyances as sixty-five years of Arab terrorism and five major wars).

That every one of these malicious slanders converged perfectly with the major themes of PLO propaganda; that Steiner's novella and play appeared at a time when Europe was being swept by a tidal wave of "literature" and films restoring Hitler to heroic status, a time when Israel was consistently represented by its enemies in the UN and the press as the inheritor of Nazism, a time when Jewish intellectuals at British and American universities, where the PLO cause is among the most popular liberal idolatries, were hastening to distance themselves from Israel—all this was a mysterious accident that Steiner could not explain except by reference to his creative *daemon.*

Whatever misgivings Updike may have had about the ability of Western journalists to make Jews into metaphors should finally have been laid to rest by their treatment of the war in Lebanon. The propaganda battle against Israel began with the invention of the figure of 600,000 homeless civilians by the Palestinian Red Crescent Society, which happens to be headed by Yasser Arafat's brother. The figure, a patent absurdity on the face of it for an area whose entire population is under 500,000, was irresistibly attractive to anti-Israel journalists for the same reason that it was invented in the first place: it began with a 6 and facilitated the licentious equation of 600,000 Palestinian Arabs with the 6 million Jews. That is why it continued to be used (for example, by Robert Fisk in the *Times* of London, and Jessica Savitch on NBC) long after it had become "clear to anyone who has traveled in southern Lebanon . . . that the original figures . . . were extreme exaggerations."[8]

The British Communist paper *Morning Star* published an editorial headed "Stop the Genocide" (June 11, 1982). Steven Benson of the Phoenix *Arizona Republic* published a whole series of pictures showing goose-stepping Israelis in German helmets guarding cattle cars and patrolling concentration camps; and his cartoonist colleague Oliphant showed West Beirut as the Warsaw Ghetto, with the PLO as the besieged Jews and the Israelis as the Nazi beasts. (Just which Jewish resistance leader of 1943 set the precedent for Arafat's daily baby-kissing for U.S. television cameras was not indicated by Oliphant or Alexander Cockburn or any of the other discoverers of Warsaw in Beirut.) Peter Taylor, reporting in the *Sunday Telegraph* on the mass rally in Tel Aviv to demonstrate support for the operation in Lebanon, found that "the towering, shrine-like podium at the rally, supporting rank after rank of sombre worthies and topped on high by an arrogant parade of flags, inevitably involved images of another place and another time" (July 25, 1982). William Pfaff (*International Herald Tribune*) declared that "Hitler's work goes on," done by "the Jews themselves." John Chancellor, musing autobiographically on the bombing of August 2, confessed that he "kept thinking yesterday of the bombing of Madrid during the Spanish Civil War." Since Chancellor was about twelve years old when Madrid was bombed by the Junkers 52s of Hitler's Luftwaffe in 1936, one may venture to guess that it was not memory that brought forth this analogy so much as a keen awareness that the short and ready way to prominence in broadcast journalism is the equation of Israelis with Nazis and Palestinian Arabs with Jews. Israel's aging *enfant terrible* Yeshayahu Leibowitz, whose claim on public attention had previously rested on his relentless insistence that Ben-Gurion hated Judaism more than any man he had ever known, became an instant celebrity in the European press by coining the epithet "Judeo-Nazi" to describe Israel's actions in Lebanon. The English writer of spy-stories, John Le Carré, held forth in the *Observer* (June 13, 1982) about how "Begin and his generals . . . are . . . inflicting upon another people the disgraceful criteria once inflicted upon themselves," and in his novel about Israelis and Arabs of the following year gave tacit approval only to those Israelis who pilloried most of their countrymen as Nazis. Nicholas von Hoffman, writing from the United States for the *Spectator*, likened Israelis in Lebanon to Nazis in Lidice and expressed the hopeful belief that as a result of his efforts and those of like-minded journalists "Americans are coming to see the Israeli Government as pounding the Star of David into a swastika."

The campaign of calculated distortion begun by the Russians in 1967 had by June 1983 become so successful that its formulas could be exported to places that had never seen Jews or Nazis—places like Kuala Lumpur, where the *New Straits Times* prognosticated that "just as Hitler's diabolical plan for a 'final solution to the Jewish problem' failed to drive the Jews out of Europe, so will fail Israel's savage efforts to uproot the Palestinians" (June 29, 1983). Every half-educated Israel-hater was soon repeating the formula with the regularity of a steam engine, and the situation quickly reached the point where Conor Cruise O'Brien proposed making this vilification a kind of litmus test for the detection of antisemitism: "If your interlocutor can't keep Hitler out of the conversation, . . . feverishly turning Jews into Nazis and Arabs into Jews—why then, I think, you may well be talking to an anti-Jewist." Some people, in reaction to the daily regurgitation of this formula in the news media and by PLO spokesmen, must also have begun to wonder whether a movement that can conceive of itself only as a mirror image of its Jewish enemy is in truth a "nation," or rather an antination, whose whole meaning and existence derive from its desire to destroy a living nation. (Ironically, none of the journalistic warriors against neo-Nazism thought it worthwhile to remark on the prominence of Nazi flags and mementos in captured headquarters of the new Jews, formerly known as the PLO, in Lebanon.)

Ordinarily, in surveying so dismal a spectacle, one can take comfort from the fact that, as Orwell liked to say, there are some ideas so stupid that only intellectuals could believe them. But the allegation that Israelis were doing to Palestinian Arabs what Nazis had done to Jews was in the summer of 1982 being voiced by prominent and often powerful politicians: Olof Palme, Andreas Papandreou, Bruno Kreisky, François Mitterrand. Even the usually sober and cautious George Shultz was infected by the plague of Holocaust-analogizing in the aftermath of Sabra and Shatilla, though he stopped short of equating Israelis with Nazis and suggested only that they resembled the nations of the world that stood idly by and did nothing while the Jews were being murdered by Hitler. For him the Israelis were not yet the Nazis, but the Palestinian Arabs certainly had become the Jews. Statesmen, as Shakespeare showed in *Julius Caesar*, are just as likely as other people to get their thoughts entangled in metaphors, and to act fatally on the strength of them.

That is why we must adhere sternly to the simple but indispensable truth that, as Cynthia Ozick has written, "Jews are no metaphors—not for poets, not for novelists, not for theologians, not for murderers, and never for antisemites."[9] The blurring of the crime that was the Holocaust is, of course, not always political and not always a weapon used against Jews or Israel. It often seems characteristic of nothing more than the intellectual vulgarity and lack of distinction that are besetting sins of our culture. That it is omnipresent no one can doubt: Go to a feminist rally, and you will see placards that read "Pornography is to women what Nazism is to Jews!"; listen to a spokesman for gays, and you will be told that their psychological and social confinement in cars, bars, restrooms, and theaters parallels the concentration of Jews in World War II; go to an antinuclear rally, and watch the protestors painting "U.S.S. Auschwitz" on the nearest Trident submarine; read a novel by William Styron, and you will get a little lecture on the parochial interpretation that has been put on the Holocaust by Jews who view it as their tragedy rather than as an instance of that enslavement that has afflicted many peoples in the past and will continue to do so in the future. None of these travesties is politically motivated, but all of them express a deep-seated wish to transform the Nazi murder of the Jewish people, a crime of terrifying clarity and distinctness, into a blurred, amorphous agony, an indeterminate part of man's general inhumanity to man. By doing so, they subserve the malignant designs of those who wish finally to release the nations of the West from whatever slight burden of guilt they may still bear for what they allowed or helped Hitler to do to the Jews of Europe, and so remove whatever impediments of conscience may yet stand in the way of the anti-Israel juggernaut. In the present political climate, whoever makes of the murdered Jews of Auschwitz and all the other killing centers metaphors for all humanity degrades rather than exalts them, and renders easier the dirty work of those who would make them the representatives not of humanity in general but of their polar opposites: the enemies of the Jews in particular. Those who deprive the dead Jews of their deaths are of necessity in collusion with those who seek to deprive the living Jews of their lives.

Notes

1. Yehuda Bauer, *The Holocaust in Historical Perspective* (Seattle: University of Washington Press, 1978), p. 32.

2. Ibid., p. 35.

3. See Benno W. Varon, "The Haunting of Meyer Levin," *Midstream* 22 (August/September 1976):20.

4. See the article on this controversy by Nissim Elnecave, "Por Qué la Iglesia Esta Especulando con los Martires Judios para Sanctificarlos como Católicos?" *La Luz*, 20 July 1979, pp. 12–15.

5. On this subject, see Cynthia Ozick, "All the World Wants the Jews Dead," *Esquire Magazine* 82 (November 1974).

6. Norman Podhoretz, "The Abandonment of Israel," *Commentary* 62 (July 1976):26.

7. For information on the AFSC campaign against Israel, I am indebted to Marvin Maurer, "Quakers in Politics," *Midstream* 23 (November 1977):36–44; and H. David Kirk, *The Friendly Perversion* (New York: Americans for a Safe Israel, 1979).

8. David Shipler, *New York Times Service*, 15 July 1982.

9. Cynthia Ozick, "A Liberal's Auschwitz," in Bill Henderson, ed., *The Pushcart Prize: Best of the Small Presses* (Yonkers, N.Y.: Pushcart Book Press, 1975), p. 127.

19

The Psychology of Antisemitism: Conscience-Proof Rationalization and the Deferring of Moral Choice

Wendy Stallard Flory

Hannah Arendt, confronted with Eichmann's own account of his role in implementing Hitler's "Final Solution," was confused and troubled to find that the evidence about his motives that she had expected to come to light did not seem to exist. She had assumed, naturally enough, that the testimony of a mass murderer must show either evidence of hatred and sadism or, in their absence, a strong awareness of guilt. In fact, Eichmann made it clear that he felt none of these. Nor was he unusual in this. Arendt discovered that even those who committed the actual murders "were not killers or sadists by nature; on the contrary, a systematic effort was made to weed out all those who derived physical pleasure from what they did. The troops of the *Einsatzgruppen* had hardly more crimes in its record than any ordinary unit of the German Army, and their commanders had been chosen by Heydrich from the S.S. élite with academic degrees."[1]

Having eliminated sadism as the main motive, Arendt could not find any adequate alternative explanation and was left in confusion to confront the discrepancy between the bestiality of the Nazi crimes and the apparent absence of bestiality in the temperaments of the murderers: "The trouble with Eichmann was precisely that so many were like him, and that the many were neither perverted nor sadistic, that they were, and still are, terrifyingly normal . . . [and] that this new type of criminal who is in fact *hostis generis humani*, commits his crimes under circumstances that make it well-nigh impossible for him to know or to feel that he is doing wrong" (p. 253). Perplexed by this anomaly, Arendt was unable to grasp what it is about the psychology of antisemitism that would explain this and tried to resolve the problem prematurely— and inevitably, unsatisfactorily—by speaking of the "banality of evil."

This phrase was a particularly unfortunate choice, the adjective ("banal") seeming to belittle or diminish an outrage of such extreme horror that surely no adjective could be extreme enough. Arendt was, of course, applying "banal" not to the evil of the Holocaust as experienced by its victims, but rather to the conception of the "Final Solution" as it seemed to have been held in the minds of those who carried it out. The phrase was inherently inaccurate. It was not the evil that was banal but the thinking of the perpetrators of the evil.

If we continue the investigation from the point at which Arendt gave up on it, we see that there are two separate points that are particularly anomalous. The first is that "the murderers were not killers or sadists by nature"—that is, they were apparently not motivated by hatred or malice; and the second is their apparent immunity to feelings of guilt. Arendt suggested that this lack of guilt feelings was the result of external influences when she said that "this new type of criminal . . . commits his crimes under circumstances that make it well-nigh impossible for him to know or to feel that he is doing wrong," yet this comes dangerously close to suggesting that we are dealing with something outside the realm of moral choice and personal responsibility. In trying to make sense of the disparity between the magnitude of the evil and the weakness of the personal animus of its enactors, she did not find the clue she needed because she was looking for the wrong thing. She was looking for an extremity of motive that would be commensurate with the extremity of its outcome. In fact, she had found the clue she needed but did not recognize it for what it was. The clue lay in her observation that the murderers were, in fact, "terrifyingly normal."

Even the most extreme form of persecution is the effect of prejudice, and the impulse to prejudice is a fundamental human tendency. It exists before any incentive to hatred and below the level of conscious moral choice at which guilt would be felt. The impulse to prejudice is not abnormal and to be denounced, but normal and to be eradicated. Until we understand this, we continue to leave our societies vulnerable to the danger of prejudice's most extreme manifestations. It is because the impulse to prejudice is instinctive that the conscience can be bypassed and prejudice can take its course, even to the extent of extreme persecution, without ever having been made a matter for moral choice by the individual. If a society is to safeguard itself against the destructiveness of antisemitism, it must raise the consciousness of its individual members by making sure that it is a matter of common knowledge that each individual is instinctively inclined toward prejudice and can be free of it only through conscious effort. To be free from prejudice means to have identified it in one's own instinctive reactions, to have made the decision that it is morally unacceptable, and to have taken whatever steps are necessary to break prejudiced patterns of thought. We must realize that what Arendt assumed was aberrant is, in fact, normal. We must learn that because the human impulse to prejudice is instinctive the tendency will usually be to justify it, and that the ability to rationalize is so sophisticated and unerring that unless there is strong moral leadership to encourage people to do otherwise they will be able to defer indefinitely making it an issue of moral choice. Under these circumstances, prejudice can intensify into the extreme of bestiality, which is no less normal for being terrifying and no less terrifying for being normal.

The historians can tell us what external forces determined the timing and particular nature of antisemitic manifestations. To determine precisely what these forces were is, of course, a complex and demanding task; yet this information, taken alone, does not answer a question of crucial importance—one that is often asked both implicitly and explicitly throughout this book—the question of why the people exposed to these external forces responded to them. The availability of the *Protocols*, of Zion for example, does not explain the fact that they were enthusiastically received.

What I have to say about the psychology of antisemitism is basic and simple, and—probably for this very reason—usually overlooked; but unless we make a place for it in our thinking, our discussions of particular manifestations of antisemitism are in danger of being unfocused and even inconclusive. I will speak first of prejudice in general rather than of its specific manifestation as antisemitism because it is essential that we understand clearly the fundamental psychology that antisemitism holds in common with all forms of prejudice before we can see the exact significance of the particular forms that antisemitism has taken, forms that are different in some ways from other manifestations of prejudice.

The real explanation for the ubiquity of prejudice is so simple that only the strength of our need for a rationalization could have allowed us to hide it from ourselves so effectively. Prejudice is simply one manifestation of the most fundamental and instinctive of all human drives—selfishness—and its persistence is the result of another human characteristic that is equally predictable—the pride that makes us ready to go to almost any length to avoid admitting to ourselves that we were in the wrong.

Prejudice is never a response to the behavior or characteristics of a group. The impulse to prejudice pre-exists. The particular kind of selfishness that generates it is the temptation to inflate our sense of self-worth by taking satisfaction from the misfortunes of others. Almost all human beings are vulnerable to this temptation to some degree, which explains such commonplace phenomena as our fascination with gossip and our avid interest in "the News," which in turn is, of course, almost entirely news about the worst kinds of things that happen to other people—about crime, corruption, natural disasters, and tragic accidents.

A similar kind of cheap satisfaction comes from dwelling on the idea that one is "normal" and an "insider" compared to other groups of people who are in some way "different" and therefore "outsiders." There is a strong tendency for people to think of any difference from the norm to which they have chosen to subscribe as automatic inferiority because this allows them to feel superior to a large number of people.

Antisemitism and racism are the result of a selfish attempt to inflate one's sense of self-worth, and often to compensate for one's feelings of inadequacy, by choosing to treat differentness as though it were a moral failing. Any attempt to identify specific personality traits of Jews or blacks or any other group as "reasons" for prejudice is bound to be spurious and is always an attempt to rationalize the real motive—a narrowminded and defensive refusal to allow others the fundamental human right to be judged as individuals.

That these so-called reasons are only rationalizations is, of course, inevitable. One can not inherit moral characteristics simply by being born a member of a particular race or group, and it is only on moral grounds that we are ever justified in arriving at a negative opinion about an individual. Since prejudice is a reaction to difference alone and not to racial, cultural, or moral characteristics, those groups who suffer most from persecution are likely also to have a very obvious kind of differentness. Blacks, for example, are not white; Jews are not Christian and celebrate the Sabbath on a different day of the week. To be obviously different is to be easily branded as an outsider, and both Jews in Europe and blacks in the United States have historically been thought of as *in* the country in which they live, but not *of* it. This is also the case with the gypsies—and it is no coincidence that they were marked out for extermination by the Nazis, together with the Jews.

Very few people are able to attain the degree of maturity that would make them completely indifferent to the appeal of the cheap satisfaction of feeling superior to "outsiders," but for many the pleasures of condescension are enough and they have no inclination to act upon their prejudices. The stimulus that intensifies prejudice and makes it active rather than passive is always fear. This is, in fact, a fear of personal inadequacy that refuses to acknowledge itself as such and claims to have discovered in the objects of its prejudice the reasons for its existence.

Of the various kinds of fear that intensify prejudice, we tend to feel most comfortable concentrating on the pathological variety. The fear of inadequacy is an intrinsic part of the individual's personality, dating from childhood, independent of present circumstances and impervious to reason or logic. There is a strong temptation to want to believe that all "real" racism or antisemitism involves an extreme and abnormal psychological state of this kind, since this belief establishes a "safe distance" between the "real" racist or antisemitic and "ordinary" or "normal" people. But in actuality, the pathological bigot is likely to be considerably less dangerous than the "normal" person who acquiesces in prejudice. "Hysterical racists" and "virulent antisemites" are relatively few in number, are easily identifiable, and pose a threat that is very much a known quantity. Prejudice will never become active persecution on a large scale without the tacit acquiescence of the majority of "ordinary people" within the society.

The two main fears that intensify prejudice in "normal people" are the fear of loss of social status (and of the respectability, esteem, or power that go with it) and the fear that comes with financial difficulties. The temptation to prejudice increases considerably when loss of social status occurs in a time of widespread social change and when personal financial difficulties coincide with national economic crises. The process by which such fears lead to prejudice in an extreme form is the same in either case. When, as often happens, people refuse or are unable to see that the fear springs from a sense of personal inadequacy, the fear is impossible to deal with and there is a strong tendency to externalize it by inventing some outside source for it—the scapegoat. Since nothing short of self-confrontation will remove the anxiety, the charade of blaming some supposed hostile influence cannot offer any possible resolution to the problem and, in fact, is likely to intensify it. The subconscious awareness of lying to oneself gives rise to further confusion and frustration, and the sense of suppressed guilt at one's self-delusion is added to the original sense of inadequacy and of being trapped by circumstances beyond one's control. Anger and hatred become a welcome outlet for these unbearable feelings and are focused with increasing emphasis upon whichever scapegoat has been chosen.

It is very important to realize that this subconscious awareness of lying to oneself can act as a positive as well as a negative force. When we follow our natural instinct and repress this awareness we force ourselves more deeply into prejudice and hatred, but it is also possible for this sense of guilt to become the means of raising us out of our prejudice. As Zvi Gitelman has mentioned, the decisive influence will be the leadership of those who are perceived as speaking with authority in the society. In times when those in power make no attempt to denounce prejudice and the pursuit of self-interest in ways that harm others, or even encourage them, instinctive selfishness will ensure that a significant number of people will give free rein to their latent prejudices and very few people will be prepared to take a stand against an abuse that the majority seems content to let take its course. On the other hand, when those in positions of influence and authority officially condemn prejudice, their example is likely to be influential because people are at least subconsciously aware that their impulse to prejudice springs from selfishness and mean-spiritedness. It is relatively easy to turn their self-consciousness about this into a recognition of their underlying guilt.

The great enemy is always the power of rationalization. Emil Fackenheim spoke of the "devil's logic"—the antisemite's infallible recourse to blaming the Jews "for their virtues as well as their vices." I believe that what he has called the "devil's logic" is precisely the power of rationalization. Working, as it does, with the full force of the subconscious mind behind it, it is unassailable by logic and will marshal any opinions as "proof," not even hesitating to hold simultaneously ones that are mutually exclusive. People can be, and commonly are, instinctively antisemitic without being consciously antisemitic. In such a case they will be able to contend quite sincerely that they are not antisemitic at all. Hence, incidentally, the very real problem with the reliability of public opinion polls on this issue. Hence also the great danger that straightforward antisemitism will be disguised, even in the eyes of the people who espouse it, as a conscientious humanitarian concern for the victims of Israel. I would suggest that what Fackenheim has described in this context as "self-righteousness" is again the power of rationalization to seem to validate a morally reprehensible impulse as a morally acceptable one.

When prejudice is at issue, our instinctive impulse is to except ourselves from blame, to concede that prejudice is a common failing of other people, but to "explain" how, in our case, what might seem to be prejudice is a justifiable response to real moral failings in the group that we are stereotyping. Logically, of course, this is nonsense. We know that it is impossible for all members of any group to share the same negative characteristics just by being born into that group. Even if we postulate the highly unlikely situation in which the majority of any group was guilty of antisocial behavior and attitudes, a society would still be guilty of a violation of individual rights and freedoms were it to act on the assumption that any individual members of that group were antisocial, not on the strength of their actions and attitudes but on the grounds that they were members of that group.

The real premise for prejudiced thinking is that differentness means inferiority. Needing to disguise the patent falsity and pettiness of this premise, antisemites are automatically alert to every opportunity to rationalize their prejudice and blind to everything that contradicts their rationalizations. If Gentiles are cheated by a Gentile, they are angry at the individual; if they are cheated by an individual who is Jewish, they are angry at that person as a Jew. When they are treated well by Jews, they are grateful to them as individuals. Instances of admirable behavior on the part of Jews, no matter how frequent, are never considered to be a refutation of negative stereotypes about "the Jews as a group."

We know that for a Gentile to say "Some of my best friends are Jews" is to invite mockery, but the impulse to mock such a comment needs to be scrutinized itself. When we automatically mock someone for saying this, we are likely to be assuming that they are insincere, so that we can find fault with their insincerity and feel superior to them. Yet the really sobering thought is that there is a good chance that the person is sincere in saying this—that people can, and often do, have good friends who are Jewish and still find this no impediment to their antisemitic prejudices. A comment that we would like to take as a reflection upon an individual is more likely to be a reflection upon the power of rationalization of people in general, ourselves included.

When we consider the different groups that were the victims of Hitler's policy of attempted extermination, it is clear that the situation of the Jews was different from that of other groups, and yet attempts to account for this difference are not always entirely conclusive. To a considerable degree, the clue to understanding this difference lies in an awareness of how the rationalizations of prejudice spring from the basic tenets that differentness is a liability and therefore inevitably undesirable and to be avoided. The case of the Jews is a serious threat to the rationalizations of prejudice in that it presents a direct affront to these tenets. Rather than avoiding differentness, religious Jews actively cultivate it; and rather than being at a disadvantage as a result of their differentness, Jews are often seen to be successful in precisely those material ways that are the real, although often unadmitted, concern of the bigot.

It is highly unusual for a group that is the victim of prejudice to present a challenge of this kind. The widespread poverty among blacks in America, for example, seems to substantiate the idea that to be different is to be at a disadvantage. Moreover, since they cannot change the differentness that marks them as a group, they cannot be accused of cultivating it. Because immigrant groups in the United States, such as the Irish, the Italians, the Poles, and the Hungarians were so ready to assimilate as soon as they were financially able to do so, their situation also seemed to support the tenet that differentness is a liability and therefore must be avoided. The gypsies were similar to the Jews in choosing to insist on their differentness, but they did not challenge the premise of differentness as liability in being content with subsistence rather than aspiring to financial success.

The situation of the Jews refuted the false logic of prejudice more drastically than the example of any other group, and this was one fundamental reason why the compulsion to destroy them was so strong. Other non-Aryans, such as the Slavs, could be classified as subhuman and enslaved, and some could even be killed without compunction, but it was not considered necessary to murder them methodically. Jewishness was an "affront" of a unique kind because it involved the cultivation of differentness in such a thoroughgoing way—in almost every aspect of life and behavior, and from such an early age (in the case of boys, almost from birth on). Perhaps this last fact functioned as a kind of perverted rationale for the decision to murder Jewish children and even infants as well as for the apparent inoperability of the usual minimal compassion that excepts babies and young children from torture and murder even when adults are slaughtered without compunction.

Perhaps the most terrifying and incapacitating thought about the Holocaust is the idea that what happened in Germany under Hitler was the result of mysterious and inscrutable forces that, because they cannot be understood, cannot be guarded against in the future. On the contrary, I believe that if we understand the compulsions involved in prejudiced thinking and particularly the inexorable way in which the power of rationalization overrides the customary processes of rational thought, we can also understand what a society can do to protect itself against a horror of this kind. Though people may pay lip service to the idea that prejudice should be condemned, they are likely to have caught themselves, at least from time to time, instinctively reacting in a bigoted way. When they think of themselves as "normal, decent people"—as most people do—they are likely to feel that these "lapses" cannot be, after all, completely unjustified. As soon as anyone in a position of authority seems to be countenancing, condoning, or even advocating discrimination, people who had before been self-conscious about resorting to derogatory stereotypes are likely to be glad for permission to cease feeling guilty of being narrow-minded and self-serving. This explains why "normal, decent" Germans neither rose up in outrage against the extermination of the Jews nor made any strenuous effort to find out the details of Hitler's "Final Solution." They were likely to have felt some degree of distaste for Jews and to have wanted to believe that their dislike was not a sign of inadequacy in them but an honest response to something undesirable. The more severe a form the persecution took, the less likely it was that an outcry would occur, because of the tendency for people to dislike those they have wronged as a way of evading the guilt. The more drastic the wrong, the stronger the need to "blame the victim."

The Holocaust occurred because, in a time of extreme economic crisis, when fears of personal and national financial ruin aggravated a normal disposition toward prejudice into an active hatred, a leader came into power who not only condoned this impulse toward hatred but *required* it, promising that it would solve the very problems that had stimulated the hatred in the first place. The German people were convinced by Hitler's rhetoric of hatred only because it sanctioned the strong impulse that they already felt to escape from fear into hatred.

The German people, held fast in the toils of Nazism, were not arbitrarily trapped by some coincidence of historical or sociological forces—by some general "tendency toward imperialism" operating on an international scale, as Arendt tried to argue in *The Origins of Totalitarianism*. The decisive forces at issue were the laws of moral choice, and the degeneration of Nazism into increasing brutality was the inevitable destructive and self-destructive consequence of lies and hatred. Whenever the operative law is moral choice, we must always pay particular attention to the motives of the individual or group under consideration. It was Arendt's failure to do this that makes her "lumping together" of Nazism and Communism so unconvincing. Although she acknowledges the existence of differences that we would expect to be significant, she does not pursue the implications of the differences. She notices, for example, that while extermination was very consciously and deliberately planned and executed in Hitler's camps, death in Stalin's gulags was usually the effect of neglect. This difference seems to me to point directly to the most crucial distinction between the motivations of Nazism and Communism. Communism at its inception was a morally acceptable system and its motives were idealistic. Its turn toward repressiveness was a perversion of its original aim—not its fulfillment. Nazism, on the contrary, was intentionally and explicitly committed to repression from the beginning. Aryan prosperity was to be achieved at the expense of the *Untermenschen*, through the enslavement of the *Ostvolk* and the extermination of the Jews. The Stalinist purges occurred because communism had lost its moral center. Once the original ideal of commitment to individual freedom became a lie, there were no longer guarantees of individual freedom, and the familiar pattern of denial, displacement of guilt, and persecution imposed itself. Nazi persecution was not, like the Stalinist actions, persecution "by default" but, rather, the consequence of a deliberate choice. The lie that must be rationalized was the cornerstone of the whole Nazi ideology—the claim that Aryans were racially superior and, for this reason, justified in enslaving or exterminating non-Aryans. The *Generalplan Ost* and the "Final Solution" needed to be planned in detail if they were to serve as a rationalization of the basic lie upon which the whole system was founded—the lie of Aryan superiority—and it is important to realize that the motive force behind these plans was not sadism but guilt. Subconsciously aware that their "justification" for persecution was a lie, and needing to suppress this awareness with a rationalization, the Nazis proceeded to "make true" their claim that non-Aryans were subhuman. In Hitler's concentration camps the separation of families, torture, rape, and starvation were all ways of trying to strip away the dignity of the victims in the hope of also stripping away their humanity. This, I believe, provides the answer to Emil Fackenheim's question of why it was necessary to torture the Jews if they were going to be killed anyway.

Arendt's notion of "the banality of evil" is itself a revision of her earlier suggestion, in *The Origins of Totalitarianism*, that the concentration camps "are more essential to the preservation of the regime's power than any of its other institutions" and that they offer a "very well-defined training . . . in totalitarian domination" without which it would have been impossible to maintain the fanaticism of the armed forces and the complete apathy of the rest of the population.[2] This idea seems not only problematic but also unnecessarily depressing in its implications, because it concludes that the endless refinements of brutality in the camps were all preconceived, planned, and voluntarily chosen. This forces us to confront the terrifying double prospect, first, that minds depraved enough to cold-bloodedly plan in detail evil of such magnitude could exist and, then, that a whole society could be totally subjected to their will. The endless refinements of torture in the camps were not evidence of the Byzantine perversions of the human mind in the grips of hatred. Except in some special cases—for example, when Jews were used as subjects of "medical experiments"—the torture was not methodically designed and implemented by calculating planners but, rather, was a spontaneous response to all of the different ways in which the humanness of the victims persisted in showing itself, even under the most degrading conditions. For the most part, and especially after the early days of the camps, the torturers were driven not by hatred but by the need to evade their sense of guilt. If the lie that these victims were subhuman was to be rationalized, every manifestation of their humanness had to be trampled upon. Since the lie could never be made true, the process of rationalization and the persecution it entailed could not stop until every Jew had been exterminated. In this important sense the brutality was not chosen but entailed. The moment of moral choice was the acceptance of the original lie. It was at that moment that the guilt of everyone involved began. So when, during Eichmann's trial, Arendt had the opportunity to examine at close quarters the workings of the mind of one of the actual "master planners," what she found was not a monstrous will to evil but a mind that seemed to her "terrifyingly normal."

I believe that it is possible to explain why the "absence of malice" in men like Eichmann is not paradoxical. Everything depends upon our recognition of the fact that the prejudice *begins* not with hatred but with the selfish impulse to reinforce our sense of our own worth at the expense of others. A sense of inadequacy aggravated by fear is likely to lead to hatred of a scapegoat, but the hatred fulfills the specific function of rationalizing the bigot's sense of guilt. Under the Nazis, antisemitism moved into its most extreme phase to the extent that *individuals no longer had to generate their own rationalizations, and therefore hatred was no longer necessary.* Once the government of the country took upon itself the responsibility of "validating" antisemitism, individuals were free to set even more distance between themselves and their sense of suppressed guilt. For the great majority of people, it was no longer necessary to hate.

In *Eichmann in Jerusalem*, Arendt includes a comment by Eichmann that illustrates this perfectly. Here, she was writing about the Wannsee Conference of January 1942, at which the undersecretaries of state, legal experts from all the government ministries, and high-ranking members of the Civil Service met to discuss how the Final Solution could be applied throughout Europe. Eichmann's account made clear that Heydrich, who called the meeting, and knowing that many of those present were not even party members, "expected the greatest difficulties"; but rather than arousing objections, "the Final Solution was greeted with 'extraordinary enthusiasm' by all present." Eichmann himself, who originally had had misgivings about "such a bloody solution through violence," found these misgivings recede: "Now he could see with his own eyes and hear with his own ears that not only Hitler, not only Heydrich . . . , not just the S.S. or the Party, but the élite of the good old Civil Service were vying and fighting with each other for the honor of taking the lead in these 'bloody' matters. 'At that moment [he says], I sensed a kind of Pontius Pilate feeling, for I felt free of all guilt'" (100–101). From this point on, it would never be necessary for him to feel hatred toward his victims—*and yet this did not make him any less responsible for their deaths.* Arendt, and probably most of those who witnessed the trial, assumed that hatred was a prerequisite for persecution. When she failed to find evidence of hatred, she was confused and tried to explain this apparent anomaly. Her attempt at explanation was unsatisfactory only because she, like the court, failed to realize that persecution does not begin with hatred and so we should not require proof of hatred to find someone guilty of responsibility for mass murder.

In her desire to be as accurate as possible in describing Eichmann's attitudes and motives, Arendt duly recorded his absence of malice. Unable to explain this she continued to insist that it be acknowledged, and her rather truculent-sounding insistence is easy to misread as a perverse attempt to minimize Eichmann's guilt. Her critics were probably all the more angry for being unable to think their way around this apparent paradox themselves. She could have avoided the controversy altogether had she simply said in a forthright way that she found the evidence confusing. She chose instead a very counterproductive approach. Since Eichmann seemed less obviously guilty than she had assumed he would, she looked for the "missing guilt" elsewhere and fell into the common fallacy of "blaming the victim." It was her decision to devote one chapter of *Eichmann in Jerusalem* to the fact that the leaders of the Jewish communities in Europe "almost without exception, cooperated in one way or another, for one reason or another, with the Nazis," that prompted the great outcry against the book. By examining the "role of the Jewish leaders in the destruction of their own people" (p. 104), she seemed to be implying that she was helping to resolve the confusing matter of Eichmann's guilt, whereas the cooperation of the *Judenräte* with the Nazis was a quite separate issue and one that could obviously not be done justice to in a brief, parenthetical commentary such as she provided. Nor was it a matter that had any bearing at all on the issue of Eichmann's guilt. He was actively involved in a plan to murder millions of innocent people; he knew that the actions he was taking would result in the deaths of these people; the fact that he had rationalized his guilt to himself and was helped in this by the propaganda of his government in no way mitigated the degree to which he was guilty.

By including an indictment of the behavior of the Jewish Councils in a work dealing with Eichmann's guilt, Arendt exposed herself to criticism on two counts. She seemed to be implying that there was a connection between these two issues where none logically existed, and, although she did not herself intend to rationalize the fate of the Jews by blaming them for failing to be better survivors, her criticisms of the Jewish leadership were bound to give encouragement to those people who did want to rationalize the Holocaust in this way.

Arendt mentions in passing some of the impediments to action that the Jewish leadership faced, but the issue of the conduct of the members of the councils is an extremely complex one and it is clearly irresponsible to arrive at conclusions about it on the basis of impressions rather than through research. After five years of investigation, Isaiah Trunk arrived at very different conclusions from those of Arendt; these are summed up, in his book *Judenrat*, in the closing words of the introduction that Jacob Robinson contributed to this study: "It would appear, then, that when all factors are considered, Jewish participation or nonparticipation in the deportations had no substantial influence—one way or the other—on the final outcome of the Holocaust in Eastern Europe."[3] This conclusion underlines yet again the overwhelmingly important point that the course of prejudice can never be influenced by the behavior of the victims.

Once we realize that prejudice is not the effect of some mysterious and unpredictable force "out there" but instead, at its root, is the manifestation of something as familiar and commonplace as selfishness, we need not feel so powerless to deal with it. The fact that prejudice has always been such a powerful force in societies does not mean that it must continue to be so. It is in the same category as all the other abuses that historically have deprived certain sections of the population of basic rights but have now been done away with. There is no reason why subscribing to antisemitic stereotypes should not go the way of accepting serfdom or slavery, making public executions an occasion for family outings, baiting the insane for entertainment, and denying women the right to vote. These are all practices that at one time were considered perfectly acceptable and yet are now seen as so much in conflict with the level of civilization we claim for our society that we find the possibility of reinstating them unthinkable. The violation of human rights through the institutionalization of prejudice and the rationalization of prejudiced thinking fall into the same category as these other abuses, and we have been slow to realize this only because we have not clearly understood the nature of prejudice. Plenty of well-meaning people who are genuinely concerned with this problem do not understand the origins of bigoted thinking, what aggravates it, and what can defuse it. As a result, they are seriously limited in their ability to move against it decisively. More often than not, those theories which even educated people accept as "reasons" for prejudice turn out to be not reasons at all but rationalizations.

If, as I have suggested, prejudice is a manifestation of selfishness, then a society can protect itself against the destructive effects of prejudice by insisting (as it does with other kinds of selfishness) that it must be rigorously monitored and restrained. We are well aware of the need to train children from a very early age to control and repress other kinds of selfishness so that they can function in personal relationships and as members of the larger society. We understand very clearly that selfishness is a normal human impulse and yet one that is unacceptable because it is both personally and socially destructive. We have failed to move decisively against prejudice because we have not understood that it is both normal and destructive in the same way as any other of selfishness. "Normal, decent, ordinary people" almost always ..... or prejudice in some form or another and, because they do not acknowledge that this is so, are not able to be adequately on their guard against it.

We cannot take effective steps against prejudice if we treat it as abnormal and something to be hidden rather than normal and something to be corrected. If we pretend to believe that prejudice is an aberration, then we force people to lie to themselves about being prejudiced. To be free from prejudice is to have transcended it by effort and by choice—and people will not make the effort if they are unaware that it needs to be made.

Notes

1. Hannah Arendt, *Eichmann in Jerusalem* (New York: Viking, 1963), p. 93.
2. Hannah Arendt, *The Origins of Totalitarianism* (New York: Harcourt Brace, 1958), p. 427.
3. Isaiah Trunk, *Judenrat: The Jewish Councils in Eastern Europe Under Nazi Occupation* (New York: Macmillan, 1972), p. xxxv.

20

Antisemitism, Sexism, and the Death of the Goddess: Some Problems with New Readings of Old Texts

Judith L. Goldstein

I am going to relate our ongoing discussion of antisemitism in the New Testament to the concurrent one of sexism in the New Testament.[1] By bringing these issues together, I hope to show how each throws light on the other. However, I also wish to point to a growing area in which people who would consider themselves feminists are formulating new anti-Jewish readings of ancient history, adding yet another set of negative characteristics to the portrait of the Jews. In spite of their sensitivity to the use of women in Western theology as "other," embodying traits rejected by dominant men (these are their terms), "Christian feminist anti-Judaism represents precisely the continuation of a patriarchal ethic of projection" (Plaskow, 1980:12).

Two basic viewpoints on whether the New Testament is or is not antisemitic are presented in Chapter 9 of this volume. The first says that the New Testament is not inherently antisemitic but that its interpretation has led to persecution of the Jews. The adherents of this view say that such New Testament readings must be corrected through additional exegeses and by incorporating historical scholarship about the social relations and the rhetoric of Jesus' time into our understanding of the texts. The other view claims that the New Testament is inherently antisemitic in some parts, and the fact that nothing can ameliorate certain of its doctrines has to be confronted. Rosemary Ruether is associated with this second viewpoint.

The corrective rereadings suggested by advocates of the first viewpoint offer a deceptively simple solution. What is involved in changing the readings of a text? What, in fact, is involved in reeducating people, given that the reinterpretation of texts such as the ones under consideration must include what has been called "consciousness-raising" in the context of feminism? Adding to our knowledge of the past is not enough to change the reading of a text that is embedded in a problematic and living present.

Ruether, the main proponent of the second viewpoint, has attributed to her feminism her sensitivity to antisemitism. What is the relation between the antisemitism of the text and the sexism of the text? What is the relation between the questions and problems feminists have with the New Testament and those that Jews and Christian theologians have with it?

Those who are concerned with the antisemitism and sexism of the New Testament question the readings of *a* text. We have to remember, however, that we always have new texts, and they contain the old. Ruether's feminist sensitivity to antisemitism has been transformed by others into a new accusation aimed at the Jews. At a time when charges of deicide have been silenced, some say that the Jews have killed the Goddess. The stance of those feminists who saw similarities between the status of women and that of the Jews has been transformed.

The charge that the Jews invented patriarchy (no less has been implied by this "new" set of arguments) is the ideological twin of the charge that the Jews invented racism.[2] Both accusations blame the Jews for creating the very institutions that persecuted them. Their persecutors are absolved. The combatting of both these charges changes the terms of the debate for Jews. New oppositions have been created; the battle lines are redrawn, and Jews face those who are attempting to co-opt the very values for which the Jews have traditionally fought. The Jews must debate not racists but those who call themselves antiracists. Jewish feminists are forced to contend with men and women who espouse the same values of equality between the sexes that they themselves support.

The Text, Antisemitism, and Sexism

In the following subsections I present a number of insights shared by critics of New Testament antisemitism and sexism.

Dualistic Thinking

While examining the New Testament's attitude toward women, Rosemary Ruether realized certain parallels with its attitude toward Jews. In her view, the Christian male establishment has incorporated certain dualisms into its thinking that consistently place women in an inferior position and men in a superior one. She describes "the basic dualities" as "the alienation of the mind from the body; the alienation of the subjective self from the objective world; the subjective retreat of the individual, alienated from the social community; the domination or rejection of nature by spirit" (Ruether 1979:45).

Jews as well as women have been the victims of these dualities, and often have been derogated for similar qualities. Both have been considered carnal rather than spiritual, evil rather than good. The process of "projection" has given them the role of representing all that the more powerful rejected in themselves. Ruether cites Tertullian "on the guilty nature of women." The term *you* in the quotation that follows refers to women, but Jews can quite effectively be substituted as the term's referent. "*You* are the devil's gateway. *You* are the unsealer of that forbidden tree. *You* are the first deserter of the divine law. *You* are she who persuaded him whom the Devil was not valiant enough to attack. *You* destroyed so easily God's image of man. On account of *your* desert, that is death, even the son of God had to die" (emphases in original) (Ruether, 1974:157).

Language

Feminists insist that the language of the text be taken seriously. Using male terms for God is meaningful and changes the relation of women to the divine. Male terms do not constitute a general reference but specifically exclude women.

One can similarly say that the term *Jews* can never be a general term of reference, can never be a general symbol, but is always specific. An argument such as the one Raymond Brown makes in explaining (away) the derogatory use of *the Jews* in John should be rejected.[3] Brown, as quoted in Chapter 9 claimed, "It is quite clear that in many instances the term 'the Jews' has nothing to do with ethnic, geographical, or religious differentiation. . . . John is not anti-Semitic; the evangelist is condemning not race or people but opposition to Jesus."

Changing the Reading of a Text

Changing the reading of texts is related to changing everyday speech as far as a program of education is concerned. This is hard. As we know from the progress of feminism, there is a continuum between pasting a sign reading "This ad insults women" on offending billboards and the reinterpretation of great literature. Placing new texts with corrective readings on the shelf next to old texts will not accomplish these changes. On such basic questions, academic and everyday discourses are continuous. Scholars have to be far less sanguine about the possibility of separating their scholarship from the distortions of popular sermons or popular readings of what they say. Ruether may say that certain tenets of classical Christianity are rooted in *apocalyptic* Judaism, but others talk simply about the Jews. I will turn to this discussion now.

Jews and the Death of the Goddess

Judith Plaskow wrote, "There is a new myth developing in Christian feminist circles. It is a myth which tells us that the ancient Hebrews invented patriarchy: that before them the goddess reigned in matriarchal glory, and that after them Jesus tried to restore egalitarianism but was foiled by the persistence of Jewish attitudes within the Christian tradition.

. . . The consequence of this myth is that feminism is turned into another weapon in the Christian anti-Judaic arsenal" (p. 11).[4] Cosmologies usually either look back to a golden age or subscribe to the notion of progressive improvement. In this developing myth, the Jews are worse than what came before *and* what came after. Or, to switch to a spatial rather than a temporal metaphor, Judaism is the valley between the two hills of matriarchy and Christianity.

Scholars who have examined the New Testament on the subject of women and Jews have attempted to locate a "really real" base that was contemporary with the society of Jesus' time, in the hope that such information would allow for new and more correct interpretations of the New Testament. These sociological/historical forays ask if Jesus was or was not part of the Jewish society of his time. They should also, but usually do not, provide a nuanced description of the Jewish society of his time. According to Leonard Swidler, "Jesus was a feminist," ahead of his time in his sympathy for women. A better understanding of Jesus' time is, of course, desirable, but we have to be wary of ideologies that create new texts while purporting to be interpretations of old texts.

Swidler's basic thesis, elaborated in *Biblical Affirmations of Women* and shared by many others writing on the subject, is worth examining.[5] He wrote, "There was a dual tradition on women in the Hebraic nation, one positive and one negative, somehow connected with Goddess worship and dominant status for women on the one hand and Yahweh worship and dominant status for men on the other, and that with the passage of time the negative came to dominate more and more. . . . Jewish women have since (the Roman Empire) basically remained severely subordinated to men, within Judaism until the most recent times" (pp. 158–159). The characterization in a phrase of centuries of turbulent history among different cultures, and in radically different social, political, and economic conditions, takes one's breath away.

Just as disturbing as the reification of such concepts as "domination" and "subordination" is the enthroning of a former matriarchy based on speculation, shaky logic, and the imposition of contemporary psychology on the "past." Again, Swidler's argument is representative of an entire genre. The argument is as follows: In the beginning was goddess worship. Male gods entered with the introduction of animal husbandry when all could see that males had a role in procreation. Before this, "there never was any question about the female's essential role in bringing new life into the world, but the role of the male and sex was not always so obvious" (p. 22). Nonetheless, male gods were still subordinate to female goddesses until the next stage when "patriarchal male-God worshipping, animal-herding Indo-Europeans" attacked from the north. Then comes a logical leap. Indo-European male gods had many of the characteristics of the Hebrew God. Therefore, Swidler asserts, although we have no idea what the connection between the two peoples might be, "it is clear that the stance of both patriarchal peoples and their theologies vis à vis the religion of the Goddess would be, and was, very similar—hostile" (p. 24).

I must leave to others a discussion of the particular historical events recounted here and will only point to a psychologism with no apparent foundation. Swidler, and Merlin Stone in *When God Was A Woman*, both assume that giving birth indicates superiority, and thus both the recognition that women give birth and the lack of acknowledgment of male paternity must mean that women were accorded more value. Most anthropologists would be suspicious of applying this assumption to the past and to other cultures in the present. If anything, the opposite has been argued. This opposing viewpoint states that women, because of the pain and messiness of childbirth, have been associated with "nature" rather than with "culture." "Culture," the domain of the artificially created, the sphere of social activities, is more valued and is associated primarily with men.[6] This opposition between nature and culture can be criticized, and has been criticized, as a particular Western category and not a universal one. Swidler and Stone might consider it the kind of thinking that arose *after* the fall of the goddess. My point, simply, is that both sides are arguing from their reading of contemporary realities, and that there is nothing in the historical record to support one view over the other. An argument that hinges on this psychologism, as Swidler's does, is a weak argument.

After setting the stage, Swidler moves on to the position of women in the Old and New Testaments. In his view, although there are positive and negative strands within the Hebrew tradition, Jesus' attitude toward women was completely positive. Any negative elements found in the Christian tradition came from elsewhere. In the presentation of Swidler's points, all the positive statements about Jesus are stated *in contrast* to the Jewish society of his time. Some examples follow: (1) Jesus used women in his teaching stories, "something unusual for his culture." (2) His images of women are never negative "in dramatic contrast to [those of] his predecessors and contemporaries." (3) He taught using balancing stories of men and women; "unlike that of other rabbis," his teaching was for both men and women (p. 164). (4) "Unlike other Jewish rabbis about whom stories of miraculous healing and raising from the dead are recorded, Jesus does heal women" (p. 180). This comparative structure has a devastating cumulative effect. References to the "other rabbis" ignores all the problems of comparison to which Plaskow refers. Writes Plaskow, "It is deceptive to speak of rabbinic opinion, customs, or sayings as monolithic. . . . [another error] lies in comparing the words and attitudes of an itinerant preacher with laws and sayings formulated in the rarefied atmosphere of rabbinic academies" (p. 11).

Plaskow points out that the institution of the Rabbinate, and any consolidation of its authority, took place well after Jesus' lifetime. I find other readings Swidler offers even more anachronistic. "Woman" encompasses all other categories in his interpretations when a better category might be the "dispossessed"; at other times his readings seem rather far-fetched, as in his analysis of Jesus' statements about the family. He discusses the following concepts. "Anyone who prefers father or mother to me is not worthy of me." (Matthew 10:34–36); "If anyone comes to me without hating his father, mother, wife, children, brothers, sisters, yes and his own life too, he cannot be my disciple" (Luke 12:51– 53). His gloss is this: "What is apparent is Jesus's setting himself the task of dismantling the awesomely powerful restrictive forces of the patriarchal family, whose most obvious victims were women" (p. 178).

In sum, I would like to suggest that new readings are not always helpful readings, and that they are often insufficiently new. The question still remains: How do you get readings relevant to a given time? How do you get minority readings of a text? Too often the attempt to discover readings relevant to the past produces interpretations that, as I have tried to show, include unexamined modern categories. Another problem is that the historical readings offered are too limited in that they produce *one* reading when there were undoubtedly many readings—minority ones as well as what Harold Bloom has called "misreadings" at any point in time.

What Is Wrong with the Reinvention of the Past

Looking for the origins of inequality or discrimination is a problematic task, for women and for Jews. "To look for origins is, in the end, to think that what we are today is something other than the product of our history and our present social world" (Rosaldo, 1980:393). We have the text, but we should remember that antisemitism, like male dominance, may always be there but may not assume the same content or form in all times and all places. We must also ask questions about the social world in which Jewish/Christian relations take place, and about what it means to be a person, female or male, Jewish or Christian, in that world. The "feminists" who look exclusively outside the church to account for its sexism are "projecting" onto the Jews. Gregory Baum makes a point, paraphrased by John Pawlikowski in Chapter 9 of this volume, that is relevant to both women and Jews. "Jesus' conflict with various Jewish factions in his own time became symbolic for the New Testament writers of the perpetual conflict between authentic and in-authentic religion within Christianity. It was the unwillingness on the part of Christians to acknowledge this and to arrive at critical self-knowledge that led to the projection of this criticism onto the entire Jewish community."

Baum's point should also resonate with scholars, alerting them to the self-deception involved in their twin goals of studying the text of the New Testament "itself" divorced from its past interpretations, and searching for its meaning in the "real" description of the society in which Jesus lived. The understanding of the New Testament and of its historical environment is inevitably colored by more recent events and by views that scholars hold about Jewish/Christian relations in their own times. In looking for origins—whether to decide if the New Testament is antisemitic or not, or if the Jews killed the Goddess or not—we must be careful not to bypass the problem of history and ongoing social relations. It is dangerous for scholars to claim an innocence they do not, and probably should not, have.

Notes

1. This paper was delivered by me in my role as discussant for the panel "Religion and Religious Establishments" (November 20, 1983) and, except for some amplification, has remained unchanged. I thank my colleague Deborah Dash Moore for discussing some of these ideas with me.

2. This charge was discussed at the Conference on Anti-Semitism by Alain Finkielkraut.

3. Father Pawlikowski told me after the panel discussion that Mr. Brown no longer holds the view expressed by him here.

4. Readers interested in pursuing these ideas should consult the excellent and important articles by Plaskow and Daum in *Lilith*, no. 7 (1980). Daum includes a bibliography on the subject. Some responses to their arguments appear in *Lilith*, no. 8, 1981.

5. A letter to the editor following the publication of the Plaskow and Daum discussion made the important point that "when we approach individual Christians, whether they be scholars or lay people, we must not make assumptions concerning their motivations" (p. 3). The authors of the letter go on to list the important contributions Leonard Swidler has made to ecumenical understanding as a "veteran of decades of pioneering work in Jewish-Christian relations" (p. 3). I want to stress that I have used Swidler's work as an example of a certain line of argument (partly because it is better than many other books more exclusively concerned with goddess feminism), and I have criticized its reliance on what I think are anachronistic interpretations of the culture of ancient peoples. I do not criticize Swidler's motivations or his arguments as antisemitic.

6. The argument relating females with nature and males with culture is found in Sherry Ortner, "Is Female to Male as Nature Is to Culture?" in Michelle Zimbalist Rosaldo and Louise Lamphere, eds., *Woman, Culture and Society* (Stanford, Calif.: Stanford University Press, 1974). Criticisms of the argument throughout Carol P. MacCormack and Marilyn Strathern, eds., *Nature, Culture and Gender* (Cambridge: Cambridge University Press, 1980).

References

Daum, Annette. "Blaming Jews for the Death of the Goddess." *Lilith*, no. 7 (1980):13.

Letters to the Editor. "Lines of Communication." *Lilith*, no. 8 (1981).

Pawlikowski, (Rev.) John T. "New Testament Antisemitism: Fact or Fable?" Paper presented at the Conference on Antisemitism in the Contemporary World, Rutgers University, November 20, 1984.

Plaskow, Judith. "Blaming Jews for Inventing Patriarchy." *Lilith*, no. 7 (1980):11–12.

Ruether, Rosemary, ed. 1974. *Religion and Sexism.* New York: Simon and Schuster.
———. 1979. "Motherearth and the Megamachine: A Theology of Liberation in a Feminine, Somatic and Ecological Perspective." *in* Christ and Plaskow, eds. *Womanspirit Rising.* New York: Harper and Row.
Rosaldo, Michelle. 1980. "The Use and Abuse of Anthropology: Reflections on Feminism and Cross-cultural Understanding." *Signs*, vol. 5, no. 3.
Stone, Merlin. 1978. *When God Was a Woman.* New York: Harcourt Brace Jovanovich.
Swidler, Leonard. 1979. *Biblical Affirmations of Women.* Philadelphia, Penn.: Westminster Press.

Part Five

Contemporary Perceptions

21

Perceptions of Antisemitism in France

Dominique Schnapper

For the European Jew, France has always played a special role. Throughout the nineteenth century and up until 1940, France was the country of emancipation, the first country of Europe whose great revolution granted legal equality and civil rights to Jews. It is not by chance that a Yiddish proverb speaks of "Happy as God in France." However, by the end of the nineteenth century this image had become ambiguous. France was also the country of the Dreyfus Affair, echoes of which resonated throughout the Jewish communities everywhere. Recently, particularly in the United States, the image of France with regard to Jews has become even more ambiguous. Let us mention the Gaullist policy, which was critical of Israel and was itself sharply criticized; de Gaulle's famous statement, "a proud and dominating people"; and the recent attacks on the Copernic Synagogue (October 1980) and on the Jewish restaurant in the rue des Rosiers (August 1982), which created violent reactions. To some Americans, France appeared, unjustly, *the* country of antisemitism.

I shall deal here not with the image foreigners have of French antisemitism but with the consciousness French Jews have of French antisemitism. Antisemitism has existed and still exists everywhere in the Christian and Muslim worlds. The real problem exists when it becomes a major political issue. I want to argue that, between the two world wars, antisemitism was one of the major political issues of the time, that at the time French Jews constantly underestimated it,[1] and that since 1945, antisemitism has *not* been a major political issue and French Jews are now constantly overestimating it.

Before World War II

It is difficult to imagine the depravity that was let loose in some of the press (*L'Ami du Peuple, L'Action Française, Je Suis Partout, Gringoire*) and in other writings in the 1930s, particularly from 1933 onward. The very fact that we now read these texts with horror shows how great the difference is between the intellectual and moral atmosphere of the two periods. Céline's sayings are well known. Here is an extract from them: "If you really want to get rid of the Jews, then, not thirty-six thousand remedies, thirty-six grimaces: racism! That's the only thing Jews are afraid of: racism! And not a little bit, with the fingertip, but all the way! Totally! Inexorably! Like complete Pasteur sterilization."[2]

Even more than Céline, whose senseless verbal violence can be explained by his own particular personality, this page of the graceful and delicate poet, Jean Giraudoux, revealed the state of mind of the intellectual class: France "had been swamped by hundreds of thousands of Ashkenazis escaped from Polish and Romanian ghettos" who,

> wherever they go, bring with them their imprecision, their underground action, their bribery and corruption. They are a constant menace to that spirit of precision, of good faith and of perfection, which characterizes the French tradition of craftmanship. This horde has managed to deprive itself of its national rights and yet to defy being expelled from every country. They choke the hospitals in their thousands, because of their precarious, abnormal physical constitution.[3]

As has been recently shown, the antisemitism of the 1930s took place in two currents. First, there was the xenophobic current, tied to the economic crisis and to people's ignorance of the principles of political economy; second, there was a deep fear of war among the French population. The Jew, in their eyes, was a foreigner who came to weaken the French economy. As a deputy said in 1931: "We are not suffering from a national unemployment crisis, but rather from a foreign invasion crisis."[4] On the other hand, the Jew was someone likely to bring France to a declaration of war, given the enmity toward Nazi Germany. As Lucien Rebattet wrote in *Je Suis Partout* (June 1938): "If all of France were as aware of the danger presented by the Jews as are the Alsatians, our country would be in a much better state."[5]

When Léon Blum became the first Jew to hold the position of prime minister, attacks on him and caricatures of him accumulated with a vehemence that was all the stronger because he was head of the Popular Front government. We have only to repeat Xavier Vallat's accusation made in the Chamber of Deputies on June 6, 1936: "For the first time, this ancient Gallo-Roman land is to be governed by a Jew." We may also repeat the so-called analysis by the same Vallat: "a man who is such an outstanding representative of a people condemned by a divine curse to remain homeless."[6] Even the excellent historian, Pierre Gaxotte, spoke of Blum in these terms: "He is the incarnation of everything which turns our blood cold. He gives us goosepimples, he is Evil itself, he is Death itself."[7]

Despite the noble declarations of Camille Chautemps, minister of the interior in 1938, according to which France would remain faithful to its traditions of hospitality, the French government nonetheless ordered its *préfets* to exercise "extreme caution" in permitting Jews ("Israelites") driven from Germany to enter France.[8]

Antisemitic agitation reached its high point after the Munich Accords. In September 1938, antisemitic gangs, denouncing the Jews for pushing the government into war to defend Jewish interests, attacked immigrant neighborhoods and looted Jewish shops, especially in Alsace.[9]

All these facts are well known. It is therefore all the more surprising when we learn of the huge discrepancy between the violence of the antisemitic campaign in the press and the relative lack of awareness of antisemitism among the native Jews at that same time. Léon Poliakov has recently stressed this fact and was the first to do so.[10] I should like to continue along the same line, relying on the systematic series of open interviews that I conducted during the academic year 1982–1983 with assimilated French Jews.[11]

On the one hand, as Poliakov has suggested, it is probable that the hatred shown by the press of the far right and the violence of the gangs may have been restricted, in their most extreme form, to a few activist intellectual and political militants. The bulk of the population probably practiced a kind of antisemitism we could define as traditional—that is, most often verbal and semiconscious. The testimony in my survey, given the absence of opinion polls from that time, shows that the secular tradition of the French Revolution remained alive, in educational institutions more than anywhere else, and that incidents in the schools and universities were usually restricted to insults or scufflings between classes.

But our analysis should go further. The French Jews had chosen to become French more than anything else; Judaism, a more or less forgotten ancestral religion, meant less to them than the vital feelings of patriotism that they shared with other Frenchmen. Moreover, for three or four generations, they had been striving to remain faithful to their origins while adopting a patriotism that was all the more fervent because of the universal values of the French Revolution. The French Jews were also fully assimilated into the education system established by the Third Republic, thus enabling them to reconcile the messianism of their forefathers with the patriotism of the French and their respect for traditional values with the need to adapt to the modern world. Therefore, *they could only underestimate French antisemitism.* To admit that there could be an antisemitism that was not merely marginal and condemned to disappear was indeed to put their very existence as "Frenchmen of mosaic faith" in question. It was absolutely necessary that they underestimate antisemitism because of the place objectively held by the Jews in society as a whole and by the definition of the Jews in a modern nation-state: the place, that is, of a purely religious group, even if in fact they were most often nonobservant. This necessity was expressed by forms of discourse, which, even when it accepted the existence of antisemitism, minimized it by various means.

Certain exchanges took the form of total denial:

Have you or your family experienced some kind of antisemitism?
No.
Never? At school?
No. Absolutely nothing, absolutely not.
At school, people knew you were Jewish?
Probably. It was not a problem before 1914, it was not a problem. There
were a few Jewish girls, we were always mixed with the others.
There was never even a remark?
Absolutely not. Nothing. Never.
And your husband?
I don't think so. We never talked about this.[12]

Others played down the episodes of World War II by describing them
as simple problems of everyday life, happily and easily solved thanks
to the help of the local population.

During [the] summer of 1941, we looked for a house to spend the holidays
and we stayed in this house for years. The Italians were here until the
end at Grenoble; it was much safer and less dangerous than with the
Germans. We have found people who had never seen Jews in their life.
They became aware that we were living like the others, that we were
neither thieves, nor murderers. We became great friends. With some of
them, we are still in relationships, especially the teacher. Really good
friends, and with the peasants too, everybody. We were not hidden. We
were what we were.[13]

They can admit that antisemitism exists, but it is taking place somewhere else; or else they reduce it to the anodyne form of "snobbish"
antisemitism, or to the "childlike" (and therefore insignificant) form of
fights between classes. Thus a man who originally came from Normandy,
where he had been aware only of "snobbish" antisemitism, declared in
an interview that it wasn't until he got to Paris that he discovered
antisemitism. He made a distinction between the two environments:
Where he came from, in Normandy, no one knew about antisemitism.

I came to Paris to study. . . . I was surprised to see that the Jews were
always together. It was a surprise for me, to see how Parisian Jews were
living in a kind of ghetto. It was not the case of my family. . . . We
knew that some people were anti-Semitic, but there was nothing violent,
nothing terrifying. When we were going to cocktail parties, we knew we
were not exactly like the others. I knew it; I can't tell you I suffered from
it. We have not really known what antisemitism was. It used to happen
in Paris at the same time. But in Normandy there was no antisemitism.[14]

The Dreyfus Affair had deeply shaken the French Jews, even if they
treated its Jewish aspect as a secondary matter. The affair was constantly
brought up during family meals. But their narratives of solemn paternal
advice and warning, and of slaps in the face during breaks between
classes—a partly symbolic violence—almost took the character of a

ritual. We find the exact same scenes in the literature of the time.[15] Is it not possible to interpret these narratives as a way of dealing with a childlike kind of antisemitism reduced in importance and made marginal and as a way of basically avoiding the question of the Jews' roots in France and of their patriotism?

> I am the son of someone who has been intimately linked to the Dreyfus Affair and I have felt its echoes again and again. My father had warned me: "You are Jewish. You will be insulted, '*sale juif*,' by some of your comrades at school. You know we are not violent. I hate fights. But if they say '*sale juif*,' you must slap in the face the comrade who said it." It happened to me three times at Janson de Sailly.[16]

There is another way of dealing with antisemitism that consists of reducing it to an episode of purely secondary importance in social life, and of showing how the virtues of the speaker and of his or her family succeeded once and for all in making it insignificant. Naturally, this procedure has the added result of raising the speaker's own esteem.

> At the beginning of the war, my brother had a captain who was very much against him just because he was Jewish. In May 1940, this captain had been wounded and John went to fetch him behind the enemy's front. First, he did not find him. He went a second time and this time, he did find him. He also found other men of the company and brought them back, too. When they were demobilized at Limoges, after the Armistice, they separated and the captain said to John: "My dear friend, for me and around me, there will be no more antisemitism." And he proved it. He really did later on what had to be done.[17]

You will note the contradictions that appear in many of these narratives. A formal denial of the existence of any antisemitism is followed by an account of episodes revealing various kinds of antisemitism, more or less serious, more or less insidious.

> Antisemitism, personally, I say it, I repeat it. I have never experienced it. Not in the *Lycée*, not in the village where people got to know us. Maybe, my husband in business.

> No, we never suffered from antisemitism. Except the case of my husband, of course.

> In the family, one never spoke of antisemitic incidents, except for the demonstrations against my grandfather, the *doyen* [president of the Law Faculty]. This is the only occasion we remember. There was the story of my uncle, who was an officer and left the army very young. I always wondered if it has some relationship, but my mother knew nothing about it.

> I have heard only about the end of the military career.[18] Otherwise, nothing.[19]

This self-contradiction betrays an underestimate of antisemitism. And in this underestimate, we can read the normal ideology of a group of people for whom patriotism—a patriotism in which, through a kind of miracle, the best of Jewish tradition harmonized with the universal principles of the French Revolution—constituted the most essential of all values. By what was nothing else than a historical miracle, the universal values of liberty and equality happened to be embodied in their homeland, which through the Revolution had given the entire world values that accorded with all that was best in Jewish tradition. Zadoc Kahn expressed this general feeling when he stated: "It seemed as though the era predicted by the prophets of Israel has finally begun." This patriotism, the rationalism of the Enlightenment, to which the French Jews subscribed passionately, made it impossible for them to think that the French could ever harbor such absurd, mean feelings as antisemitism. They were so thoroughly assimilated that they refused to see antisemitism other than a peripheral phenomenon involving only isolated individuals, morally condemnable, and indeed condemned by eternal justice and history. Paradoxically, the Dreyfus Affair did not alter this feeling. The victory of the *Dreyfusards* and the exculpation of Captain Dreyfus reinforced the feeling that this hostility was merely the death rattle of prejudices belonging to another age. Because their conduct was above reproach, the French Jews could only be recognized for what they were—namely, patriots. The Jews had enthusiastically undergone the process of assimilation to French culture that society as a whole, with its tradition of cultural centralization, demanded of them. And now this very process of assimilation and the objective position it gave them in French society prevented them from recognizing antisemitism in its full force and in all of its aspects. Their behavior was in this respect no different from that of the great majority of the French population.

After 1940

The year 1940 marked the death of a certain type of "Israelite," of "assimilated Jew." French Jews were deported like any other Jews, and this common fate, created at Auschwitz, caused a radical break with the past. Since 1940, and even more so since 1945, even the most assimilated French Jews, French as they may be, no longer believe that France is the country of miracles. For people like these patriots above reproach, the attitude of the French government in 1940 was perhaps just as shocking as the revelation of Hitler's genocide. As much as the unprecedented attempt to exterminate the Jews, the tragic madness of which exceeded the bounds of historical consciousness, it was the attitude of the government and of part of the people of France—who had ceased to be the champions of the rights of man and had given up defending both French Jews and foreigners who had believed they had found in

France a refuge—that shattered once and for all what seemed in retrospect to be no more than a tragic illusion. What is more, Jews of French ancestry have now become a tiny marginal minority in French Jewry, which is now made up of people from North Africa and of descendants of immigrants from Central Europe.

These two fundamental facts—the attitude of the French government in 1940 and Hitler's genocide—have given a new meaning to every kind, every trace, of antisemitism. The Jewish population deciphers every event that is tied to the fate of the Jews in the light of the genocide. Any action, any attitude that can be interpreted (even unfairly) as being antisemitic is considered to be part and parcel of the sort of behavior and attitudes that led to the genocide. The large place occupied by the genocide in the collective memory of the Jews makes any form of antisemitism and, even more so, any attack on the physical integrity of the Jewish population a foreshadowing of some new deportation. Every antisemitic incident, whatever its cause and its meaning, becomes immediately overblown.

We know how intense was the emotion felt by the Jewish population at the time of the attack against the synagogue on rue Copernic in October 1980. For the first time since the war the physical integrity of a Jewish group had been directly threatened. Most striking with regard to the thesis of this chapter is that this attack, which inquiries showed could be attributed to international terrorists, was, for young Jews who had not known the war period, a time to reconsider their own identity as French Jews. Shmuel Trigano interpreted the feelings of other intellectuals of his generation when he brought to question, following Copernic, the entire history of the Jews of France and even that of Western Jewry:

> The explosion at rue Copernic brought an end to a epoch. . . . Copernic suddenly revealed to the Jews, not by the symbolism of words but by a concrete fact, the terrible [precariousness] of their situation in France and more generally in the West. . . .[20] What is being questioned here is not an ideology or a party. It is the very framework of Jewish life, the very principle of French political culture and if we can say modern culture to the extent that the French model served as an historical framework for modernity.[21]

The objective gap between the event itself—a terrorist attack that, in an attempt to destabilize French democracy, was directed against a population whose capacity for emotion and a strong response was only too well known—and the reaction of a young intellectual who brought to question the history of Jews in the framework of the modern state may be analyzed as one of the expressions of the extreme sensitivity of French Jews to any actions that in reality or in the imagination can be associated with antisemitism.

After the discovery of the genocide in 1945, the Jews in France had the illusion that, since the "price had been paid," antisemitism was over with once and for all. This illusion lasted for a generation. There was a sort of a taboo on Jewishness and Jewish problems. The reemergence of some forms of antisemitism—albeit in a form not comparable to that existing before 1940—made the Jews even more sensitive to an evil they thought had completely disappeared.

Moreover, the very fact that the incidents taking place were incomparably less numerous than they had been during the 1930s instilled an even bigger meaning in each of them. We know that the indignation suffered was proportional not to the magnitude of the phenomenon but, rather, to its emotional meaning. The Jews will no longer consciously tolerate antisemitism, which has become unacceptable to people who think of themselves as the survivors of the genocide.

The French Jews have increased in number and have become more active in politics and religion, and more ambitious in general, since the arrival of the Sephardim from North Africa. And they are convinced that the timid, discreet behavior that the assimilated Jews exhibited before 1940 was, in fact, a moral mistake and a political failure, and that the attacks against them should have been countered by more attacks.

> In 1944–45 and then after the Armistice, things turned around. There was no antisemitism, or when any sign of it did arise, I let them have it.

> Look, we won't put up with it anymore. Jews are now organizing to fight antisemitism much more than they used to do, before the war, say.

> I am convinced that this minority needs to defend itself against antisemitism, which does exist—make no mistake about it—though in a different form than in the past. The antisemites no longer talk about putting us in camps or burning us alive, but they have other, much more subtle ways, much more scientific ways of inflicting harm on the Jewish minority.[22]

The present overestimate of antisemitism is partly due to the underestimate of antisemitism that prevailed before the war. In retrospect, the error committed by the Jews (like the French in general before 1940) appears to be part of a tragedy. Later generations have accordingly decided firmly that they would avoid this error. We cannot blame Americans for repeating what the French Jews have been saying—that France is dangerous for them. Although France stood out for decades as the country in which Jews were most free and most happy, today it seems to some foreigners that France was the very incarnation of all that Jews should flee from.

Yet France is currently witnessing a strong revival of ethnic and religious consciousness among the Jews, now a large and vibrant community that acts and expresses itself with complete freedom. The Jews are no longer too shy to express their Jewishness, and they meet with no restrictions in doing so. As evidence, I could cite the enormous increase in Hebrew studies at all levels, the rise in the number of students of Jewish culture and history, and the ever-growing number of scholarly works and compilations devoted to Jewish problems. We can also observe a proliferation of associations of all sorts: religious, cultural, and political (and the diversity of political opinions among young Jews and their passion for independence only serves to encourage this proliferation), not to mention public demonstrations and increased attendance at religious services. This revival has even reached the grandchildren of assimilated French Jews, whose grandparents would probably have looked with astonishment upon the renewal of interest in Judaism, which in their time had been reduced to a family memory.

We might also observe certain former leftists from the 1970s who are now devoting themselves to the study of the Talmud, and ex-Communists who have been given positions of responsibility with the community organizations. Their path often begins with an interest in the State of Israel; they start to learn Hebrew and then join Zionist associations. Some of them go from political activism to religious practice, which initially may be symbolic (refusal to eat pork or shellfish, fasting on *Yom Kippur*) and later somewhat stricter. A few end up by adhering to Orthodox Judaism. Many, it is true, are content to remain more or less active, more or less critical of existing Jewish institutions. Indeed, such returns to Judaism may take any of a variety of forms.

Jews are also taking an active part in French intellectual and political life. For instance, Jacques Wahl, Simone Veil, and Lionel Stoleru have exerted some influence in Giscard d'Estaing's government, as have Robert Badinter, Laurent Fabius, Jack Lang, and Jacques Attali in the present government. Laurent Fabius was nominated prime minister in July 1984 by François Mitterrand. His Jewishness was mentioned, but both the mass media and public opinion, according to national polls, were very supportive of him and stressed his youth, his ability, and his personal style, which differed greatly from that of the former prime minister. It would still be difficult for a Jew to be elected president—but the incredibly violent reactions to Léon Blum, who, after all, had been elected by the French voters in 1936, are simply unthinkable today. Jews are no less important in intellectual life. I would even say that, in most current intellectual and political milieus, it is actually rather fashionable to be Jewish. To take a famous example, Bertrand de Jouvenel recently discussed the fact that he himself is half Jewish (by his mother)—a fact that, to my knowledge, he had never mentioned before.

We must remember, above all, that the two attacks which shocked Jewish opinion (rue Copernic and rue des Rosiers) were the result not of French antisemitism but of international terrorism. These attacks were unanimously condemned by all political, religious, and moral authorities of the nation. It is true that Valéry Giscard d'Estaing did not give the impression that he understood Jewish sensitivities; he did not understand that such incidents immediately reminded the Jews of their parents' experiences—experiences that left an indelible memory that makes any form of antisemitism a foreshadowing of the genocide. However, if Giscard d'Estaing showed a lack of personal sensitivity, as a statesman he declared himself entirely on the side of the Jewish population. In order to put this criticism of the former president into perspective, we must remember that in the 1930s a candidate for the legislature was elected on an antisemitic platform.

Today all French politicians, including those of extreme right and the Moscow-linked Communist party, condemn antisemitism. But in fact, things are never that simple, and in certain cases we know that some forms of anti-Zionism are nothing but a disguise for antisemitism. Of course, one may, without being antisemitic, criticize Begin's actions during the Lebanon War in 1982. Yet, strangely enough, the Israelis were accused in the mass media of "genocide," in spite of the fact they were fighting an armed adversary; the Palestinians in June were compared to the Warsaw Ghetto, even though the Israelis had encouraged the civil population to leave the town. The attitude of the mass media created a general feeling of discomfort among many French Jews by giving them the impression that antisemitism, which is forbidden by law and to a large extent socially "unfashionable," was in the process of reawakening in its new and Zionist disguise.

But the fact remains that, whatever the deep feelings are, antisemitism does not nowadays express itself and is certainly not a political or even social issue in France. If all Jewish institutions are protected by the police, they are protected not against the French population but, rather, against international terrorism. Forty years ago, the French police played a slightly different role.

If French Jews seem to be unanimous in affirming that antisemitism has increased during the last few years, their *behavior* is different from the expressed opinions. Though France is a country that everyone is free to leave, the figures of French *aliyah* have always been very low (except during a few months after the Six-Day War). On the basis of the survey whose results are published in *Jewish Identities in France*, it appears that *aliyah* is never the result of antisemitism but, rather, of religious needs. The interviewees, who are actually planning their *aliyah*, do not refer to the problem of going against the grain in a predominantly Christian society or to the hostility of non-Jews; they refer only to religious grounds—Israel is the Promised Land.

> The Torah tells us that only in the land of Israel can the Torah come true and its laws be applied; that's the main thing. Beyond that, the environment there is basically Jewish and much more conducive to religious practice. Religiously speaking, I think I could find myself much more easily in Israel than in France.[23]

> If you really want to live a fully Jewish life, then it's obvious that you've got to live there.[24]

One last point is merited. "Normal" xenophobia (in the statistical meaning of the term) does not lack for objects other than the Jews, in a country where the number of foreign workers is above 4 million. Between the wars, xenophobia focused on Italians and on Jews from Eastern and Central Europe. But now, with the children of immigrant workers, especially North Africans, it has found new fields. Henceforth, the French population is able to vent its hatred of foreigners on *les Arabes.*

The revival of French Jewry achieved partly through the influx of North Africans; the awakening of Jewish consciousness, particularly in the political form of "militant Jews"; the reverberation of events in Israel and of the Middle Eastern crisis; and the living memory of Hitler's genocide explain the extreme sensitivity of the French Jews toward all forms of antisemitism and their tendency to overestimate its importance and meaning. It is precisely because the French Jews have this self-consciousness and because antisemitism has grown considerably weaker that they tend to overestimate it in the postwar period. This attitude also has a kind of exorcising function. In reality, it is probably impossible to struggle against Nazi or Communist antisemitism. In those countries where the struggle may take the form of political action, of writings, of organizing colloquia, Jews endeavor to exorcise the ghost of total antisemitism. To exaggerate a relative evil is to conjure up an absolute Evil. Happy are the French and American Jews who are free to exaggerate antisemitism.

Notes

1. This statement, of course, does not concern the recent emigrants, driven out from Central and Eastern Europe, who for obvious reasons have a strong awareness of antisemitism.

2. Louis Ferdinand Céline, *L'Ecole des cadavres* (Paris, 1938), quoted by Michael R. Marrus and Robert O. Paxton, *Vichy, France and the Jews* (New York: Basic Books, 1981), p. 264.

3. Jean Giraudoux, *Pleins pouvoirs* (Paris, 1938), p. 76.

4. See Michel Winock, *Edouard Drumont et Cie* (Paris: Seuil, 1982), p. 101.

5. Lucien Rebattet, quoted in Pierre Marie Dioudonnat, *Je suis partout 1930–1946* (Paris: La Table Ronde, 1973), p. 240.

6. Xavier Vallat, quoted in Léon Poliakov, *L'Europe suicidaire, 1870–1933* (Paris: Calmann-Lévy, 1977), p. 331.

7. Pierre Gaxotte, quoted in Winock, op. cit., pp. 124–125.

8. See R. Schor, *L'opinion française et les étrangers en France, 1919–1939* (Nice: Thése, 1980). See also Michel Winock, op. cit., p. 101.

9. Paula Hyman, *From Dreyfus to Vichy: The Remaking of French Jewry, 1906–1939* (New York: Columbia University Press, 1979), p. 229.

10. Poliakov, op. cit., pp. 307–308.

11. *Enquête ethnologique sur les communautés juives; Mission du Patrimoine, 1981–1983* (interviews with G. Namer, L. Valensi, N. Wachtel).

12. Ibid.

13. Ibid.

14. Ibid.

15. One can find more or less the same scene in the novels of Pierre Hirsch, Edmond Fleg, Emmanuel Berl, André Maruois, Maurice Sachs, and André Spire. See Pierre Aubery, *Milieux Juifs de la France contemporaire à travers leurs ecrivains* (Paris: Plon, 1957), p. 17.

16. See *Enquête ethnologique.*

17. Ibid.

18. The father had to leave the army because of the Dreyfus Affair.

19. Ibid.

20. Shmuel Trigano, *"La république et les juifs* (Paris: Les Presses d'aujourd'hui, 1982), pp. 15, 18 [translated by Dominique Schnapper].

21. Ibid., p. 33.

22. See Dominique Schnapper. *Jewish Identities in France: An Analysis of Contemporary French Jewry* (Chicago: University of Chicago Press, 1983), pp. 84–85.

23. Ibid., p. 23.

24. Ibid., p. 25.

22

Problems of Perceiving and Reacting to Antisemitism: Reflections of a "Survivor"

William Safran

Antisemitism is a hardy weed. We know that it exists, but the explanations for its existence, growth, and spread are varied, and there are disagreements about what would be required to eradicate it. Often the prescriptions for its removal have turned out to have no effect or, worse, have made it stronger. Writers on the subject must guard against two dangers: the paranoid tendency to see all criticisms of Jews and Israel as inspired by antisemitism and the opposite tendency to view antisemitic manifestations as departures from an evolving norm of human relationships based on tolerance, rationality, functionality, and equality. This writer in particular is subject to a set of conflicting impulses: As a European-born Jew, a veteran of concentration camps, and hence a "survivor," he is sensitive to the antisemitic phenomenon; as a social scientist, he must admit that antisemitism is not always present, does not necessarily color his professional colleagues' relationship to him, is not everywhere equally strong, and sometimes is hardly, if at all, the motive force behind human attitudes and actions.

This chapter will focus on the problem of perceiving antisemitism and on some reactions to it. In doing so it will lean upon experience, which has taught us the following: (1) Antisemitism is likely to continue to exist as long as there are Jews, or—as suggested by recent events in Poland—as long as there is a memory of Jews; (2) if one rationale for judeophobia is no longer relevant or sensible, another one will be found quickly; (3) it is not always easy to determine what kinds of attitudes or forms of behavior are openly antisemitic, unconsciously antisemitic, or tending to encourage antisemitic behavior in others; (4) there is considerable uncertainty about what historical, demographic, sociological, or ideological factors promote or moderate antisemitism;[1] and (5) there is equal uncertainty about the utility of particular reactions on the part of Jews—whether they serve to weaken or strengthen antisemitism, or make no difference.

It is possible to argue that certain forms of acceptance, and even official legitimation, of Jews may stem from a basic antisemitic impulse— that is, from the reluctance to consider Jews as "normal" social beings or from a vestigial racial definition of Jews—and hence a vestigial racism. In the Soviet Union, Jews are considered a nationality, but they are deprived of the means of promoting their national culture. In West Germany, the Jewish religious community is subsidized by provincial governments, despite its small size; old synagogues have been restored, and the whole Jewish community has been put under a form of *Denkmalsschutz* (the protection accorded to historic monuments)—as if to indicate that Jews are considered archeological relics or anthropological curiosities rather than a vibrant people, while authorities do little to punish war criminals or prevent the desecration of Jewish cemeteries. In France, Jews still tend to be defined (especially by "enlightened" intellectuals) in terms of their "origins" or in terms of reactive impulses to antisemitism, as if Judaism had no independent existential reality and as if Jewishness were a protean mass shaped by others.[2] Such an attitude may not be *inherently* antisemitic but, rather, an expression of an intellectual xenophobia inspired by Jacobinism and, as such, may be manifested in equally reserved attitudes toward Frenchmen of Italian, Polish, or even Breton "origins"; moreover, outward forms of Jewish behavior *have* often been conditioned by antisemitism or by an effort on the part of Jews at propitiating actual or potential antisemites.

Still, such a definition of Jews may have an antisemitic effect: Once Jews equip themselves with the cultural-linguistic baggage appropriate for their trip as Jews (i.e., by speaking Hebrew or teaching their children to do so), they depart from the stereotype of *Israélites*, become *Juifs*, are perceived to be exhibiting a form of cultural "ingratitude," and become the object of suspicion.[3] Statements emanating from the Vatican that label as "Jews" those converts to Catholicism who had been saved by monks and nuns during World War II may be inspired largely by a desire to clean up the image (and self-image) of the Roman Catholic hierarchy; the assertion of French Cardinal Lustiger that, although a Catholic clergyman, he would always remain a Jew may have been inspired by deep emotion and genuine goodwill; and the assurances of "Jews for Jesus" that one may embrace Christ, yet remain a Jew, may be aimed at those who wish to gain salvation and continue to eat bagels and lox; yet all these reflect a *racial* definition of Jews that may be used by others for *racist* purposes.

In the United States, which has not been particularly Jacobin, there are many liberals, especially in university towns, who are overtly philosemitic and yet harbor attitudes that may derive from a latent antisemitism. They have many Jewish friends, participate in interfaith gatherings, vote for Jewish candidates for political office, and have no difficulty in advocating full equality for Jews. But the Jews they like, and wish to treat as equals, are denatured Jews—that is, those who behave like Protestant or Catholic middle-class Americans and whose Jewishness is a thin layer of their being, having no remarkable attitudinal or behavioral consequences, who attend religious services (preferably in Reform temples) once a week or less often, and whose Jewishness is either a matter of vague origins or of cultic adherence connected with basic rites of passage. The understanding and tolerance of many of these well-meaning liberals does not easily extend to Jews whose Jewishness is manifested in excessive religiosity or to communal Jewish orientations that are too much connected with culture and folkways or, worse, with matters pertaining to Israel. It may be true that these liberals feed upon an evolving set of *Jewish* attitudes: The Jews with whom they associate have encouraged them to think that "normal" Jews, if given half a chance, *are* like Protestants and *could* be redefined in the de-ethnicized terms that are not offensive to their neighbors.[4] In any case, the refusal to accept Jews outside the confines of standard definition (i.e., as anything other than a variant of a liberal U.S. Protestant sect) constitutes a subtle, and perhaps subconscious, form of antisemitism.

In view of the diffusion of secularism and racial tolerance, the antisemitism of intellectuals is no longer significantly inspired by theological or racial arguments; this development, however, has facilitated the introduction of another basis for their antisemitism: that which is derived from the difficulty of placing Jews into an orderly taxonomy, and the related difficulty of making scientifically valid generalizations about them. These difficulties are particularly irritating to social scientists, many of whom have a "nomothetic" rather than "idiographic" approach to social reality. Since Jews cannot be conveniently typologized, the Jewish reality becomes elusive and mysterious, and this situation weakens the barriers to wild imaginings and devil theories. Among the Gentile academics I have known, there are those who are quite rational and scientific in their judgments about most sociopolitical matters but who have harbored a variety of interesting beliefs about Jews—for example, that the majority of Jews have money; that the "Jewish establishment" exacts an annual tithe from every Jew, a "Diaspora tax" that goes automatically to the support of Israel; that the Mossad (the Israeli intelligence service) is behind every crisis in the world; that physical attacks against Jews in Europe are deliberately engineered by Israeli *agents provocateurs* in order to "Zionize" assimilated European Jews; that rabbis in the Diaspora take orders from, or at least periodically check their opinions with, the rabbinical establishment in Israel; that Jews in the Western democracies vote in accordance with more or less explicit instructions from the Israeli government; and so on. None of these academics would admit to being antisemitic, and on a certain level of consciousness, they are not antisemites; in fact, they all have Jewish friends, and would willingly hire, protect, and promote Jewish colleagues. Their antisemitism is subliminal; and since it has not been particularly harmful, it does not matter, perhaps, that little can be done about it.

Although in our era of enlightenment old-fashioned theological or racist doctrines no longer serve as the buttresses of antisemitism for anyone who is reasonably well educated, racialist and theologically derived critiques of Jews manifest themselves in liberal intellectuals' critiques of Israel. There is no doubt that some Gentile critics of Israel exist who are not, or who do not believe themselves to be, antisemitic. Nonetheless, anti-Zionism cannot be separated from antisemitism, if only for the following two reasons: The evils that had once been attributed to Jews have come increasingly to be attributed to Israel, and the treatment that was once considered appropriate for Diaspora Jewry—isolation, delegitimation, and ultimate extinction—is now increasingly considered appropriate for Israel.

The contention that anti-Israel attitudes are often translations of antisemitism gains substance once it is understood that the critics of Israel use the same language—and the same double standard—as the erstwhile critics of Jews. To the extent that their attitudes are inspired by theology, antisemites *must* be anti-Zionist because the very existence of Israel disconfirms a fundamental hypothesis of "normative" Christianity: that Judaism has been transcended by Christianity, and hence that Jews who do not accept the "truth" are condemned to eternal homelessness and moral or mental decay—that they have become, in Arnold Toynbee's words, the carriers of a "fossilized" civilization who cannot revive anything, including an independent political system.[5] Moreover, Israel's evolving culture and the behavior of Israelis in their own society have put in question long-held stereotypes of antisemites— for example, that Jews lack fighting abilities, make poor farmers, are bereft of creativity, and are incapable of making material sacrifices for the common good. It is therefore not surprising that many of the evils once attributed to Jews tend nowadays to be attributed to Israel: mendacity, cruelty to women and children (a modern variant of ritual murder?), the exploitation of Gentiles (the Arabs as the Israelis' *shabbes goyim*), and the desire to dominate. Intellectuals who voice these criticisms do not, of course, use the crude language of street antisemites; instead, they cloak their (often subconscious) antisemitism in the form of pseudo-humanitarianism—for instance, as a concern with the underprivileged masses of the Third World, and therefore an interest in opposing those who are allegedly their chief victimizers—namely, the Zionists. Ironically, many anti-Zionists use a racial argument reminiscent of that of the antisemites of the nineteenth and early twentieth centuries. However, the notion of Jews as an extra-European, "oriental" race tending to subvert European civilization by corrupting the blood of pure "Aryans" can no longer be used by those who express their antisemitism in terms of anti-Zionism. Accordingly, the racial definition of Jews is inverted: Israelis have become the (white) European imperialists who subjugate the "people of color" in the Third World, including the Arabs. In this argument, the fact that a majority of Jews in Israel are "Orientals" tends to be ignored, except when it is necessary to point out that the Israeli "ruling circles" are not democratic and oppress their own co-religionists. Alain Finkielkraut recently wrote that

> the Jews are the eternal object of hatred by humanity, which always waits for the opportune moment to proclaim its hatred. . . . There have been alternations in this relationship. . . . The authentic popularity of Jews in the Europe of the past twenty years and their present disrepute proceed from exactly the same sentiment, the same Christian complex: [in the past] one loved [in the Jews] the martyr and the image of the persecuted, and nowadays one rejects them for having betrayed their supposed vocation. It is the identification of genocide with the passion of Christ and with the crucifixion to which Jews have owed their recent prestige, and it is their infidelity to this image that provides the items for the bill of indictment drawn up by the opinion-makers. Temporarily deified by Auschwitz, the Jews incur the risk, via Israel, to return to their destiny as deicides.[6]

This statement, to be sure, reflects a degree of paranoia, but it also reflects a quite realistic perception of an antisemitism that consists of the refusal to accord to Jews the right to be "normal." In the past, Jews, individually and collectively, had been regarded as subhumans, God-killers, corrupters of Gentile humanity. In more recent years, they have been glorified as objects of pity. The establishment of Israel did not restore "normalcy" to Jews, as many Zionists had hoped. For the legitimacy of the state of Israel was made to hinge upon the Israelis' behaving like ideal-type Socialists, altruists, and angels—showing the way by making compromises and (as politicians and journalists have been putting it incessantly) taking the kinds of "risks for peace" that no other nation would be called upon to take. But once the Israelis were perceived to have misbehaved (i.e., actually to be fighting when in danger of attack), they departed from the expected Jewish vocation, and became (again) the object of Christian hatred. A similar double standard has been manifested by those who are not much bothered by the spectacle of Western European, Black African, or Communist countries' trading with South Africa, but who are visibly upset by Israel's doing so.

There are those who argue that the application of an exceptionally high moral standard to Israel's behavior is a form of flattery of the Jews, that it implies a belief that Jews are more civilized than others, that more can be expected of them, because Jews, viewing Israel as "a light unto the nations," have expected more of themselves. Others, on the contrary, suggest that such an expectation is antisemitic, in that it implies a refusal by Gentiles to grant to Jews the same right to behave as mortal humans that is accorded to non-Jews: to fight in their self-defense, to punish their enemies, to derive benefits from their victories, to protect their interests, to harbor resentments, and occasionally to make mistakes.

It is true that for some two decades after its establishment, many Western intellectuals, politicians, and clergymen refrained from criticizing Israel, just as they refrained from criticizing Jews too much. The Holocaust was still too recent, and it was not fashionable to be openly antisemitic. Moreover, many were probably hoping that the "Jewish problem" would disappear from Europe with the removal to Israel of some of the Jews whom the Holocaust had spared and the disappearance, through assimilation, of the remainder. In the same way, many who had refrained from attacking Israel may have thought (or hoped) that the "problem of Israel" would disappear if and when the numerically stronger Arabs conquered the diminutive Jewish state. The subsequent indifference of many members of the Western (and especially European) elite to threats against Israel and the increasingly open hostility to that state since 1967 have perhaps been inspired by deep disappointment over the failure of the Arabs to put an end to it. With the passage of time, as it became clear that the State of Israel was behaving in an inappropriate fashion—it did not go under; and as the memory of the Holocaust receded, the constraints of morality and good taste against overt expressions of antisemitism have become relaxed. The Holocaust itself has been approached from a revisionist perspective, making it appear less horrible.[7]

Antisemites have tried to make it easier for themselves by dealing with the Holocaust in one or more of the following ways: (1) denying its historicity; (2) minimizing its criminal nature nature by obscuring the distinction between murderer and victim; (3) attempting to break the causal connection between antisemitism and the Holocaust, thereby salvaging a modicum of respectability for the former; and (4) making questionable and often grotesque comparisons between the Holocaust and other events, thus depriving the former of its uniqueness, adding to the murder of Jews the insult of depriving them of their history, and weakening an important constraint against future antisemitic outrages. Specifically, in recent years the Holocaust has been compared to the destruction of Dresden, the war in Vietnam, the bombing of Hiroshima, the stockpiling of nuclear weapons, the Irish potato famine, the pollution of the environment, the inflicting of a large number of casualties by one side on another on World War I battlefields, and the Israeli Army's invasion of Lebanon.[8] The systematic mass murder of Jews has been "explained" as the inevitable consequence of bureaucratization, mechanization, massification, and/or the spread of secularism, as well as a manifestation of (German and other) totalitarianism, with the Jews being only incidental victims. In the proliferating number of university courses and seminars that now constitute a part of a veritable "Holocaust industry," professors have managed to deal with the murder of 6 million Jews by presenting it as a problem of theology, metaphysics, and even aesthetics. The transformation of the Holocaust into a sociodrama and, worse, into a soap opera where the "human-interest" angle is more important than history, in both the academies and the media, has the effect of decriminalizing and defactualizing mass murder, falsifying Jewish history, raising doubts about Jewish moral claims upon Gentiles, and, ultimately, disarming those who fight against antisemitism. Some of the falsifiers of the Holocaust may not have been motivated by antisemitism so much as by an understandable desire to exculpate themselves and the culture to which they belong, and in whose names the crimes had been committed. But there is no doubt that their revisionism has been *used* by antisemites.

There are similar uncertainties with respect to a number of other events and actions. Thus it is a matter of controversy whether or not General de Gaulle's statements about Jews being "an elite and domineering people" reflected an antisemitic mentality or not (especially in view of the fact that during World War II quite a few Jews had rallied around him, and had been openly welcomed, in London). But his extended remarks about the problematic relationship between Gentiles and Jews, which was blamed largely on the Jews ("wandering here and there," and "provoking" others, etc.),[9] echoed traditional stereotypes about Jews. Perhaps de Gaulle picked on the Jews because they did not behave the way Jews (in this case, Israelis) should have behaved: waiting until threatened with defeat, and coming as supplicants to France, asking to be "saved" from utter extinction by the leader of a great military power. Perhaps Israel was resented, not because it was a Jewish state but because as a small country, its victory was particularly galling to the general since it provided an unfortunate juxtaposition to the military decline—and the lack of victories—of France, with its glorious martial tradition. De Gaulle's behavior was in some ways reminiscent of that of British colonial officials—and finally of the British foreign minister after World War II—with respect to the Jews in Palestine. Some colonial officials doubtlessly resented the fact that they had to deal with Jews; but others probably resented the *Yishuv's* behavior because it was insufficiently obsequious and therefore inappropriate for (the usually "primitive") inhabitants of a colony.[10]

Could one describe as antisemitic acts the issuance of false papers to murderers of Jews by the Vatican and the Red Cross, and their subsequent employment by the CIA and other federal agencies? Officially, such actions were taken not for the sake of helping out, let alone rewarding, these criminals for their anti-Jewish activities but for reasons of national interest or on "humanitarian" grounds; still, one is entitled to assume that antisemitic motivations played a role in some of these decisions. In 1981, when Pope John Paul II appointed a Jewish convert, Jean-Marie Lustiger (whose mother had died in Auschwitz), as archbishop of Paris, many Jews were confused as to the implications of this act. On the one hand, there is nothing to suggest that the pope wished to offend the Jews; on the contrary, the act could be interpreted as a friendly gesture toward Jews, particularly inasmuch as the newly appointed cleric openly avowed his Jewish descent. On the other hand, the appointment served as a bitter reminder of the fact that so many young Jews who had not been deported and had not perished were nonetheless lost to the Jewish community. Their lives had been saved by Christians, as had their souls.

How does the recent canonization of Father Maximilian Kolbe relate to antisemitism, if at all? Kolbe had volunteered to take the place of a condemned man (not a Jew) and died at Auschwitz. The Vatican's action could be interpreted as a gesture quite neutral with respect to Jews: The Church desperately needed a saint, and a Polish one would come in particularly handy. But Kolbe's background had been bereft of any love for Jews; indeed, just before the war he had published a broadside against "fanatical Jews" and "international Zionism," and had asked that Jews be "eliminated" from Polish life.[11] Thus the beatification could be interpreted as an expression of a Vatican belief that Jew-haters are not *ipso facto* undeserving of sainthood.

While he was chancellor of Austria, Bruno Kreisky was noted for the frequency and vehemence of his attacks on the State of Israel, which on occasion spilled over into gratuitous attacks on Jewish attitudes and behavior.[12] It is possible to find pathological, ideological, or pragmatic explanations—to argue that the attacks stemmed from self-hatred, that they were motivated by the deep concern of a true Socialist for persecuted Palestinian Arabs, or that whatever may have been his private feelings, it was politically opportune to propitiate a society still imbued with antisemitic feelings and containing an oversized share of Nazis. But there is no doubt that Kreisky's statements provided ammunition for antisemites.

Another example of the unintended spreading of antisemitic stereotypes is James Michener's recently published novel, *Poland*.[13] Michener is not an antisemite; yet in portraying the Jews of Poland essentially as moneylenders, and in ignoring not only the long tradition of Jewish scholarship but also the noncommercial Jewish contributions to Polish civilization, he appears to have swallowed the antisemitic portrayal of Jews (by "local [Polish] authorities") with uncharacteristic ingenuousness.

How is one to interpret the failures of the West German judicial establishment in prosecuting and convicting those who had murdered Jews during the Hitler regime? Have the West German judges, in handing down light sentences or acquittals, shown approval of Hitler's antisemitic policies? Or is their behavior to be attributed primarily to a reluctance to stir up old emotions and unsettle a rather fragile sociopsychological equilibrium among Germans? Is the failure of the authorities in the Bavarian village of Oberammergau to expunge the references to the Jews' perfidy and collective guilt for deicide from the famous Passion Play to be attributed to antisemitic convictions, or merely to a concern with the promotion of tourism? More seriously, have the antisemitic campaigns periodically sponsored by government officials in postwar Poland, as in 1968 and 1981, been inspired by a deep hatred of Jews, or by overriding political calculations; that is, did they represent a pragmatic utilization of widespread antisemitic sentiments for purposes of political mobilization?

In the United States, high government officials and politicians, in hinting that Jewish opponents of the AWACS sale to Saudi Arabia might be putting Israel's interests ahead of those of the United States, were not specifically setting out to harm Jews, but they were using latent antisemitism for tactical reasons.[14] In American and other Western universities, some professors may refuse to cancel their classes or reschedule examinations on Jewish holydays because they are hostile to Jewish students; many others may refuse to do so in order not to upset their tight schedules. But no matter what the motivations, the effect is the same: to put observant Jews at a disadvantage—in other words, it is antisemitic.

It is clear from the foregoing that not all actions having an antisemitic effect have been inspired by the same kind of antisemitic intent. One may posit a range of behavior patterns: (1) calculated and deliberate antisemitic behavior, stemming from deep anti-Jewish sentiments; (2) consciously antisemitic actions, inspired not by hatred of Jews but by cold political or economic calculation; (3) actions undertaken in the clear awareness of their possible antisemitic side effects; and (4) actions in which the promotion of antisemitism is an unintended and unforeseen consequence. Such distinctions must be kept in mind if antisemitism is to be intelligently countered.

The uncertainties about what kind of behavior is prompted by antisemitism, or by some other impulse or rationale, are matched by an almost equal uncertainty about what causes, promotes, moderates, and nullifies antisemitism. Does the pervasiveness of Catholicism or Christian fundamentalism encourage antisemitism, and does secularism or rationalism promote tolerance? Is antisemitism less likely to occur in republican and economically advanced systems than in authoritarian and economically underdeveloped countries? Are Jews less likely to provoke the hatred of Gentiles if they assimilate to Gentile culture than if they remain relatively insulated from that culture and retain their particularism? The evidence is far from conclusive; yet the behavior of individual Jews, and of Jewish organizations, has often been based on incomplete or questionable causal analyses.

The differences of opinion concerning the major causes of antisemitism have been reflected in a continuing controversy about the appropriateness of Jewish reactions. To put it simply: If antisemitism is attributed to factor X—say, the excessive concentration of Jews in a small urban area—then, logically, Jewish policy aimed at reducing antisemitism should be to eliminate factor X—that is, to promote the dispersal of Jews to the suburbs or the countryside. A recent article has stated the following:

> Jews have tried conversion, pretended invisibility, adapted to the cultures of their persecutors, assimilated, deepened their Jewish commitment, hunkered down in self-ghettoization, fought back, passed, championed social

and political panaceas, have self-hated and self-loved, made alliances with other discriminated-against groups, with the rich and powerful, and the poor and powerless, with radicals and with reactionaries, courted Christians and atheists, have dispatched emissaries to monarchs, tyrants, popes and presidents, have paid for bribes, showered philanthropy, have bloc-voted and bullet-voted, contributed to political parties, churches, civil-liberties organizations and have supported a plenitude of Jewish defense organizations.[15]

It is possible to classify these responses as follows: (1) group or organizational responses; (2) individual Jewish accommodation; (3) collective Jewish adaptation to the surrounding culture and environment; and (4) attempts to change that environment.

The remainder of this chapter will concentrate on the response of individual Jews and, specifically, that of Jewish intellectuals. Whereas in earlier periods, and particularly in Europe, there were many Jewish intellectuals who thought that they could eliminate antisemitism by fighting for rationalism, universalism, liberalism, or socialism, Jewish intellectuals today overwhelmingly seem to prefer to accommodate individually to the thinking that is current in their professional environments.

There are numerous examples of such behavior. One Jewish university professor, who was conducting a class on the Holocaust, objected to the speech of a prominent guest lecturer on the grounds that it had been "too Israel-oriented" and "too Zionist," and had "ignored the wider philosophical implications" of the event. Another Jewish professor was a cosponsor of a conference on "Genocide and Omnicide," in which the Holocaust was compared to nuclear proliferation, in which the plenary speaker was a well-known Jewish professor who had been excoriating Israel for many years, and in which a commentator was chided for introducing the "extraneous" subject of Israel. A third Jewish professor publicly suggested at a symposium on international politics that it was difficult (in the United States and Europe) to publish anti-Israel books because the Zionists control the publishing houses. A fourth Jewish professor, at an ACLU forum on religious celebrations in public schools, argued that Christmas was a "universal" holiday whose celebration in public schools was a normal and legitimate part of American education. There have been other Jewish professors who have publicly criticized Jewish vulgarity (but not the vulgarity of other groups), poked fun at Jewish (but not African, American-Indian, or other) "tribal" rituals, and written that Jewish (but not necessarily other) festivals are mostly based on myth, and if not that, on events that recall bloodthirstiness. Jewish professors in the United States, France, and Britain are prominent as signatories of manifestos and as participants in street demonstrations relentlessly protesting this or that policy on the part of Israel (but not Soviet policies in Afghanistan or Poland). There are Jewish academics who would readily associate with the activities sponsored by the American

Friends Service Committee but not those sponsored by Jewish groups. There are Jewish academics who explain the anti-Jewish actions of Idi Amin and of the Ayatollah Khomeini in terms of the quest of these leaders for the liberation of their countries from Western imperialism,[16] and who lend the prestige of their names to the publications of anti-semites.[17] Finally, there has been a growing number of Jewish scholars who have distorted the facts about the Holocaust and disseminated various revisionist theses about that event.[18]

It would be unfair to suggest that these activities have been prompted by Jewish self-hatred, or by a conscious desire to feed the flames of antisemitism. The basic explanation is found in the professional status of these Jews as academics and the occupational diseases to which this status has exposed them. Jewish intellectuals, like Gentile ones, are given to universalism and therefore tend to downplay their own Jewishness and the relevance of Jewishness in general to the important issues of the day. They embrace the currently popular theses about "modernization," and hence are embarrassed by Jewish "tribalism." Some Jewish social scientists and philosophers are constantly engaged, like their Gentile colleagues, in systematizing, generalizing from, and abstracting reality, and thus are tempted to be receptive to the revisionist theses about the Holocaust—that is, to look upon it not as unique but as *sub specie aeternitatis*, as a link in a long historical chain of policies of "population control,"[19] as proof of the death of God or of the evils of capitalism, or as the consequence of nationalism. To the extent that Jewish intellectuals, particularly progressive ones, are secularist and rationalistic, Judaism, like some Christian sects, is seen by them as obscurantist and mystical, and those who practice it are seen as backward. To the extent that Jewish intellectuals are sympathetic to or supportive of the Third World, they share the guilty consciences of their Gentile colleagues and therefore their views about Israel's alleged guilt for oppressing Arabs, who, in this connection, are invariably striving for freedom and democracy. To the extent that Jewish intellectuals share their colleagues' belief that modernization is a necessary step toward the ideal type that is "modernity," they inevitably also come to believe that self-avowed Jews (i.e., those whose Jewish identity goes beyond a mere confession of origin and touches upon meaningful Jewish culture) are guilty of adhering to a "primordialist" communal identification and therefore of behaving in a retrogressive fashion. To the extent that Jewish intellectuals are Marxist, they take a dim view of those who are consciously Jewish because the latter have not yet transcended Judaism and hence are still committed to the capitalist order, because their behavior is bourgeois, and because, as defenders of Israel, they are defenders of imperialism.[20]

Intellectuals can no longer easily accept the old theses (promoted by Werner Sombart and others) that the Jews had to prey upon Gentiles because their religion (the Talmud?) required such exploitation or because their merchant status made it inevitable. In most Western democracies, the proportion of academics among Jews has been increasing relative to the proportion of business people; and the people Jews confront, and must adapt to, in the academy are neither naive consumers nor competing merchants but, rather, fellow intellectuals and students. Since the professional success of these Jews depends upon the intellectual merchandise they buy and sell, they are often the medium for the dissemination of Gentile conventional wisdom. This includes references to the (Jewish) Bible as the "Old Testament," to the Jews as a "race," to "Jehovah" as a jealous and punishing God (as contrasted to the loving God of Christians); standard Christian interpretations of the Pharisees and of *lex talionis* (an eye for an eye); and, in a more contemporary context, the characterization of PLO killers of Israeli children as "freedom fighters" rather than as terrorists. Such interpretations, which often contain antisemitic overtones, may be resorted to quite unthinkingly and innocently. This sort of imitative behavior applies not merely to Diaspora intellectuals but to an increasing number of Israeli scholars as well, particularly those who have significant links with the Euro-American academic community.

Several generations ago, the internalization of antisemitic stereotypes gave rise to a form of self-denigration that frequently resulted in conversion and even, in a famous aberrant case (that of Otto Weininger), in suicide. For nearly three decades, the State of Israel provided for many Jewish intellectuals an antidote to the internalized antisemitic poison, insofar as the character of its government and people confounded so many stereotypes. Its society was Socialist; many of its leaders had emerged from the kibbutz, had experience as farm laborers, wore open-collared shirts, spoke succinctly and directly, did not appear to have too much sense of history, were not religious, and did not manifest the traditional Jewish neuroses. But the victory of non-Socialist parties, and more particularly the leadership of Begin, embarrassed many American Jewish intellectuals and weakened their sympathy to Israel—not merely because of Begin's policies but as a consequence of the reemergence of features that many had hoped would no longer be associated with Jewish statesmen: a short stature, an urban, lower-middle-class intellectual background, a public observance of Jewish rites and customs (including the wearing of a skullcap on formal occasions), a memory of Jewish *Leidensgeschichte*, a frequently articulated concern with the fate of all Jews, and a Yiddish accent. Of course, an articulation of these discomforts cannot easily be expected, since it would constitute an admission that the self-image of so many enlightened Jews had been conditioned by antisemitic stereotypes.

Sometimes the alignment of the thinking of Jewish intellectuals with that of antisemites may have nothing to do with ideology or cultural embarrassments but is instead coincidental. Thus when a gentle, and deeply religious, Hebrew University professor compared the State of

Israel to the Nazi regime by saying that "the Israeli government has done [some] things the way the Nazis have done them in the countries they had conquered, with the only exception that we [Israelis] did not build extermination camps,"[21] he was surely inspired by pangs of conscience and by the desire to shock his countrymen. But others may have more selfish motives for their adaptability—the quest for a large and sympathetic general readership, for speaking engagements, grants, and academic promotions. This kind of intellectual servility, which serves the purpose of individual survival, is a variant of the caricature of *Judenrat*, or more accurately of *Hofjuden* ("Court Jew"), behavior. The world is not particularly friendly to or patient with Jews, and one must try to save oneself by accommodating to this reality—that is, by making oneself useful to the *goyim* and showing oneself to be a "good" Jew.[22] Of course, just as American Gentile antisemitic scholars can hardly be compared to "Hitler's professors," Jewish accommodationist intellectuals cannot be quite compared to the *Judenräte* in terms of their impact. Nor would it be fair to compare the Jewish accommodationist intellectuals to the members of the *Verband nationaldeutscher Juden*, who, by distancing themselves from *Ostjuden* and by demanding that Zionists be deprived of German citizenship, sought to deflect the wrath of antisemites away from themselves. But such accommodationist behavior nonetheless constitutes a kind of *trahison des clercs juifs*; for "good" Jews, in attempting to convince Gentiles that they do not personally conform to the Jewish stereotype, do not destroy that stereotype but merely represent an exception that proves the rule; that is, they do not counteract the antisemites, and may actually be their unwitting tool.

Notes

1. See Helen Fein, *Accounting for Genocide* (New York: Free Press, 1979).

2. This was, for instance, the opinion of Jean-Paul Sartre, in *Réflexions sur la question juive* (Paris: Gallimard, 1954). He later modified his views.

3. See William Safran, "France and Her Jews: From 'Culte Israélite' to 'Lobby Juif,'" *Tocqueville Review* (Spring/Summer 1983):101–135.

4. Will Herberg, *Protestant, Catholic, Jew* (Garden City, N.Y.: Doubleday Anchor, 1960). On the theme of "ethnic amalgamation," see, especially, pp. 188–194.

5. Because Jews had rejected Jesus, they "were thereby putting themselves permanently in the wrong and on the shelf." On Toynbee's view of Judaism as a "petrified religion," see Arnold Toynbee, *Study of History*, vol. 5 (Oxford: Oxford University Press, 1948–1961), p. 126. See also Franklin H. Littell, "Christian Anti-Semitism and the Holocaust," in Randolph L. Braham, ed., *Perspectives of the Holocaust* (Boston and The Hague: Kluwer-Nijhoff, 1982), pp. 42–48.

6. Alain Finkielkraut, "L'opium des journalistes," *Regards: Revue Juive de Belgique*, no. 219 (October 8, 1982):14.

7. See Lucy S. Dawidowicz, "Lies About the Holocaust," *Commentary* 70, no. 6 (December 1980):31–37.

8. For a particularly obscene analogy, see Helmut Schödel, "Bruder Eichmann, Bruder Sharon," *Die Zeit*, 4 February 1983, p. 12. This is a polemic in the guise of a drama critique.

9. Although the overall tone of de Gaulle's speech was meant to be sympathetic to Jews, it did suggest that they were "immodest" in their territorial claims. The full text is in *French Foreign Policy: Official Statements, Speeches, and Communiques, July–December 1967* (New York: Ambassade de France: Service de Presse et d'Information, 1968), pp. 135–136.

10. See Richard Crossman, *Palestine Mission* (New York and London: Harper & Brothers, 1947), pp. 169–170.

11. Christopher Hitchens, "Holy Men," *Nation*, 15 January 1983.

12. Kreisky asserted that "if the Jews *are* a people, they're a nasty one" ("Die Juden—ein mieses Volk," *Der Spiegel*, 17 November 1975). On another occasion, he referred to Begin as a "political grocer." See Robert S. Wistrich, Bruno Kreisky, and Simon Wiesenthal, *Midstream* (June-July 1979):26–35.

13. James Michener, *Poland* (New York: Random House, 1983). Cf. the review by Haskell Nordon, "James Michener's Poland," *New York Times Book Review* 20 November 1983, p. 43.

14. See the interview with Nathan Perlmutter in "The New Anti-Semitism: A Symposium," *Moment* (January-February 1982):15–23.

15. Nathan and Ruth Ann Perlmutter, "Hating Jews," *Moment* (September 1982):51.

16. See Richard Falk, *Human Rights and State Sovereignty* (New York: Holmes & Meier, 1981).

17. See, for example, Noam Chomsky's preface to a book by a French history professor who argued that the story of the Holocaust was a gigantic fraud: "Quelques commentaires élémentaires sur le droit à la liberté d'expression," in Robert Faurisson, *Mémoire en Défense contre ceux qui m'accusent de falsifier l'histoire: la question des chambres à gaz* (Paris: La Vieille Taupe, 1980).

18. Hannah Arendt, in her *Eichmann in Jerusalem* (New York: Viking Press, 1963), has attempted to exculpate the Germans by inculpating their Jewish victims as much as possible. She distorts and exaggerates the role of the Jewish leadership, and reduces the positions of Nazi murderers to those of mere cogs in a bureaucratic machine, so that evil becomes "banal" and clear guilt no longer exists. The refutation of these arguments by Jacob Robinson in *And the Crooked Shall Be Made Straight* (New York: Macmillan, 1965) has not affected the status of Arendt as a cult figure among many Gentile (and Jewish) intellectuals. In the opinion of both Arendt and Bruno Bettelheim (in various writings), Nazi Germany was a totalitarian system as far as ordinary Germans were concerned; but for Jews it was apparently *not* so totalitarian, because the latter could have escaped Germany or resisted the Nazis without too much difficulty (e.g., by acquiring guns).

19. George Kren and Leon Rappoport, in *The Holocaust and the Crisis of Human Behavior* (New York: Holmes & Meier, 1980), and Richard Rubenstein, in various writings, appear to endorse the views of Arendt and Bettelheim. Moreover, for Rubenstein the Holocaust constituted a form of "triage."

20. An interesting if highly confused analysis is that of Abram Leon, *The Jewish Question: A Marxist Interpretation*, 2d ed. (New York: Pathfinder Press, 1970), pp. 248–249, et seq. In this book, the evils of the bourgeois class are attributed to the Jews collectively, as a "people class," and Zionism, in allegedly sanctioning the oppression of another people (which therefore constitutes another

class), is the ideology of that class oppression. See also M. J. Rosenberg, "To Uncle Tom and Other Jews," in Jack Nusan Porter and Peter Dreier, eds., *Jewish Radicalism: A Selected Anthology* (New York: Grove Press, 1973), pp. 5–10.

21. Meir Uziel, "Perakim mitokh vikuah be'arba eynayim im Professor Leibowitz" [Segments from a tête-à-tête with Prof. Leibowitz], *Ma'ariv*, Sof shavu'a [weekend supplement], 22 July 1983, pp. 7ff.

22. On this point, see Aviva Cantor Zuckoff, "The Oppression of America's Jews," in Porter and Dreier, *Jewish Radicalism*, pp. 29–49.

23
Attitudes Toward Israel and Attitudes Toward Jews: The Relationship

Earl Raab

Negative feelings toward Israel do not coincide with negative feelings toward Jews, according to the evidence. And yet there is evidence that negative attitudes toward the State of Israel may constitute a major new watershed of international antisemitism. Because of the importance of Israel to Jews everywhere—and because the creation of Israel was partly a response to the Nazi Holocaust—there has been a tendency to equate hostility toward Israel with antisemitism. Of course, "hostility toward Israel," like antisemitism itself, is a mixed bag whose contents need separating. But on the face of it, the automatic connection is not there.

In the Yankelovich poll of September 1974, for example, Americans were asked whether they thought it would be good or bad to have a Jew as president, *and* whether they would identify with the Israelis or the Arabs in case another war broke out. The same proportion of those who approved of a Jewish president as of those who disapproved of a Jewish president identified positively with the Israelis. And the same proportions of those who approved and disapproved of a Jewish president identified positively with the Arabs.[1] In their analysis of a comprehensive 1974 Louis Harris survey, Seymour Martin Lipset and William Schneider found no significant correlation one way or another between sympathy for Israel and conventional antisemitism. Nor was there a significant correlation between antisemitism and support for the PLO or between the belief that Jews have too much power in this country and support for Israel.[2]

The question of "Jewish power" is of particular interest, especially as it relates to the perception of how American Jews use that "power" on behalf of Israel. There has long been concern about the large proportion of Americans who consistently say that the American Jews feel closer to or more loyal to Israel than to the United States. That, of course, raises the specter of "dual loyalty," which has always been a staple of hard-core antisemitism.

In earlier years the "disloyalty" question was usually a pure function of antisemitism, the point of reference being the lack of Jewish loyalty to anything other than the Jewish clan itself. Modern right-wing antisemites then attempted to establish a link between that disloyalty and radicalism or communism. Thus, in various surveys from 1938 to 1940, anywhere from a quarter to a third of all Americans believed that Jews were "less patriotic than other citizens." In one 1940 study, about one-fifth of all Americans believed that Jews tended to be communistic or radical; Jews were at the top of that list, just below Russians.[3] After World War II, there was a severe drop in the proportion of Americans who thought of Jews as more radical or communistic than other Americans.[4] However, since the establishment of the State of Israel, anywhere from a quarter to a third of Americans have agreed with the proposition that Jews are more loyal or closer to Israel than to the United States.[5] That is about the same proportion of Americans who thought the Jews were disloyal in the 1930s, usually in connection with some kind of radicalism. But there is a drastic difference between the two phenomena. In the 1930s the suspicions about Jewish loyalty were directly associated with antisemitism. Today, that does not seem to be the case.

There is an obvious explanation for this disparity and for the current correlation between antisemitism and belief about Jewish loyalty to Israel. Americans overwhelmingly disapproved of radicalism and communism in the 1930s, and any perception of Jewish involvement with radicalism could serve either as a cause of antisemitism or just as a convenient article of antisemitic belief. But Americans have overwhelmingly approved of Israel, as we shall see, so Jewish activity on behalf of Israel has been considered generally benign.

In November 1956, only 12 percent of Americans thought American Jews had complicity in "the trouble in the Middle East," and only half of those thought that there was anything wrong with such an involvement.[6] In October 1974, Yankelovich found that about one out of ten Americans thought that the close ties of American Jews to Israel was bad, about three out of ten thought the close ties were positive, and the rest were indifferent. Even more significant, the ratios were about the same for all other ethnic groups mentioned. Americans felt a little more favorable about Irish ties to Ireland than about Jewish ties to Israel and a little less favorable about the national ties of Greeks, Blacks, Germans, and Spanish-speaking people than they did about Jewish ties to Israel.

Such findings are obviously governed by the circumstances. Americans did not have benign thoughts about such close national ties when they applied to the German Americans in World War I, Japanese Americans in World War II, or Iranian Americans during the hostage crisis. The point is that circumstances in the United States have been favorable to Israel. Therefore, the perceived connections between American Jews and Israel have not triggered a backlash.

There is reason to believe that many Americans *do* have some resentment about a Jewish political power used on behalf of Israel (a power that so many of them are willing to term "too much") and about the concept that Jews have "more loyalty" to Israel than to the United States. However, even that portion of the American public is not pushed into active hostility toward American Jews on this account, as long as those Americans themselves so predominantly sympathize with Israel. Therefore, a paramount factor to be considered is the stability of those sympathies and of the favorable circumstances of U.S.-Israeli relations. There are three axes around which sympathy or antagonism for Israel can turn, and each of them has a different implication for antisemitism. One is nationalist Zionism and nationalist anti-Zionism. The second is political anti-Zionism, which has more to do with Jews than with the Israel it invokes. The third axis turns more pragmatically around perceived mutuality or antipathy of interests.

Nationalist Zionism and Anti-Zionism

The definition of Zionism is associated with a vast body of literature and a long history of debate among Jews. One of the subjects of that debate has had to do with the manner in which Zionism does or does not relate to the Land of Israel. But within the limited context of Zionism/anti-Zionism and antisemitism, it is possible to posit a core definition of nationalist Zionism which holds that the State of Isarel belongs where it is, that it exists for Jews everywhere, and that it must be a Jewish state. This definition of nationalist Zionism has an ideological cast beyond simple patriotism and nationalism—although many Israelis embrace the premises of core Zionism for security reasons, if for no other reason. For example, it is not likely that, on pragmatic grounds alone, many Israeli Jews would feel secure in any Middle East government that was not Jewish. For a mixture of ideological and security reasons, there are a number of non-Israelis who would embrace the principles of core nationalist Zionism, including some Christian fundamentalists and most Diaspora Jews.

The Arab world is, of course, the source of nationalist anti-Zionism. To begin with, there is a clash of Israeli and Arab nationalisms that, although similar to other nationalist clashes that have taken place in the world's history, are among the most inconsolable. David Ben Gurion stated it simply to the Zionist Action Committee in 1938: "[The Arabs] do not acknowledge our right to a homeland because, in their eyes, this is their homeland."[7] Moreover, this nationalist clash, whenever it became aggravated, inevitably brought with it mutual hositilities and prejudices between the peoples involved. In 1912, Rabbi Abraham Isaac Kook, chief rabbi of Palestine, objected in a Jewish journal in Palestine to an emerging "mentality of hatred for the Arabs."[8]

Despite the resistance of many Israelis and Arabs, the nationalist conflict engendered prejudicial anti-Arab and anti-Jewish feelings. Under much less desperate conditions, the United States' wars with Germany and Japan resulted in similar tendencies within the United States. The historian of the Arab nationalist movement, George Antonius, wrote in 1938: "The development of Zionism in the post-war [World War I] period has been one of the main psychological factors in the deplorable growth of antisemitism."[9] Antonius knew that the term *antisemitism* had been created to apply specifically to the Jews. He also knew that *Zionism* was the proper name for Jewish nationalism in the Middle East, as well as source of anti-Jewish feeling among Arabs.

The antisemitism and anti-Arabism engendered by this nationalistic Zionism and anti-Zionism would not, under other circumstances, deserve wide attention or have reverberations on the world scene. But this regional antagonism is being acted out on the world scene. Indeed, the clashing Arab/Israeli nationalisms often seem the smallest part of the conflict raging in that area. As one result, the nationalist anti-Zionism has been attached to, used to fuel, and often confused with another quite different kind of anti-Zionism, one that might be called political anti-Zionism.

Political Anti-Zionism

There is a symmetry between nationalist Zionism and nationalist anti-Zionism, the latter being directly addressed to the core attributes of modern Zionism. But there is no such symmetry with political anti-Zionism, whose source of antagonism is not Zionism but the *Protocols of the Elders of Zion*. The logic of political anti-Zionism is built around the classic conspiracy theory featuring a cabalistic Jewish world power on the *world* scene. Plagiaristic czarist agents brought that theory to an art form in the creation of the *Protocols*. Hitler used the theory, the *Protocols*, and occasionally the term *Zionism* in his war against the Jews.

Of course, one recognizes political anti-Zionism, so described, as a near-euphemism for political antisemitism. But political anti-Zionism has an identity of its own; it is a political antisemitism that uses Israel as a key ingredient in its image of a cabalistic Jewish world power. The chief sources of this political anti-Zionism are the Soviet Union, anti-American Third World ideologues, and Arab propagandists, in that order. Political anti-Zionism is the form in which political antisemitism is used by the "left wing."

Political antisemitism on the left was foreshadowed not so much by its antinationalism as by its taste for a statism bereft of mediating groups. The first watershed of modern antisemitism, it has been noted, was the kind of nonpluralistic European nationalism that, ironically, was associated with the liberation of the Jews from the ghetto. That was the import of Count Stanislas de Clermont-Tonnerre's famous statement demanding individual and religious liberty for the Jews, but also demanding of the Jews that they become "French people" rather than constituting themselves as a separate community. It was, of course, a tragic flaw of European nationalist liberalism, which became a fearful right-wing instrument.

But another watershed of modern antisemitism was prefigured when Lenin outlawed antisemitism in the Soviet Union at the same time that he began to disband Jewish community organizations. This ideological antipathy to Jewish life was less redolent of Clermont-Tonnerre than of his contemporary, Jean Jacques Rousseau, who insisted that nothing should intervene between the individual and the benign state. Yet, compounded from whatever historical tendencies it possesses, political anti-Zionism, like old-fashioned political antisemitism, is a largely fictional device that is mainly used as an instrument in the retention or acquisition of political power. The Soviet Union, the prime ideological source of political anti-Zionism, has uses for that instrument on both domestic and world political scenes. The ideology, which is simple enough, gets repeated day after day in the official press and literature of the USSR. There is little deviation from the formula, as Lev Korneev expressed it in 1982:

> An important role in the psychological war of imperialism is alloted to Zionism, whose ultimate goal in political practice is the achievement of maximum dominance for the Jewish bourgeoisie in the system of capitalism and the liquidation of the countries of socialism. With the support of all the other forces of world reaction, the subversive activity of Zionism has now acquired very impressive dimensions. On account of this, a correct analysis of complicated world problems and important international events will hardly be possible if the degree of participation in them of Zionism is not taken into account.[10]

Korneev continued in the formula with a clear identification of Zionism with the "fascist" state of Israel, and proceeded to delegitimize both Israel *and* the Jews. He further maintained that Israel calls together

> people who live in more than a hundred countries, and who are in no way connected with each other. . . . The Jews ceased being a people, they lost their common language, and the Jewish ruling clique was turned, in the course of centuries, into a special type of intermediary cosmopolitan group in which rabbis, merchants, usurers and other such exploiters dominated. . . . Centuries-long practice over the whole earth allowed Jewish merchants, usurers and bankers to concentrate in their hands incalculable wealth; it is not for nothing that the name Rothschild became the synonym for the man of unlimited wealth.[11]

The more naked words *Jewish* and *Jewry* began to appear on their own as the linkages were established in this conspiracy theory: "The position of Jewish capital is very significant in France, England, Sweden, Australia, Holland and several other countries. At the same time, the Jewish bourgeoisie is American, English, French and so on, that is, part of the plutocracy of the country in which it resides. Thus, Jewry has a double character, which is expressed in its ideology and political character."[12]

This is the package of political anti-Zionism as it is produced, used internally, and exported by the Soviet Union. It is, in fact, old-fashioned political antisemitism, with the added ingredient of Israel. *However, Israel is not the prime target of political anti-Zionism, as it is in the case of nationalist anti-Zionism.* As Yuri Ivanov, a leading Soviet theorist on Jewish matters, put it: "Zionism is the ideology, the complex system of organizations and the political practice of the big Jewish bourgeoisie which has merged with the monopolistic circles of the United States and other imperialistic powers. . . . The ruling circles of Israel entered the international Jewish concern as junior partners."[13]

Although Israel is not the chief target of political anti-Zionism, the existence of Israel provides this new version of political antisemitism with a seeming credibility it would not otherwise have, especially for the left wing, and establishes a link in the conspiracy web that serves the ideological purposes of Third World anti-American rhetoric around the world, even when that rhetoric is not strikingly pro-Soviet. It is, after all, a fact that Israel and the United States are close allies. It is also a fact that Jews around the world support Israel politically and financially. These facts are a cause of embitterment for Arab nationalists, and they are carefully noted by Third World ideologues who have taken up the cause of Arab nationalism and who typically describe Israel as a "handmaiden of U.S. imperialism."

Jordan's representative at the United Nations, Hazem Nuseibeh, spoke at the UN debate on December 15, 1980, in this fashion: "The representative of the Zionist entity is evidently incapable of concealing his deep-seated hatred towards the Arab world for having broken loose from the notorious exploitation of its natural resources, long held in bondage and plundered by his own people's cabal, which controls and manipulates the rest of humanity by controlling the money and wealth of the world."[14]

Just as the links among "international Zionism, the United States, and imperialism" are constantly made part of the weave of conspiracy theory by some Arab spokespersons, so have they become useful for the non-Arab ideologues of Third World anti-Americanism. In a characteristic article entitled "The Class Origins of Zionist Ideology," by a professor at Tuskegee Institute, the author stated: "It was somewhat symbolic that the original draft of [Herzl's] *The Jewish State* was entitled *An Address to the Rothschilds* and intended for the private use of the Rothschild family. . . . That Zionism expressed the interests of Jewish finance capital did not negate the fact that Zionism also was an ideology of world imperialism."[15]

Similar expressions have been found all over that ideological landscape. At one point, the Student Non-violent Coordinating Committee (SNCC) published a cartoon depicting a hand with the Star of David and a dollar sign on it pulling nooses around the necks of Nasser and Muhammed Ali; the SNCC then asked the readers whether they knew "that the famous European Jews, the Rothschilds, who have long controlled the wealth of many European nations, were involved in the original conspiracy with the British to create the 'State of Israel' . . . ?"[16]

It is not that all Arab nationalists or Third World anti-Americanists embrace political anti-Zionism. However, it is important to note that the currency of political anti-Zionism, as distinct from nationalist anti-Zionism, is a grave potential source of political antisemitism in the world today.

Attitudes Based on U.S.-Israeli Relations

It is important to note that sentiments about Israel and about the Jews in the United States do not turn primarily around *either* the axis of nationalistic anti-Zionism or that of political anti-Zionism. The attitudes of most Americans about Israel are primarily shaped by pragmatic considerations of "U.S. national interest." A common misperception is that Americans were most sympathetic to Israel at the time of its creation, following hard on the U.S. war against Nazism and the revelation of the Holocaust. Distance from that period, according to that misperception, has eroded American sympathy. But overall American sympathy for Israel has increased with the years. Thus, six surveys of American sympathy between the years 1947 and 1949 show a median of 33 percent of Americans favoring the Israelis and 12 percent favoring the Arabs. A review of 15 surveys between 1970 and 1983 shows a median of 47 percent of Americans favoring the Israelis and 7 percent favoring the Arabs.[17]

It may be that the 24 percent of Americans who said they were more sympathetic to the Israelis in November 1947 were a somewhat more solid and less changeable bloc than the 49 percent who said they were more sympathetic to the Israelis in February 1983. (At both times, 12 percent said they were more sympathetic to the Arabs.) After all, this growing American proclivity to "sympathize" with the Israeli cause carries with it a limited commitment. We know, for example, that the portion of the American public who sympathizes with Israel will typically retreat when asked whether we should be militarily involved on Israel's behalf, even to the extent of selling arms. But, although the American public's willingness to send arms to Israel has varied more than the "sympathy" quotient in the face of differing circumstances, that index of support has also generally risen over the years.

There have been a number of signs that the American public's attitudes toward Israel, have, from the beginning, been shaped by strategic considerations, as signalled by the U.S. government. In November 1947, when the U.S. government announced its approval of a UN partition plan that would include Israel, 65 percent of the American public said they approved. But in April 1948, when the U.S. government announced that it opposed that same plan, only 26 percent of the American public approved.[18] In 1968, when the members of one representative American sample were asked whether they were willing for the United States to send arms to Israel, only about a quarter replied in the affirmative; but when the same people, at the same time, were asked whether they would be willing to send arms to Israel "if the Soviets were arming the Arabs," the affirmative answer more than doubled. Moreover, American public support has remained stable in its support of Israel, despite its disagreements with specific Israeli actions and oral postures. Accordingly, a Gallup release of July 1982 reported that

> although as many Americans disapprove as approve of Israel's invasion of Lebanon, the action appears not to have altered Americans' basic loyalties in the Middle East. . . . In an analagous situation last summer, a *Newsweek* poll conducted by the Gallup organization found that America's reaction to Israel's bombing of PLO positions in Beirut was more critical. Fifty percent said the bombing was not justified and 31 percent said that it was. But that survey, too, found no change in Americans' basic sympathies.

There is much evidence on that score. In a July 1981 Yankelovich poll, Americans were virtually split on such questions as whether Israel was wrong in its attitude toward a Palestinian state on the West Bank or whether Israel treated Arabs badly, but these same Americans still registered their sympathy for the Israelis over the Arabs by a five-to-one ratio.

In sum, these cues suggest that American support for Israel has less to do with any intrinsic emotional ties to that country, or with Zionist ideologies, than with perceptions of U.S. national interest. The term *national interest* is a commodious one. National interest is not just a matter of rarefied geopolitics or military strategy, although Israel is prevalently seen as the only politically stable and militarily viable ally of the United States in that area. That perception has to do with U.S. national security, and with the inhibition of Soviet expansion in the area; but it also has to do with access to oil, the U.S. economy, and American jobs. Finally, it has to do with peace, another popular aspect of perceived U.S. national interest.

The perception of Israel as a free, Western-style, democratic society—the only one in the Middle East—not only affects Israel's ability to complement those other U.S. goals in the Middle East but it is significant in itself as well. Israel's political and public culture is familiar and qualifies Israel as part of that circle of wagons known as the association of free societies, patently important for the United States. American sympathy for Israel is predominantly based on some combination of these perceived elements of U.S. national interest, rather than on sentiments related to the Holocaust or to core Zionism.

This favorable American attitude toward Israel serves as a natural deterrent against negative attitudes about Jews spilling over to negative attitudes about Israel, especially among those who have some strong sense of investment in the "U.S. national interest." That favorable attitude would include the great majority of Americans, notably the segment of the ·population that has been most prone to conventional antisemitism in the past. The ideology of the rampant right-wing antisemitism of the 1920s and 1930s centered on the Americanism and anticommunism that now calls for support of Israel. Yet a reversal of this predominantly favorable attitude toward Israel would not necessarily create, in itself, a wave of antisemitism in the United States. But the deterrent would no longer be present if such a reversal occurred, and there would be the added phenomenon of American Jewry promoting an Israel seen as antipathetic to the United States.

In Summary and Foreboding

With respect to the relationship between attitudes toward Israel and attitudes toward Jews, the evidence adduced leads to some hard conclusions about today's situation, but it can only provide some softer suggestions about the possible permutations of tomorrow. Jews tend to have a sense of "foreboding" that can be pushed over into paranoia but more often is a fairly sensible concern about the evil potential in currently satisfactory but volatile situations.[19]

Antisemitism is not today a serious source of anti-Israel feeling, primarily because, within perceptions of the U.S.-Israeli alliance, conventional antisemitism tends to be tied to values that would lead to support of Israel or, at least, would deter antagonism to Israel. But despite the evidence that within large statistical groupings there does not seem to be a significant relationship between antisemitism and anti-Israeli feelings, to believe that hard-core antisemites find it easy to be partial to a Jewish state would be contrary to good sense. There is evidence, indeed, of a relatively small pocket of population in which a relationship exists between the two attitudes. In one 1981 survey, it was found that 23 percent of the population was counted as antisemitic because its members held so many negative beliefs about Jews. Almost the same proportion, the 20 percent of the population that was "highly favorable to Israel," were among those counted as antisemitic. But among those "unfavorable to Israel," 32 percent were antisemitic. In short, there is undoubtedly a hard core of antisemites in the United States whose negative attitudes extend to the Jewish state. But it is a small core, and one that does not yet seriously affect the general climate of favorable American feelings toward Israel.

Anti-Israel feeling is not today a serious source of antisemitism. This converse disconnection is an even more direct result of the prevalent climate of partiality toward Israel. It is not possible now to disentangle the primacy of antisemitism or of anti-Israelism in the hard core that is both antisemitic and anti-Israel. But because of the prevailing circumstances with respect to U.S.-Israeli relations, that hard core is not a major factor today in this country. And for the great bulk of the American population, there is today no significant connection between negative feelings toward Israel and negative feelings toward Jews.

Parenthetically, the same evidence on that score suggests that neither is there a significant direct connection between positive feelings toward Israel and positive feeling toward Jews. Indeed, in the aforementioned 1981 survey, only 6 percent of the population said that the existence of Israel made them think more highly of Jews, and a slightly smaller percentage said that Israel's existence made them think less highly of Jews. But whatever the significance of such a subjective self-analysis, certain indirect effects cannot be cavalierly discounted. There has been some evidence in the past, for example, that Americans who know Jews best, in a friendly context, tend to be more sympathetic to Israel. To paraphrase a Hadley Cantril premise about public opinion: When attitudes are not highly structured, they tend to move in the direction of attitudes held strongly by friends and associates. But what is even more powerfully (if indirectly) true is that the image of the American Jews as familiarly integrated into the U.S. culture can presumably buttress the image of Israel as a Western democratic society, one component of perceived U.S. national interest in Israel. When Americans were asked in a Cambridge Survey to compare Israelis and Arabs on a number of cultural characteristics, the item on which the Americans rated Israelis most favorably had to do with which group was "most like Americans." On that item, Israelis were favored by a five-to-one ratio.[20]

There are undoubtedly such indirect effects. But they do not disturb the present evidence that antisemitism and anti-Israel feeling are not to be equated, and that neither is the prime source for the other in the United States today.

The Foreboding Syndrome. The favorable American climate toward Israel is reversible. Prevalent negative attitudes would not only remove a deterrent but would also be likely to provide a stimulant to antisemitism, presumably built around American Jewish activity on behalf of an unpopular Israel. The foundation underlying antisemitic views is reflected in the fact that between one-quarter and one-third of Americans have been consistently willing to say that American Jews are more loyal to or closer to Israel than to the United States. The Cambridge survey twice (in 1974 and 1975) put the question in a most abrasive way: "Some people forget they are Americans when they rush to defend Israel." In both cases, a third of the Americans responded in the affirmative.[21]

It is noteworthy that the one apparently sharp break in the continuing favorable Gallup poll measurements of American attitudes toward Israel came in September 1982. As earlier observed, Gallup had indicated in

July of that year that basic American support of Israel over the Arabs had remained steady in the face of a number of Israeli actions of which the American public disapproved and in the face of Israel's incursion into Lebanon. But in September 1982, the ratio of approval for Israel over the Arabs, which had been 49–10 in July 1981, dipped to 32–28. This followed a series of highly publicized rows between the governments of the United States and Israel, culminating in President Reagan's proposal for the future of the West Bank, which the Israeli government rejected abruptly and with an unusually strong personal attack on the president.

Israel's importance for "U.S. national interest" had been impugned. The ratio of approval for Israel over the Arabs snapped back quickly in the Gallup survey of January 1983 to a ratio of 49–12, as the air cleared between the two nations. Nevertheless, the episode provides support for the premise that circumstances touching on perceptions of U.S. national interest will largely determine the U.S. commitment to Israel. There also emerges an understandable uneasiness about the deterioration of goodwill toward American Jews under those circumstances.

It is conceivable but not too likely that U.S. policymakers will "abandon" Israel in the foreseeable future; the logic and tradition of that alliance are strong. But it is more conceivable that the United States' general circumstances at some given point could limit its ability to support Israel. There are strong veins of American sentiment that can only be described as isolationist, antimilitary, or at least opposed to active U.S. military involvement abroad.

If the United States' support of Israel were to waver on this account, or indeed on the additional account of domestic economic stress, American Jewish activity on behalf of restoring that support would predictably become even more vocal—and it is likely that such activity would be seen as contrary to U.S. national interest. The resentment that has been muted could, indeed, be reactivated.

The formulations here are functionally tied to the question of American antisemitism. The same equations are not applicable to France and the fourth largest Jewish community in the world. "French national interest" is differently perceived. Currents of pro-Arab, Third World, anti-American thought are, of course, much stronger. Susceptibility to left-wing political anti-Zionism is greater. However, many observers are similarly convinced that the future of antisemitism in France is tied to Middle East politics. As Henry Weinberg put it, "The renewed attacks on Jews during the recent Israeli action in Lebanon suggest that the potential for anti-Jewish violence in the context of the Arab-Israeli conflict may become a permanent feature of life in France. In the end, the place of the Jew in French society will to a large extent be determined in a region distant from France's boundaries. As a senior French Jewish statesman phrased it in response to a question about the future of French Jewry: 'Everything depends on events in the Middle East.'"[22]

Since the 1930s, no one has been foolish enough to say "it can't happen here." The possibility of the emergence of political antisemitism in the United States must always be kept open. But, in the modern world, political antisemitism *means* political anti-Zionism. Israel cannot be left out of the equation. As long as the U.S.-Israeli alliance is convincing, and made convincing by U.S. policymakers, right-wing political anti-Zionism is less likely in the United States. Nor is the ascendancy of left-wing political anti-Zionism any more likely in the United States' foreseeable future than the ascendancy of *any* left-wing political ideology. Less unlikely is that certain American streams of isolationist, antimilitary, and anti-American thought could hasten the deterioration of U.S. support of Israel under certain circumstances, with negative results for American Jews.

In any case, the signs suggest that antisemitism is not and probably will not be at the genesis of any widespread antagonism toward Israel; rather, any political antisemitism in the future will find its *basis* in antagonism toward Israel—and, more precisely, in the activity of Jews supporting an Israel toward which there has developed antagonism or apathy.

Notes

1. The hazards of survey information, especially in the face of different languages and time situations, are well known. However, in the case of the Middle East, the same questions have been asked so often by the same organizations over the course of so many different time situations that a comparison of the results is *often* useful. In other cases, survey material is no more than, but also no less than, suggestive. In most cases, where such material is used, the date and source are listed in the text and not endnoted. For other material, references are made to two compilations of survey results: Charles Herbert Stember et al., *Jews in the Minds of Men* (New York: Basic Books, 1966); and Seymour Martin Lipset and William Schneider, "American Opinion Towards Israel and Jew" (unpublished manuscript, American Enterprise Institute, n.d.).

2. The correlations are as follows: (1) conventional antisemitism and sympathy for Israel $= -.07$; (2) conventional antisemitism and perception of Jewish power $= -.04$; and (3) conventional antisemitism and support of the PLO $= -.09$.

3. Stember, op. cit., pp. 116, 158.

4. Ibid., p. 162.

5. Jews more loyal to Israel than to the United States:

Year	Agree (%)	Source
1964	30	NORC
1974	26	NORC
1974	26	Harris
1974	34	Yankelovich
1977	27	Yankelovich
1979	29	Gallup
1980	34	Gallup
1981	34	Gallup

| 1982 (March) | 30 | Gallup |
| 1983 (January) | 37 | Gallup |

6. Stember, op. cit., p. 189.

7. Quoted in Elyakim Rubenstein, "Zionist Attitudes in the Arab-Jewish Dispute of 1936," *Jerusalem Quarterly* (Winter 1982):140.

8. Quoted in Ben Zion Bokser, "Rabbi Kook, the Arabs and the Japanese," *Judaism* (Spring 1983):185.

9. George Antonius, *The Arab Awakening* (New York: Capricorn Books Edition, 1965), p. 265.

10. Lev Korneev, "For Whom is this Profitable? The Psychological War of International Zionism," *Neva* (May 1982).

11. Ibid.

12. Ibid.

13. Yuri Ivanov (Adviser on Jewish Affairs to the CPSU Central Committee), *Beware Zionism* (Moscow, 1969).

14. Institute of Jewish Affairs, *Research Report* (December 1981):10.

15. Stephen Halbrook, "The Class Origins of Zionist Ideology," *Journal of Palestinian Studies* (Autumn 1972):87, 106.

16. *SNCC Newsletter* (June-July 1967).

17.

| | More Sympathy for: | | |
Date	Israelis (%)	Arabs (%)	Source
Nov. 1947	24	12	Stember (p. 179)
Feb. 1948	35	16	Stember
June 1948	34	12	Stember
July 1948	36	14	Stember
Oct. 1948	33	11	Stember
March 1949	32	13	Stember
Feb. 1969	43	4	Gallup
Feb. 1970	38	2	Gallup
Aug. 1970	47	6	Harris
July 1971	46	7	Harris
Oct. 1973	47	6	Gallup
Nov. 1973	48	7	Roper
Dec. 1973	41	6	Roper
Dec. 1973	50	7	Gallup
Jan. 1976	56	9	Yankelovich
Jan. 1977	47	6	Gallup
June 1977	43	5	Gallup
Oct. 1980	45	13	Gallup
July 1981	49	10	Yankelovich
Sept. 1982	32	28	Gallup
Jan. 1983	49	12	Gallup

Source: *Midstream* (February 1983).

18. Stember, op. cit., p. 178.

19. Earl Raab, "Anti-Semitism in the 1980s," *Midstream* (February 1983).

20. Lipset and Schneider, op. cit., p. 17.

21. Ibid., p. 53.

22. Henry H. Weinberg, "French Jewry: Trauma and Renewal," *Midstream* (December 1982).

24
American Jewish Organizational Efforts to Combat Antisemitism in the United States Since 1945

Leonard Dinnerstein

Antisemitism has plagued Jews in the United States since colonial times, but until about forty years ago American Jewish organizations had been rather timid in protesting it. The American Jewish Committee and the Anti-Defamation League, both started before World War I, were not sitting on their hands for forty years; but it was not until after the formation of the American Jewish Conference in 1943 that American Jewish organizations made really concerted efforts to reverse the growing antisemitic trend in the United States.

The worst period of American antisemitism occurred between the ends of the two world wars. The dissemination of the *Protocols of the Elders of Zion*, which suggested that there was a Jewish plot to take over the world, the inauguration of quotas in colleges and universities, the vitriolic attacks of Henry Ford in his *Dearborn Independent* newspaper, and the rise of the Nazis and the German American Bund are some of the more easily remembered events of the era. But the 1920s and 1930s were also times of increased discrimination in housing and employment, which combined with a growing belief not only that Jews held too much power in the United States but that they constituted a menace to society as well. Jewish leaders and organizations became increasingly terrified by the evidences of American antisemitism but did not seem to know how to counteract them. Some Jews believed that if they all behaved themselves then American antisemitism would subside, so they admonished coreligionists to speak softly, play down parochial concerns, and not do anything that might attract negative attention because the behavior of one, as Louis D. Brandeis often remarked, reflected on all members of the group.

But the with the advent of World War II, and then the increasing knowledge of Hitler's barbaric policies toward coreligionists in Europe, leading American Jews finally coalesced and proclaimed their devotion to the idea of a Jewish state in Palestine after the war ended. That sixty-three of sixty-four Jewish organizations could agree on even one issue seemed almost miraculous at the time, but the unification also provided the stimulus for further joint activities.[1]

One of the major concerns of all the Jewish organizations was how to combat the growth of American antisemitic activities and beliefs. For although the United States was at war with Germany, Hitler's attitudes toward Jews did not seem to be at odds with those held by Gentile Americans; hostility toward Jews increased, rather than decreased, during the war. Poll takers noted that Gentiles thought Jews had too much power in this country, that they ought to be excluded from certain towns, and that, after the Germans and Japanese, they constituted the greatest menace to American society. When Bess Myerson became the first Jewish "Miss America" in 1945, several people suggested that she change her Jewish-sounding name. And she made far fewer personal appearances than her predecessors because many corporate sponsors did not want their products promoted by a Jew.[2]

That some efforts had to be made to stem further development of American antisemitism was universally agreed upon by leaders of the American Jewish organizations. The example of what happened in Europe during World War II convinced them that passivity and timidity were valueless and that quiet efforts with friendly Gentiles would not suffice to turn the tide. Thus, in 1944, several major Jewish defense organizations, including the American Jewish Committee, the American Jewish Congress, and the Anti-Defamation League, along with nearly a score of local groups, banded together to form the National Jewish Community Relations Advisory Council (generally known as the CRC in Jewish circles) as a coordinating and clearing agency to promote harmonious intergroup relations and a respect for cultural pluralism in the United States. Moreover, the individual Jewish agencies themselves took a much more militant stance against antisemitism. They established new departments and divisions, conducted investigations into the causes of antisemitism and the means of combatting it, and took a much more active role in promoting legislative changes. The larger agencies, like the American Jewish Committee, the American Jewish Congress, and the Anti-Defamation League, favored "scientific" analyses of the problem by individuals professionally trained in history and the social sciences as one facet of their campaigns.[3]

Almost all of the community leaders viewed their efforts as part of a broader job in which it was stressed that prejudice toward anyone because of race, religion, or national origins constituted a major social problem about which all citizens should be concerned rather than a parochial one of interest only to Jews. Their underlying rationale, of course, was that by attacking the overall problem of prejudice they would have an easier chance to recruit non-Jewish allies to the cause. But they were also right on an ethical basis alone, and they knew this. Antisemitism is only one manifestation of prejudice, and no Jewish organization could protest its existence while sanctioning any other kind of bigotry.[4]

Once the major decision was made to fight vigorously against American antisemitism, the CRC went into action on local, state, and national levels. The larger agencies expanded their organizations for the broadened campaigns and moved simultaneously on several fronts. The most important areas included education, employment, housing, public accommodations, and immigration. Bias in these spheres, it was felt, prevented Jews from earning a decent living, residing in desirable neighborhoods, and, of course, entering the country. Hence several efforts were made to obtain antidiscrimination laws in which race, religion, creed, and national origins could not be legally sanctioned causes for discriminating against otherwise qualified people.

Early successes in obtaining antidiscrimination in employment and higher education came first in New York and then in other states. By 1950, New Jersey, Massachusetts, Connecticut, Rhode Island, Oregon, and the state of Washington had already passed laws prohibiting employment discrimination. Thereafter other states followed suit, and once that occurred, Jewish agencies throughout the nation monitored and complained about illegal practices wherever they were found. In time, bastions of discrimination such as American Telephone and Telegraph, major legal firms, and leading industrial concerns changed their hiring practices.[5]

The same was true in higher education. The American Jewish Congress led the fight to ban discrimination in colleges and universities, and in 1948 New York became the first state to prohibit student selection on the basis of race and religion. The next year, Massachusetts and New Jersey passed even more stringent legislation in this sphere. Subsequently, groups such as the Anti-Defamation League and the American Jewish Committee campaigned to require colleges and universities to consider applicants for admission strictly on the basis of individual merit. In 1950, the Anti-Defamation League issued a report indicating that 102 discriminatory questions had been removed from the application blanks of 43 colleges in the states of New York, New Jersey, Colorado, Montana, Massachusetts, Oregon, and Washington.[6] Some of those eliminated included such questions as "What was your mother's maiden name?" "What is your religion?" and "Has anyone in your family ever changed religions?" By 1979, when Harold Shapiro became president of the University of Michigan, an economics professor there wrote: "What is expecially to be noted is the fact that Prof. Shapiro's religious affiliation did not seem to enter into consideration. The selection was made on its merits, and the qualms of yesteryear about appointing a Jew to the highest post in one of the most distinguished universities in the country was not an obstacle."[7]

In housing and resort accommodations—two other areas of widespread prejudice—the Jewish organizations sought legislative corrections and were sometimes successful. First, they analyzed the situation; then they prepared detailed arguments and proposed bills for legislative consideration; later, they lobbied to obtain passage of these measures. They also employed other devices. In 1948 both the American Jewish Congress and the American Jewish Committee submitted "friends of the Court" briefs to the United States Supreme Court urging that restrictive covenants in housing be declared unconstitutional. The Court so ruled. Thereafter, and probably before as well, major Jewish organizations regularly submitted "friends of the Court" briefs in cases arguing against released time for public school students for religious activities, against school prayers, and against quotas in educational admissions policies.[8]

Where the resorts and social clubs were concerned, the Jewish agencies had to do a good deal of public relations negotiation. They had to convince owners that such terms as *Gentile clientele, strictly Christian,* and *discriminating Christian People* were not only undemocratic and contrary to the highest ideals of the nation but bad for business as well. In states where public accommodation laws existed, complaints to the appropriate officials usually led to investigation and action. In other cases, negative publicity and discussions with travel agents and those who planned conventions urging them not to send clients to places that discriminated resulted in some reforms. Not until the 1964 Civil Rights Act barring discrimination in public accommodations, however, did such policies become illegal throughout the nation.[9]

The Jewish organizations did not rely strictly on legislation and court decisions to combat antisemitism in the United States. Certainly legislation contributed to a lowering of the barriers against Jewish opportunities, but they did not, by themselves, eliminate prejudice. To accomplish that, the organizations resorted to a traditional Jewish way— education. Jews have great faith in, and respect for, education. Scholars have always been highly respected in the culture; they were often the ones, at least in Eastern Europe, to whom people went for answers to difficult problems. Thus it seemed only natural for the Jewish agencies to sponsor studies by American scholars into the causes of antisemitism and the possible methods of combatting them. These studies have been carried out continually since the end of World War II; in tandem with various smaller pamphlets and handouts, they have resulted in the widely praised *The Authoritarian Personality* by T. A. Adorno et al. and the major University of California series of sociological studies on antisemitism such as Glock and Stark's *Christian Beliefs and Anti-Semitism,* Selznick and Steinberg's *The Tenacity of Prejudice,* and Quinley and Glock's *Anti-Semitism in America.*[10] Furthermore, polls have been sponsored to check out how other Americans feel about Jews and Jewish activities. "Do Jews have too much power?" "Would you mind living or working with Jews?" and "Would you accept a Jewish son or daughter-in-law?" are just some of the questions that have been posed.

Jews and their organizations have also honed their political skills in an effort to obtain desired goals and to prevent any legislative or administrative encouragement of antisemitism. They frequently exercise their constitutional rights to petition and advise elected and appointed public officials about group interests. Factual details on subjects of concern to American Jews are continually being presented to public officials, who are also honored and entertained by different Jewish groups. Financial contributions are made to support the campaigns of friendly and potentially friendly politicians, and even where Jews do not constitute a significant proportion of the voting population, politicians are wary of offending them. As one Republican politico put it, "Everyone loves to be loved. You don't want to displease any group of constituents if you don't have to. It's not likely that Jews could affect my reelection chances, but I sure don't want to experiment. Jews are a bloc, vocal and well-informed." A border state Democrat echoed these sentiments: "Jews are a small, influential group in my constituency . . . active in all areas of political life. They feel very strongly about Israel, and though they couldn't cause me any real election problems, you like to have them on your side. You sure don't want them against you. If they come to me on an issue, I like to go along unless there is good reason not to."[11]

The leading Jewish agencies are increasingly concerned that some inadvertent act of a Jew, an untoward event in the Middle East, or a major domestic economic or social crisis will set off a new wave of antisemitism. In a recent analysis of antisemitism in the United States, the researchers noted that Jews are much more sensitive than non-Jews to existing prejudices. And despite the fact that repeated surveys show a tremendous decline in antisemitism in the United States over the past thirty-five years, many Jews simply refuse to believe that they have nothing to worry about. "Jewish perceptions" about the level of anti-semitic beliefs, as Gregory Martire and Ruth Clark have written, "are sharply at odds with the views actually expressed by non-Jews."[12]

I might add that, in many cases, Jewish perceptions are also at odds with the findings of the polls and surveys. This fact was acknowledged in the *Joint Program Plan* of the Community Relations Council in 1982. The first paragraph in the booklet's overview reiterated the major concern of all Jewish organizations:

Although all the standard measurements with one exception do not indicate a dramatic upsurge in anti-Semitism in the United States this past year, most American Jews, from grass roots to national leaders, believe that the threat to their security is real and growing. They perceive a dramatic increase in overt anti-Semitism and in the growth of anti-Semitic orga-nizations. They believe that more and more Americans are feeling in-creasingly hostile toward Jews. While such fears are chronic among Jews, they have become more pronounced during the past year.[13]

Such a paragraph confirms what psychologists had already found to be true: that people believe only what they want to believe, that factual statements to the contrary are rejected out of hand. Thus, while all impartial surveys find antisemitism in this country to be waning in strength, many apprehensive Jews are reaching just the opposite conclusion.

That antisemitism has actually weakened as much as it has is due, in considerable part, to the unstinting efforts of the American Jewish Committee, the American Jewish Congress, the Anti-Defamation League, and the local agencies of the Community Relations Council, which have been zealous not only in monitoring indications of prejudice but in reeducating all Americans to the importance of tolerance and understanding. To be sure, since the 1960s they have had a favorable national climate of opinion in which to disseminate their messages, but they have also made the most of their opportunities. Groups of non-Jewish community leaders are given all-expense-paid tours to Israel to see how a democratic, socialist country is being developed; scholars' and laypersons' conferences with Jews and Episcopalians, Lutherans, Methodists, and Baptists have been held; interfaith activities of all kinds have been sought after and promoted. Intercultural education, "brotherhood kits," civil rights programs, and the like have been developed and distributed. Attempts have also been made to eliminate hostile references to Jews in religious textbooks. All of these activities were designed to promote interfaith tolerance and understanding and to minimize group tensions and conflicts.[14]

In addition, the leading Jewish organizations have been a primary force in promoting civil rights for all groups. Generally, until about the late 1960s, they worked with black groups such as the NAACP and CORE to promote integration and equal rights and equal opportunities for blacks and whites. It thus came as a shock to the Jewish organizations, and Jews in general, when black hostility toward Jews manifested itself after the passage of the Civil Rights Acts in 1964 and 1965. A CORE leader in a New York suburb publicly declared that Hitler did not kill enough Jews,[15] a school strike in New York City pitted a predominantly black local community against a predominantly Jewish teachers' organization, and what was viewed by the blacks as hostility against them was interpreted at first by the teachers' union as a conflict between labor and management.

The school strike definitively divided New York City's Jews and blacks, but the major break came because the goals of the two groups were so far apart. The Jews for the most part believe, as Nathan and Ruth Ann Perlmutter recently wrote, that "it's the individual's own qualifications, characteristics and actions which in each instance determine his rights and his responsibilities under law."[16] But for the blacks, *affirmative action* are the key words. Whereas most Jews feel that they will succeed if given an equal opportunity, most blacks think that they have been handicapped by centuries of degradation and therefore need more assistance than white people. Some Jewish organizations agree but practically have apoplexy when the word *quota* appears. As Charles F. Wittenstein of Atlanta's Anti-Defamation League observed, "We don't think a racial quota is ever benign because, while conferring a benefit on one race, it imposes a disability on another."[17] Yet another Jewish leader, Rabbi Alexander Schindler, president of the Union of American Hebrew Congregations, recognized "that affirmative action is the Israel of the black community."[18] Given the past history of both groups in this country, that conflict must exist in this area is understandable.

Many of the leading black and Jewish organizations are still trying to cooperate in promoting positive intergroup relations.[19] But when Jesse Jackson used the term *hymies* to refer to Jews during his 1984 campaign for the Democratic presidential nomination and tolerated a man on his staff, Louis Farrakhan, who threatened the Jewish people, he reawakened the fears of Jewish people that many blacks tacitly accepted the negative stereotyping about them.[20]

During the past decade, antisemitism has also manifested itself among several members of the women's movement. Despite the fact that many Jews are prominent feminists (or perhaps because of that?), resentment and hostility have arisen. In November 1982, *Sojourner,* the publication of the Ohio State University Center for Women's Studies, prominently featured an article entitled "Anti-Semitism: The 'Invisible' Form of Bigotry." Sigrid Ehrenberg, the author, explained how it was that "the more open Jewish feminists become as Jews within the movement, the more aware they become of anti-Semitism within the movement."[21] Careless, or deliberate, scheduling of feminist meetings on important Jewish holidays like Rosh Hashanah (the New Year) or Yom Kippur (the Day of Atonement), comments at meetings such as "Israel has no right to survive," "Zionism is racism," and "Jews don't have to worry about the Klan, since Jewish cartels run the world" are pejoratives by anyone's definition. The scapegoating of Jewish women at the August 1980 United Nations Women's Conference, which met in Copenhagen, also reflects the fact that age-old prejudices have not been eliminated and that "sisterhood" is not always meant to include Jewish women along with other females.[22] In fact, it seems that many feminists are able to overcome only a few of the stereotypes with which they were brought up; in antisemitism they seem to have found a socially acceptable outlet (at least among many women's groups) for their other "hang-ups" and frustrations.

Despite the outbursts of black and feminist wrath in recent years, the Jewish organizations have generally been successful in combating manifestations of antisemitism since the end of World War II. The reasons for their success are several. First, the climate of opinion was right. Immediately after World War II we had political leaders like Harry S. Truman who lent their prestige to the cause of civil rights. Second, after having fought a world war to promote democratic ideals, few, if any, responsible individuals chose to publicly oppose those goals. Third, and this is particularly important, Jewish organizations united to some extent and worked zealously to obtain nondiscriminatory legislation. As was not the case in previous decades, they no longer felt that they had to remain quiet lest they incur the opposition of American antisemites. And with increasing success, their organizations grew and thrived. Finally, the passage of the Civil Rights Acts in the mid-1960s combined with an expanding economy and the various protests of the decade to produce a tolerance of diversity hitherto unknown in American society. All of these factors provided opportunities for Jews that simply did not exist beforehand.

Yet a stray slur, a bigoted remark, or several daubs of swastikas on a building can escalate in the minds of apprehensive Jews into huge threats. One student at the University of Massachusetts claimed that any crisis, be it in Grenada or El Salvador, increases her anxiety. She told a reporter that "some students equate the state of Israel with Jewish students and when global conditions deteriorate 'people need a scapegoat' which translated into increased anti-Semitism."[23]

With the advent of Ronald Reagan's presidency and the severe curtailment of economic benefits to the poor that followed in 1981 and 1982, a rash of antisemitic vandalism occurred in Montgomery County, Maryland, which borders on the nation's capital. The policy chief attributed the outbursts to the fact that "there are more people who need government aid, and with the economy the way it is, people are frustrated; they're striking out in anger."[24]

Newspaper tales and individual experiences have a way of taking on lives of their own and do not always jibe with factual details. In 1982, for example, the specific number of antisemitic incidents fell 14.9 percent from the previous year, according to an Anti-Defamation League (ADL) report. These 829 incidents had been reported in 35 states, compared to a total of 974 in 1981. How significant they were is difficult to evaluate without knowing more of the details. But the ADL believes that collecting and reporting these statistics are important in alerting officials of this country to possible escalations in prejudicial thought and behavior.[25]

Most of the Jewish organizations are ever vigilant to the need for minimizing antisemitism and increasing harmonious relations between Jews and non-Jews. While preparing this chapter, I had on my desk two pamphlets. One, used by the ADL, is entitled "Human Relations Materials for the School, Church and Community."[26] It has about seventy pages and lists the publications, films, and teaching materials that have been prepared to expose prejudice and promote tolerance. These materials are available to schools, churches, and community organizations.

The other booklet is the 1982–1983 *Joint Program Plan* for the National Community Relations Advisory Councils (CRCs).[27] In its fifty-five pages it offers a guide to Jewish agencies throughout the country about the major issues of concern to Jewish groups in the current year, including a summary of each issue and the "action goals" recommended for individual group use and/or consideration. I found this program plan extraordinarily impressive. The topics listed for 1982–1983 include Israel (as usual), Soviet Jewry, Social and Economic Justice, Energy, Jewish Security and Individual Freedom, and Church-State Interreligious Relationships. In their specific "action goals" the groups recommended, among other things, that Jewish communities make efforts to oppose social budget cuts, that the federal government maintain its responsibility "to mount and regulate the basic welfare programs of the nation," that the federal government "demonstrate, through vigorous enforcement, its commitment to the spirit and the letter of civil rights legislation," and that Jewish communities "actively seek out coalitions to develop strategies to achieve equal rights for women."[28] The CRCs also called for a coalition of "like-minded groups" to impress upon Congress and other opinion leaders "the unconstitutional and divisive aspects of proposed legislation and constitutional amendments on prayer in the schools" and reiterated its opposition to tuition tax credits for students in private schools and attempts to "Christianize" the political process. It further recommended "cooperating with Christian churches in their efforts to educate their constituencies to those distortions about Jews and Judaism in church teaching that have fostered anti-Semitism."[29]

The CRCs program made perfectly clear why its choices have been shaped as they have. "We have learned," the Overview section candidly observed, "through bitter experience that deteriorating economic and social conditions as well as political conditions can lead to hostility, severe tensions, alienation, polarization, and fierce conflicts among groups in society. Such developments foster situational anti-Semitism and jeopardize the security of Jews in their individual pursuits and the Jewish community in its collective role."[30]

And from the evidence we now have, we can say that the major Jewish organizations should be quite pleased with the results of their endeavors. A 1983 article in the *Women's American ORT Reporter* commented that "the three major American Jewish defense organizations [American Jewish Committee, American Jewish Congress, and Anti-Defamation League] have been so successful in educating the American public that anti-Jewish educational, employment and housing policies, as well as negative anti-Semitic stereotypes, have declined dramatically since 1945."[31] This is not to say, of course, that antisemitism has disappeared in this country. Stereotypes that have taken root over twenty centuries are not easily abandoned, and the image of the Jew as "Christ-killer" still occasionally emerges in Christian thinking. But the statistics do show that constant, unified, and vigilant efforts, sharply focused, can over time make a tremendous impact in curbing, and beginning to turn around, prejudices that threaten the existence of the Jewish community in the United States.

Notes

1. Zvi Ganin, "The Diplomacy of the Weak: American Zionist Leadership During the Truman Era, 1945–1948" (Ph.D. dissertation, Department of History, Brandeis University, 1975), pp. 15, 25. This was subsequently published under the title *Truman, American Jewry, and Israel, 1945–1948* (New York: Holmes & Meier, 1979).

2. *Tucson Citizen*, 25 December 1979, p. 16A.

3. Philip J. Baram, *The Department of State in the Middle East, 1919–1945* (Philadelphia: University of Pennsylvania Press, 1978), p. 285; Stanley High, "Jews, Anti-Semites, and Tyrants," *Harper's Magazine* 185 (June 1942):22–29; "Summary of Polls on Anti-Semitism, 1938–1942," prepared by Richard C. Rothschild (unpublished, 1943, located in Blaustein Library, American Jewish Committee, New York City), pp. 22, 23; Wilson Whitman, "O Little town . . . (restricted)," 157 (December 25, 1943):751; Charles Herbert Stember, *Jews in the Mind of America* (New York: Basic Books, 1966), p. 128; Earl of Halifax, "Weekly Political Summary," 7 October 1945 (British Public Record Office, Kew, FO 371/44538, Document # AN3069).

4. Baram, *Department of State*, p. 264; *American Jewish Year Book* (cited hereafter as *AJYB*) 47 (1945–1946), pp. 280–281; 40 (1947–1948), pp. 200, 201, 207, 211; Naomi W. Cohen, *Not Free to Desist* (Philadelphia: Jewish Publication Society of America, 1972), pp. 151, 334; *New York Times*, 27 January 1945, p. 30; 5 January 1948, p. 2; 22 January 1949, p. 5.

5. Leonard Dinnerstein, "Anti-Semitism Exposed and Attacked, 1945–1950," *American Jewish History* 71 (September 1981):138; *AJYB* 58 (1957), p. 126; 59 (1958), p. 80; Cohen, *Not Free to Desist*, pp. 424, 427; *New York Times*, 13 July 1953, p. 14; 17 November 1954, p. 34; 20 January 1957, p. 58; 27 May 1957, p. 23; 29 September 1957, p. 59; 29 June 1959, p. 23; 21 October 1965, p. 47; 21 May 1967, p. 70; 30 November 1967, p. 29; 31 October 1971, III, p. 3.

6. *AJYB* 53 (1952), p. 91; Dinnerstein, "Anti-Semitism," pp. 138–140.

7. William Haber, "New U of M President: In an Era of Academic Justice," *Jewish News* (Southfield, Michigan), 3 August 1979, p. 1.

8. *Shelley v. Kraemer*, 438 US 1 (1947); *Zorach v. Clausen*, 343 US 306 (1952); *Engel v. Vitale*, 370 US 421 (1962); *Defunis v. Odgaard*, 416 US 313 (1973); *University of California Regents v. Bakke*, 438 US 265 (1977).

9. *AJYB*, 58 (1957), p. 131; *New York Times*, 6 August 1948, p. 20; 21 December 1952, p. 20; 2 January 1953, p. 14; 11 March 1953, p. 52; 25 February 1955, p. 23; 19 December 1959, p. 27; 6 August 1965, p. 24; 2 January 1966, p. 88.

10. T. W. Adorno et al., *The Authoritarian Personality* (New York: Harper & Bros., 1950); Charles Y. Glock and Rodney Stark, *Christian Beliefs and Anti-Semitism* (New York: Harper & Row, 1966); Gertrude Selznick and Stephen Steinberg, *The Tenacity of Prejudice* (New York: Harper & Row, 1969); and Harold E. Quinley and Charles Y. Glock, *Anti-Semitism in America* (New York: Free Press, 1979).

11. Marvin C. Feuerwerger, *Congress and Israel* (Westport, Conn.: Greenwood Press, 1979), p. 84.

12. Gregory Martire and Ruth Clark, *Anti-Semitism in the United States* (New York: Praeger Publishers, 1982), p. 7.

13. National Jewish Community Relations Advisory Council, *Joint Program Plan, 1982–1983* (New York), p. 5.

14. Cohen, *Not Free to Desist,* pp. 454, 456–457; *AJYB,* 55 (1954), p. 89; *New York Times,* 20 January 1960, p. 52; 11 March 1964, p. 9; 29 October 1966, p. 29; 20 November 1966, p. 10; 17 December 1966, p. 23; 20 December 1966, p. 45; 14 January 1967, p. 33; 6 February 1969, p. 24; 18 November 1969, p. 8; 18 September 1970, p. 24; 14 March 1972, p. 18; 29 April 1972, p. 36; 8 June 1972, p. 50; 30 September 1973, p. 49; 28 October 1973, p. 87; 27 March 1974, p. 46; 2 May 1975, p. 40; 2 November 1975, p. 28; 23 November 1975, p. 60.

15. *AJYB,* 68 (1967), p. 77.

16. Nathan Perlmutter and Ruth Ann Perlmutter, *The Real Anti-Semitism in America* (New York: Arbor House, 1982), p. 275.

17. *Wall Street Journal,* 29 May 1984, p. 18.

18. Ibid.

19. Cohen, *Not Free to Desist,* p. 406; *New York Times,* 14 June 1954, p. 14; 29 August 1966, p. 1; 27 June 1967, p. 18; 14 October 1967, p. 8; 13 September 1968, p. 31; 30 April 1971, p. 181; 17 November 1973, p. 18; 21 July 1974, p. 51; 13 November 1974, p. 22; 25 January 1975, p. 35; 16 March 1975, p. 51; 12 September 1975, p. 66.

20. *Wall Street Journal,* 29 May 1984, pp. 1, 18.

21. Sigrid Ehrenberg, "The 'Invisible' Form of Bigotry," *Sojourner* (November 1983):82.

22. Ibid., p. 83.

23. *Sunday Republican* (Springfield, Mass.), 11 December 1983, p. B-1.

24. *Washington Post,* 1 December 1982, p. C-1.

25. *New York Times,* 11 January 1983, p. 6.

26. *Human Relations Materials for the School, Church and Community* (New York: Anti-Defamation League of B'nai B'rith, n.d.).

27. National Jewish Community Relations Advisory Council, *Joint Program Plan, 1982–1983.*

28. Ibid., p. 38.

29. Ibid., p. 55.

30. Ibid., p. 8.

31. David M. Szonyi, "Anti-Semitism: Time for Clear Thinking," *Women's American ORT Reporter* (Winter 1983), n.p.

Contributors

Edward Alexander, Professor of English, University of Washington and Tel Aviv University

John S. Conway, Professor of History, University of British Columbia

Michael Curtis, Professor of Political Science, Rutgers University

Leonard Dinnerstein, Professor of History, University of Arizona

Emil L. Fackenheim, Professor of Philosophy, The Hebrew University and University of Toronto

Wendy Stallard Flory, Department of English, University of Pennsylvania

Zvi Gitelman, Director of the Center for Russian and East European Studies, University of Michigan

Judith L. Goldstein, Associate Professor of Anthropology, Vassar College

Nathan Glazer, Professor, Graduate School of Education, Harvard University

Arthur Hertzberg, Rabbi Emeritus, Temple Emanu-El, Englewood, New Jersey, and Professor of History, Dartmouth College

Paul Johnson, British author and journalist

Michael R. Marrus, Professor of History, University of Toronto

Ronald L. Nettler, Fellow, Truman Center, The Hebrew University, Jerusalem

John T. Pawlikowski, OSM, Department of Historical and Doctrinal Studies, Catholic Theological Union

Terence Prittie, British author and journalist (deceased)

Earl Raab, Director of the Jewish Community Relations Council, San Francisco

Stephen J. Roth, Director of the Institute of Jewish Affairs, London

William Safran, Professor of Political Science, University of Colorado

Dominique Schnapper, Professor at Ecole des Hautes Etudes en Science Sociales, Paris

Dan V. Segre, Professor of Political Science, Haifa University

Emmanuel Sivan, Professor of History, The Hebrew University, Jerusalem

Norman A. Stillman, Associate Professor of History, State University of New York, Binghamton

Robert Wistrich, Professor of Jewish History, The Hebrew University, Jerusalem

Rivka Yadlin, Fellow, Truman Center, The Hebrew University, Jerusalem

Index